HIGH FLIGHT

HIGH FLIGHT

*Aviation and the
Canadian Imagination*

Jonathan F. Vance

PENGUIN
CANADA

PENGUIN CANADA

Published by the Penguin Group

Penguin Books, a division of Pearson Canada, 10 Alcorn Avenue, Toronto,
Ontario, Canada M4V 3B2
Penguin Books Ltd, 80 Strand, London WC2R 0RL, England
Penguin Putnam Inc., 375 Hudson Street, New York, New York 10014, U.S.A.
Penguin Books Australia Ltd, 250 Camberwell Road, Camberwell,
Victoria 3124, Australia
Penguin Books India (P) Ltd, 11, Community Centre, Panchsheel Park,
New Delhi – 110 017, India
Penguin Books (NZ) Ltd, cnr Rosedale and Airborne Roads, Albany,
Auckland 1310, New Zealand
Penguin Books (South Africa) (Pty) Ltd, 24 Sturdee Avenue, Rosebank 2196,
South Africa

Penguin Books Ltd, Registered Offices: 80 Strand, London WC2R 0RL, England

First published 2002

1 3 5 7 9 10 8 6 4 2

Copyright © Jonathan F. Vance, 2002

Author representation: Westwood Creative Artists
94 Harbord Street, Toronto, Ontario M5S 1G6

Printed and bound in Canada on acid free paper ∞

National Library of Canada Cataloguing in Publication

Vance, Jonathan Franklin William, 1963–
High flight : aviation and the Canadian imagination / Jonathan F. Vance.

ISBN 0-14-301345-9

1. Aeronautics—Canada—History—20th century. 2. Aeronautics—Social
aspects—Canada—History. I. Title.

TL523.V36 2002   629.13'0971   C2002-901939-7

Visit Penguin Books' website at **www.penguin.ca**

CONTENTS

PROLOGUE

I HAVE NEVER LIKED FLYING. IN FACT, THE ENTIRE EXPERIENCE, from my first glimpse of the airplane on the tarmac to the heavy braking and rapid deceleration on landing, fills me with dread. But I spent my childhood building model airplanes and reading comic books about fighter pilots, I love going to air shows and aviation museums, and I have passed countless hours over the past two decades chatting with veterans of the Royal Air Forces about their experiences. I may dislike the act of flying, but I am fascinated by the notion of flight.

This book is not a history of flying, and indeed I have gone out of my way to avoid writing one. Canada has been blessed with many fine aviation historians—Frank Ellis, Fred Hitchins, Larry Milberry, K. M. Molson, Peter Pigott, Wayne Ralph, Shirley Render and the many people whose articles have filled the Canadian Aviation Historical Society's journal—who have enriched our knowledge of airlines, aircraft types, aviation policy and pilots. I am deeply indebted to their work for making mine easier.

Instead, this book is a history of the *idea* of flight, an attempt to convey the perceptions of flying held by a generation that did not yet know how the new technology would change their lives. To put it another way, I have not been preoccupied with what happened to aviation in Canada but with what people *imagined* would happen. Most Canadians of the first half of this century regarded the new technology with keen interest but with little personal connection. Nevertheless, they knew that significant technological changes were under way that, for good or ill, would reshape their world. The airplane, the first new machine of the twentieth century and the fulfilment of one of humanity's most ancient and enduring wishes, would, in many ways, lead that reshaping. We can see from the twenty-first century how aviation changed the twentieth and how unrealistic were the predictions of aviation enthusiasts. But it is much more interesting to take ourselves back to the earliest days of flight to see how people thought their world would change in the air age. We can glimpse their hopes for the future and their fears; we can sense the promise of aviation and its peril.

As the reader will see, the number of Canadians personally involved in flying (a group that I call the air lobby) was relatively small, at least until the 1930s. Nonetheless, they took it upon themselves to educate the mass of Canadians who were not airminded (to use their contemporary term), who were uninformed and perhaps uninterested in the great potential of aviation for improving their lives, their country and their world. The public preconceptions about aviation were often misleading, contradictory and unrealistic but were so strongly held that the air lobby had to address them in spreading the gospel of flight. Their proselytizing efforts constitute the other half of my story.

To get a sense of prevailing opinion regarding aviation, we could do worse than to look briefly at the writings of Stephen Leacock, who was always able to look at things in two very different ways. As an economist, he saw the world through the lens of the dismal science, applying a practical and sometimes hard-nosed intellect to any problem that had an economic dimension. As a humorist, he brought both a devastating wit and a deep affection to his subject matter. Like most people of the early twentieth century, Leacock cast a skeptical eye on aviation and its supposed impact on the world. The professor in him had some very definite notions about the implications of flight for business and the economy, but Leacock the humorist found intense amusement in the popular assumptions that had come to surround flying.

In "The Man in Asbestos," a Rip Van Winkle character awakens centuries in the future, when all forms of transportation have been eliminated as risky and pointless. What was the point of travelling? asked his guide. "It's just the same being here as being anywhere else." No good ever came from the airplane or the railway or the automobile: "It brought into every town a lot of people from every other town. Who wanted them? Nobody." Excerpts from the *Midge's Corners Metropolitan* (formerly the *Midge's Corners Sentinel and Advocate*) from 1930 demonstrate the transformation of rural life that the airplane had wrought: "the top of Joe Thompson's barn...has been adapted for the purposes of an aerodrome. We congratulate the young people in helping to encourage aeronautics in this section. We are informed that it is in the air that the aeronautic society of the corners will soon put up an aerodrome, the need for which is felt by all the farming community." It was a far cry from the early days of Midge's Corners, when Ed Wildman's new top buggy so impressed the local paper.

"The Last of the Rubber Necks" takes the reader on an air bus in 1950, when a round-the-world sightseeing trip costs five dollars. The passengers are effusive at the opportunity. "I've just been dying to go for a long time," burbles one woman, "but of course my husband is always so busy that it's hard for him to get the time. You see it takes a whole day." Another passenger intimates that air boats will soon make the trip in half a day but declares that he prefers the old-fashioned, slow airliners that take a full day to circle the globe: "After all, there's nothing like taking things easy." However, he does admit that "it gets a little monotonous for the children, doesn't it?" Down the aisle, a man marvels at how air travel helps him to know the world better: "So that was Germany, eh? Much flatter than I thought. And Poland looks a good deal yellower than I had supposed. Nothing like foreign travel for clearing up your ideas. I don't think you can understand foreign nations in any real sense without actually seeing them." Another woman finds the great landmarks of England whizzing past: "Well, I'm certainly glad to have seen Westminster Abbey. I don't think anyone's education is complete without seeing it. Didn't you feel a kind of thrill when you heard it go by?" Perhaps the highlight of the trip, though, is an opportunity to drop bombs on one side or the other (it doesn't particularly matter which) of a Chinese rebellion, through the courtesy of the airship company and the International Friendship Committee.[1]

In these few sketches, the ever-perceptive Leacock deftly lampoons the hopes and dreams of the air lobby. The social revolution that the mobility of the air age would create, the necessity of even the smallest community to have an airfield to avoid being left behind, the airplane's ability to shrink both time and space, the enthusiasm of women and children for flying, the air highway as a path to greater international understanding and world peace, the notion that flying was a means of personal improvement—all these ideas were characteristic of the air age. Although most of them proved over-optimistic and unfounded, by the mid-1930s they had coalesced into an ideology of hope in the promise of technology, the ideology of air-mindedness. But it all began nearly a century earlier, with a balloon, an aeronaut and a beautiful summer afternoon.

HIGH FLIGHT

· 1 ·

BALLOONATICS AND AERONAUTS

FILLING THE BALLOON.

EAGER NEW BRUNSWICKERS STARTED TO GATHER AROUND lunchtime, and by late afternoon most of the vantage points around Saint John's Barrack Square and Parade Ground were thronged with spectators. That day, August 10, 1840, Louis Anselm Lauriat, the celebrated balloonist from Boston, would ascend in his *Star of the East*. The weather was ideal, very clear with a gentle breeze from the southwest ("the atmosphere as serene as a young maiden after plighting her troth," recorded one newspaper), and there was a buzz of excitement as Lauriat made his final preparations. Just after five o'clock, he commanded his assistants to cast off the ropes, and the *Star of the East* rose, slowly and tentatively at first, but gradually with more assurance. From the basket suspended beneath his balloon, Lauriat waved his hat and bowed gravely to the people below. They watched in fascination as the balloon drifted north, then wafted to the east as the wind pushed it away from the city. The spectators in Barrack

Square could see it for nearly an hour before it disappeared. As he drifted over the farmlands east of Saint John, Lauriat ascended farther, reaching a height of some seventy-three hundred feet. After nearly ninety minutes in the air, he brought the *Star of the East* to a safe landing in a farmer's field twenty-one miles from the city. He packed up his balloon, collected his meagre earnings (very few spectators had purchased tickets to the event, but an appeal for donations brought in enough money to cover Lauriat's expenses) and returned to Boston by steamer. The "intrepid Aeronaut," as the papers called him, was gone, but he had brought the air age to British North America.[1]

During the next seventy years, a legion of aeronauts would follow Lauriat, hoping to take advantage of the public's interest in balloons, dirigibles and airplanes. Many were charlatans—had they not been selling tickets to flying displays, they would have been hawking snake oil or perpetual-motion machines. Others were genuine pioneers, with a deep passion for flight and a determination to finance further experiments by mounting demonstrations for the general public. They were exotic characters such as Madame Lowanda, the Bird Boy and Professor Thaddeus Sobieski Constantine Lowe, and they elicited in observers a curious mixture of fascination, admiration and disdain.

The aeronauts rarely failed to attract a crowd of people, drawn to see them by a variety of motives. For many, idle curiosity or the prospect of a pleasant diversion brought them out on a sunny afternoon; some likely nursed the secret hope that they might witness some dreadful accident. A few, however, joined with the aeronauts in envisioning wondrous things for the future of air travel. Despite the primitive technology, they confidently predicted an era when opulent airships, carrying hundreds of passengers and thousands of pounds of cargo, would crowd the skies; when travellers would board a flying machine for intercity jaunts as readily as boarding a train; when time and space would be compressed by flying machines that knew no earthly obstacles; when people would see their world from the vantage point of the gods. In these predictions, we see the first vague outlines of the dreams that would come to dominate the air age.

, , ,

As long as humans have walked the earth, they have probably longed to rise above it. Religion, myth and legend are filled with tales of creatures endowed with the power to ascend into the heavens. Muhammad's flight from Mecca to Jerusalem and back on a fanciful flying creature; Pegasus the winged horse; angels and fairies; the winged bulls of Assyria; the legendary flying carpet; the winged gods Mercury and Hermes—all bear witness to the human desire to break the constraints of earthly existence.

The transition from fancy to reality, though, was not so simple, for it was not entirely clear how an ordinary mortal could be lifted into the air. The mythical Daedalus and Icarus attempted to imitate the birds by crafting wings of feathers and affixing them to their backs with wax, a proposition that anticipated one of the most enduring assumptions about the best way to achieve human flight, the ornithopter concept. For centuries, monks, nobles, scientists and artisans alike firmly believed that the best way to achieve artificial flight was to imitate the birds, by using human strength to operate mechanical wings. Leonardo da Vinci was the most sophisticated of these thinkers, filling page after page with intricate sketches of avian anatomy and flying machines patterned after birds. Da Vinci wisely declined to test his ornithopters himself, but other budding aeronauts were less reluctant. Indeed, the annals of early flight are filled with intrepid pioneers plummeting to their deaths in primitive ornithopters or jumping from towers wearing cloaks stiffened into wings.

Roger Bacon, the thirteenth-century English philosopher, scientist and Franciscan monk, knew of these attempts and may even have witnessed one himself. Such failures impelled him to the conclusion that the obstacle was weight: the devices were simply too heavy to rise into the air using human strength alone. He therefore turned his mind to a lighter-than-air flying machine, writing of globes made from thin copper and filled with "thin air or liquid fire" that would rise into the air and float in the atmosphere. Bacon may have been first to conceptualize the hot-air balloon in any detail, and as the centuries passed, the lighter-than-air principle seemed to offer the best prospect for success. In 1670, Francisco de Lana, a Jesuit, envisioned a small boat that would be carried aloft by four copper spheres emptied of air. He reasoned that if air had weight, the absence of air must have no weight; therefore, the globes would rise. De Lana overlooked the matter of air pressure, but he and Bacon were on the right track in assuming that gases had different weights and, therefore, different lifting properties. However, it would be another hundred years before this notion was successfully put into practice by the French Montgolfier brothers, who sent the first human aloft in 1783, in a silk-and-paper balloon elevated by hot air. At the same time, their compatriot Jacques Charles was getting better results (if less publicity) in a balloon filled with hydrogen, a newly isolated element available only since 1766.

News of these developments reached British North America. In October 1784, William B. Jarvis, later secretary and registrar of Upper Canada, wrote to his brother in Parr Town (Saint John), New Brunswick, of witnessing the ascent of Vincenzo Lunardi in a balloon ("cheating the Turnpike" by avoiding road tolls, as Jarvis put it) in London, England, the previous month. Thomas G. Ridout, later a successful banker and member of the Family Compact, wrote to his relatives in Upper Canada of watching the ascent of a balloon over London, England, from atop St. Paul's Cathedral in 1811. Eight years later, a number of newspapers in Lower Canada carried accounts of flights by French balloonists touring the United States (one angry crowd in Philadelphia reportedly tore apart a balloon when the promised ascent did not occur).[2] In 1820, the Quebec *Mercury* reported the launch of small balloons from the Champs de Mars. One landed on a roof, leading police to warn that they would prosecute balloonists under the ordinance that prohibited the discharge of combustible devices within city limits. Another came to earth near a carriage, so frightening its occupant that he fainted. On regaining consciousness, he declared "that he had been visited by the Devil who had come for the purpose of clawing away his soul."[3]

The Halifax *Nova Scotian* was less preoccupied with the supernatural, but was equally skeptical of the notion of flight. A few years before Lauriat's ascent, the paper published a long article titled "Chronology of the Art of Flying," from tower jumpers and de Lana to Jacques Charles and the Montgolfiers. But the editor pointed out that "balloons have not justified the expectations they raised. They have conferred little or no value upon science, and their principal value is derived from the opportunity they give of seeing almost a whole kingdom at a glance. The aeronaut has only the power of ascending or descending. Nor can he reach any given point, unless the current of wind in which he happens to set sail sets directly towards it." Shortly afterwards, the paper backed up its skepticism by describing in gruesome detail the death of Robert Cocking, an English landscape painter with more money than sense, who plummeted from an ascending balloon wearing a parachute of his own flawed design.[4]

Despite such tragedies, it was clearly only a matter of time before the ballooning craze swept Canada. There were a number of attempts to launch unmanned balloons in the 1830s, in Montreal, Kingston, Halifax and Fredericton, but not all were successful. One plan to launch three balloons in Montreal in October 1834 as a charity fundraiser had to be cancelled when the unruly crowd pushed its way into the launching area and burst one of the balloons. Two years later, the celebrated American balloonist Charles Ferson Durant was given the opportunity to become the first man to go aloft in Canada, when a wealthy Montrealer offered him $500 to make an ascent in the city. Durant declined, declaring the sum to be insufficient, and missed making his mark in Canadian aviation history.[5] The honour went instead to Louis Anselm Lauriat in 1840.

The balloon that propelled Lauriat into posterity was not markedly different from that built by the Montgolfiers, although rather more utilitarian. By the mid-nineteenth century, the aeronaut's vehicle had evolved into a fairly simple device. A small wicker or wooden basket was suspended beneath a large bag made of canvas, silk or some other strong fabric, held within a mesh of rope. Lift was occasionally provided by hydrogen but more often by coal gas, which was much cheaper and easier to produce. Large quantities of gas to inflate the balloon had to be available on site, and the inflation process could take many hours, depending on the ambient temperature and other climatic factors. During inflation, volunteers were enlisted to control the ropes that tethered the balloon to the ground. Once it was aloft, altitude could be controlled by dropping ballast (to ascend) or releasing gas (to descend). In the event of an emergency, a rope attached to a ripping panel allowed the aeronaut to deflate the bag quickly. The bag would then be transformed into an immense parachute that, in theory, would float the pilot safely to the ground. Beyond these basic means of control, balloons were entirely dependent on the weather. Low cloud made it pointless to attempt an ascent, as did any form of precipitation. In the air, the balloon was completely at the mercy of the wind, which might carry both aeronaut and vehicle into trees, buildings or a nearby lake.

As the technology of ballooning improved, the craft became slightly less unwieldy. By the early twentieth century, the round balloon had been replaced by a sausage-shaped gasbag, usually about sixty feet long and eighteen feet in diameter. Suspended below the bag was a triangular wooden frame, thirty to forty feet long and two feet high, with a propeller at one end, a small internal combustion engine in the middle and a rudder at the other end. The pilot, still known as an aeronaut, sat astride the frame and controlled the rudder by means of a long cord. Because it could be guided, the craft became known as a dirigible (from the French *diriger*, "to steer"). The aeronaut also had to operate a hand pump to keep oil circulating into the engine, listen for any sounds of engine trouble and monitor the pressure of the bag by periodically tapping it with his finger. His other primary task was keeping the airship level, which he did by moving back and forth along the frame.

Clearly, ballooning had come a long way since Bacon and de Lana had theorized about lighter-than-air flight. But in these early days it was not entirely clear that history was being made, and balloon ascents were little more than entertainment gimmicks. As local fairs competed with other forms of entertainment to draw a crowd, they resorted to ever stranger and more spectacular displays, and balloon ascensions fitted the bill nicely. By the late nineteenth century, any decent Victoria Day celebration, agricultural society exhibition or fall fair had to feature a balloon ascension (preferably with aerial acrobatics and a parachute jump), along with fireworks, brass bands, Wild West shows, pig races, strongmen and perhaps even Private Smith, the fastest walker in the world. Most aeronauts, such as Madame Carlotta (her real name was Mary, but Carlotta looked so much better on the handbills), Professor Ayres and Miss Mandell and her dog, Aerio, were entertainers, not engineers or inventors; their priority was drawing crowds, not improving aviation technology.

For this reason, the deficiencies of early balloons all too often got in the way of the show. At the Niagara Fair in September 1850, hundreds came to see Ira Thurston (who was to die in a balloon accident in 1858) make an ascent, but hours of waiting in the hot sun brought only "grievous disappointment." The balloonist was unable to get his craft airborne, leading the editor of the St. Catharines *Journal* to demand refunds for the thwarted spectators. When Professor Lowe was unable to get his craft airborne at the Ottawa's Victoria Day celebrations in 1858, the *Tribune* sullenly declared that "the Balloon affair, as everybody expected, was a failure." Indeed, the long waits involved in balloon ascents led the editor of a Hamilton newspaper to observe resignedly that "in such matters there is often much wearisomeness and disappointment, in protracting the time for exhibiting the spectacle."[6]

But if getting up was difficult, getting down could be positively hazardous, as the American aeronaut Charles H. Grimley discovered in Ottawa in 1877. The bright sun shining on his balloon *The City of Worcester* made it look like a ball of fire, and local farmhands took cover as he floated toward them. It was some time before Grimley could convince one to emerge from hiding, grab hold of the tether rope and haul him down. The farmer refused to allow him to deflate the balloon in his field, fearing that the gas would explode and kill his family, huddled in terror in their farmhouse. All was made well when Grimley was greeted by a local worthy and invited to a nearby tavern "to refresh the inner man."[7]

Mishaps like these did nothing to dispel the skepticism evinced earlier by the *Nova Scotian*. In 1875, after a balloon dumped its hapless crew and passengers in Lake Ontario, the Toronto *Globe* published a caustic attack on ballooning and all connected with it: "Improvements in their construction and management cannot be said to have kept pace with those of other things that could be mentioned...as far as the purposes of peace are concerned these balloons are still little better than mere toys, and there is at present little prospect of their soon, if ever, becoming anything better ...even for amusements they are risky, and we should think, upon the whole unpleasant." As for the balloonists who spent chilly hours drifting in the lake, had they drowned, "their fate would have called forth little sympathy and very little surprise. They had turned themselves into mere advertising agents, and proposed to earn their coppers by risking their necks."[8] The editor of the London *Advertiser* was just as dubious about the new technology. An 1888 exhibition of ballooning, acrobatics and parachute jumping had been a huge success, but he doubted that the balloon "will ever become of practical use... [but] will remain what it is—a scientific toy and the apparatus of the professional gymnast." Twenty years later, the same criticisms could be heard. In July 1908, at least six contestants in a Chicago balloon race came to earth in southern Ontario and Quebec. One deposited its occupants in a tree in West Shefford, Quebec, before disappearing into the sky again, leading a local newspaper to declare that despite some possible utility in war-gaming and map-making, "balloon-ing will always remain a sport and nothing more."[9]

Even after dirigibles replaced balloons, the same problems plagued planned ascents. In 1909, when the much-ballyhooed Knabenshue dirigible remained aloft for only three minutes, the London, Ontario, crowd was almost as disappointed as the pilot, Leo Hess, whose contract stipulated that he would not be paid unless he remained in the air for eight minutes. A planned ascent in Toronto was such a fiasco that exhibition organizers ordered the aeronaut from the grounds, perhaps to save him from the wrath of disappointed spectators.[10] An exhibition by James C. Mars, in a Strobel dirigible, proved an exercise in frustration for visitors to the Victoria Fair and Horse Show in September 1909. On the twenty-second, Mars got his airship off the ground, albeit after dark, leading the *Colonist* to rank the flight as "one of the best [attractions] offered at the fair, both from its novelty and also by reason of the skill displayed by the aviator." Mars's perfor-mance would, in the writer's view, prove "that aerial navigation has come to stay." The following day, the editor had much less reason to be optimistic. The scheduled afternoon flight was not attempted, one of Mars's assistants claiming that the wind was too strong, and a short ascent after dinner failed to soothe the ruffled feelings of the spectators, few of whom elected to stay around for the flight. The editor roundly condemned the aero-naut because "an admission fee was charged to those who wanted to go into a tent and look at a gas bag and a whirling motor... faith has not been kept with the public in this matter, and the responsible people are acting for the public and should see that they are given what they are promised." The exhibition's secretary brandished a signed contract in front of Mars (who had already come before the courts in a dispute with a business partner over ownership of the dirigible), insisting that he would have the sher-iff seize the airship unless the contracted flights were made. This appears to have had the desired impact: Mars ascended in his dirigible on schedule, much to the delight of the crowds.[11]

On other occasions, more was lost than a few idle hours. In September 1888, a butcher named Tom Wensley was one of several strong young men holding the tether ropes of a balloon at the Central Canada Fair in Ottawa. Sadly, Wensley either did not hear or ignored the command to cast off ropes and started ascending with the balloon. At about a thousand feet, he lost his grip and plummeted to his death, the first aerial fatality in Canada. Press reports suggested that he might have acted with intent, claiming that Wensley had had a dream in which he saw himself flying through the air.[12] Twenty years later, the Calgary Fair was struck by disaster when Capt. Jack Dallas's airship was caught in a sudden squall. A toppling pole burst the bag, which Dallas and his assistant, Bert Hall, were inflating, and a spark ignited the gas, sending a fireball fifty feet into the air. Dallas and Hall were burned, and one fair-goer was killed by falling debris. In 1909, a Nassr dirigible had been contracted to put on a flying display at the Ottawa exhibition, but on the first day it brushed against a power line, electrocuting one of the assistants and injuring two others. Later that day, the airship had another accident that disabled the propeller, and as it was being pulled back to the exhibition grounds it ran into power lines again. This time, the sparks ignited the balloon and the gasbag went up in a sheet of flame.[13]

Such mishaps were widely reported in the press, and the balloon began to work its way into popular culture in a manner that would not have pleased the serious, air-minded Canadian. Indeed, for many people, the likelihood of travel by air was so remote that the balloon became a sort of shorthand for anything too improbable or fantastic to imagine. As Ida Chesley pondered her potential suitors in the novel *The Banker's Grandchildren*, she admitted that she "would as soon have thought of flying off in a balloon for the purpose of exploring the 'Milky Way,'" as of marrying a handsome but poor young clerk. In James De Mille's *A Comedy of Terrors*, Mrs. Lovell, horrified at the prospect of a balloon flight, remonstrated that "I'd just as soon think of allowing myself to be fired from a cannon." A mysterious appearance or disappearance could rhetorically be explained the same way. "Where, then, was Savareen?" queried the narrator of a typical Victorian Canadian melodrama. "Had he sunk into the bowels of the earth, or gone up, black mare and all, in a balloon?"[14]

Nevertheless, despite the delays, disasters and disdain, the crowds never stopped coming. In 1874, some ten thousand people gathered at the Dominion Day celebration in Brockville, Ontario, to witness an ascent by Professor Squires. The balloon struck the spire of the Methodist church, heightening the crowd's enjoyment. As the local newspaper reported, "Women grew white with terror, brave men trembled. There at a height of eighty feet above the earth was a fellow hanging by a few slender threads above and around him, the glittering steeple sheeted with tin, below the cold stone battlements of the tower, on which to fall was instant death." In 1884, an excited throng crowded an Ottawa fairground to see Madame Lowanda, one of the few women aeronauts and a veteran of more than thirty ascents. With the "adventurous young aeronaut placed in full command of the apparently unwieldy monster," the *Queen of the Air* slowly ascended, Lowanda scattering advertising leaflets as she drifted upward. Much to the relief of her husband, who had no fear of ballooning but was concerned for her safety once she returned to the ground in unfamiliar environs, she landed without incident at Aylmer.[15]

Gradually, the enthusiasm generated by these early flights spread, and the use of the balloon as a metaphor for the impossible was supplanted by the notion that it was a harbinger of a new age. People began to make astonishing predictions about the future of air travel. In 1889, the London *Free Press* enthusiastically reported that a Boston consortium was planning to construct an airship using the vacuum principle. It was to be built entirely of thin steel plates, with internal bracing to withstand atmospheric pressure when the vacuum was achieved. The promoters confidently predicted that it could carry two hundred passengers and five hundred tons of cargo, with electrical motors giving it a speed of seventy miles per hour. Twenty years later, a budding engineer was claiming that a leviathan half a mile in length and six hundred feet in diameter could carry ten thousand tons of cargo or fifteen thousand passengers and could give the railways and steamship lines a run for their money.[16] The Charlottetown *Daily Patriot* reported the plans of Boston millionaire Charles J. Glidden to inaugurate passenger and freight dirigible service linking the cities of New England with Saint John, Montreal and Quebec City. A rival group, the Eastern Transit Company, applied to the Connecticut legislature for permission to operate balloons between Connecticut and the Maritimes. One confident Calgarian even applied to the provincial government to lease land on Cascade Mountain to develop as an airship station.[17]

One of the most remarkable exercises in futurism, well known in Canada at the time, came from the pen of Rudyard Kipling. "With the Night Mail," written in 1905, looked ahead to the year 2000, twenty years after the dirigible had succeeded the airplane (one character speaks derisively of the era "when men still flew tin kites over oil engines") as the only means of bulk freight transport and the carrier of 98 percent of the world's air passengers. Everything on earth is administered by the Aerial Board of Control, established in 1949 with the motto Transportation is Civilization, which had outlawed war as injurious to air traffic and commerce. The story describes a journey from London, England, to Quebec City on a mail carrier, a steel-sheathed dirigible over two hundred feet long that cruised above the clouds at nearly 250 miles per hour, sharing the sky with airships known as Hudson Bay furriers, Keewatin liners, Ungava petrol tanks and Athabasca grain tubs. It is indeed a brave new world, made better by aviation technology.[18]

But it was not all about cargo and trade. Other prescient souls envisioned a new age of aerial romance developing once the airship had supplanted the ocean liner as the preferred means of transport. "Come, Josephine, in My Flying Machine" importuned one ballad of courtship in the clouds that was all the rage before 1914. A poet looked forward to the day when honeymooners could begin their married lives above the clouds:

In an airship swift, we'll drift, drift, drift
Across the cloud flecked sky.
While on earth below the autos slow,
Go crawling snail-like by,
Close to the moon, we'll spoon, spoon, spoon,
As we roam the Milky Way
In our aerodrome, 'neath the heaven's dome,
10,000 miles a day.[19]

For the citizens of Prince Edward Island, the airship offered the hope of a somewhat different relationship, the end of their isolation from the mainland. Confidently predicting that "the day is rapidly approaching when air-ships will be numbered among the fleets of the nations as well as among the passenger and mail carrying transportation facilities of the world," the Charlottetown *Daily Patriot* observed that "the solution of continuous communication between Prince Edward Island and the Mainland, in the winter season is in sight." Airships could ply the skies between PEI and Nova Scotia, at any hour of the day or night, in all but the strongest of winds. The journey between Charlottetown and Halifax would take only a few hours; hourly crossings between Cape Traverse and Cape Tormentine would take just a few minutes, so there would be virtually no danger of accident and would cost the government no more than the icebreaker service. The *Patriot* urged the government to take up the challenge so "passengers could hear the captain of the airship shout 'all aboard,' and with their valise in one hand could hasten up the passage way, board the airship and in less than ten minutes be safely landed at Tormentine, ready to take their train to all the centres of either Canada or the United States." A reader agreed: "A flying machine as we have them today would...give us that communication so desirable....I do not see, sir, why the experiment could not be made between the Island and the mainland, for commercial, mail and passenger purposes."[20]

But such prognostications were all too often overshadowed by the cold, hard realities of early airships. It was one thing to put on a successful dirigible display at a regional fair, but quite another to construct an airship of practical value. Indeed, every high-flying dream in the daily press was more than matched by accounts of commercial airships falling to earth. The crash at Echterdingen, Germany, on August 6, 1908, of LZ4, a dirigible built by Ferdinand Graf von Zeppelin, the German nobleman whose name would become synonymous with airships, led the Calgary *Herald* to sniff, "Judging by the way these airships get smashed up when anything happens to them, they cannot be very safe things to travel round in." The Victoria *Colonist* concluded from the wreck of the German airship *Deutschland* in Osnabrück on June 26, 1910, that "the air is not yet ready to surrender itself to the purposes of navigation." The ignominious failure of Walter Wellman's attempt to cross the Atlantic in a dirigible later that year drew even more sniggers. Noted the *Colonist*, "Theoretically... [the dirigible] is revolutionary. Practically it generally proves a disappointment." In 1912, when an American dirigible came to grief in Atlantic City, the Calgary *Herald* observed sourly that "people talk glibly of the possibility of being able to book a passage in a balloon from New York to some port in Europe, with a reasonable chance of reaching their destination in safety. Such enthusiasts are about one hundred years in advance of the science on which they rely."[21]

And so to many, it was already clear that the airship was not the way of the future. Just months after telling the reading public about a monster, fifteen-thousand-passenger dirigible, *Queen's Quarterly* presented a dissenting opinion.[22] This writer believed that the lighter-than-air machine faced a doubtful future, especially given the recent rash of airship failures. In his view, and in the view of many others, the way to the skies lay with the airplane.

✻ ✻ ✻

On September 29, 1907, at the Nova Scotia Provincial Exhibition in Halifax, yet another eager crowd gathered to witness the ascent of a dirigible. Thomas Scott Baldwin (he used the title captain, without any apparent legal right to do so) had flown his *California Arrow II* four days earlier, so the townspeople had every hope of another flight. They waited for most of the day, but by late afternoon the wind was still about ten knots, well above the seven knots that Baldwin deemed acceptable for a safe ascent. Gradually, the crowds melted away, some to return the following day, others to dismiss Baldwin as just another huckster.[23]

In the crowd was a gentleman who had travelled some distance for his first glimpse of an airship in flight. Alexander Graham Bell did not record his impressions of Baldwin's failure, but he would later state that the dirigible, although "of the greatest importance to mankind," was "on the wrong basis, being lighter than air."[24] Ballooning was, he believed, a blind alley.

Flight had exercised a hold over Bell since his childhood. He would haunt the slopes of Edinburgh's Corstorphine Hill, kicking through the heather and gazing up at the birds that wheeled overhead. Bell's trusty amanuensis, Thomas Watson, recalled the inventor's fascination with the anatomy of a very dead seagull while on a beach stroll and later promised Bell he would turn his mechanical skills—Watson had built a very light steam engine that Bell thought would be ideal for a flying machine—to the conquest of the skies once the telephone business was up and running. Watson never did join forces with his old mentor again, but Bell constantly turned ideas about flying over in his head, occasionally committing them to paper in a hurried sketch or a frantic scribble.

Bell was probably aware of flight experiments around the world, if only because they were reported in the daily press. Such reports were usually undiscriminating, although in hindsight it is easy to pick out the crackpots and frauds. A gentleman in Belgium claimed to have invented a small flying machine that would allow any man to fly "with the swiftness of a swallow and the vigor of an eagle." All he required was deep-pocketed investors. A Spanish farm labourer was reported to have devised a successful ornithopter. With fans on his feet and hand-powered wings on his back, he claimed to have soared to a height of six hundred feet. He, at least, was not looking for any money.[25]

It is difficult to judge how such reports might have affected Bell. His thinking on aviation remained scattered and haphazard until 1891, when he acquainted himself with the aviation experiments of his old friend Samuel Pierpont Langley, a respected physicist and secretary of the Smithsonian Institution. From that summer, Bell was hooked; more and more, he spent his hours pondering propellers, testing steam jets, building miniature rockets and experimenting with wing shapes. One pictures him in his laboratory in a cheerfully agitated state, filling his notebooks with tiny lines of commentary, quickly scribbled calculations and rough sketches. To read Bell's laboratory notes from the period is to get a glimpse into the workings of his mind.

On March 29, 1894, for example, he was grappling with the relationship between weight and velocity in airborne objects. Employing the somewhat dubious analogy that it required less power to drive a lead bullet through the air than a mass of feathers of the same weight, he deduced that a heavy flying machine would move through the air better than a light one. Furthermore, as a bullet moves through the air without wings, "Could not a heavy machine...be kept up without wings at all" if it had sufficient velocity? he mused. Was the true function of wings not support, but guidance? He wondered why a bird in flight remained on a constant plane, rather than bobbing up and down with every flap of its wings. His answer: they were kept in the air by their velocity. "Will conclude these notes," he wrote triumphantly, "with thought with which I commenced them and which grows more evident the more I ponder over it—*Velocity is itself an element of support.*"[26] In these feverish notes, we can see Bell's creative process at work. Using a combination of trial and error, empirical observations, ratiocination and analogies, he valiantly tried to understand basic aerodynamics. On this day, Bell was wrong, at least in that he did not yet appreciate how a wing creates lift, one of the basic aerodynamic forces. In another sense, though, he was looking beyond aviation to rocketry.

Few people were privy to Bell's laboratory notes, but occasionally he would write short essays on the future of air travel. In 1892, he dictated an article that began with an imaginary flight from Boston to New York. The passengers took their seats in a carriage, which then rose vertically before moving off horizontally. On arrival, the machine hovered over the airport and gradually descended. A rope was tossed out and the carriage secured to the ground so the passengers could alight. In 1896, he told an American journalist that it would not be long before a person could dine in New York and breakfast in Ireland or England after a flight across the Atlantic.[27]

At about the same time, other aviation pioneers were taking their thinking in different directions. In Germany, Otto Lilienthal was working with gliders and demonstrated that a curved wing surface was more efficient than a flat one. This work would be carried on and refined by Octave Chanute, who established a research camp on the shore of Lake Michigan to test his powered gliders. Sir Hiram Maxim, better known to the world for developing the machine gun, was having some success with huge kites powered by steam engines. Samuel Langley came very close to achieving artificial flight in 1903, but repeated launching accidents wrecked his flying machine, his credibility and his will to continue.

In Dayton, Ohio, Orville and Wilbur Wright had followed these developments with growing interest. The brothers had been interested in flying as children, when their father bought them a small helicopter toy. In the late summer of 1896, as Orville lay prostrated by typhoid, Wilbur and their sister Katharine took turns by his bedside, keeping an eye on his fever and feeding him milk and beef broth. This gave Wilbur time to think, his thoughts focused by a news report of the death of Otto Lilienthal, and from that point the brothers began to take notice of any aviation news items that appeared in local papers. In 1899, Wilbur wrote to the Smithsonian Institution requesting copies of any publications on aviation and received a package of pamphlets by people such as Lilienthal and Langley, as well as a reading list of other works. They devoured everything they could find on the subject, putting other people's theories to the test and, when they were found wanting, returning to the essentials of flight for inspiration. In an astonishingly short period of time they were building and testing gliders at Kitty Hawk, North Carolina, chosen because of its favourable climatic conditions. Successful but not entirely satisfactory glider flights in 1900 and 1901 sent them back to Dayton to verify their calculations, and better-than-expected flights in 1902 convinced them that it was time to take their next step: the addition of an engine to their glider. In September 1903 they crated up their new Wright Flyer and set out for Kitty Hawk. More tests and tinkering followed, and on December 17, 1903, assisted by the men of the U.S. Lifesaving Service Station at Kill Devil Hills, Orville coaxed the Flyer into the air for a grand total of twelve seconds. The dream had finally been realized—powered flight was now a reality.

The flight elicited barely a glimmer of interest in Canada (outside the small community of aviation enthusiasts), in large part because the Wrights were careful to shield the details of their accomplishments from the prying eyes of competitors. A few reports did leak out, however. The Toronto *Daily Star*, with more relief than enthusiasm, informed its readers that "A Flying Machine at Last Succeeds." The London *Advertiser* reported erroneously that the aircraft had flown three miles into the face of the wind before it "gracefully descended to earth." In fact, the flight was just over a hundred feet. The error originated with some overzealous newspapermen in Norfolk, Virginia, who heard of the flight but were unable to confirm the details, so they simply made them up.[28]

Alexander Graham Bell followed all these developments with interest, but his attention might have remained unfocused without the intervention of his wife, Mabel, who shared Bell's passion for science and technology. She had the same questing mind and unbounded curiosity as Alec, but a stronger leavening of common sense. It was that element which would ultimately help bring powered flight to Canada, to the unlikely setting of Baddeck, Nova Scotia, where their estate, Beinn Bhreagh (Beautiful Mountain, or the Bell Palace, as it was dubbed by a local newspaper), would become a magnet for the small but growing community of aviation enthusiasts.

Among this group were four men whom Bell hoped would help him achieve his dream of artificial flight. They were young, energetic, technically and scientifically minded—veritable personifications of the new twentieth century—and excellent foils to Bell's brilliant but occasionally undirected Victorian mind. Casey Baldwin, a native of Toronto, and Doug McCurdy, born in Baddeck, had both attended the School of Practical Science (later the Faculty of Applied Science and Engineering) of the University of Toronto. Baldwin's consuming interest in aviation was fed by McCurdy, a year behind Baldwin at university but just as passionate about flying. The son of Bell's secretary, assistant and photographer, McCurdy had grown up watching Bell experiment with his enormous kites at Beinn Bhreagh. Tom Selfridge, an artilleryman from California, had met Bell in Washington and received an invitation to Baddeck to observe the experiments for the U.S. Army. The fourth man, Glenn Curtiss, from Hammondsport, New York, was a mechanical genius with a passion for speed; it was on a motorcycle of his own design that he set a world record for the fastest mile in 1907. He owned a chain of bicycle stores and manufactured light and powerful aero engines (among his customers was Capt. Thomas Scott Baldwin, whom Bell had hoped to see make an airship ascent in Halifax). Of the four, Curtiss was the least interested in aviation; he had little confidence in aviators, but Bell knew that as an engine builder he was without peer.

Bell and his four young associates worked independently of one another at Baddeck for most of the summer, until Mabel Bell observed, "What a fine thing it would be to unite these unusual men with their different abilities into still closer relations." She offered $35,000 to cover expenses and pay the salaries of Baldwin, McCurdy and Curtiss.[29] Accordingly, on October 1, 1907, the Aerial Experiment Association (AEA) came into being "for the purpose of carrying on experiments relating to aerial locomotion with the special object of constructing a successful aerodrome." The five would first attempt to complete Bell's pet project, a giant, tetrahedral human-carrying kite, and "Afterwards each associate in turn should have the assistance of the others in the construction of a machine according to his fancy." Just two months after its founding, the first goal was attained. On December 6, 1907, the *Cygnet*, carrying Tom Selfridge, was pulled into the air by a small steamer and remained aloft for a full seven minutes. The flight was a complete success, but Selfridge was unable to cut the towline in time and the *Cygnet* was wrecked as the steamer dragged it across Bras d'Or Lake.

As the laboratory staff replaced the tetrahedral cells that had been destroyed, Baldwin, Curtiss, McCurdy and Selfridge relocated to Curtiss's motorcycle factory in Hammondsport "to construct a gliding machine with which the younger members could indulge their impatience to be flying." Over the next few months, the AEA recorded a string of successful flights, first with Selfridge's *Red Wing*, and then with Baldwin's *White Wing* and Curtiss's *June Bug* (Bell thought its wings resembled those of an insect in flight). Before McCurdy's *Silver Dart* was completed, tragedy struck. In August 1908, Selfridge was summoned back to Washington to join the army's new aeronautical board. He was invited to accompany Orville Wright on a number of demonstration flights, but on September 17, 1908, at Fort Myer, Virginia, Wright's aircraft crashed; Orville was seriously injured, and Selfridge became the first fatality in an airplane crash.

Selfridge's death did not deter his associates. Though the AEA was intended to exist for only twelve months, Mabel Bell offered another $10,000 to extend its life for a further six months so that the *Silver Dart* and two tetrahedral kites, the *Cygnet II* and the

Oinos, could be completed. The *Cygnet* was the first to be readied, and on February 22, 1909, a new engine was mounted to it for a test flight on the ice at Baddeck. The engine turned out to be severely underpowered and, try as they might, they simply could not get the *Cygnet* to lift off the frozen lake. Cold, frustrated and a little dejected, the members of the AEA trudged back to Beinn Bhreagh to prepare for the next day.

It dawned cold and clear, with wisps of cloud drifting overhead and hardly any wind. The crew transferred the *Cygnet*'s engine to the *Silver Dart*, replaced the transmission with a lighter one and installed a propeller that had been tested on an iceboat. About 1 P.M., the aircraft was wheeled from its shed onto the frozen lake, to a spot about a mile from Beinn Bhreagh. A good number of people had gathered (schoolchildren had been let out of class for the occasion), and the crew was about to summon a policeman to keep the crowd away from the flying machine when the wind shifted slightly. They quickly moved the *Silver Dart* up the bay, and before the crowd could follow, McCurdy opened the throttle and the aircraft began to slide along the ice. It gathered speed for about ninety feet and then, in the presence of 147 witnesses (whose names were duly recorded for posterity), the *Silver Dart* slipped into the air. McCurdy took the aircraft up to forty feet, flew for about half a mile, and lightly landed the *Silver Dart* back on the ice. It was all over in ninety seconds, perhaps before many of the spectators realized that they had been watching history in the making.

The local community reacted warmly to the flight of the *Silver Dart*. The Baddeck Board of Commissioners passed a resolution congratulating "the bold aeronaut Douglas McCurdy, a Baddeck boy born and bred." A newspaper in Windsor, Nova Scotia, pointed out that McCurdy had flying in his blood, for he was a distant relative of Jean-Pierre Blanchard, who made the first balloon flight across the English Channel in 1784 (and whose wife became the first woman to die in an aviation accident when she fell from a burning balloon in 1819). Elsewhere in Canada, there was less interest. Press reports were scant; in fact, the loss of the *Silver Dart* in a crash at Petawawa in August 1909 (while performing demonstration flights for the Department of Militia and Defence) drew rather more interest from the press. Nearly a month passed before the achievement was mentioned in the House of Commons, and then finance minister W. S. Fielding admitted that the government, while appreciative of the work of the AEA, had no particular interest, beyond bringing it to the attention of the War Office and the Admiralty in London.[30] Bell tried to create some enthusiasm with a major speech at the Canadian Club of Ottawa on March 27, but without success. Everyone agreed that the flight was remarkable, but there was little consensus on what would come of it.

On March 31, 1909, the Aerial Experiment Association passed into history. But its spirit lived on, for that summer the Beinn Bhreagh community formed the Social Aero Club. At first, it was nothing more than a congenial gathering: the laboratory staff and others would assemble weekly for the reading of the *Beinn Bhreagh Recorder*, the newsletter of the estate. There would be coffee and refreshments, parlour games and the occasional guest speaker or debate before the party broke up in the wee hours of the morning. But Bell and McCurdy suggested that the group be put on a more formal basis. McCurdy believed it entirely apt that Canada's first aero club be situated in Baddeck, the centre of Canadian aviation at the time, and be affiliated with the International Convention of Aero Clubs. As the parent club in Canada, it would draw members from all provinces.[31]

In fact, Baddeck had been beaten to the punch. Just a few weeks after the *Silver Dart* flight, the American journal *Aeronautics* reported the establishment of an Aero Club of Canada in Winnipeg, and in September 1909 an informal meeting was held to create the Aeronautical Society of Canada in Toronto; by early 1910, it had six members (including three who had already flown) and a library. Similar organizations at McGill University, Montreal, and in Oshawa, Ontario, followed. Nevertheless, the

Hon. William McCurdy presented a bill in the Nova Scotia legislature to incorporate the Aero Club of Canada at Baddeck. "Since
the birth of the human race," he intoned, "when man observed
the great birds floating in the regions above with such ease, and
moving with such grace and rapidity, there has been a certain feeling of humility at his helplessness to soar aloft...No doubt but
from earliest times to the present man has dreamed of his ability
to float through space with the utmost ease....At last heavier-
than-air machines of aerodromes driven by gasolene [*sic*] power
have been successfully constructed, which are comparatively free
from accident in the air, and cannot easily be injured or disabled
by projectiles from an enemy. Such machines are bound to be of
great service for aerial locomotion both in time of peace and in
time of war."[32] At least in the view of the Baddeck aviation community, the air age had truly come to pass.

, , ,

William McCurdy's confidence in aviation was one thing, public
attitudes quite another. The general public continued to regard
anyone connected with flying machines with considerable suspicion. Bell would later recall that people looked at him strangely, as
if he had taken leave of his senses, whenever he talked about his
experiments with powered flight.[33] Great scientists like Lord
Kelvin thought Bell was doing grievous damage to his reputation
by associating himself with fancies like flying machines, and even
Bell's closest associates were aware that aeronautics was a far from
respectable pursuit. As Baldwin told a crowd at the University of
Toronto shortly after the successful flight on the *Silver Dart*, "only
a few years ago intelligent people scoffed at the idea of flying, and
a man needed a good deal of courage to profess his faith in its ultimate accomplishment...Sweeping criticism had put the problem
in a class with perpetual motion. Scientific men felt it was an
unsafe field in which to risk their reputations, and a popular feeling
existed that flight involved some inherent impossibility and was in

general a subject to be avoided." Baldwin might well have wondered how much these attitudes had been changed by the flight, for a year later a Toronto newspaper asked the question, "Why, Casey Baldwin... [do you] waste time in airship-making?"[34]

For most people, the airplane remained, like the balloon, a form of entertainment or gimmick. The first flight over Edmonton in 1911, for example, was less about aviation than property sales: if the pilot could land in a lot designated by a local realtor, he received title to the land. Other real estate agents liked the aerial motif so much that airplanes cropped up in their advertisements for days afterwards. The first intercity flight in Canada, between Montreal and Ottawa in 1913, was mounted not to test the potential of the new technology but as a publicity stunt to promote the launch of a new newspaper. In 1913, the American aviator Cecil Peoli dressed up in a Santa Claus suit and circled above Fletcher's Field in Montreal to draw attention to a sale at a local department store.[35] In short, airplanes did the same things that balloons and dirigibles had done in previous decades—everything but demonstrate that a flying machine could have practical value.

Even the great air shows of the pre-war era had little impact on such notions. The biggest of them was held at Montreal's Lakeside Park in the summer of 1910, the first international aviation meet ever in Canada. It ran for over a week and drew as many as ten thousand spectators on a good day, including Jean Bruchési, the archbishop of Montreal, the American senator William Jennings Bryan and the tobacco magnate Sir William Macdonald. The stars of the show were the American pilot Walter Brookens and Jacques de Lesseps, the French aviator and son of the promoter of the Panama Canal, with a supporting cast of lesser-known pilots, balloonists and stuntmen. Their display flights certainly moved observers. One reporter called it "an epoch-making day in Canadian history," and struggled for words lavish enough to capture the import of the event: "Away above thousands of eyes there sailed under the cloud-clothed skies the dream of ages realized. The very heart stood still. The pulses seemed to cease their beat.... In the bowl of heaven in its impish fancy there floated in spectral reality a human being in a machine of human invention. Now it dips, then it rises. It is not in a land of dreams one lives to see gravitation defied. One almost fancied that outraged Nature would hurtle it from her glowing space to earth below."[36]

But daily newspapers more often reported on flying machines coming to grief. Airplanes, like balloons, still displayed a marked reluctance to leave the ground. "The aviator... who was scheduled as one of the big crowd drawers, and who was to have made a flight twice each day, only flew twice," noted the editor of the Calgary *Herald* in 1911. "The slightest breeze proved sufficient to deter him from taking to the air. The first day, when there was no wind... it was too muddy. Other times... it was too windy. In his tent, adjoining the track, however, he gathered considerable money, charging ten cents per look at the mechanical bird." It was no better in Vancouver when the Pacific Aviation Company came to town for what was billed as a Grand Easter Holiday Carnival of Flying-Machines. The advertised three days of flying yielded only two short flights (and at least four minor accidents), which little pleased the thousands who had turned out for the show and led the local press to call into question both the skill and courage of the pilots. Their attempts to awe the crowds went from bad to worse, reported the Vancouver *Province*, with the final day's efforts being "the poorest of the three very disappointing, would be hair-raising, mid-air maneuvers."[37]

Nor were spectators shy about venting their rage on aviators who failed to deliver the promised flight. At a Montreal park in September 1912, a Boston pilot, George Grey, declined to take to his aircraft because of a dispute over fees with exhibition organizers. The crowd, estimated at five thousand, left the park in disgust but got their revenge a week later when Grey was booked to appear at Lafontaine Park. When he again refused to fly, blaming poor-quality gasoline, the angry crowd attempted to pull his aircraft to pieces. Grey escaped injury, thanks to quick action by the local police, but his flying machine did not.[38]

Even when aircraft got into the air, they seemed maddeningly reluctant to remain there. On Dominion Day 1912, an immense crowd turned out in Sault Ste. Marie, Ontario, to see Lincoln Beachey pilot a Curtiss biplane, which crashed into a billboard after flying less than a mile. In Ingersoll, Ontario, another large crowd waited all day to see Charles Frank Morok fly a Curtiss, but Morok failed to appear; he had accepted a booking in Chatham the same day. There, twelve thousand people watched him coax the airplane twenty feet into the air, but after travelling some six hundred yards it crashed heavily. The pilot was uninjured. A local newspaper acidly concluded that the airplane was "apparently 'of the earth, earthy,' and strictly refused to make overtures for a speaking acquaintance with the clouds. Its most spectacular act was an attempt to plough up the Chatham Driving Park with its propeller, an attempt that failed lamentably, there being more resistance to the sod that the wooden blade would stand." The good citizens of Chatham gamely invited Morok and his partner, Fred Hoover, for a return engagement on August 21, 1912, but things were no better. Hoover barely got the airplane off the ground before it ripped through two fences and collapsed in a heap. The fair committee, which had signed a contract stipulating that Morok and Hoover would be paid only if one of them made a flight, promptly directed the sheriff to seize the wreckage of the aircraft, in an effort to recover the costs of bringing it to Chatham.[39]

Such incidents were of great concern to air-minded Canadians, the engineers, aviators and journalists who were convinced that flying had a bright future in Canada if only it could be allowed to develop safely. They became the harshest critics of the state of aviation. In their observations, we see the same concerns that would be raised by the air lobby in the 1920s. They invariably counselled patience: as "an airship meet cannot be carried on schedule time like horse races," spectators were advised that delays and cancellations should not be allowed to spoil their enjoyment of the event. There was still much work to be done before flying was safe, reliable and predictable. The public should applaud advances but should not expect too much too soon. Progress would likely be incremental. The Calgary *Herald*, which always worked hard to foster air-mindedness in its readers, asked for forbearance at the constant delays in Didier Masson's planned flight from Calgary to Edmonton in 1911: "Aviation as a sport has not yet reached the precision of croquet. It is, in fact, as unstable as the winds of sunny Alberta.... Air flight exhibitions cannot yet be organized to take place on a schedule."[40]

But air enthusiasts feared that aviators themselves were guilty of impatience. Lamenting that the use of the airplane for entertainment was detrimental to the long-term development of aviation, they warned that in the rush to make money, aviators were not taking sufficient care in constructing their crafts. The resulting collection of machines could hardly inspire confidence in the spectator. A journalist at Lakeside Park in Montreal thought Doug McCurdy's *Baddeck #2* looked "very clumsy, weighty and complicated," while the Wright aircraft resembled "a huge orange-box with the sides knocked out." "To the ordinary observer," noted the Calgary *Herald*, "there is nothing about an airship but...dingy canvas slats held clumsily together by criss-cross wires.... The present flying machines are far from being the last word on the subject. They are full of imperfections and experimental fittings. With the exception of the motor, any ordinary school boy with a pair of scissors, a jack knife, a few lengths of fretwood, an ordinary tool box and a ball of string can manufacture an aeroplane equal in flying capacity to any of those in use." The following year, the same newspaper took up the argument again. "There is no good reason for building aeroplanes with wood work on them that would make any conscientious carpenter blush with shame, with metal work that any good ornamental iron worker would improve by 50 per cent and with covering of which no upholsterer or sail maker would be guilty. The haste to get to flying and to win the large prizes offered for various flights has been provocative of these things, and as a result, most of the prizes have been premiums on daring, rather than substantial recognitions of scientific or engineering ability applied to aeroplanes. . . . The sooner the crude little aeroplanes, built by adventurers, are replaced by the production of skilful and thorough designers, the better chance this country will have to lead the world in aeronautics."[41]

Air-minded Canadians also argued that flying displays were doing little to advance the cause of aviation. "*Radical* improvements will have to be made before the aeroplane will be more than a dangerous toy, to be used only by men who do not value their lives very highly," F. O. Willhofft wrote in *Queen's Quarterly*. "The wonderful performances that we read about every day do not mean much more to the development of the science of flying than running Niagara Falls in a motor boat means to the development of the motor boat industry."[42]

The worst offenders, in their view, were the very people who were aviation's most public face: not the Bells and Baldwins who laboured to solve the problems of control and reliability but the Beacheys and Hoovers who flew their aircraft into the ground in front of thousands of spectators. Commenting on the death of the American airman Eugene Ely (a regular at Canadian air displays) at an air show in Oregon in 1911, the Edmonton *Journal* noted that "as in the case of most of the others [aviators who had died in flying accidents], it was not in attempting anything which was likely to show any real progress in the mastery of the air that his career was terminated. . . . If this pure dare-deviltry could be eliminated, the fatalities among airmen would soon decrease very materially, while it would also help bring aeroplanes into more general use. This is not likely to happen so long as it appears to be [an] extremely perilous mode of travel." After the American aviator John Bryant was killed in a crash in Victoria in August 1913, the *New York Times* calculated that since the newspaper began keeping track five years earlier, 308 people had died in aircraft accidents, 85 in the first eight months of 1913 alone.[43]

So the true visionaries of the air were careful to temper the excitement engendered by early air shows with a dose of reality.

Doug McCurdy believed that the risks associated with landing an aircraft were "so many that the management of the craft while in the air was often only a secondary matter, and in any case the anticipation of trouble in landing almost destroyed what pleasure might be gained from the aerial trip." There had been so many accidents that "the public has lost confidence in aviation." Jacques de Lesseps concurred, declaring in 1910 that "aviation is thus far only a sport. When it becomes safe it will be time to consider its commercial possibilities."[44]

, , ,

Everything that the critics said was, of course, quite true. The technology was so very primitive that the airplane had demonstrated little practical value beyond entertainment. Yet the potential of flight was catching on, despite its actualities; the realization of one of humanity's oldest dreams was beginning to move people's hearts and thrill their souls. The new frontier was about to open up, kindling a sort of romance that neither trains nor automobiles had created. Musings on the future of aviation were not yet common before the First World War, but those that survive foreshadow the discourse of air-mindedness that would so dominate the 1920s and 1930s.

At the most basic level, the balloon and the airplane became potent symbols for modernity, particularly when contrasted with the relics of the Old World. When Anna Jameson, whose *Winter Studies and Summer Rambles in Canada* provides a fine glimpse of Upper Canada in the 1830s, watched a balloon ascent from an ancient amphitheatre in Verona, Italy, she was profoundly struck by "the comparison between ancient and modern times." The Maritime poet M. H. Nickerson, looking for a modern counterpart to Hermes, the winged god, could think of nothing more appropriate than a balloon.[45] Advertisers, too, fixed on balloons and airplanes as an assurance that their products were the newest of the new. A group of nattily dressed men admiring airplanes

overhead proved that J. N. Harvey of Vancouver sold only the
most modern in men's clothes. Ghirardelli's ground chocolate was
clearly the finest beverage for truly modern men like the one piloting the airplane in the advertisement. And there was no better way
to launch the brand-new Montreal *Daily Mail* than by delivering
it to prominent politicians in an "ultramodern Depperdusan [*sic*]
monoplane flown by the Air-man Robinson... the latest and most
powerful long-distance machine.... The newspaper freight was as
modern as the machine that carried it."[46]

It went without saying that the new age of the air would be a
distinct improvement over the old one. A. Y. Jackson, who complained sourly that the air age would spoil the skies for painters
("just imagine when the aeroplanes and dirigibles get busy at
ninety miles an hour; won't we see the poor old cumulus stirred
up like custard, and flung all over the sky," he wrote in 1910), was
not convinced, but his skepticism was often overshadowed by
breathless enthusiasm. When Cecil Peoli, widely known as the
Bird Boy, appeared in Charlottetown, one journalist saw the dawn
of a new day: "The Provincial Exhibition of 1912 will go down in
history as being the first at which airplane flights were given, and
the revolutionizing possibilities of the science of aviation were
demonstrated to the thousands of interested Prince Edward
Islanders who can now look forward to the day when that nine
mile strip of water which divides us from the mainland need no
longer be considered a barrier.... The faith of the believer in man's
ultimate conquest of the air, was strengthened, from the mind of
the skeptic, the mists of doubt, were cleared away... gleams of
light, reflected from the polished surface of the motor, helio-
graphed their message of assurance with the aid of the autumnal
sun, to the gazing multitudes on the earth below."[47]

The *Patriot* was most interested in aviation's potential to end
the isolation of Prince Edward Island, but it was already becoming clear that the airplane had the potential to shrink time and
space in a broader sense. The Halifax *Herald* extrapolated from a
French pilot's flight that a businessman could breakfast in Chicago

and lunch in Ottawa, and marvelled at "how these aeroplanes, when perfected, are going to make our huge country look almost as small as a map in a school-boy's hands." It was impossible to predict the extent of that potential, as the *Herald* admitted: "What is the speed limit of a winged gas engine? Nobody knows. The development of the science of flying has been so wonderful in the last few years that even expert aviators will not hazard a guess. All they can say is that the aeroplane is responding as nothing else is to the demand of the modern speed mania for fast, faster, fastest. And what is inconceivable speed today may see, what?— 200 miles an hour tomorrow."[48]

The *Herald* focused on the practical transportation value of the airplane and on its potential to accelerate the pace of business by making travel easier and quicker. However, the airplane's ability to shrink time and space implied something even more significant: flying machines allowed the individual to break free of the earth, to escape the trials and tribulations of life on the ground. In *A Comedy of Terrors* (1872), a melodramatic novel by James De Mille, more famous for his aptly titled *A Strange Manuscript Found in a Copper Cylinder*, the intrepid Grimes concocts a plan to escape from Paris, which is encircled by Prussian armies. He must use all his powers of persuasion to convince his fellow travellers to accompany him, urging them that "a balloon is the safest and the easiest mode of travel that has ever been invented.... You only get into your balloon, let the wind be fair, and the weather any ways be moderate, and let a cool head have the navigation of her, and I'll bet any money that you go by that balloon easier, pleasanter, quicker, safer, and altogether happier than by any mode of conveyance known to mortal man." High above the Paris mob, the Prussian army and a legion of shadowy spies and agents provocateurs, one is "free as a bird possessed of all the inalienable rights of man, such as life, liberty, and the pursuit of happiness." In the end, his friends consent, and the balloon becomes their agent of deliverance. "In a brief period of time," Grimes muses to his reluctant passenger, "you will soar aloft beyond these transitory troubles, and find yourself in the midst of a celestial calm. No matter where the wind may blow us, there we may go, and we will find safety and peace."[49]

Here we see the first glimmerings of the notion that thanks to the flying machine, the vast distances of the earth became insignificant and the tribulations of life on the ground were easily escaped. The resultant feeling of freedom led people to equate flight with a perspective unlike anything humans had known. This feeling impressed itself strongly on a newspaper reporter known only as Mary Elizabeth, when she flew over St. Catharines, Ontario, on a publicity flight in 1914: "We could see many miles inland, for the day was clear and ideal for flying. To look down upon the country from the mountain top is a wondrous picture, but to sit in space and feel that utter detachment from everything and gaze upon the land is beyond everything. We do not properly appreciate the old world we live in until we have looked at her from afar, detached and flying through the air above her."[50]

As they ascended, people were powerfully struck by two impressions. First, the signs of earthly existence quickly shrank to insignificance. "Higher and higher we rose," wrote one traveller of an ascent over Paris, "till the city lay spread out like a map beneath our feet. It looked like a toy city, or like the models of the French seaports and arsenals, which are shown in the Musée de Marine, in the Louvre."[51] At the Canadian National Exhibition in Toronto in September 1885, a reporter for the *Mail* made an ascent with Madame Carlotta Myers, the noted American balloonist, and marvelled at seeing the earth from above: "The thousands of upturned faces visible in the grounds when the balloon first began to ascend were blurred and indistinct, while their owners seemed dwarfed to the dimensions of Lilliputians. The public buildings in the city shrank to comparative insignificance, and the island itself looked so small that the finger of one's hand seemed to cover it." Grace Denison, the Toronto journalist and an editor of *Saturday Night* magazine, went for a balloon ride while on holiday in Germany and was struck by the same realization: "I drank in the picture of far-off, tiny Hamburg, its toy churches and houses, its ships in harbor, like specks upon the bosom of the Elbe; its wee lakelets, like two bright silver dollars among the green, the river winding like a silver ribbon round the green islands that lay like patches of moss upon its surface." A journalist writing in the London *Free Press* remarked on "the look of entire independence and freedom from the trammels of conventionality enjoyed by the balloonist.... What is in reality a busy mart of trade, appears from the height of two thousand feet to be a densely wooded glen, the arcadian ideal of an artist, with here and there a pile of bricks and mortar that apparently could only have found a place by being dropped from the clouds.... The money maker who rears a mansion knows not that he dwells in a cabin but a foot and a half in height, nor does he of the fustian coat suspect his cottage to be the embodiment of a poetic ideal."[52] The enraptured prose is even more telling because the reporter never actually ascended in a balloon; the scheduled flight was cancelled, and the reporter wrote from his imagination. Nevertheless, his account accords with countless others written later; clearly, the perspective made possible by flight had already left its mark on the imagination.

Connected with this new vision was a heightened sense of superiority: only the chosen few could view the earth from the vantage point of the gods. Edward Allen Talbot, the brilliant but dissolute Upper Canada inventor and journalist, observed that ordinary pedestrians could not appreciate the beauties of Upper Canada but that "an Aëronaut, in his towering flight... might, from his lofty balloon, perceive many picturesque and romantic spots."[53] And there is an unmistakable hint of envy in Alonzo Cinq-Mars's tribute to Georges Mestache, who became the first pilot to fly over Quebec while Cinq-Mars was stuck on the ground: *"Pour moi, pauvre mortel à la terre rivé, | En aviation je ne suis arrivé | Qu'à faire s'envoler dans le ciel bleu mon rêve."* The balloon even became a metaphor for omniscience for a local historian, who applied it to those who study the past: "far preferable appears the unprejudiced birdseye view of them which we can still obtain if the glass is rightly focussed through breaks in the rolling vapors of time while seated at our ease in the balloon of tradition."[54]

These notions of superiority and omniscience were radical, but new advances in aviation technology were already starting to seem commonplace. Almost every day, the newspapers told of a new aerial first, a new obstacle overflown, a new record set. "Really, these air-ship records are growing monotonous," complained the Calgary *Herald*. "Let's have a real good bicycle race for a change." The editor of the London *Free Press* observed that recent achievements in aviation are "received to-day with little show of surprise." Commenting on a circuit race in which eleven aviators flew across the English Channel, the Calgary *Herald* noted that "Flight Has Been Rendered Quite Common By Today's Result."[55] The fact that aviation accomplishments no longer inspired awe suggested that there was a growing acceptance of the new technology. Alexander Graham Bell drew the analogy between flying machines and automobiles, observing that the airplane, now used mainly for pleasure purposes, would soon come into widespread commercial use. He believed that an aircraft like the *June Bug* could be manufactured and sold at a profit, even at $1,500 below the price of many automobiles. Ten years from then, predicted the Calgary *Herald*, "the flying machine will probably be as common in the air as automobiles are now on the streets."[56]

That day, air travel would be a natural part of life. "Flying through the air would become one of the popular pleasures in the near future," predicted a young Hamilton aviator named John Burton in 1909, "as soon as the people became accustomed to the use of the aeroplane and have confidence in it enough to try one...the exhilaration and thrills of joy which run through one's veins during a flight is not to be experienced in any other sport." In the post-apocalyptic world conjured up by the Nova Scotia writer Percy Blanchard, flying machines have indeed become a way of life. A tiny aircraft resembling a dragonfly brings the mail, while a slightly larger craft operates something akin to a bus service, carrying passengers safely and smoothly from place to place. A giant dirigible provides a stage for the local orchestra, which serenades the citizens from a height of five hundred feet.[57]

The writer Frederick Nelson looked ahead twenty years to 1928, when flying had become a way of life around Toronto.[58] The city extended as far north as Newmarket, but travel from the suburbs to downtown was a breeze, thanks to the dirigibles of the Toronto and District Airship Company; airplanes were also available for commuters who wished a speedier trip. The immense Dominion Hotel had its own fleet of airships, stored in hangars attached to the building. Each ship carried fifty guests at a time on sightseeing trips to Niagara Falls, depositing them gently back at their hotel at the end of the day.

Looking ahead to 1927 from 1913, Rev. Hugh Pedley, a Congregationalist minister from Winnipeg, envisioned a time when travelling by air was second nature to Canadians. For personal travel, there were small and speedy airplanes, powered by light, reliable gasoline engines and flown by pilots who had to meet rigorous standards before being allowed to take to the air; clergymen used airplanes to minister to their flocks, and young adventurers raced them on weekends. Commercial airships carried some forty passengers between Montreal and Winnipeg (with stops at Ottawa, North Bay, Port Arthur and Kenora) in about thirty-six hours. Lifting them above the dust and smoke of the cities, they moved soundlessly and without vibration, allowing travellers to have a meal more delightful and a sleep more restful than any obtainable on trains or ships.[59]

The Dominion in 1983, a futurist work by a Peterborough writer who went by the nom de plume Ralph Centennius, looked even further ahead to a day when the complex railway engine, the dangerous ocean liner and the unreliable balloon had been supplanted by the "magnificently simple" rocket car. Canada's rocket cars were manufactured at St. Mangan, on the Gulf of St. Lawrence; each carried fifty passengers in incredible luxury. They took off from broad metal slides and quickly accelerated to cruising speed of sixty miles per minute. The passenger could leave Halifax ("one of the greatest carports in the world") and arrive in Ireland within thirty minutes, or Constantinople in less than three hours. It was "a splendid apparatus...which brings all the ends of the earth together and makes the whole world a public park, the most distant parts of which can be visited and returned from in the course of a single day."[60] This was the future that the Charlottetown *Daily Patriot* conjured up when it predicted the onset of a new disease: "aeroplanitis...arises not from sailing aloft, but from failure to do so. In this fact lies hope that the malady will not become permanently menacing to the public. Someday all may fly."[61]

, , ,

There was no question that aviation had progressed dramatically in just a few decades, in spite of the aerial shenanigans of pilots who caused so much concern to the air lobby. But there were still only a handful of Canadian pilots in 1914 (although a steady stream of American aviators came north to ply their trade), and the aero clubs established with such confidence after the flight of the *Silver Dart* had quietly collapsed. Doug McCurdy spent much of his time after 1909 in the United States, where aviation found a more congenial atmosphere, while Casey Baldwin stopped flying in 1911 to turn his skills to other engineering projects. Bell continued to speak publicly in support of flying but wound up his aviation experiments in 1912. The Canadian Aerodrome Company that the three of them had founded with such high hopes withered through lack of interest. Indeed, Canadian aviation seemed to be stagnating as the energy and enthusiasm of the early days dissipated. Flying remained, as one amateur poet put it, "an infant in the lands of dreams."[62] If the technology was to progress and the dreams of the air lobby were to be realized in the foreseeable future, a catalyst would be needed. In the summer of 1914, few people could see one coming.

· 2 ·

SOON SHALL THE
SKY BE OURS

FOR BILL LAMBERT, AN AMERICAN WHO JOINED THE ROYAL
Flying Corps (RFC) in Toronto in 1917, the sight over Hangard,
southeast of Amiens, was bewildering: the sky around him was
filled with airplanes. A dozen S.E.5 single-engine fighters of 24
Squadron had taken off in the afternoon of April 12, 1918, for an
operational patrol over the battlefield, and encountered as many as
thirty German machines. Minutes after the two forces met, smaller
groups of airplanes joined the fray. Soon they had coalesced into
an immense swarm of aircraft, clustered in an area about two miles
across, between six and ten thousand feet high. Everywhere
Lambert looked, airplanes were hurtling through the sky like
insects, twisting, turning, spiralling. Machine-gun bullets

streamed in all directions, and puffs of smoke or flame signalled that some had hit their marks. Above and to the east, one of Lambert's squadron mates pursued an Albatros scout, which eventually crashed into the ground. Below, George Foster of Montreal and Con Farrell of Regina also scored hits on German aircraft. Lambert squeezed off a burst at a fighter that crossed in front of him; the pilot slumped, and the aircraft spun to the ground. The American craned his neck to look for another target, but as quickly as it began it was all over. As if by magic, the sky had cleared of aircraft, and Lambert, now alone, flew back to his base.[1]

Just a few years earlier, even Bill Lambert, who had lived and breathed aviation since the day he heard of the Wright brothers' flight at Kitty Hawk, could not have imagined such a sight. Before 1914, the airplane was a fragile, unstable craft, reluctant to leave the ground and then apt to crash at any moment. Only the prescient few foresaw the days of speedy, agile machines that could be guided through intricate manoeuvres by expert aviators.

When the First World War began, many people predicted that it would bring an end to experiments in aviation; instead, it became the catalyst that air-minded Canadians were looking for. The demands of wartime so accelerated the pace of technological change that it became a commonplace to assert that the war been flight's salvation. But the war in the air also had cultural significance out of all proportion to its impact on the conflict. Of the many facets of the air war, two generated sustained popular interest: the exploits of the legendary fighter aces over the Western Front and strategic bombing. The strong emotional appeal of both stemmed from the fact that the air war offered an antidote to the frustrations of the land war. In contrast to the massed infantry offensives, which were often all too costly and inconclusive, the air war harkened back to a time when individual action could decide the course of events. Strategic bombing also held the promise of bypassing the land battle and winning the war from the clouds. The complexities of the air war were reduced to two very simple stereotypes: a contest between chivalrous fighter pilots, jousting in the skies according to a well-understood code of ethics; and a simple morality play, in which evil German aircraft and Zeppelins* bombed innocent civilians and drew Allied bombing as a form of divine retribution. Before 1914, aviation was seen as the harbinger of a wonderful new age; when that new age arrived during the First World War, the airplane was suddenly transformed into an antidote to modernism.

, , ,

In 1911, an editorial in a Regina newspaper remarked optimistically, "The mastery of the air is a distinct triumph for the men of the twentieth century," but concluded with a warning: aviation "should be so used as to confer blessing only and not provide an additional curse on mankind."[2] That sentiment would be echoed by many others in succeeding decades, but even in 1911 the Pandora's box of military aviation had already been opened. Primitive rockets had been used in China since the 1100s, and references to rockets and aerial bombs began appearing in European accounts in the fourteenth century. In 1794, just a decade after the Montgolfiers' pioneering flight, the French army used a manned hydrogen balloon as an aerial observation platform in the war against Prussia, an experiment repeated in wars in Algeria in 1830 and in Italy in 1859. During the U.S. Civil War, the Union leadership sanctioned the establishment of a balloon corps, organized by none other than Professor T. S. C. Lowe, but the experiment, although successful in tactical terms, was never popular with the army and turned out to be a personal and financial disappointment for Lowe. The French, on the other hand, solidified their leadership in aeronautics ("aerostation," to use the contemporary term) with their extensive use of balloons during

---

* Zeppelin is the trade name of a German company that manufactured airships. As contemporaries generally applied the word to any German airship, I have also done so.

the Franco-Prussian War. Particularly dramatic was the aerial escape of the French cabinet minister Léon Gambetta from the besieged city of Paris in September 1870.

This use of balloons was not the only example of military aviation familiar to Canadians. A Maritime volunteer with the Canadian contingent in South Africa wrote home describing a balloon used as an observation platform to locate Boer positions, and at least one Canadian officer noted that flying machines would have been useful for similar tasks during the Russo-Japanese War.[3] Indeed, by the time the Regina editor issued his warning, there were already indications that balloons and airplanes had opened up a whole new range of possibilities in warfare. "To a nation going to war, a machine of this kind would be invaluable," observed one budding pilot in 1909, "and to the man who could offer to any government an aeroplane which would be capable of flying over the forts and entrenchments of the enemy, take photographs of the armaments, and thus secure complete and authentic plans of the enemy's batteries and so forth, it would give anything he demanded."[4]

Not all governments were as forthcoming as this prescient soul might have wished. Air-minded individuals continually prodded and cajoled the great powers to explore the military potential of the new technology, and the United States, Britain, France, Germany and Russia did show some limited interest in flying experiments before the First World War. Germany, the world leader, had more than 230 serviceable military aircraft in 1914; the United States Army, the first in the world to purchase an airplane, had only a dozen.[5] Still, at a time when airplanes were country-fair sideshows that regularly came to grief, it is remarkable that armies and governments showed any enthusiasm at all.

In Canada, the Department of Militia and Defence invited Doug McCurdy and Casey Baldwin to demonstrate a Canadian Aerodrome Company machine at Petawawa (clearly stating that the department would provide no financial assistance for the tests). On August 2, 1909, the *Silver Dart* made three successful flights but was badly damaged on the fourth, when McCurdy struck a hillock while attempting to land. A few days later, in front of dignitaries from Militia and Defence, McCurdy coaxed the *Baddeck #1* into the air but was unable to keep it aloft; soon after taking off, it pulled up into a stall and dropped to the ground. The crash seems to have confirmed the skepticism of Militia and Defence. As one aviation booster later put it, "the 'Colonel Blimps' of those days shrugged their shoulders, said 'I told you so,' and resumed their customary somnolence, refusing to be disturbed by any new fangled notions." According to a news report, deputy minister Eugène Fiset believed that Canada was too small to invest in military aviation, especially as the technology was unproved. Baldwin and McCurdy's allies tried to convince the government to vote an annual subsidy to support their aviation research, but the cabinet demurred. Sam Hughes, the minister of Militia and Defence, later chided McCurdy that "the aeroplane is an invention of the devil, and will never play any part in the defence of a nation, my boy!"[6]

So it was no surprise that military aviation in Canada was still non-existent by 1914, albeit not for lack of trying on the part of the air lobby. Air-minded Canadians' tactics, from flying exhibitions to fear-mongering, hammered home the point that aviation would change the face of war. Since the summer of 1910, when Canada hosted its first international air show, bombing displays had become commonplace. At the great Montreal show, one newspaper promised that "a scenic fort will be constructed filled with soldiers. A mighty aeroplane will skim through the air, and shots will be fired by the military men.... Then the aeroplane will drop a huge sandbag into the fort, which striking dynamite in the fort, will cause an explosion and blow the fort down." To demonstrate the airplane's utility in naval warfare, a flying exhibition at Port Stanley, Ontario, in 1912 featured the American aviator Walter Brookens hurling mock bombs at a plywood battleship anchored offshore.[7]

Air power also became a standard subject of futurist writing in

Canada before 1914. Alexander Graham Bell, whose personal notoriety guaranteed him a ready audience, was fond of giving detailed descriptions of how the art of war had been altered by the coming of the air age. In speech after speech, he predicted that the airplane would be not simply an adjunct to the land battle, but would become a strategic weapon. Air power, he declared, had taken over from sea power as the dominant element in world affairs; the first nation to command the air would control the globe. Once the greatest maritime power, Britain was in danger of seeing its paramountcy slip away unless it established itself in the air. Bell warned that Graf von Zeppelin's airships could sail over London and drop bombs with impunity; the city could be devastated by a rain of explosives, and Britain's navy, for centuries the nation's first line of defence, could do nothing to stop it. The East Huron MP Thomas Chisholm, in an effort to convince the government to fund McCurdy and Bell's aviation experiments, told the House of Commons that airships would one day circle the globe in seventy hours and be able to sink even the mightiest dreadnought.[8] His scenario was not dissimilar to that described by W. H. C. Lawrence's futuristic tale of the Anglo-American war fought on Canadian territory, in which several British ships were sunk by dynamite balloons launched by the Americans. In the apocalyptic battle described in Nova Scotian Percy Blanchard's novel *After the Cataclysm*, terror is spread by airships dropping "rock rending explosives,"[9] the same nightmare conjured in a remarkable epic poem by Lt.-Col. J. R. Wilkinson. In fifty-eight stanzas of florid overwriting, he envisioned an Armageddon in which the most potent agents of destructions were airships:

> And I saw lines of airships advancing,
>   Soaring like mighty birds of prey;
> And rent asunder were the lurid clouds
>   That obscured the red god of day.
> And I saw them glide on to each other,
>   The opposing lines up on high,

And the trumpet call from balloon to balloon
    Manœuvred them through the sky.
And still dropping their horrid explosives
    Below to the shattered plain,
They seek by quick aerial manœuvres
    Advantageous positions to gain.
And thus rising, poising, and advancing,
    Pausing in close column and line,
The strange scene was awesome and wonderful,
    And immeasurably sublime.
Fiercely on each other with quick-fire guns
    Destruction they now madly pour,
And infernal machines and magazines
    Add their terrible, deadly roar.
And out on the vast aerial spaces
    It echoed and rolled away,
A shuddering and horrible tumult,
    Lost in distance grim and gray.
And contending there for the mastery,
    Some collided with ruinous crash,
And fell from the fierce crimson clouds above
    To the earth with a horrid crash.

And thus they fought in the aerial plains
    To cover their own below,
And to hover o'er, and hurl destruction
    On the contending mammoth foe.[10]

Wilkinson, like Bell, Lawrence and Blanchard, clearly saw the implications of war in the air: there would be no safe ground.

, , ,

The early days of the First World War gave little sign that such an eventuality was on the horizon. Naysayers in Canada and Britain argued that experiments in aviation must cease so that energies could be put to more useful purposes. The first weeks of the war suggested that their advice had merit: the first British reconnaissance mission, on August 19, 1914, was a disappointment, both pilots getting lost without locating the units they were sent to find. Days later, a German reconnaissance pilot reported a mob of panicked and disorganized British soldiers, but his seemingly demoralized enemy had been engaged in a soccer game. A Canadian Aviation Corps was conjured out of thin air in September 1914, with a strength of two officers (a third was later taken on) and an American-made Burgess biplane that even its manufacturer admitted was badly in need of reconditioning. It was not a happy experiment. The much maligned Burgess was damaged in transit and never flew again. By the time Lieut. W. F. N. Sharpe of Prescott, Ontario, was killed in a training crash in February 1915, his commander, Capt. E. L. Janney of Galt, Ontario, had already been struck off the strength of the Canadian Expeditionary Force and the Canadian Aviation Corps had ceased to exist.[11]

Despite these early disappointments, airplanes were starting to prove their worth in modern battle. It was the Allies' great good fortune that the weather in August and early September 1914 was ideal for flying, so British and French reconnaissance pilots could watch the German invasion forces sweep across northern France. Their reports allowed commanders to respond quickly as the situation evolved and to move reinforcements to where the danger was greatest. The "Miracle of the Marne," which cost Germany its best chance to win the war, would not have been possible without aerial reconnaissance.

But the end of the war of movement in the fall of 1914 did not mean the end of the airplane's usefulness. As the opposing armies dug into the line of trenches that eventually stretched from Switzerland to the English Channel, strategic and tactical reconnaissance, pinpointing everything from supply dumps to machine-gun posts, remained vital, particularly for the Allied armies, which did not have the luxury of being dug in on the high ground as the Germans frequently were. At first, the armies relied on hastily trained observers to sketch or describe what they saw as they flew over enemy lines—the eyes of the army, many writers called them—but aerial photography soon supplemented their work, providing images for the commanders on the ground. Over the course of the war, the British took half a million aerial photos, which they could compare over time to discern changes in the enemy's defensive positions. Just as important was artillery spotting, both locating enemy batteries and directing the fall of shot on targets. It was a complicated technical exercise that used wireless transmitters, Very lights or signalling lamps to convey locations or map references, but one soldier-poet put it in romantic terms:

> The great guns swing to the call and beck
> Of the men who traverse the upper air,
> And that soaring speck is the great guns' eyes...
> Death's controlled by a man-made bird,
> And a bird-like man, o'er the German line.[12]

By mid-1915, observation and artillery-spotting aircraft were becoming so important that they became targets, first from ground fire and then increasingly from armed scout aircraft. Once the "eyes of the army" went up with an escort of fighters to defend them against enemy aircraft, escalation became inevitable. More and larger squadrons were thrown into the air war on the Western Front, and with astonishing rapidity technological improvements began to reach the battlefield: machine guns with interrupter gear that allowed the weapon to be fired through the airplane's propeller without damaging it; more powerful and reliable aero engines that provided better range; improved airframe designs that gave greater manoeuvrability and resilience; and specialized aircraft to replace the general-purpose machines in use at the beginning of the war.

This mad rush to develop more and better aerial weapons was just the catalyst that the air lobby had been looking for before 1914, but even those intimately connected with aviation were surprised at how quickly the technology was improving. Billy Bishop, the native of Owen Sound, Ontario, who would soon become the most famous war pilot in Canada, remarked that "seeing the modern war-aeroplanes riding through howling storms reminds one that it was not so long ago that a ten-mile breeze would upset all flying-plans for a day at any aerodrome or exhibition field." Alexander Graham Bell was just as impressed by the rapidity of progress: "A year of war has done as much to improve them [flying machines] as a decade of peace," he declared in 1916, and there were few who could argue with him.[13]

By then, it was a rare day when clear skies were not dotted with aircraft. Training flights were a common sight over rear-area bases in France and England, and Britain's ports were now home to growing numbers of flying boats to keep the sea lanes free of German naval units. One observer later remarked that before 1914, not one Canadian in a hundred had seen a flying machine; by the third year of the war, the men and women of the CEF could see them on any given day. Descriptions of aerial combat—or simply of aircraft passing overhead—began to crop up in their diaries and letters. They would write of hearing the sound of a far-off aero engine and searching the sky for the black speck of an airplane; of watching the patrols fly over in neat formation; of trying to follow the course of a dogfight. Underlying their observations was a deep sense of wonder that said as much about their own war as it did about the war in the air.

By the time aircraft appeared in significant numbers over the battlefields, both sides were dug in. Activity was infrequent in some areas but in the bloodiest sectors, the armies periodically hurled themselves across the barren and blasted No Man's Land—thereafter the symbol of the futility of trench warfare—and onto the barbed wire and machine guns of the foe. Casualties were so enormous that it was often impossible to bury all the dead, whose bodies mingled with the mud of the battlefield. The senses of the front-line soldier were assaulted by the crash of artillery shells; the whine of machine-gun bullets; the stench of decaying flesh; the bloated and discoloured corpses; the fat, repulsive rats that fed on them; the sickly smell of poison gas. "A modern battlefield is the abomination of abominations," wrote Coningsby Dawson of the Canadian Field Artillery in 1916. "Imagine a vast stretch of dead country, pitted with shell-holes as though it had been mutilated with small-pox. There's not a leaf or a blade of grass in sight. Every house has either been levelled or is in ruins. No bird sings. Nothing stirs. The only live sound is at night—the scurry of rats. . . . It's like walking through the day of resurrection to visit No Man's Land."[14]

The desolation of this wasteland, from which all points of reference had been obliterated, produced in many soldiers a profound disorientation. Its numbing sameness imparted a surreal confusion as the soldier's horizons shortened to the few yards of trench on either side of him. Was there another world outside the trenches? On the fire-step of a much battered trench, any other experience seemed remote. Even death came randomly, from an enemy rarely seen. And then, above the devastation, would appear an airplane.

Judging by their letters and diaries, soldiers were fascinated by aircraft. Most of them had probably never seen an airplane in flight before they enlisted, but there was more to it than that. Soldiers were powerfully struck by the contrast between the air and the ground. They described air combat as pretty, thrilling or exciting, words that few of them would apply to the Poor Bloody Infantry, and were astonished at how easily the airplanes flitted around the sky. Frank Walker, a stretcher-bearer from Charlottetown, was mesmerized by the sight of an Allied scout plane flying over his aid post in Ploegsteert Wood in August 1915: "He managed his machine with the skill of a wizard," he recorded of the pilot. "The spectacle is, of course, a daily occurrence here. But I cannot get over the wonder of it."[15] The "Sunny Subaltern" whose letters filled two best-selling volumes, was just as fascinated by the agility of two aircraft locked in mortal combat: "I watched one of the prettiest fights I have ever seen—our plane manœuvring and trying to climb, while the fast Hun fighter crept nearer and nearer—watched them dip and turn, each trying to jockey for position.... For I suppose five minutes they twisted, dived, climbed and slipped." Stuart Ramsay Tompkins, a trench-mortar officer from Alberta, found aerial combats a welcome diversion from his dismal surroundings. "It is great on a clear day like this to see the aeroplanes circling overhead," he wrote in February 1917. "They are certainly the wonders of the war."[16] In all these comments, it is hard to miss the theme shared by countless other letters and diary entries: an unmistakable envy at the airplane's freedom from the stagnation of the trenches.

The contrast between earth and sky held considerable appeal on the home front as well. For popular songwriters, the dashing airman was the ideal figure to be celebrated in a vaudeville ditty. "They flirt with the stars, play tag with the moon," went Morris Manley's "Up in the Air" (1918), "they're all flying heroes, they'll win the war soon / When they loop the loop they never seem to care / To them it's great fun, to bring down a Hun!" Sometimes hard-pressed to find a suitable subject in the infantryman mired in mud, poets also saw in the aviator a figure more amenable to poetic flights of fancy. In "To the Absent," Jesse Edgar Middleton, a prolific writer of war verse, waxed poetic about a member of the Toronto Mendelssohn Choir who was serving in the RFC ("*Libera Me*, the airman sings, / And his eyes are brimmed with a soldier dew, / The shrapnel whines in his far-spread wings / As he circles wide in the wintry blue"), while "The American Aviator" paid tribute to a Yale man who won his wings to become "Full brother to the Matterhorn / A sword-point in the blue."[17]

The contrast between the air and the ground war was also a useful recruiting tool. By 1917, young airmen were being killed at an alarming rate, and the RFC required a constant supply of volunteers to keep its squadrons up to strength. A British recruitment and training organization, officially designated Royal Flying Corps, Canada, was created in December 1916 to tap Canadian manpower reserves for potential pilots. Its propagandists quickly realized that there was no better way to attract recruits than by comparing life in the trenches to life in the air. "Up in the air there are none of the objectionable features of trench warfare," observed Randolph Carlyle in a rosy article that carefully skirted around the fact that the life expectancy of a fighter pilot was rather lower than that of an infantry officer. Fl. Lt. Ward Maclennan, writing in *Queen's Quarterly*, was less disingenuous, noting that, whatever dangers the pilot faced—Maclennan himself would die in action before his article went to print—"he does not have to put up with the heart-breaking conditions of mud and wet under which the rest of the army labours." Indeed, more than a few soldiers applied for transfer to the RFC after catching a glimpse of aircraft flying overhead. As Billy Bishop recalled, "It was the mud, I think, that made me take to flying....I had succeeded in getting myself mired to the knees when suddenly, from somewhere out of the storm, appeared a trim little aeroplane. It landed hesitatingly in a near-by field as if scorning to brush its wings against so sordid a landscape; then away again up into the clean grey mists....I knew there was only one place to be on such a day—up above the clouds and in the summer sunshine."[18]

For men like Bishop, the transformation from soldiers into aviators involved instruction in map-reading, meteorology, wireless telegraphy, aerial photography, engine mechanics, airframe design, aerodynamics, gunnery and, of course, pilot training. It was a challenging program that quickly weeded out those who were intellectually or physically unfit, creating a group of highly motivated pilots and observers keen to sally forth and meet the Hun. When they received the long-awaited postings to operational squadrons, they realized just how different was the life of the aviator from the life of the infantryman. While not luxurious, the average front-line airfield was comfortable. There were hot meals and fully stocked bars, dry beds and clean clothes, gramophones and concert parties. All in all, it was quite a civilized existence—Billy Bishop even claimed to have gone into action once in his tennis whites, as he and his squadron mates were interrupted in the middle of a match.

More important, the new pilot's first trip over the battlefield was a revelation. To the infantryman looking over the parapet at No Man's Land, the battlefield was an oppressive emptiness. The enemy positions might be visible as indistinct mounds in the distance, but more often there was, quite literally, nothing to see. For the infantryman-turned-pilot, however, this disorienting void became a world of space and clarity. No longer was the pilot constrained by the physical limitations of the battlefield that had hindered his sight and movement while he was in the trenches. As Hartley Munro Thomas, a Montreal native who reached the front as an air observer in June 1917, put it, "There is an expansive feeling of vastness—itself very vague—when you rise into the air.... You tear along at a hundred miles an hour, up and down, round and round, and you never see the slightest hint of a limit to the sky, for literally there is none."[19]

Connected to this physical liberation was the pilot's broadened vision. Everything was laid out beneath him with, on a fine day, incredible clarity and brilliance. The pilot "sees more of what is going on than any other soldier," observed Ward Maclennan.[20] Trench lines were discernable, enemy strongpoints could be pinpointed, and the green and productive fields away from No Man's Land could be seen. Walter Jamieson, a Toronto native who served in the balloon section of the Royal Field Artillery, was amazed on his first flight in an observation balloon, two thousand feet above the battlefield: "The country immediately below, and for some miles, was clear-cut as a cameo, a marvellous photographic map showing every road, canal, railroad, etc., perfectly." Canon Frederick George Scott, who usually toured the front lines in a motorcycle sidecar, experienced the same sense of awe at seeing the battlefields from an airplane: "A most wonderful panorama spread below us. The great plain beneath us was marked off like a chessboard in squares of various shades of yellow and green, dotted here and there with little villages surrounded by the billowy crests of trees."[21] Official Canadian war artists who painted aviation subjects, such as Franz Johnston (a future Group of Seven member) and C. R. W. Nevinson (a Briton and part of the Vorticist movement, influenced by Futurism), were fascinated by the pilot's aerial view of the world and executed works with suggestive titles—*As It Looks Over the Side* and *Over the Houses*. Fred Varley (a founder of the Group of Seven) chose an equally revealing title for one of his aviation sketches: *The All-Seeing Aviator*.

Varley's title captured what many believed was the true gift of the pilot. From ground level, a major attack appeared to be simply a mass of men moving aimlessly forward; distances and direction were difficult to gauge, and it was sometimes impossible to determine if the correct objective had been reached. But from the vantage point of the clouds, things made sense. Billy Bishop was captivated by the battle going on beneath him on the Somme. "I could not believe that the little brown figures moving about below me were really men"; their movements seemed so calm and orderly from the air, even though it was "one of the tensest, bitterest [battles] of the entire world-war." Harry Quigley, a pilot who had a short but illustrious career in post-war aviation, flew over the front in the summer of 1917: "We were up over 2½ hours and working between 400 and 600 ft. We could see every man in the attack and saw them take trench after trench until all objectives were reached. It certainly was a fine show and I believe I had the best seat in the house. I wouldn't have changed places with the Corps Commander that day."[22] For Bishop and Quigley, height had transformed the muddle of the land battle into a rational, comprehensible sequence of events, more orderly and intelligible and at the same time less real and threatening.

The height that gave the pilot greater vision and comprehension marked his superiority over the earthbound. Billy Bishop admitted to feeling "a great and tender pity for all the millions of people in the world" who had not had the chance to fly. Later in the war, he had to drive through the city of Arras, and remarked sourly that it was "vastly different from flying...threading your way tediously in and out of the marching troops and the interminable traffic of offensive warfare." Many other pilots felt, at least unconsciously, the same sense of superiority implied in Bishop's comments: ordinary people were condemned to live in mud and slime or to travel at a snail's pace through the impedimenta of the land war. The pilot traversed a different world, not of monotonous browns and greys but of brilliant blues, vivid greens and dazzling whites. "We found ourselves in a sort of gorge," recalled Ward Maclennan of one memorable flight, "which seemed to run for miles between huge banks of white clouds. Far below us as we looked down the lane between the clouds lay a bright green strip of fields. On either side, almost touching the wing tips of our machine, was an impenetrable mass of snowy white cloud-bank. Far above us as we looked up through the cañon walls was a strip of bright blue sky. This gorge of clear air between the clouds, although very narrow, extended several miles back to the aerodrome. It was great."[23]

The aviator's ability to rise into a better world produced many invidious comparisons with those lesser mortals condemned to remain on the earth. The poet T. A. Browne, who probably never flew himself, contrasted "the free unrutted tracts of air, / The clime of cloudland and of boundless space," and the "grimy earth" and "the gray abysses far below." The future governor general Georges Vanier did get a chance to fly, when he and three fellow officers of the 22nd Battalion visited the RFC base at Hendon in August 1915. The experience was a revelation: "The take-off is the most impressive moment: it is taking flight towards the unknown. Our bodies seem to leave us and become part of our souls."[24] His sense that flying elevated the individual to a higher level of existence also impressed itself on others. "Nothing is freer than spaces of heaven, / Far from the puny desires of the crowd," wrote Hartley Munro Thomas. Indeed, much of Thomas's aviation poetry has a marked disdain for the earthbound and their "puny desires." In "Above the Clouds," he observes that the airman has loftier concerns than other people: "We are not as the rest," he writes haughtily, "Counting life by wealth or years." His verse "Children of the Air" is just as dismissive of the non-flier: "Oh, who would be a groundsman when the sky is clear?" he wonders. Only the weak and stunted, he concludes: "Leave the earth to the plodding ones. / Ours the wind against the eyes! / Ours the conquest of the skies!"[25]

But it was not just pilots who accepted the superiority of the aviator over lesser mortals. Jack Turner, an infantry officer who wrote about flying from the perspective of the trenches, viewed the aviator as "god-like—poised on the ether's rim," while the New Brunswick artilleryman H. A. Boone wrote of seeing "a fine performance in the air by one of these almost superhuman men with his machine." Georges Vanier watched an Allied reconnaissance aircraft fly over the trenches at Kemmel, near Ypres, in October 1915, and was both fascinated and humbled. "Another of our pilots flew a superb complete reconnaissance of the German lines," he recorded in his diary. "Shells exploded quite close to the plane. What bravado! Compared to the work that we are doing, these pilots are superhuman."[26] Norah Holland, a Toronto writer who had two brothers at the front and was a cousin of the Irish poet W. B. Yeats, also conferred on the pilot power that approached the divine:

> High o'er the mountain steep
>   Our wingèd fleets shall sail,
> The serried squadrons sweep,
>   White-pinioned down the gale.
>
> We are the lords of the land,
>   We built us towns and towers,
> The sea has felt our hand—
>   Soon shall the sky be ours.[27]

Flying, then, was more than a means to wage war more efficiently; it was a spiritual experience that brought the pilot close to divinity. A tribute to Hartley Munro Thomas observed that flying "had released him in some way from the fetters of our mortal life, and given him a vision of another land." That land, what Thomas called the dominions of the clouds, was reserved for gods and aviators whose airplanes allowed them, in the words of the trench poet Kim Beattie, to "pass in the path of the bannered sun, / With God and the gray cloud witness."[28] Many a pilot or passenger was powerfully reminded of the hymn "Nearer My God to Thee" while in the air, and Harold Price, a devout Toronto Methodist who joined the RFC in 1916, likened the sky to "that magic sea over which I have so often longed to sail. Below me stretch[ed] billow upon billow of big fleecy clouds of wonderful whiteness. Above was the great blue vault of heaven and the powerfully dazzling sun. The earth was gone, and all its troubles. I was alone with God, and truly in his sanctuary, his glorious temple. It was hallowing, and it filled me with awe and wonder, and a great reverence for my Heavenly Father."[29]

, , ,

Price's ruminations, with their timeless religiosity, stand in stark contrast to the meaning of flight in pre-war discourse. Before 1914, the flying machine was a metaphor for modernity; it was the newest of the new, the symbol of progress in the twentieth century. This interpretation did persist into the war years; for some people, the airplane did come to symbolize the industrial war of the modern age. John Turnbull, who painted aviation subjects for the Canadian War Memorials Fund, executed works in the Futurist tradition. Where Nevinson painted aircraft with sweeping, avian wings above verdant, agricultural landscapes, Turnbull depicted them above urban areas. For him, they were not quasi-birds in harmony with the natural world but ultramodern machines to be rendered in sharp angles and discordant colours.

But Turnbull was in the minority, for his Futurism did not meet the needs of the time. The war was too modern already; the industrial age had transformed battle into mechanized slaughter in which the human element was insignificant. What was needed was something that could act as a familiar talisman in this bewildering new age of anonymous modern warfare. This need produced an ironic consequence: a quintessentially modern weapon was transformed into an anachronism. The airplane was no longer the twentieth century's first new machine but the steed that carried the cavalry of the clouds into battle. The aviator was not the master technician but a medieval knight in armour. In taking to the air, the fighting man regained a measure of the individualism lost in the ground war. The war in the air pointed not to the future but to the past.

For Canada, the war sat uneasily between the traditional and the modern; it was a modern war that could be understood only in traditional frames of reference. Canada built an army of more than 600,000 men, many times larger than any it had ever fielded, yet was determined that individuality, the identity of each citizen-soldier, not be lost. The nation embraced the cult of the service roll, which demanded that the name of each soldier be recorded for posterity. This listing of names—on local service rolls, in special editions of newspapers or in souvenir volumes— became a means to deny the character of mass war: however large the CEF became, it was still composed of individuals. But the practice had an unintended consequence. The long lists of names actually emphasized the anonymity of modern battle, particularly when the newspapers began printing the growing casualty rolls in ever smaller type. Anxious Canadians searching the dense columns for names of loved ones could not but realize that each man was a very small cog in a very large machine.

One way around this dilemma was to focus on individual acts of gallantry, and the daily press devoted much space to the exploits of particular soldiers. But there was so little continuity— gallant soldiers came and went, hero of the day; even Victoria

Cross winners rarely became household names. The newspapers quickly moved on to new stories, and the repetitive nature of their award citations might well have minimized, quite unfairly, the soldiers' bravery in the public eye.

And then the flying ace appeared on the horizon, figuratively as well as literally. Here was a character to counteract the depressing anonymity of the war. The early aces of the war were lone hunters, going out at dawn or in the late afternoon to fight the enemy individually. Albert Ball, Georges Guynemer, Werner Voss—these were the embodiment of the air ace. And there was no gainsaying their appeal. Who would not want to meet the enemy in single combat, where skill and wits decided the issue, instead of a mass infantry attack, where one's fate was beyond one's control? Don Brophy, who enlisted directly in the RFC and never experienced life in the front lines, admitted that he would welcome a tour of the trenches to see what they were like, but "I would rather be in the Flying Corps where you are an individual, and not just part of a machine."[30] When he wrote this diary entry in December 1915, a year before he was killed in a flying accident, it still had some validity. But by 1917, Ball, Guynemer and Voss were all dead, and for the next two years the war in the air would be characterized by mass, rather than single, combat. The most successful pilots, like Mick Mannock, James McCudden and Manfred von Richthofen, would make their mark while leading large squadrons of aircraft. Billy Bishop's lone dawn raid that won him the Victoria Cross, whether real or invented, was romantic but rare. Much more common were the huge dogfights like the one Bill Lambert witnessed over Hangard.

Single combats might have been increasingly infrequent after 1916, but the individuality of the air war grew ever more prominent in the public mind. Although RFC policy officially prohibited the press from identifying pilots, Canadian newspapers rarely observed the regulation, particularly when the experiences of a local airman could be showcased. Such articles, usually based on letters home, catered to a growing public interest in aviation and provided readers with stories that were very different from those of the ground war. In the pages of the *Canadian Magazine*, Randolph Carlyle noted that "the airman still fights singly, and in no other fighting is the individual left to his own resources." Even though the pilot flew as part of a fighting patrol or squadron, observed Charles Grey, the influential editor of the British journal *The Aeroplane*, "his safety depends on his own personal initiative to a far greater degree than if he were fighting on the ground." Lord Montagu of Beaulieu, who visited Canada in December 1917 to promote aviation for the British government, told an Ottawa audience that "in flying you are master of your own machine, you are to a large extent master of your own fate. You are, in the air, to a large extent what commanders of destroyers are on the sea, quite independent of other control, and it is up to you—to use a Canadian phrase—it is up to you to do well or ill."[31]

Clearly the air war produced a myth of exaggerated individualism that often bore little resemblance to reality. But it also provided a response to the modernity of the war. Since August 1914, propagandists on both sides had presented the war as a medieval morality play, pitting good against evil. Britain relied heavily on the image of St. George slaying the dragon of Prussianism, Germany on the Teutonic knight of the Middle Ages. For a generation raised on Siegfried or Ivanhoe, these familiar images offered reassurance in a confusingly modern war.[32]

It is impossible to state with any certainty when or with whom the "knights of the air" image originated, but by mid-1916 it had permeated the rhetoric. "We have gone back some centuries," observed Montagu, "to the time when knight would ride out against knight in a single combat, man against man." In his poem "Dawn Patrol," Kim Beattie conjured up an image of one of those single combats:

> A Knight of the Air's in the wraith-wisps,
> > Riding the vapouring spires,

He's screaming alone through the cloud void,
Scolding with snickering wires.[33]

Frank Walker, who watched an aerial battle over the Somme in September 1916, wrote enthusiastically that "no grander tournaments were ever staged in the old days of Chivalry, than what these 20th-century knights pull off so nonchalantly in the sky."[34] Hartley Munro Thomas, too, was drawn to the medieval motif. He described air fighting as "chivalrous battle above the grey vast" and used images drawn directly from the Middle Ages: "Let us join in noble sport. / Ladies, grant us smiles as due / For the jousts we fight for you." In "Chivalry of the Air," he went so far as to minimize the differences between airmen on opposing sides:

Sons of the ancient Liberty!
   And you, our foemen, sons of Teuton Lords!
Sing to the new-born chivalry
   That the sky life now affords.

Free is the cult of the aeroplane,
   As you, our foemen, learn with us flying there.
Bold in heart, in will, and in brain,
   Are the knights of the cloud and air.

In an obituary address, the Reverend David Christie called Alan MacLeod, the Manitoba native who won the Victoria Cross for saving the life of his observer, "the finest flower of chivalry. The old days of knighthood are over, but for the very fairest blossoms of the spirit of knighthood the world has had to wait till the twentieth century."[35] That MacLeod was felled by influenza rather than a German bullet did not fundamentally alter his character. He died nobly, an antidote to the uncertainties of the modern age.

, , ,

But the air war served as an antidote in another sense as well. Once the trench lines of the Western Front solidified, it became more difficult to find a strategic advantage over the enemy. The senior commanders in the field believed that the war could be won only on the Western Front, and that all resources had to be channelled there to secure a decisive result. Of course, they differed over means. Field Marshal Douglas Haig, the British commander-in-chief, sought the big breakthrough that would allow his troops to burst through German lines and deliver a knockout blow. When his offensives achieved only modest gains, his answer was not to change the tactics but to increase the scale. Offensives failed, in Haig's view, when they did not marshal enough men or firepower; increase the number of infantrymen or artillery pieces, and an offensive would succeed. The War minister, Earl Kitchener, and the Chief of the Imperial General Staff, Sir William Robertson, favoured attrition—limited offensives that would draw the enemy into battle and force them to expend more men. The victor, in the contemporary jargon, would be the nation that could bleed its enemies white. Dissenting voices, particularly those of the British prime minister, David Lloyd George, and Winston Churchill, his minister of Munitions, believed that the war could only be won away from the Western Front; decisive action there was impossible, so it had to be sought elsewhere. They proposed campaigns in the Dardanelles, Salonika, Italy, Palestine, Mesopotamia, even an amphibious landing on the north German coast, to bring the war to a speedy and successful conclusion.

Other strategists, however, had a radical idea. The airplane had already shown some utility as a tactical weapon against enemy trenches, gun emplacements and supply depots near the front lines. From hand grenades or homemade bombs tossed haphazardly out of the cockpit, tactical air power had evolved to the point where bombing or strafing could have a real impact on ground operations. But such tasks merely accepted the assumption that the Western Front had to be the main battlefield.

Instead, why not bypass the battlefield altogether? Why not use the freedom and vision that the airplane conferred to craft a war-winning weapon? The new technology could carry the war right into the enemy's capitals and fulfill the predictions of the pre-war futurists by raining bombs on Berlin, London or Paris until the enemy capitulated.

Alexander Graham Bell, who had been making these arguments for more than a decade, finally found a ready audience for his theories. "The power that secures supremacy in the air will ultimately have all other methods of warfare at its mercy," he told the Halifax *Herald* in 1915. A year later, he dictated a long essay that foreshadowed the character of aerial combat in the Second World War. Contrary to what skeptics had said before the war, he wrote, aircraft and dirigibles were here to stay. "These two classes of machines will ultimately decide the fate of war...there will now be a struggle among the nations for the supremacy of the air." He remained dubious about the value of the airship but admitted that it would be a useful observation platform for the navy. Granted, it had great weight-carrying capacity, but because of its size and slow speed it would have to work at night, under the protection of "a cloud of small fast flying machines." Here, Bell found the future of aerial warfare. "I am inclined to think that we are about to witness a development of differentiation of functions of flying machines. We will have many small, fast-flying machines for scouting purposes alone and larger weight-carrying flying machines will be developed for offensive purposes...the larger dirigible balloons, and the large weight-carrying flying machines will have to be protected by numerous smaller flying machines as an aerial guard. The individual units of the aerial guard will make up for their weaknesses in offensive power by their speed and numbers. They will constitute as it were the mosquito fleet accompanying and protecting the larger machines."[36]

Before long, others had picked up Bell's theme. Sir Frederick Benson, an Ontario native who had decades of service with British cavalry regiments, told a reporter that the decisive actions of war

would be fought in the air. Gen. F. O. W. Loomis, commander of
the Third Division, predicted that "on aircraft will depend the
outcome of this war to a great extent." Lord Montagu agreed,
telling a Montreal audience "that aircraft are likely to become the
most competent source from which we can hope for victory."[37] As
the war dragged on, bringing little sign that the stalemate on the
Western Front could be broken, people pinned greater hopes on
the air weapon. In July 1917, just a few weeks before the opening
of the Passchendaele offensive that would enter the lexicon of war
as a synonym for pointless slaughter, the Manitoba *Free Press*
reported on American plans to construct a huge air fleet of fifty
thousand bombers that would pound the enemy into submission.
This fleet never materialized, but the predictions continued.
"They [aircraft] constitute a new and formidable arm of attack,"
observed a Toronto newspaper in 1918, "with ... air raids far into
the enemy country and with each week the air forces of all the
nations grow steadily more powerful and aggressive."[38]

The only problem was that Germany had been more successful than the Allies in opening a second front in the air. Admittedly,
things had not started off well for the German air services. The
first bombs dropped on British soil fell on Christmas Eve 1914
but did no damage; another single-plane raid the following day
was equally ineffective. By that time, the British had launched a
series of raids on German Zeppelin sheds. Three were unsuccessful, but in the fourth, on the night of October 22–23, 1914,
Sopwith biplanes from the Royal Naval Air Service station at
Antwerp destroyed the brand-new Z-9 at Düsseldorf. The war was
less than three months old, but the Z-9 was the sixth German dirigible lost.

However, the British failed to press the advantage, and the
emboldened German airship service seized the initiative. They
strengthened their defences and, on January 10, 1915, extracted
from Kaiser Wilhelm permission to begin a limited aerial bombardment of England. The first raid came nine days later, killing
four civilians and injuring sixteen. The British public regarded the

raid mostly as a curiosity, and the loss of a number of German dirigibles in succeeding months may have given Britons a false sense of security. But the night raiders returned in mid-April, and thereafter with increasing regularity. On May 31, 1915, bombs fell on east London. Only seven people were killed, but four of them were children, including a little girl and her baby sister, burned to death when incendiary bombs hit their home in Stoke Newington. A week later, after a raid on the northeastern city of Hull, enraged townspeople attacked businesses operated by people with German-sounding names. Calls for retaliation grew in intensity, but that did nothing to halt the bombing. By September 1915, the raiders came five times in a single week.

The growing ire was partly assuaged in the fall of 1916, when the British air defences began having more success in stopping the Zeppelins. The first airship to be shot down on British soil fell on September 2, 1916, and on October 1, L-31, commanded by Heinrich Mathy, perhaps the most reviled of German airship captains on account of his intemperate boasting in American newspapers, was shot down in a sheet of flame over Hertfordshire by Lieut. W. J. Tempest, a Yorkshire-born horse breeder who had been homesteading near Perdue, Saskatchewan. With these successes, the British public began to feel that the air offensive had been blunted. In fact, it was only being redirected. In early 1916, the German army brought Gotha twin-engine bombers into limited production. They were ungainly-looking machines, as most of the early bombers were, that carried fewer bombs than a Zeppelin and were slower than most of the British aircraft that would be sent up to meet them. But they were well armed, reliable, could operate at altitudes of up to fifteen thousand feet, and were relatively easy to manufacture. By the spring of 1917, they were picking up where the Zeppelins had left off.

The first Gotha raid came on May 25, 1917, at Folkestone, the main embarkation port for British troops heading to France. In ten minutes, twenty-one Gothas dropped 139 bombs on the town and nearby Shorncliffe camp, home of a Canadian base: 95 people were killed and nearly 200 injured, more than in the previous eight Zeppelin raids combined. Two weeks later more than 160 Londoners were killed, including fifteen children who died when the Upper North Street School in Poplar was devastated by a bomb. In January 1918 one of the aptly named Giants, an immense multi-engine bomber introduced in the autumn of 1917, dropped a single bomb in front of the Odhams Printing Works in central London. The explosion collapsed a wall, tipping the huge printing presses into the basement, where more than 500 people had taken shelter. The blast also ignited rolls of newsprint stored in the basement. The resultant inferno killed 38 people and injured 85.

Compared with the big bombing raids of the Second World War, the Poplar and Odhams tragedies seem minuscule, but at the time they were nightmares worse than anything the pre-war futurists had conjured up. The few high-profile victories over Zeppelins could not hide the truth that the air defences were usually powerless to stop the raiders, even in daylight. Panic was gripping the British public. It is a sign of the near hysteria that on the same night as the Odhams bombing, fourteen people were killed in panicked crushes at two separate air-raid shelters.

In the end, the German air offensive had a negligible impact on the war. The engines of the bulky airships were notoriously unreliable, and fewer than half of the raiders that left their bases actually reached their targets. Furthermore, any damage was purely random. Not only were the Zeppelin crews unable to hit specific targets, but they were often unable to locate major cities. The Gothas and Giants were generally more accurate but were no more successful in producing a decisive result. The offensive killed and wounded a few hundred civilians, and fears of raids may have increased absenteeism in British factories in 1918. But it inflicted no serious damage on military or industrial facilities and did not divert significant British resources from the Western Front to home defence duties. On the contrary, it was the German army and navy that wasted experienced crews and scarce resources that might have been used more efficiently elsewhere in the war effort.

But the offensive had a significant influence on popular attitudes toward aviation. In a war that Allied propagandists had already constructed as a struggle between good and evil, the quintessentially modern bombing campaign fitted comfortably into the medieval morality play. As a demonstration of the evil of Kaiserism, the bombing of English cities was just as effective as the image of bayoneted babies, violated nuns or French children with their hands cut off.

The offensive was simplified into two basic themes: the deaths of non-combatants; and the vengeance to be wrought on the enemy by Allied pilots. Not surprisingly, the deaths of women and children outraged public opinion. Headlines such as "Resume Murder of Tots," "Nursery a Slaughterhouse after the Zeppelin Raid," "20 Baby-Killers Sweep Over British Capital" and "Air Vultures Rain Death on Innocent Purchasers of Food" were common in Canadian newspapers.[39] Journalists referred not to the deaths of women and children but to the "midnight murdering" of non-combatants; the raids were "a slaughter of the innocents" and "an organized attempt to murder women in their homes and torture children in their cots."[40] Particularly poignant was the case of Caroline and Henry Good, who were found burned to death in their home in Ball's Pond Road in the London suburb of Dalston; they were kneeling side by side, possibly in prayer, Henry's arm around Caroline. An inquest into their deaths, which hardly seems to have been necessary, determined that the couple had been "murdered by some agent of a hostile force."[41]

Poets, too, found the air raids appealing, and often used the death of non-combatants as the climax of their work. In James L. Hughes's poem "An English Volunteer," an older man is convinced to enlist by news that his mother has been killed in an air raid.[42] Jesse Edgar Middleton's poem "The Zeppelin" begins with a newly married couple celebrating their wedding night, but the happiness is soon shattered by an air raid:

One sudden blaze of Hell, one roaring blast!
   The devil laughter of a coward foe!
Then dreams and love and life itself are past.
   What fool can say that God would have it so,
Our God, who made the flowers and the sea?

Even more terrifying is Walter Brindle's "Air Raid," which begins with three little girls playing in the street outside their home. All is innocent bliss until a German airplane appears overhead:

Then a quiet little bomb
From a quiet aeroplane,
Fell down in a quiet little way,
And death came with it.
And it fell rushing down,
And landed with a crash,
On that quiet little town,
Where those quiet little girls were at play.
As each fond little mother
Rushed out to the door,
She gazed on destruction dire,
For she saw each little daughter
Lying quiet on the ground,
Some were dead, others maimed,
Some on fire.[43]

The deaths of non-combatants, described in lurid detail and horrifying imagery, brought calls for Allied pilots to become avenging angels and visit death upon enemy cities in retaliation for German raids. Lord Montagu laid out the Allied thinking in a speech in Ottawa in December 1917: "We do not think it pays from any point of view—I will put it quite bluntly—to waste bombs in killing women and children. We do not think it is the best thing to do from the military point of view. Of course it is not right from the moral point of view. But we are quite ready to carry out reprisals if the reprisals are worth doing from a military point of view, and we are going to bomb, and we have bombed, German munition-making towns, and if we have killed citizens other than those actually fighting, well, they have done it to us and they must suffer what they give us...we want to do the Germans as much harm as is possible, and not merely to kill women and children, which seems to be in some cases the Germans' only object." Before his Canadian tour was over, however, Montagu's position had changed slightly, from a reluctant admission that bombing was necessary to a keenness to carry it out. "When we bomb a German town—as I hope we shall do more," he told a Toronto audience a few weeks later, "we should do more to bring an early victory and stop the war than by any kind of peace propaganda and hard warfare at the front." The following spring, the Toronto *Daily Star* quoted approvingly the undersecretary in the British Air Ministry: "We have started bombing German towns. We mean to continue bombing German towns, just as the Germans bomb our towns...it is, unfortunately, one of the new phases of warfare invented by the Germans and carried out by them."[44]

Judging from contemporary accounts, these policies were heartily approved in Canada. In 1915, Canadian newspapers reported gleefully on plans to construct a huge, bomb-carrying flying boat that would be used to retaliate against Germany for the "wholesale murder of innocents and non-combatants" in Britain. Twenty would be built by the Curtiss factory in Toronto, and the *Globe* reported proudly that this avenging angel would be christened the *Canada*. George Palmer's poem "Air Reprisals," written when the public was vociferously demanding retaliation raids, sums up the public mood:

> Bomb Potsdam and Cologne,
> Bomb those who're near the throne,
> Bomb them in a way they'll understand,
> That at the bombing game

We can do just the same,
But we'll drop them with a still more lavish hand.[45]

By the war's end, the Allies were indeed dropping bombs more
lavishly, although not to the extent that Palmer might have
wished. The Independent Air Force, created in the summer of
1918 to mount a strategic bombing offensive against Germany,
devoted most of its resources to tactical operations in support of
ground forces. British engineers were developing a new bomber,
the Handley Page V/1500, for the express purpose of attacking
enemy cities, but the Armistice came before it entered service. As
a result, German civilians never experienced anything like the
Zeppelin and Gotha raids.

Because the Allies were unable to mount a significant strategic
air offensive, public opinion had to be satisfied with other forms
of retaliation. Mary Josephine Benson's poem "The North Sea's
Emptiness" is a bitter verse in which the mariners on a fishing
smack refuse to rescue the crew of a downed Zeppelin, deciding
that death on the empty sea is a just fate for terror bombers. The
poem was inspired by an event in January 1916—the captain of
the fishing trawler *King Stephen* refused to pick up the crew of the
stricken airship L-19, fearing that the airmen might overpower his
crew. Public opinion and press were fully behind the captain, if
international law was not, and the Toronto *Evening Telegram* probably spoke for most Canadians in praising the crew of the *King
Stephen* for having "left baby butchers to die" on the North Sea.[46]

But the exceptional *King Stephen* episode hardly assuaged public feelings. Much more satisfying were the downings of German
dirigibles by Allied fighter pilots. If the fighter aces of the Western
Front were noble warriors jousting in the clouds, the Zeppelin-
busters were St. George going forth to slay the dragon.

Once again, facts were rarely permitted to stand in the way of
a good myth. In June 1915, the Allied world was captivated by
accounts of Reginald Warneford's destruction of LZ-37 over
Belgium. The Ottawa *Citizen* reported that "never in fiction has

anything more remarkable in an aerial duel been imagined" than the contest between the immense airship and Warneford's flimsy monoplane.[47] The Manitoba *Free Press* reckoned it "a story that makes the wildest tales of Verne insipid," and Jean Blewett cast the tale into romantic verse in "What Time the Morning Stars Arise":

Ah, yonder sweeps a Zeppelin!

A bird with menace in its breath,
    A thing of peril, spoil and strife;
The little children done to death,
    The helpless aged bereft of life.

The moan of stricken motherhood;
    The cowardice beyond our ken;
The cruelty that fires the blood,
    And shocks the souls of honest men.

These call for vengeance—mine the chase.
    He guides his craft—elate and strong.
Up, up through purple seas of space,
    While in his heart there grows a song: . . .

Old Britain hath her battles won
    On fields that are a nation's pride,
And oh, the deeds of daring done
    Upon her waters deep and wide!

But warfare waged on solid land,
    Or on the sea, can scarce compare
With this engagement, fierce yet grand;
    This duel to the death in the air.

He wins! he wins in sea of space!
    (Why prate we now of other wars?)

Since he has won his name and place
  By deathless valor 'mong the stars?[48]

It is an appealing characterization, although the real Warneford
was by most accounts reckless, cocksure and little loved by his
squadron mates. Just as far off the mark was the report, passed on
hastily by many Canadian newspapers, that Warneford was a
Canadian; the closest he had come to Canada was having two
cousins living in New Brunswick.[49]

The following year, Wilfred Campbell gave heroic treatment to
another Zeppelin buster, William Leefe Robinson, who brought
down the first airship to be destroyed on British soil. For
Campbell, Leefe Robinson had a score to settle "in the vengeful
race / With the sinister fleets of night." He flew, calmly and
serenely, over London until he spotted his prey, an airship sailing
scornfully "o'er a people's defenceless despair." In an instant, Leefe
Robinson was pouring his "death-dealing rain" into the body of
the dirigible. The poem's denouement comes as a foregone conclusion to this timeless tale of hunter and hunted:

Then I hover and listen, till I see the far glisten
Of a flame-flash blanching the night;
  And I know that my hate,
  That has lain in wait,
Has won in the grim air-fight.

Then I curve and slant, while my engines pant,
And the wings of my great bird tame;
  While the sinister Hun,
  In his ill, undone,
Goes out in a blinding flame.[50]

Such scenes made a deep impression on the Canadian public,
which had been denied the satisfaction of seeing German cities
bombed from the air. The downed Zeppelin became a useful

visual metaphor for the triumph over German militarism. When the Aero Club of Canada produced its special airmail stickers in 1918, it rejected a conventional image of a mail plane cruising over the Canadian landscape; instead, it chose a drawing of a British scout aircraft shooting down a German airship "in a blinding flame."

, , ,

Despite its popularity in wartime Canada, this mythologizing of airmen as medieval knights or avenging angels did not sit well with everyone at the sharp end. The perpetually sour George Kendall Lucas, a former law student from Markdale, Ontario, was one pilot who objected to the rhetoric of the air war: "The newspapers are full of special articles...about the 'cavalry of the air,' 'our super-men,' 'the freedom of the blue,' etc., etc. It's all bunkum, merely an advertising dodge.... There are more heavers of fertilizer in the Air Service than any place I ever struck." Bogart Rogers, a Californian who joined the RFC Canada in 1917 and learned to fly in Ontario, agreed: "Callousness and a hard-boiled and unsympathetic attitude were the best friends of a successful ace," he observed. Duncan Bell-Irving, one of three Vancouver brothers who served in the RFC, was also put off by the idolatry of the air aces: "Our officers are a bit disgusted at the 'Write Up' aviators get. I heard that an R.N. aviator got a V.C. for destroying a Zeppelin. If it had not happened that the bombs ignited the gas successfully nothing would have been heard of the exploit, while the man would have been just as brave."[51]

Nor were the great aces comfortable with the aura of chivalry. The war in the air might have been cleaner and more romantic than fighting on the ground, but it demanded every bit as much brutality and ruthlessness. The tales of opposing pilots waving jauntily to each other after a joust in the clouds were nonsense, they argued; the only good enemy was a dead enemy. The object of the game was not to hit the plane, Billy Bishop told a luncheon in London, Ontario, in 1917, but to kill the pilot: "There is one way to [bring down enemy aircraft], and that is to hit the man... with a concentrated fire in some vital spot. You must hit him in the head or the upper part of the body with a concentrated fire of bullets." In his best-selling memoirs, he described in some detail his satisfaction at seeing an enemy aircraft go down in flames, a feeling that he ascribed to "this new Hun hatred [that] had become a part of my soul" after a few weeks in combat. "Anything goes in the air," Raymond Collishaw, the Nanaimo-born pilot who became the most successful Royal Naval Air Service ace of the war, told a Toronto audience shortly after the war; air fighting was a cold-blooded business that had no room for mistaken displays of chivalry.[52]

But few Canadians were prepared to hear such truths. They found in the pilot the ideal antidote to the frightening uncertainties of modern war, a figure who could be everything the war was not. In an age of modern weapons, the aviator had the power to turn back the clock to a time when combat was clean, clear and simple. Free of the suffocating constraints of the trenches, he sailed aloft in a realm of clarity, cleanliness and order. Varley called him the all-seeing aviator; in the ferment of war, the pilot had become divine.

· 3 ·

THE WORLD AT
YOUR FEET

THE CROWDS AT TORONTO'S CANADIAN NATIONAL EXHIBITION
were better than usual on the last Monday in August 1920, some
estimates putting attendance at over 100,000. People packed the
midway and stood in long lines in front of the stalls that sold pop-
corn and hot dogs and candy floss. They waited patiently to get
into an exhibition of the war art commissioned by the Canadian
War Memorials Fund—it was drawing rave reviews—and to
inspect the live pheasants brought in by the Department of Game
and Fisheries. Henry Ford was in town to promote his new gasoline engine and to take in the automobile exhibits and perhaps a
car race. Forty-two Victoria Cross winners and their families were
being recognized at a soldiers' show, and the crowd cheered lustily

when the band struck up "O Canada" in their honour. The shouts of hawkers, the laughter of children, the clatter of the rides, the grunting of livestock—all added to the excitement of that warm summer afternoon.

And then in the distance came the sound of aircraft engines, and three planes came into view, flying in a neat V formation. As they passed over Sir John Eaton's yacht, Billy Bishop, in a Sopwith, peeled off into a series of vertical banks and loops while Billy Barker, in an Avro, executed a spinning nosedive. In the Curtiss Canuck, Forde McCarthy dived and looped over the waterfront. Eventually, they all descended, skimming so low that they almost went out of sight behind the breakwater before climbing again, engaging in a series of mock dogfights that Bishop easily won in the nimbler Dove. Then Barker did a succession of low loops over the midway and as far as the boardwalk, pulling out of the last loop only a few feet above the buildings. As the *Globe* reported, the airplanes "skimmed so close to the ground that the crowd thinned in fear, and then, as if mocking the terror they had created, they darted back to the heavens." One journalist remarked on the war pilots' tendency to "go crazy" in the air and attempt every conceivable stunt. Another simply called the display "one of the most reckless flying exhibitions seen in Toronto."[1]

These writers were not alone in their belief that pilots posed a danger to themselves and others. CNE organizers eventually fired Bishop and Barker, in part because of their tendency to dive perilously close to the crowds, but plenty of pilots were doing the same thing across Canada.[2] At country fairs, agricultural exhibitions, fundraisers or on their own initiative, they re-enacted dogfights, performed aerobatics or tossed their airplanes around the sky with an abandon that left spectators shaking their heads. For these former war pilots, barnstorming was the only way they could indulge their passion for flying.

The war years had demonstrated the practical utility of the airplane, both as a weapon and as a vehicle for aerial observation and photography. It had also given the country what it lacked before

1914: a large cadre of experienced, skilled pilots who could put aviation to practical good. Lionized as war heroes and elevated to celebrity status, they could command an audience whenever they spoke or acted. But here were some of Canada's greatest aces, returning flight to the circus sideshow days of the pre-1914 era. There is no doubt that performing intricate aerobatic manoeuvres at air shows, renting out their war-surplus aircraft for commercial purposes and engaging in unusual publicity stunts provided a congenial alternative to a sedentary peacetime existence; but these things also convinced the public, already conditioned to see aviators as separate from the rest of society, that pilots were strange aerial drifters of dubious character and that aviation was still little more than entertainment.

Not until the late 1920s did these attitudes begin to change, in large part because of a mushrooming public interest in long-distance flights. The rush to be the first to fly from somewhere to somewhere else may seem futile to modern sensibilities, but in the late 1920s it captured the spirit of a restless, inquisitive, thrill-seeking age. The accidents and disappearances of aviators merely heightened the appeal and confirmed to many people that pilots were hotheaded daredevils. But a number of remarkably successful long-distance flights transformed the image of aviators. No longer were they regarded as merely unstable and reckless; on the contrary, their stature in the public eye began to return to what it had been during the war years. The pilot came to be seen as a divine figure who transcended both time and space in a flimsy flying machine. Like the crazy barnstormer of the early 1920s, the long-distance flier of the late 1920s became a symbol of the times.

, , ,

The transition to peace was not an easy one for many Canadians. For more than four years, the nation had lived in constant stress. The fate of the British Empire seemed to hang in the balance, and with it the entire Christian West. The stakes were enormous and justified virtually any constraint on people's lives. Prohibition was invoked because a drunken worker was an unreliable worker; alcohol was banned in order to beat the Hun. Censorship, administered by the government and abetted by a willing press corps, ensured that Canadians heard only what was good for them to hear. Compulsory military service, as divisive as it was, ensured that citizens lived up to their civic obligations. The lid was clamped down on labour unrest, too. There were isolated outbreaks, but workers generally accepted the argument that they should put off their demands until the enemy was defeated. Rationing, restrictions on civil liberties, the disenfranchisement of voters were all justified on the grounds that during wartime, the needs of the individual had to be subordinated to the needs of the nation. A deep emotional commitment was also demanded. Business as usual, the slogan adopted by Britain early in the war, was not meant to be taken literally. It did not mean that one should carry on as if nothing had happened. Rather, it preached stoicism. In Canada no less than in the mother country, one had to keep a stiff upper lip. To be light-hearted and carefree was to be suspect—not necessarily disloyal, but shallow or callous, in failing to take the war seriously.

And then it was over. On November 11, Canadians poured into the streets to celebrate. The merrymaking was real enough, but in truth it took some time for the realization to sink in: the war was really over; things could get back to normal. Once the crushing burden of wartime pressure had been lifted, four years of pent-up energy manifested itself first in a restlessness that pervaded the country. After years of restraint, many people wanted to enjoy their newfound freedom but were not quite sure how to go about it. Some were inclined to turn the clock back to before 1914; when that proved impossible, they cast around for someone to blame. Others were determined to push the limits of acceptable behaviour, to bring forth a new world from the crucible of war.

Among the most restless were the pilots who had been so lionized during the war. For them, the Armistice of November 1918 was a double-edged sword. It meant an end to the fighting, but it also meant an end to flying. They had grown accustomed to flying whenever they wanted and to having an airplane at their disposal with no worry about the cost of gasoline, oil or repairs; all that was taken care of by the squadron mechanics. Even when no combat patrols were scheduled, it was easy to justify a short hop to test a recently repaired engine or a patched control surface. But now those days were gone, and it soon became apparent that there would be few jobs for pilots in any post-war Canadian air force after "this devastating peace broke out," as one airman put it.[3]

Soon after the war ended, however, the Imperial Munitions Board decided to dispose of the aircraft used to train pilots for the RFC in Canada. The most common type was the Curtiss JN-4 Canuck, as the Canadian-made version was known (the same aircraft manufactured in the United States was known as the Jenny). This nimble two-seater was reliable, easy to maintain and inexpensive. Across the country, entrepreneurs bought up the aircraft and marketed them at fire-sale prices. In the spring of 1919, a Toronto entrepreneur was advertising Canucks at $2,000 apiece. "This is the big year for profitable local flying," he predicted. "Keep in the game and be ready for the wonderful aerial developments ahead."[4] For the demobilized pilot with a little private capital or a few investors, the Canuck offered a way to keep flying. All they needed was enough money for gas and oil, spare parts, unexpected repairs and a little profit. Airmail contracts were still years in the future, and the provincial governments were just beginning to think about getting into the aviation business. With few stable sources of revenue, many pilots turned to the one pursuit with any hope of remuneration: entertaining the public. And so was born the aerial barnstormer, taking the nickname from the itinerant showmen who criss-crossed rural America, performing in barns, town halls or any other venue that would have them. Typically, the aerial variant buzzed a small town to draw the people into the streets, sometimes dropping handbills to advertise their services. He landed in a nearby farmer's field and offered rides, either for a flat fee or for a certain sum per minute or per pound of the passenger's weight. Once the interest and disposable income of that town was exhausted, he would move on to another.[5]

The enterprising aviator could also take advantage of any large public gathering to earn a few dollars. In Winnipeg, the short-lived Veteran Aeroplane Company offered $10 flights to crowds attending the city's Peace Day celebrations, held in July 1919 to mark the signing of the Treaty of Versailles that officially ended the war. To emphasize that fair-goers would get more than a calm, sightseeing flight, the firm's advertisements promised "Thrills of War in Times of Peace." Depending on the season, pilots might also travel the circuit of country fairs, bidding for contracts with fair organizers and performing aerobatics for the crowds. Within a year of the war's end, every fair and exhibition worth its salt had to feature an aerobatic display.

Across the country, promoters promised air shows that would chill the blood and thrill the soul. When the Quebec Provincial Exhibition Committee contracted Georges Vézine to perform in June 1919, they carefully stipulated the stunts he was to do, including loops, spinning dives, stall turns, spiral descents, Immelman turns, half rolls and "racing with auto and horse and other tricks anywhere above the City." In May 1919, the American stuntman Ormer Locklear suspended himself from the wing of an aircraft as it flew fifteen hundred feet above Toronto; this "flirt with eternity," observed the *Globe*, caused onlookers to "hold their breath and gasp." In June 1919, the good people of Victoria were promised a sensational air show "of the most daring character" that would include "Freak Flying, as practiced by war pilots to relieve the monotony of everyday flying."[6] At Minoru Park in Vancouver, the site of some of Canada's first air shows, an "aviators' carnival" on Dominion Day 1919 featured a trio of stunt flyers, a wing walker and the obligatory race between an automobile and an airplane.

It was perhaps inevitable that fair-goers would come to expect ever more dangerous stunts; and pilots had to up the ante if they were to win contracts. Harry Fitzsimmons, who had formed the Lethbridge Aircraft Company with John E. "Jock" Palmer, another wartime pilot, decided that wing-walking might put them ahead of their competitors. While in California shortly after the war, Fitzsimmons had seen Ormer Locklear pioneer the art, and he and Palmer set to work practicing. Soon their wing-walking feats were the talk of air shows around Alberta. It wasn't long before Locklear climbed from one airplane to another in mid-flight, using a rope ladder, and Canadian barnstormers were quick to copy him. As they had in the pre-war era, critics deplored the risks, but as long as they brought in contracts, pilots were happy to oblige.[7]

Many aviators also found that they could pick up extra income by renting out their aircraft for sales gimmicks. Stan McClelland in Saskatoon turned his Curtiss into an aerial billboard, plastering it with advertisements for M. K. Thomson Jeweller, the Savoy Café and Central Pharmacy. Russell Smith of Ottawa started the Aerial Services Company to do airborne advertising and promised prospective clients he could "'bomb' every city, town and village in Western Canada with advertising literature.... Do it the aerial way. Make your personal appeal direct to the consumer."[8] In May 1919, Roland Groome, described by press accounts as "the daring young performer in the aerial business," delivered a special edition of the Regina *Leader* from the Saskatchewan capital to Moose Jaw, Indian Head and Qu'Appelle. The paper's editor proudly if incorrectly proclaimed that this was the first time in Canada that an aircraft had delivered newspapers. When Ernest Hoy made his pioneering flight over the Rockies from Vancouver to Calgary in August 1919 in an aircraft provided by the B.C. branch of the Aerial League of Canada, he carried with him sweaters from Universal Knitting in Vancouver to be displayed in the window of the Diamond Clothing Company in Calgary. Probably to the League's chagrin, the Calgary *Daily Herald* seemed less interested in the significance of the flight for future air travel than in the fact that Hoy had apparently made the first delivery of merchandise by air.[9]

What is striking about all this activity is how little attitudes toward aviation had changed since 1914, even as the technology had improved dramatically. It existed to thrill the crowds or to sell sweaters, not to bring about some radical transformation in the human condition. The air lobby feared that once the novelty of these stunts wore off, public interest in flying would evaporate.[10]

They were also concerned about the image of the pilot. During the war, the aviator had become a heroic cultural icon. In the early post-war years, the dashing fighter ace became the reckless stunt flier; an eager public lapped up his aerial daredevilry but had doubts about his respectability and sanity. The escalation of stunting merely pushed aviators ever farther toward the margins of society. Then, at the height of the barnstorming era, a new mania took hold: the race to be the first person to fly from one place to another. And the biggest challenge was the Atlantic Ocean.

, , ,

Long before Walter Wellman came to grief in his airship in 1910 eight hundred miles into his planned flight from New York to Europe, aviators had dreamed wistfully about hopping the Atlantic. "In the annals of modern daring," observed a Toronto editor, "there is no more thrilling venture than ... the non-stop air crossing of the broad Atlantic."[11] For Canadians, there was more at stake than merely crossing a body of water. The biggest threat to the British Empire was its very success: the far corners of the greatest empire the world had ever known were separated by days or even weeks of travel. The steamship had been a marked improvement over sail, and the advent of the transatlantic telegraph cable after 1858 had made near-instantaneous communication possible, but the airplane had the potential to bring a real revolution in imperial relations. Once the Atlantic could be crossed by airplane, Canada and the mother country would be just hours apart.

Beyond the consequences for imperial unity, Canadian interest was also fanned by the colourful characters, big money and great risks that characterized the contest. In 1913, the British newspaper magnate and aviation enthusiast Lord Northcliffe had announced a prize of £10,000 to the first person to fly between North America and Great Britain or Ireland, but the coming of war had temporarily put paid to those attempts. However, the war had also fostered technological developments that brought the flight within reach. The multi-engine bombers intended for British reprisal raids against Berlin had both the range and the load-carrying capacity to cross the ocean, as did the big flying boats built to protect the coasts of North America and Britain. Northcliffe announced in July 1918 that the prize money was still up for grabs, and on November 4, 1918, Britain's Royal Aero Club and the Air Council lifted the wartime ban on long-distance attempts. On November 15, the Club received its first official entry. When the British government released Royal Air Force officers to enter the fray, the trickle of applicants turned into a flood.

Rumours—if not airmen—flew: French pilot René Fonck, the highest-scoring Allied ace of the war, would make an attempt in a huge British-built seaplane. Another behemoth, a five-engine Caproni triplane, was being readied for an Italian crew. The New York department store magnate Rodman Wanamaker, who had backed a similar attempt in the summer of 1914, was paying for a new Curtiss flying boat, to be flown by a British pilot. Raymond Collishaw would lead a crew of three in a Canadian-made Handley Page bomber. A British-Canadian consortium would field a heavily modified Fairey biplane. Most of these schemes were ill-prepared, underfunded or simply over-optimistic and never got beyond wishful thinking.

By the spring of 1919, the field had been whittled down by accident and withdrawal to a handful of legitimate challengers. Four of the teams were British. The biggest was a leviathan, a Handley Page V/1500 bomber, the largest aircraft flying in 1919, with a cosmopolitan crew led by Mark Kerr, a Royal Navy admiral. John Alcock and Arthur Whitten Brown were to fly in the

Atlantic, a Vickers Vimy two-engine bomber developed too late to see service during the war. Alcock was an experienced aviator with a pre-war pilot's licence, seven kills and more than a year as a prisoner of the Turks. Brown, born in Glasgow of American parents, had also been a prisoner and had used the idleness of captivity to become an expert navigator. The other *Atlantic* entered was a Sopwith biplane flown by Harry Hawker, a flamboyant Australian reputed to be the highest-paid pilot in the world. Ill health had kept him out of the RFC, but he was one of the best-known pilots in Britain. His navigator, Kenneth Mackenzie Grieve, was quiet and reserved, a study in contrasts to the flashy Hawker. The fourth British entrant was the *Raymor*, a Martinsyde biplane to be flown by Freddie Raynham, a British test pilot and Hawker's longtime rival in pre-war record attempts. Every time the two had gone head to head, Hawker had emerged on top, so Raynham was determined to even things up. Navigating the *Raymor* would be Fairfax Morgan, a naval aviator who had lost a leg in the war. Jolly and quick-witted, Morgan soon became the most popular of the airmen in the race.

But these efforts, which involved some of the biggest aircraft manufacturers in Britain, were dwarfed by an immense operation organized by the U.S. Navy and with the virtually limitless resources of the U.S. Treasury behind it. Though not entered for the *Daily Mail* prize, the American team was determined to be first across the Atlantic, sending four NC (denoting Navy Curtiss) flying boats from Newfoundland to the Azores and thence to Portugal. A chain of American warships, sixty-six in all, would be spaced at fifty-mile intervals, so the crews would merely have to fly from one floating beacon to the next until they reached their objective. Almost as an afterthought, the U.S. Navy also dispatched a blimp, the C-5, to Newfoundland, to attempt a crossing at the same time.

Beginning in the early spring of 1919, the contenders converged on Newfoundland in what must have been one of the strangest friendly invasions ever to hit the island. Hawker and

Grieve were the first to arrive, followed by the *Raymor*. The two crews attracted a fair amount of media attention, although W. P. Beazell of the Toronto *Mail and Empire* could not get more than two consecutive sentences out of Hawker or Grieve, which he found both intriguing and frustrating: "Their indifference to the dangers of failure and even more to the glory that will attend success has been the most striking aspect of their demeanor." Hawker even received an offer from an Irish veteran in Manitoba, who had put in fourteen years as an army bugler, to fly across the Atlantic with them and serenade them with his cornet when the going got tough. He assured the pair that he had a sufficiently varied repertoire for a landing in either Dublin or London.[12]

Then, on May 2, the U.S. Navy arrived with one ship, the *Aroostook*, anchoring at Trepassey Bay; within days, seven more had arrived. They brought supplies, spare parts, temporary buildings, aviation fuel and oil, and mechanics and crewmen. Soon there were as many American seamen in the area as Newfoundlanders, and the NCs had not even arrived yet. They were having their own trouble. On March 27, a storm had hit their base at Rockaway, Long Island, severely damaging NC1. The navy decided to cannibalize NC2 to provide spare parts, so only three flying boats left Rockaway on May 8. NC1 and NC3 arrived in Halifax harbour without incident, but NC4 experienced engine trouble and did not leave Rockaway until May 14. When it finally reached Newfoundland, the other two flying boats already had a four-day head start in their preparations. It was beginning to look as if the three NCs would need every safeguard the navy had put in place for them.

The other competitors were later getting to Newfoundland. Alcock and Brown arrived in Halifax on May 10, but it was another two weeks before they set up shop in Newfoundland. The Handley Page arrived about the same time. The C-5, on the other hand, drifted into St. John's on May 16. Supremely confident, the captain, Lt. Comdr. Emory Coil, gave people to understand that as soon as routine servicing was complete, he would cast off for

England. But Coil hadn't given enough account to Newfoundland weather, the bane of all transatlantic fliers. Soon after the airship was secured, as if to mock Coil's confidence, the wind picked up. The C-5 bucked and heaved against the mooring cables as the crew nervously watched the darkening skies. Under normal circumstances, they should have taken the C-5 up to ride out the storm in the air, but the carburetors had been removed for servicing and the engines were unusable. The only way to save the ship was to remove the ripping panel and deflate the gasbag. But the cord on the panel broke when it was pulled, and despite the frantic efforts of crew and onlookers the heavy cables snapped one by one as the airship jerked in the wind. When it was thirty feet off the ground, the crew abandoned the C-5 to its fate. It was last seen over Signal Hill, drifting bravely out to sea.

On the same day that the C-5 began its unmanned crossing, the naval flying boats were making final preparations, and in the early evening of May 16 all three were away. Despite the exhaustive preparations, things went wrong almost from the beginning. With its mismatched wing cannibalized from the fourth Curtiss, NC1 never did fly properly; by noon the next day, it was miles off course and unable to find any of the deployed warships. The crew set down on the water, intending to get their bearings and take off again, but they misjudged the height of the seas. The aircraft bounced from crest to trough until, with a sickening crunch, the entire tailplane broke off. Now virtually helpless, the crew was very lucky to cross paths with a tramp steamer bound for Gibraltar. NC3 ran into precisely the same trouble. Hopelessly lost, its crew also tried to land to get their bearings, but the swells stressed the airframe so badly that the Curtiss was no longer flyable. It was a credit to the skill of the crew that they were able to sail the NC3 (backward, as it happened) to the Azores.

That left NC4, the newest and fastest of the flying boats, to carry the hopes of the United States. Both aircraft and crew were more than up to the task. Compared with its sister ships, NC4 had an uneventful flight, reaching the Azores fifteen hours and eighteen minutes after leaving Trepassey. On May 27, the Curtiss resumed its journey, and nine and a half hours later touched down in the mouth of the Tagus River at Lisbon, Portugal. The U.S. Navy had completed the first aerial crossing of the Atlantic, a remarkable achievement, but Canadians were unimpressed. After all, it was made in stages, and as the Calgary *Herald* remarked, "It is the non-stop flight that interests the people." Moreover, flying from warship to warship might be safe, but it was not in the same class as setting out to face the elements with only one's wits and courage. "A fine accomplishment," sniffed the *Globe*, but it lacked "every element of the dramatic interest" of the other flights being attempted.[13]

Back in Newfoundland, Harry Hawker also thought the Americans unsporting; their effort was simply not in the same class as his own, he believed.[14] He grew even more frustrated on May 17 when he heard news—later proved inaccurate—that the American flying boats had reached the Azores. He had to move fast if he was to have any chance of being first across. On Sunday morning, May 18, even though the weather reports remained discouraging, Hawker and Grieve climbed into the *Atlantic*, splashed down the runway and vanished into the clouds. After the Americans' sledgehammer effort, this was real drama, thought the press. "In the history of travel since its earliest records there has been nothing more dramatic or more romantic than this flight," observed the *Globe*. It was "a feat which for many a day will furnish a theme for poetry and song." On May 19, reports placed the aircraft 150 miles off the Irish coast. As one newspaper reported, "not only local but long distance telephones were busy with eager enquiries. The whole country awaited the final word that the brave little craft had actually landed in Ireland."[15]

But that word never came. On Tuesday, May 20, the Admiralty announced that the pair must have come to grief soon after taking off from Newfoundland; it was thought that the intense cold had congealed their engine oil and rendered their wireless set unserviceable. By Wednesday, most people had given up hope.

When Hawker had roared away, an irate Freddie Raynham

immediately ordered his aircraft made ready. He wasn't about to play second fiddle to Hawker again. In his haste, he ignored all the warning signs around him. The weather had cleared, but the airfield, never very good at the best of times, was still sodden and treacherous. More significantly, the wind was blowing toward the rear quarter of the aircraft rather than the nose. In his desperation, however, Raynham ignored the fundamental laws of flight, loaded up a few supplies, bundled his one-legged navigator into the Martinsyde and taxied down the field. The airplane didn't want to leave the ground, but Raynham abruptly wrestled the *Raymor* into the air. Just as abruptly, it plummeted back to earth and smashed nose-first into the mud. Morgan was badly injured and had to return to England; he talked about opening an air service between St. John's and Montreal, but doctors told him he would never fly again. Raynham found another navigator and tried again, but that attempt was no more successful. With that, Raynham washed his hands of the whole business and returned to England.

Then, on May 25 came the news the world was waiting for: Hawker and Grieve were saved. They had long since been given up for dead—by their employer, by Northcliffe and by the British government, but not by Hawker's wife, Muriel. She was convinced that they had been picked up by a vessel without wireless communication, which is precisely what happened. The aircraft had developed engine trouble not long after taking off, and by the time they were a thousand miles from Newfoundland, it was clear that the engine would not hold out. Hawker turned toward the shipping lanes and luckily came upon a Danish steamer bound for Scotland. At 8:30 A.M. on May 19, he ditched the Sopwith in front of the *Mary* and he and Grieve were pulled aboard. The world remained ignorant of their fate for six more days, until the freighter neared Scotland and was able to send a message with signal flags.

When they finally got back to London, Hawker and Grieve were heroes. Huge parades were held in their honour, they were feted by royalty and congratulations poured in. The daily press in Canada could scarcely contain itself. The *Border Cities Star* rated their attempt "quite the most thrilling affair in the history of air navigation," and contended that no news since the Armistice of 1918 had brought such joy to the world. "Romance still lives," gushed the *Globe*, "the golden age is not behind us; we are living in it, and its vista stretches into the years, with inspiration beckoning man to attempt still greater deeds than those he has yet accomplished...the Anglo-Saxon race has lost none of the attributes of courage that have given leadership in all which count for the advancement of the race so far as the mind of humanity can plan and the body of man can endure." Prime Minister Robert Borden complimented the pair on their "magnificent gallant attempt," and Billy Barker congratulated his old friend Hawker "on his fine effort and failure, which is glorious."[16] Barker's message may well have rankled; it was a fine effort to be sure, but it was still a failure.

By now, only two teams remained in the race. The huge Handley Page had arrived in Newfoundland on May 26. The ground crew was under the direction of Ernest Stedman, Handley Page's technical chief, who would go on to become a leading member of Canada's air lobby. They set up shop at Harbour Grace, pulling down three houses, a shed and several stone fences to create a runway. It was no easy task to reassemble in the open air a flying machine with a 126-foot wingspan and a weight of sixteen tons, and the trial flights were not entirely satisfactory. By July, the aircraft's manufacturer decided to send the crew to New York City to drum up some sales and make the trip worthwhile. On the way there, though, the bomber force-landed at Parrsboro, Nova Scotia, on July 4, and it was more than three months before spare engine parts arrived from England and repairs were completed. It flew from Parrsboro on October 9 with twelve people aboard (a Canadian record for passengers carried in a single flight) and reached New York without further incident. But a month later, on the way to Chicago, the ill-starred bomber crash-landed in Cleveland; the manufacturer recalled the crew to England and wrote off the wreckage.

The last hope, the Vickers Vimy *Atlantic*, was ready for its first flight on June 9, but the weather refused to co-operate. Heavy winds and rain whipped the makeshift airfield, and conditions over the ocean were likely to be even worse: towering cumulus clouds, thrown up by the Gulf Stream, that could jostle and buffet even the biggest aircraft; violent thunderstorms that bathed the sky in eerie white and red light; ice that could quickly coat an airplane, robbing it of lift and eventually forcing it down into the sea; and drenching rain squalls that threatened to drown the engines. Not until June 14 did Alcock decide it was safe to fly. He and Brown packed the *Atlantic* with some food, coffee and letters, topped up the tanks and trundled off down the field about 2 P.M. The Vimy struggled for height and then disappeared below the hills. The crew was sure it had crashed, but seconds later a cheer went up as the Vimy reappeared, ascending slowly toward the east.

Brown would later recall the flight as his single most terrifying experience. Soon after leaving Newfoundland, one of the engine exhausts burned off, so the roar was deafening. Then there was a dizzying spin out of a cloud bank, from which Alcock recovered with barely a hundred feet to spare. To avoid more thunderheads, Alcock climbed higher, but the control surfaces, engine intakes and instruments began to ice up. Finally, at 8:15 A.M., he peered through the gloom and thought he could make out some islands. Soon a larger land mass came into view, and ten minutes later the Vimy crossed the Irish coast. They circled the town of Clifden and gently put the aircraft down on what they discovered too late was a peat bog. The wheels dug in and the stalwart Vimy ignominiously buried its nose in the peat. But Alcock and Brown had done it. They had bridged the Atlantic in a single hop.

The press was ecstatic. Long articles described the flight in minute detail, but many observers were more fascinated by its implications. "The meaning of the achievement is almost too great to be grasped," wrote the Ottawa *Journal*. "Distance has been obliterated. The Atlantic has been bridged and America brought within a day's journey of Europe. The world has been drawn together, its far corners picked up and brought within a narrow circle." A paradigm shift was under way: "The time will come," predicted the Regina *Morning Leader*, "and it may not be long, when the trip from America to Europe, and from Europe to America, by air will be regarded as quite as commonplace a journey as the crossing of the continent by railway or the ocean by steam vessel...in the not distant future, thousands of airplanes and dirigible airships will fly to and fro over land and sea."[17] The *Globe*, in a long, congratulatory editorial, summed up what was for many people the significance of the flight: "In the annals of peaceful conquests for the benefit of the human race none ranks in daring...[Alcock and Brown] have opened to all the world of commerce, science and travel possibilities so great that the mind is almost dazzled by the vision of the aerial future.... Time and space have been eliminated, and the ends of the earth linked by hours, and not by weeks or months as in the days before two gallant men set out to meet the rising sun in the hope that it would shine upon the beginning of a revolutionary era in transcontinental travel.... The visions of seers and prophets...are in a fair way to complete fulfilment within a very short time." The world was shrinking; "Europe suddenly seems very near. The Atlantic crossing, formerly a matter of about a hundred hours at the best, is reduced to sixteen." The next day, the paper predicted that air travellers would soon be reserving their staterooms for transatlantic aerial voyages. Within a year or two, a Victoria newspaper asserted confidently, there would be a regular transatlantic service for passengers and mail.[18]

, , ,

Eight years later, the world was still waiting, for the Atlantic had not been kind to aviators after Alcock and Brown. There were the high-profile airship crossings, by the British R-34 (in 1919) and the German LZ-16 (in 1924), but none of the heavier-than-air attempts generated the same excitement as the season of 1919. A

Portuguese crew flew from Lisbon to Rio de Janeiro in 1922, and in 1926 and 1927 four other crews would make successful crossings of the south Atlantic, but these flights elicited barely a flicker of interest in Canada. A successful flight between the Orkney Islands and Labrador by two U.S. Army Air Service biplanes in 1924 as part of a round-the-world flight was scarcely more noted, perhaps because it was backed by the same concentration of resources as the NC flight. Half a dozen attempts also came to grief, although Canadians barely noticed them.

But the Atlantic still exerted a strong pull on aviators; after all, the Raymond Orteig Prize of £10,000, announced in 1919 by a Franco-American hotelier for the first non-stop flight between New York and Paris, was still up for grabs. By 1927, aircraft with the capability to make the crossing in a single hop were being manufactured. On both sides of the Atlantic, the pretenders to the throne began to gather. The best known claimant was Richard Byrd, who in 1926 became the first man to fly over the North Pole; in the spring of 1927 he and his crewmen were in New York readying a Fokker monoplane christened *America* that was funded from the very deep pockets of Rodman Wanamaker. Also in the race were Clarence Chamberlin and his millionaire backer Charles Levine, who planned to fly to Germany in their Wright-Bellanca *Columbia* (the same airplane that Toronto-born Errol Boyd would use in 1930 to become the first Canadian to fly the Atlantic). The naval aviators Noel Davis and Stanton Wooster, with six-figure sponsorship from the American Legion, were readying a converted army bomber for the hop. And on the other side of the ocean, Frenchmen Charles Nungesser and François Coli, who had distinguished themselves as fighter pilots on the Western Front, were making preparations for an east-west crossing.

Then, during a ten-day period in April, disaster struck. On the sixteenth, Byrd's Fokker crashed on its first test flight; damage to the aircraft was considerable, and pilot Floyd Bennett was seriously injured. On the twenty-fourth, the *Columbia* lost part of its landing gear on takeoff and came down heavily. Then, two days later, on their final test flight before leaving for Paris, Davis and Wooster struggled to get their converted bomber into the air, but it was too heavily loaded. The aircraft crashed into a bog at the end of the runway and both pilots drowned.

With the field thinned, the press focused more closely on the surviving teams. Chamberlin reported that he and his navigator, Lloyd Bertaud, were ready to take off any day; Nungesser and Coli were waiting for better weather, while Byrd admitted that he might abandon his attempt altogether, because he had been unable to find a replacement for Floyd Bennett. The following day, the press had decided that the race had come down to "two sky goliaths... [who] await the magic word that sends them hurtling through space." On the west side of the Atlantic were Chamberlin and Bertaud, but in Paris the French pair was quickly emerging as the sentimental favourites. Nungesser was described as "the wildest man in the air" or "the handsomest officer in the far flung French fighting arm," and the press made much of his recent marriage to a beautiful American heiress. He had downed forty-five enemy aircraft during the war and spent a few years as a barnstormer in France before moving to the United States and becoming a Hollywood stunt pilot. His companion François Coli was just as dashing; dubbed "the 'one-eyed' devil" by the press on account of a war wound that had left him blind in one eye, Coli smiled broadly in press photographs that accentuated his eye patch. "Men of high exploit, these, and fearless," concluded the Toronto *Daily Star*.[19]

By the time Canadians awoke to their morning papers on Monday, May 9, the French pair were off in their stubby single-engine biplane christened *L'Oiseau Blanc*. They had left Le Bourget airport in Paris on Sunday morning, the overloaded plane struggling to gain altitude, and headed toward the west. The Canadian papers reported optimistically on Monday that they had covered two-thirds of the distance to their goal, and there were a number of unconfirmed sightings of the aircraft over Newfoundland and Nova Scotia, but by Tuesday they were twenty-four hours overdue, and by Wednesday they were all but given up for lost. There would be a persistent rumour that Nungesser and Coli had come down somewhere in the Newfoundland interior, but their fate remains a mystery to this day.

The public mood was sobered by the tragedy, but the other claimants were undeterred. "The loss of life in long distance experimental flights will not hinder their repetition or postpone the conquest of the air," predicted the Toronto *Daily Star*. "The march of invention will go steadily forward until the difficulties are overcome."[20] The contest was still on, only now there were three horses in the race. On May 13, Richard Byrd confirmed that he would go ahead with his attempt, and Chamberlin and Bertaud claimed to be ready to go as soon as the weather improved. And for the first time, Canadian newspapers mentioned a third contestant, a former airmail pilot from Lincoln, Nebraska, named Charles Lindbergh. The papers could say little about Lindbergh beyond the fact that he declined to reveal his plans.

Among these internationally renowned aviators with their millionaire backers, Lindbergh was different. Born in Detroit in 1902, he had been bitten by the flying bug during the war but did not get his opportunity until he washed out of the University of Wisconsin in 1922. Taken on as an unpaid assistant to a barnstormer, he eventually turned to wing walking and parachute jumping before getting a chance to fly the mail. With a scant $15,000 put up by supporters in St. Louis, Lindbergh had ordered a stripped-down Ryan monoplane from a little aircraft company in San Diego. It had no radio, no sextant, no running lights, no fuel gauge, minimal instrumentation—it was little more than a flying gas tank. Still, Lindbergh figured it would get him the 3,600 miles to Paris with room to spare.

Before long, Lindbergh became a bona fide celebrity. After his flight from San Diego to New York broke existing records, the press began to take an interest in him. He was very different from anyone else involved in the race. Reports referred to him as a "strapping youth" who was "unassuming and nonchalant...good looking, pink-cheeked." He didn't make a fuss about things, and his determination to fly alone evoked the romance of the quest. A lone wolf, they called him.[21]

But the weather reports were still unfavourable, so the gladiators waited. Byrd continued test-flying the *America*, while the *Columbia* camp dissolved into bickering over how the prize money would be divided up. All the while, Lindbergh casually went about his business. His mother came from Detroit to visit. He remembered that he should update his passport. He had lunch with Col. Theodore Roosevelt Jr. He even spent an afternoon at Coney Island. Those closest to him knew that his nerves were jangling, but he kept up an air of modest nonchalance. The Canadian press was intrigued by the tall flier, but found his unassuming character a little odd. They weren't quite sure what to make of him, so adopted the moniker conferred by the American press: the Flying Fool.

And then he was off. On May 20, at 7:51 A.M., he motioned for his ground crew to remove the wheel chocks, and the Ryan slowly began to trundle down the sodden field. By the halfway mark, the *Spirit of St. Louis* still had not gathered enough speed to lift its two tons of weight. Finally, with barely a thousand feet of grass left, Lindbergh muscled the aircraft off the ground. It lurched over the telephone wires at the end of the field, struggled for height and eventually headed out toward Long Island. All this was reported in great detail in Canadian newspapers. He was a "dark horse ... scarcely considered a candidate until a week ago," which was certainly true, but it was perhaps unfair to call him "foolhardy as always" for his close shave on takeoff. They concluded that "Lucky Lindy" got off the ground—only just—to begin his "lonely challenge to death."[22]

By Saturday, Lindbergh had effectively taken over Canada's major daily newspapers. Despite confirmed sightings over Nova Scotia, which suggested if nothing else that Lindbergh was indeed a legitimate contender, the press's characterization of him had not changed. "'Flying Fool' Lindbergh Keeps to Schedule," read the

headlines; a smaller article carefully provided the French transla-
tion, "le Fou Volant." The fact that he buzzed St. John's harbour
was taken as further proof that Lindbergh was "still his old auda-
cious self."[23]

But against all odds, on May 21, 1927, as a calm, clear night
settled over Paris, the *Spirit of St. Louis* touched down at Le
Bourget airport. The haggard Lindbergh clambered out of the
cockpit, to be greeted by a crowd nearly driven mad by excitement
and anticipation. As many as 200,000 people jammed the airport
and attacked the *Spirit of St. Louis* in an attempt to get souvenirs;
only a concerted effort by the Paris police prevented the aircraft
from being torn to pieces.[24]

When the wire services reported Lindbergh's arrival in Paris, his
conquest of Canadian newspapers was complete. The major dailies
filled page after page with maps, line drawings, photographs, long
interviews with acquaintances and Lindbergh's own account of the
flight. They trumpeted his achievement in huge headlines and lav-
ished praise on him in editorials. Letters to the editor extolled his
virtues, while amateur poets waxed eloquent about him in rhyming
couplets. Canadians were eager entrants to the *Spirit of St. Louis*
poetry competition, which drew more than four thousand sub-
missions from around the world; one of the more earnest efforts
was by Ontario's own Edmund Vance Cooke, who managed to use
Lindbergh's name twenty-three times in four short stanzas.[25]
Lindbergh was also exploited in the most crassly, commercial way.
Every manufacturer with a connection to the flight—SKF
Bearings, B. F. Goodrich Silvertown tires, Stromberg carburetors,
Franklin air-cooled engines, Gargoyle Mobiloil, even Waterman's
fountain pens—used Lindbergh's name as an endorsement. Party-
goers danced the Lindy Hop, while gramophones cranked out the
new hit song "Lucky Lindy" (with the rather more sombre "The
Lost French Fliers" on the flip side). You could even buy the Lucky
Lindy Lid, a hat adorned with wings and a propeller.

Beyond the fountain pens, hats and songs, a deeper transformation was under way, one that would go far beyond the image of

a single pilot. Gone was any suggestion that Lindbergh had been foolhardy. Now he was characterized as skilled, cautious and calculating. Lindy's luck, in the view of the Montreal *Gazette*, was "the synonym of good judgement as well as superb skill and dauntless courage...a triumph of aeronautical skill and judgement." The Regina *Leader* observed that "the world almost stands aghast at his performance...his feat leaves people almost breathless for the daring, the courage, the consummate skill it represents."[26] Across the country, the message was the same: Lindbergh had not succeeded in a foolhardy act by sheer luck; his success was a product of painstaking preparation, attention to detail, keen judgment and skill.

In the days following his flight, Lindbergh became almost transcendent, seen to embody virtues so enduring, so treasured, that he was almost superhuman. He had given the lie to the supposed frivolity of the age. No longer was flying a pointless pursuit, merely cheap entertainment. Now it took its place with the great epics of the age, its practical value demonstrated. "Apart from the aviation side of the feat, the moral and other effects of Captain Lindbergh's flight cannot readily be appreciated," observed the Ottawa *Citizen*. "The feat is within measurable distance of becoming a daily affair and that the oldtime and much beloved pastime of annihilating distance has been indeed worth while." Those who had viewed Lindbergh as foolhardy in the past had merely been short-sighted; they had failed to see that he was blazing a trail that soon all could follow. Out of successes like Lindbergh's, predicted the Ottawa *Journal*, "will come a passenger-carrying 'plane bridging the oceans and spanning the continents."[27]

Just as significantly, Lindbergh had reawakened the spirit of the quest. There was a danger, mused one editor, "that the ancient virtue of hazard and adventuring is being bred out of humanity," for that virtue had been the spur to progress: "Take from the world its great adventurers down through the ages and at once the human race would be robbed of its present-day civilization." But Lindbergh's "personal daring may fan into flame the spirit of adventure in the hearts of his fellow man." Lindbergh's flight was a feat of the spirit that would move people to emulation. "Dead indeed to the spirit of romance must be he to whom the sheer adventure of the flight of the youthful Lindbergh does not make an appeal and awaken a thrill," proclaimed the *Globe*. "This, then, his gift to all the world at large," wrote an amateur poet from Toronto, "A gift time cannot spend, but will endure / To hearten all the youth of every land / Some place in life by courage to secure."[28]

Though he did not win the *Spirit of St. Louis* poetry contest, Bliss Carman's entry was a stirring summation of the meaning of the flight. It came at a time when the world was beset with "the petty quarrels of nations, / Sick with the sickness of hate / And the yellow streak of despair." The fate of nations lay in the hands of "palaverers of politics... Wagging their heads together / Over their mouldy maps, / With envy, suspicion and greed / In their bloodless veins." All was "money-lust, / Lawless, low-browed, impious." And then into this grim world burst a man, "the eternal spirit of youth, / Carefree, confident, modest." He was not interested in gain or favour, publicity or fame, but only in the quest. His weapons were not treaties or armaments, but "the language of the open smile / And the honest heart, / The chivalry of our hope." And when he succeeded, Lindbergh gave meaning to life again:

> We were sick of strife and chicane,
> Wars and rumours of wars,
> And then in an hour made whole
> And glad,—with the gladness of souls
> When earth was new,
> And the stars of morning sang...
> The whole world bathed once more
> In the golden purpling glory of day.
> Even so even now hope and promise revive
> In the hearts of men.[29]

, , ,

In July 1927, Charles Lindbergh visited Ottawa to help celebrate Canada's sixtieth birthday. The government had laid on a full slate of events to mark the Diamond Jubilee of Confederation, but the young flier stole the show. He arrived with a flight of aircraft just after noon on July 2 "and was the centre of everything through the remainder of the time," according to Prime Minister Mackenzie King, who was captivated by the pilot. There is no indication that King had any previous interest in flying, but Lindbergh made a huge impression on him. He observed that the transatlantic flight was "the single greatest exploit in the world's history," and expressed interest when a Toronto reporter told King that he was related to Lindbergh through the pilot's mother. When the prime minister met the pilot in Ottawa, he could scarcely find a superlative sufficient to describe him. "A more beautiful character I have never seen," he recorded in his diary. "He was like a young god who appeared from the skies in human form—all that could be desired in youthful appearance, in manner, in charm, in character, as noble a type of the highest manhood I have ever seen." King noted proudly that after the official dinner in honour of Lindbergh and the new American ambassador, he took responsibility for ushering "this young ambassador of Heaven" out a rear door, for the crowds packed around the front entrance were too dense to get through. "He is more truly the god-man, than anything I have ever seen," mused King. The next day, fifty thousand people turned out to pay their respects to Lieut. Thad Johnston, a member of Lindbergh's escort flight who was killed when two of the planes collided over Rockcliffe. King confided to his diary that he had found the previous few days to be very moving: the Diamond Jubilee, Lindbergh's visit and Johnston's crash (even though an American official put it down to pilot carelessness) and funeral filled the prime minister with awe. It "was like Heaven itself coming near to earth, as if we were entering on a higher and loftier experience than ever before. Indeed it seems to me as if

Lindbergh was as a young god from the skies, bringing anew the message of Peace and Goodwill."[30]

The rhetoric is vintage King but entirely in keeping with public sentiment. Lindbergh was more than just a media darling; he was a spiritual figure of Christ-like proportions. Alcock and Brown had enjoyed a measure of notoriety, but they were never more than human. They demonstrated pluck, perseverance and courage, but their achievement, however remarkable it was, never went beyond the practical. Canada was not ready to worship a pilot in 1919. It was too restless and fickle; and weightier issues, including a summer of explosive labour unrest, commanded attention.

By 1927, though, calm had been restored to the workplace, political stability had returned, the economy was back on track and relative social peace reigned. For some, life was becoming too comfortable. Pursuits excused as harmless fun in 1919, when people deserved a chance to be carefree, were seeming frivolous and pointless or even symptomatic of moral decay. What if the country was sinking back into an Edwardian decadence of shallow thrill-seekers, conspicuous consumers and revellers in vice?

And then came Lindbergh, and suddenly the airplane was no longer the toy of the monied classes and the aimless barnstormer, and the pilot was no longer little better than the flapper, the marathon dancer and the flagpole sitter. Lindbergh had demonstrated the practical value of flight, but that was of less consequence than the moral value, a fact that comes out in many of the tributes. Claude-Henri Grignon's *Le Secret de Lindbergh*, a highly romanticized homage to the pilot published in 1928, is the story of a man marked for greatness from an early age, who was drawn to flying as a way to realize his destiny.[31] The names of Lindbergh's competitors hardly ever appear in the narrative; the text is sprinkled with great names, but they are literary giants, not the pioneers of science and technology. The implication is clear: Lindbergh is a giant of the soul and spirit rather than of the machine. In Grignon's entirely typical interpretation, flying became a spiritual journey that allowed humans (at least vicariously) to escape from a shallow and materialistic society to the realm of the divine. As one journalist put it, "we have taken Lindbergh to our hearts because in our hearts we can fly on unclipped wings as far as love and fancy will take us, fly radiantly and unfrightened through the darkness and the light to that ultimate destination of the spirit... [Lindbergh] is the symbol of those inner flights he has inspired in all of us."[32]

This, indeed, is the characterization that re-emerged in Canadian culture after 1927: aviators were simply on a different level, actually as well as figuratively, than lesser earthbound species. In cultural terms, the aviator emerged as an individual who was not quite mortal. At each stage of a flight, the pilot became more and more distinct from those who were left behind.

The first assumption was that flying was more than just another form of travel. Trains, automobiles and ships were mere conveyances, each with its own annoyances. "The train oscillates, its wheels grind; it roars through gas-filled tunnels, clangs over bridges, and is constantly lurching around the curves of its crooked course. The motor-car, even on the best of roads, encounters jams, interruptions, dust and smell; the ocean-liner so rocks and rolls that many of its passengers suffer intensely from sea-sickness." But to fly was to escape all this: "Travel by air avoids all those unpleasant experiences; riding at an altitude of 3,000 feet, above the noise and the dust and the odors of the earth, the sensation of movement is almost noiseless and imperceptible; the view beneath is like an animated relief-map of mountains and valleys, fields and forests, lakes and rivers, of indescribable interest and beauty. No objects flash half-seen past the traveller's window, there is no such thing as train-sickness, no sea-sickness, no fatigue." The journalist Agnes Laut, who travelled by air to the far north, was also struck by the superiority of flight: "I could not but compare the trip by airplane through the pure, washed morning air at 95 miles an hour to the grinding along at 3 miles an hour on a train in the company of drunkards."[33]

Because flying was such a superior form of travel, it followed that people who could fly were superior to those who could not. Pilots remarked that the moment their machines left the ground, they experienced a sensation of liberation. "We lurched forward," wrote Bev Shenstone, the first person to get a master's degree in aeronautics in Canada, of a flight in 1928. "Bumps, teeth-rattling bumps, wheels splashing mud, speed, a lurch, all-howling road, another bump (superb one) and then perfect smoothness." Here, Shenstone appreciated what generations of pilots and passengers have remarked upon: the takeoff was immediately followed by a feeling of calm as the aircraft's wheels left the ground. "The rush of air past the face," noted one pilot, "is tangible evidence of victory over earth's statical forces, the deep throated roar is a song of man's triumph over all physical limitations."[34]

On one level, this heady feeling was a practical consequence of flying; the earth's physical obstacles were no hindrance to the aviator. "Comparisons of explorers taking years to thread the maze [of valleys and rivers], of steel pushed foot by foot through a hell of rock and hazard" had no place in the world of the pilot, wrote journalist Jack Paterson. "Such things, commendable in their time, now were merely part of a sordid earth while we moved through a new and glorious world of space." Private and commercial pilots in the settled parts of the country found that the airplane freed them from thoroughfares growing clogged with automobiles.[35] Indeed, escaping the discomforts of the modern city accounted for much of flying's appeal. As the advertisement for a passenger aircraft reminded potential customers, "Up above the choking dust of time-wasting traffic...up where the air is clean and blue...up with the birds is where you travel when you fly in a Rambler." A British Columbia poet referred to the airman as ascending "above the city's noise and reek."[36] What is striking in all of these comments is the strong contrast between ground and air: sordid earth versus glorious space; choking dust versus clean blue air. The message is explicit: taking to the air brings the pilot to a higher mode of existence.

But liberation meant more than simply escaping physical limitations. It also meant escaping spiritual limitations: liberation of
the body was the means to liberate the soul. In 1941, John
Gillespie Magee would describe this as "slipp[ing] the surly bonds
of earth," but six years earlier the poet Annie Charlotte Dalton
addressed an airman in similar terms, saying, "you go free of earth
and our duress," where the imagination was unfettered and where
there were no boundaries to thought or action.[37] The pilot's vision
was almost unrestricted, and many aviators observed that flying
gave them a heightened sense of consciousness.

In taking off, the pilot was not simply leaving the airfield, but
rather rising above earth's concerns. "Always a smile and never a
care," chirped a jaunty post-war song, "No more trouble and no
more care / When you're flying way up in the air."[38] Douglas
Hallam, a leading member of the air lobby who piloted flying
boats in the First World War, likened flying to leaving "my pack
of mouldy troubles far away below." His sentiment was shared by
Sydney Cleverley of the Toronto Flying Club in 1932: "When one
is piloting an aeroplane the present is the only thing that matters.
On the ground you may be unhappy about yesterday, you may be
uncertain about tomorrow, but in the air your mind finds itself...
[flying is] that healer of mind,—that builder of character,—
...that creator of constant cheerfulness." It became customary to
interpret flying as an antidote to the troubles of everyday life. "A
man suffering from blue-devilled melancholy need only fly
once...to find himself whole again," as one newspaper editor put
it.[39] The almost medicinal virtues of flying gave the pilot a certain
moral superiority over those condemned to remain on the ground,
whose minds had not yet found themselves and who were not yet
whole. That sense of superiority grew as the pilot ascended and
gave flying its heady appeal.

As earthly concerns diminished in significance, so too did the
human presence on the landscape: locomotives became puffing
toy trains, roads looked like strips of tape, tiny towns appeared as
children's toys, and lakes and ponds looked like scattered coins or

bits of broken glass. The heroes of Billy Bishop's novel *The Flying Squad* look over the side on their first flight to see "the radial-car tracks, and on them several cars very much like super ants in the midst of the procession. Over to the westward...the locomotive...could be seen crawling along the railway, moving like a caterpillar between two thin strands of silver wire."[40] As the poet Wilfrid Gibson put it, to fly was to become "a new Gulliver looking down / On Lilliput, toy dwellings row on row, / And tiny toy-like people scurrying round / In fussy little cars through street and square." A Winnipeg journalist, invited by Western Canada Airways to take a flight over the city, felt the same sense of superiority over earthbound creatures and their works: "Street cars ran along down there like they were silly little models.... The Parliament Building simply couldn't have cost all that money—it would be crushed if I dropped my bunch of keys on it.... With a leg long enough, I could kick over that apartment block down there as I would kick a pebble on the road."[41]

In all these observations, life on the ground is inconsequential when viewed from the air. Doctor Blythe in L. M. Montgomery's *Rilla of Ingleside* observed that "when I have watched one of those bird-men out of sight I come back to earth with an odd feeling of being merely a crawling insect." Indeed, an anonymous "flying versifier" quoted by Douglas Hallam observed rather smugly that "I have known the freedom of the air, / Not crawled on earth like some coarse, dull, fat slug."[42] The Vancouver poet A. M. Stephen made the same point in "Lords of the Air," which drew a strong contrast between the old men who creep close to the earth and "love their good, brown clay," and the young men of the air who "tread the shining blue / On a breath of space, as the gods might do." Herbert J. Brooks distinguished between the farmer, who plods home after a day's work, and the pilot, whose workday ends with an exhilarating flight through the clouds.[43] The subject of Edna Jaques's "A Housewife Salutes a Flier" addressed an aviator in similar terms: "How could you know the love of common things, / There with the sun against your gray white wings,... /

Winging across the hills and looking down, / Upon the red-roofed houses of the town." The very same notion was expressed by the poet Eva Phillips Boyd:

> Toy cattle grazed, play windmills turned,
> And threads of smoke, from hearth fires burned,
> Showed where they spent their little days.
>   "Oh, look!" I called, "Look up and praise!
> For life is more than work and food!
> Oh, see how big and good it is!"[44]

In all these poems, those who creep on the ground are unimportant, preoccupied by "common things" and "their good, brown clay," spending "little days" going about their trivial tasks. The pilot looks down both physically and morally, seeing how much more there is to existence than grubbing for work and food. In the words of a rather less subtle poet, "Sticking to Earth– / What could be stupider! / We're for rebirth / Encompassing Jupiter."[45]

More significant in cultural terms was the ability of the pilot to rise above the clouds into the calm of the upper air. The storm clouds parallel the constraints of earth; they are suffocating and dangerous, but the pilot escapes them and enters a realm not visible from the earth. There, the pilot became more divine than human. "How many experiences are open to the pilot that are denied to the non-flyer!" wondered an essayist who went by the nom de plume Callisthenes. "On a day when clouds are grey and all-covering he can fly through them to where everything is bright and sunlit and blue—and the greyness above is changed to the whitest of white beneath." Above the clouds, wrote an air-minded journalist, was "a season of bright sunshine missed by those on the earth." The caption of a photograph of aircraft above the clouds made the same point: "Above the clouds! All sunshine overhead but darkness prevails for the mortals below."[46] Sailing in bright sunshine above a blanket of fleecy white clouds, pilots who were inclined toward religion might easily have believed that they had

ascended into heaven. Above the clouds, pilots could "scan
Creation's pages, / And trace the wondrous pathway Thou hast
trod." *"L'homme, dans ces hauteurs, rêve de l'Infini,"* wrote Marie
Sylvia, a nun and poet; but aviators did not just dream of the
Infinite, they became the Infinite.[47] An air-minded poet from
Nova Scotia felt that unity with the divine when he entered the
clouds: "Here you forget the strife, / Here you can live the life, /
Far from the mammon crowd, / With God alone." For Frances
Beatrice Taylor, the pilot stood at the pinnacle of evolution, at the
point where the human became divine. "He shall be our peer and
liege and brother," intones a heavenly voice in her tribute to
Lindbergh. "He shall go with the gods on the hills eternal."[48]

⟩ ⟩ ⟩

In the 1930s, an American doctor summoned up the ghost of
Charles Darwin to argue that pilots had evolved from birds, while
everyone else had evolved from fish.[49] The element of predestina-
tion to this otherwise bizarre notion was entirely in keeping with
the popular understanding of flying. In the nineteenth and early
twentieth centuries, balloonists and pilots were rootless showmen
who appeared in town, made their ascents and then left with their
earnings. In many accounts, they appeared as a sort of *deus ex
machina*, although the machine was notoriously fallible.

The First World War increased exponentially the number of
pilots in Canada but did little to alter the aura of separateness that
had come to characterize the pilot. Indeed, the exploits of
Canadian pilots at the front merely enhanced their distinctiveness.
As the war in the air evolved into a morality play, the pilot was
increasingly characterized as a figure who stood apart from, and
indeed above, society. *"Il regardait plus haut que les gens de son âge,"*
wrote the poet Alonzo Cinq-Mars in a tribute to fallen airman
Pierre Hamel, *"et les calculs humains ne l'importunaient pas."*[50]

The process of separation continued in the post-war era. The
barnstormers of the 1920s were the heirs of the aeronauts of the

1880s and the birdmen of the 1910s, and just as disreputable. But with the great long-distance pilots, this was to change. Alcock and Brown, and then Lindbergh, transformed the popular view of the pilot. Their flights were not country-fair sideshows or commercial stunts; they were epics of exploration that ranked with the voyages of Columbus and Magellan—demonstrating the ability to transcend time and space and to draw continents together.

Though their exploits captured the imagination of a generation, they did little to convince people of the practicability of flight. Lindbergh was lionized because his feat seemed so impossible; he put the aviator on a lofty pedestal, which implied that flying was for only a handful of remarkable individuals. As long as such attitudes held sway, it was unlikely that aviation would move beyond the chosen few.

· 4 ·

AN AIR-MINDED PEOPLE

IN HIS PIN-FEATHER STAGE

IT WAS A STRANGE CONTRAPTION, THE FLYING MACHINE described in the Sault *Daily Star* the day after Lindbergh reached Paris. It looked a little like a bicycle, with pedals to provide propulsion and handlebars that served as rudder controls; the wings folded up for easy storage. There was no engine and indeed no indication how the machine would get off the ground. In many ways the thing was a throwback to the bizarre ornithopters of centuries past that their designers claimed could be vaulted into the air by human power alone. Nevertheless, the editor confidently predicted that in the not-too-distant future, everyone would have a personal flying machine "to ride down to work as handily as he now travels on bicycle or in his flivver."[1]

Reading this editorial, one might well wonder if aviation was regressing to the days when the laws of aerodynamics were understood imperfectly, if at all. Yet the airborne flivver—cheap, easy to maintain and simple to fly—symbolized the future of aviation, at least for many air-minded Canadians: one day everyone would fly, and there would be as many aircraft in the sky as automobiles on the ground. The airplane would be the great agent of democratization, ensuring that personal mobility of the most modern kind was available to all.

But before that day, a few things had to change. Ironically, what made aviation so appealing was the very thing that stood in the way of its broad acceptance: its romance, danger and excitement. The hijinks of the barnstormers had convinced many Canadians that pilots were venal and barely sane, while the great long-distance fliers had fostered an image of the pilot as closer to the gods than to other humans. Both images created an unintended side effect: Canadians loved reading about flying, but would never dream of climbing into an airplane. Flying was for the god-like or the marginalized.

If flying was to progress, these attitudes had to be changed. The adjective used at the time was "air-minded"; it referred to an enthusiasm for flying, a belief in the future of aviation and excitement at what the airplane could do for Canada. To achieve air-mindedness, people had to be made alive to the potential of flight to improve the human condition. The air lobby had to mount a huge public relations campaign to make flying appeal to the mass of people who had never flown or even seen an airplane. That campaign focused on a number of themes. Air enthusiasts emphasized the safety of flying over other forms of transportation, thereby undermining the stereotypes of the pilot as either daredevil or demigod. They predicted that it would soon be as natural to fly as it was to drive and that anyone could fly an airplane. They played up the enthusiasm of Canadian youth for flying: aviation was Canada's destiny, they argued, for Canadian youth would make it so. Once this public relations effort was successful, the aviation lobby believed, Canadians would be an air-minded people, and flying could work its magic on the nation.

, , ,

It looked as if the air lobby would have an easy time of it, for Canadians were deeply interested in flying and all that went with it. The celebrity of wartime aces, the popularity of barnstormers and post-war air shows, the public's fascination with the exploits of the long-distance fliers, the adulation of the aviator as an immortal—all these pointed to a public apparently ready and willing to embrace aviation.

But it was one thing to join the throng at a local air display or devour news reports of Charles Lindbergh's flight; it was quite another to go up in an airplane or to make flying a part of one's life. Indeed, despite its apparent popularity, flying touched the lives of very few Canadians. It had been said that in 1914, not one Canadian in a hundred had ever seen an aircraft in flight, and the war had changed this less than one might imagine. In 1919, John Armistead Wilson, the Scottish-born engineer who was to become one of the foremost proponents of air-mindedness, estimated that 90 percent of Canadians had never seen an airplane and so were not alive to its potential.[2] Five years later, he pondered the impact of the war on public views of flying. "People instinctively dread new inventions which threaten to disturb the even tenor of their ways. Aviation was new; their fathers had never flown and when they were young no such thing had been dreamt of...people on the whole treated it [flying] as one of the many unpleasant and unnatural accompaniments of a state of war, with no relation to ordinary peaceful life." In 1926, Donald MacLaren, the fighter ace from Alberta who would also become a significant figure in post-war Canadian aviation, recalled the days when a man waving a red flag ran along in front of a railway engine because of the distrust of the then-new technology. "There are a great many people waving the red flag in the face of 'Aviation' to-day," he wrote. "People who have not had the opportunity of becoming closely associated with its possibilities and through their ignorance distrust it."[3]

Other like-minded individuals agreed. Stephen Leacock would later write that the pioneering long-distance flights had attracted much attention but had done little to awaken people to the practical advantages that airplanes could bring to Canada. A government memorandum observed in 1924 that "people had little confidence in the new form of transportation and flying was considered by the public generally as a stunt, with no application in everyday life."[4] Senator J. A. McDonald argued that aviation would never progress in Canada until the majority of people stopped believing that flying was a game for supermen engaged in extraordinary tasks. Billy Bishop, one of the high-profile members of the air lobby, thought that the intense press coverage given to trail-blazing flights underlined their exceptional nature and did not tell people that flying could be a part of their own lives. "Although I am sure from the past that we are an air-minded race," he told the Empire Club in 1936, "the average Canadian, leaving out the north country, sees an aeroplane so seldom that he still regards flying as a dangerous sport or experiment."[5]

Bishop's point was crucial to the air lobby's plan: inside every Canadian was an air-minded person trying to get out. To assist in their liberation required a massive education campaign. "One of the most important factors in the introduction of civil flying in Canada... is to win the confidence and acquire the co-operation of the public," said Norman Yarrow in 1921. "To accomplish this a great deal of educational work must be carried out, and much reliable propaganda spread."[6] But how to get the message across? Before 1914, aviators and air-minded persons often seemed to be working at cross purposes, with air boosters calling for care and prudence while pilots regularly crashed to the ground. In May 1920, while serving as a flight commander with the then Canadian Air Force, Don MacLaren proposed a detailed propaganda campaign to educate the public about the possibilities and advantages of aviation and to boost confidence in its reliability and safety. The scheme required the creation of a number of highly organized groups co-ordinated by a central office in Ottawa, staffed by four people experienced both in flying and publicity work. The senior director would oversee the operation; the deputy director would be responsible for the most significant aspects—liaison with the press, generating a weekly aviation newsletter and writing special articles on flying to be supplied free to Canada's daily newspapers. The third staff member would be responsible for cinema and photographic propaganda, making available films and still photos to cinema operators, educators, public officials and local aviation boosters for dissemination. The fourth staff member would co-ordinate exhibitions of the latest aviation technology across the country, preferably in connection with demonstration flights, which might also scatter propaganda leaflets. Competitions in speed, reliability and load carrying should be encouraged, suggested MacLaren, for "the public are keenly interested in Aerial Races and competitive meetings." Finally, the office would dispatch paid lecturers, armed with lantern slides or newsreels, to sing the praises of aviation to people across the country, and especially to high school students.[7]

This ambitious scheme required a large, efficient organization. The first step was to establish lobby groups to spread the gospel of flight. Many of the organizations that had been formed earlier were either moribund or non-existent by the war's end, but air-minded Canadians lost no time in breathing new life into them. The Aero Club of Canada, chartered in 1917, informed the government in February 1919 that its two thousand members were ready, willing and able to take a leading role in fostering aviation; so was the Aerial League of Canada, established in 1919 with branches in Toronto, Montreal, Vancouver and Victoria. These would be joined by a host of similar organizations in succeeding years: the Canadian Air Service Association, established in Calgary in January 1920 to bring together former war pilots; the Canadian Air Force Association, which held its first national convention in June 1921; the Commercial Air Pilots' Association of Canada, with the purpose of improving standards in aviation; and the Air Force Club of British Columbia (later the Aero Club of Vancouver), created in 1923 under the Vancouver fighter pilot Duncan Bell-Irving, both as a veterans' organization and to spread the message of flight through lectures, guest speakers and radio talks. Three years later, MacLaren attempted to establish a National Aeronautical Association of Canada, which he envisaged as "a clearing house whence the truths of Aviation may be circulated among the citizens of the Nation, most of whom are waiting to be educated." It was all a means, as he put it, to "Nationalize the Airmindedness of the Dominion."[8]

But it was the Canadian Flying Clubs Association, established in 1929, that eventually emerged as the most successful aviation lobby in the country. Since the early 1920s, the air lobby had been urging the federal government to provide more support for civil aviation, and on September 23, 1927, the minister of National Defence, J. L. Ralston, finally announced a program of government assistance to airplane clubs: the government would pay $100 toward the training costs of each pilot who qualified for a licence; the student would cover the other $150. The upshot, as the air lobby had hoped, was an explosion in the number of active flying clubs across the country. On May 1, 1928, the Toronto Flying Club became the first in Canada; it was followed the same month by clubs in Saskatoon, Montreal, Hamilton, Winnipeg and Regina. Later that summer came clubs in Edmonton and northern Alberta, Victoria, London, Windsor and Calgary, and by the end of 1928 there were sixteen clubs with twenty-four hundred members. In the empire, only Britain could boast more light airplane clubs than Canada, and the CFCA rapidly emerged as a key player in the air lobby's education campaign.[9]

Perhaps because of the proliferation of aviation organizations, the central office conceived by MacLaren never came into being. However, one would be hard-pressed to come up with a promotional idea that aviation groups did not exploit. For example, they joined forces with local business interests to found a number of journals devoted exclusively to flight. Vancouver's *Western Canada Flyer and Sportsman* (later *Canadian Flyer and Motor News*) and Toronto's *Aviation News* were early examples, but the real boom came in the late 1920s. *Aircraft and Airways*, which boasted that "copies of this Journal are read by 90% of Canadians interested in

Aeronautics and its Associate industries," appeared in 1928 and was quickly subsumed into the *Canadian Air Review*, billed as an "all-Canadian publication devoted exclusively to aviation." There was also a trade and technical journal called *Commercial Aviation*, published in Montreal to further the development of aviation in Canada and encourage the export of Canadian aviation products. But the most successful and influential of these journals was *Canadian Aviation*, which published its first issue in June 1928. Its aim was to lobby unabashedly for the creation of an aviation infrastructure, as its founders, the Aviation League of Canada, pointed out in a letter to the Ontario Provincial Air Service: "The aim and object of the publication will be to arouse public interest in aviation which will result in the installation of air ports and the necessary equipment for same in municipalities with a population of 10,000 or more."[10] It was an impressive publication with articles that ranged from general interest ("Nature's Wonders Viewed from the Air") to the specialist ("Engine Cowling Is Major Development in Field of Aviation") and editorials that sang the praises of flight. Few readers, after scanning the progress reports, business forecasts, flying club news, optimistic opinion pieces and advertisements, could fail to have been impressed by the energy and efficiency of the aviation sector in Canada.

But these publications were largely preaching to the converted, those already convinced of the value of flying. The real target was the general public, who could be reached more efficiently through the daily press. Shortly after the First World War, aviation boosters experimented with special supplements to daily newspapers that would promote flying to a mass audience. In December 1919, the Montreal entrepreneur Maj. K. E. Clayton-Kennedy convinced a number of big dailies, including the Halifax *Herald*, the Ottawa *Journal*, the Toronto *Globe*, the Manitoba *Free Press*, the Edmonton *Journal* and the Vancouver *Province*, to publish a special aviation number highlighting the work of private flying companies, developments in other countries and predictions for the future of aviation in Canada. In succeeding years, similar aviation inserts would appear in major newspapers, often linked to a local event such as an air show or airport opening. These special issues were not always a success. One contributor caustically wrote to Clayton-Kennedy that "it is impossible to become enthusiastic about the special aviation numbers...no one has been found who read the article. Even the members of the Aero Club of Canada in Toronto were unaware of its publication."[11]

A more effective means of reaching the public, concluded the air lobby, was through regular features in Canada's daily newspapers. Some papers, particularly those in western Canada, had already proved themselves to be air-minded and could be counted on to champion the cause of aviation with news stories or favourable editorials. But through the 1920s, more and more papers in central and eastern Canada devoted attention to aviation news. Surveys of the major papers reveal that hardly a day went by without at least one article on flying, and a big story such as the Lindbergh flight could headline for days; at such times it was not unusual for aviation to be virtually the only story on the front page. As a measure of the growing public interest, many papers featured regular columns on flying; and by the mid-1930s, probably every significant newspaper in the Dominion could boast a weekly or even a daily column on flying. The first may have been George Wakeman's column in the Calgary *Albertan*, which he claimed was intended "to keep the reading public in touch with aviation. Thus endeavouring to promote their support and confidence, which will be essential to the various aviation concerns, when they do get into future operations."[12] At about the same time, the Edmonton *Journal* introduced a column called "Wings of the Empire," which originated in the news bureau of the British journal *The Aeroplane*. Many other similar features were to follow—Arnold Sandwell's "What's Up in the Air?" (Montreal *Daily Star*), "Sky Notes from the Four Winds," John E. Thompson's "Skyways and Byways," "Along the Air Lanes" (all in the Winnipeg *Tribune*), Errol Boyd's "Wings Over Toronto" (Toronto *Daily Star*), Percy Coles's "Cloud Combing" (Toronto *Evening Telegram*),

Jack Meele's "Sky Lines" (Vancouver *Sun*). The impact of these columns is difficult to judge, but *Canadian Aviation* was surely right to observe in its inaugural issue that there was rarely a day when air activities did not figure prominently in the daily press.[13]

Perhaps taking a lead from MacLaren's scheme, members of the air lobby were also active in public speaking to promote interest in aviation. These engagements were most effective when a celebrity was involved—the visit of a transatlantic flier could work wonders to stir local interest in aviation matters. In January 1927, Sir Alan Cobham, the great English pilot who flew thousands of miles in the 1920s to lay out the empire's air routes, spoke at Windsor Hall in Montreal while on a visit to Canada to encourage aviation "by explaining away the hazards and defects with which it is credited by the general public." He told a large audience that "the public have a misconception of flying hazards," but assured them that "future generations will be born with an aviation mentality."[14] When a Cobham or a Lindbergh was not available to fan the flames of enthusiasm, it was up to lesser-known pilots and air lobbyists to do the work. People such as Ernest Stedman and J. A. Wilson eagerly took up the challenge, spending untold hours talking to service clubs, citizens' organizations, business luncheons and professional bodies about the potential of flight.

Aviation boosters also seized on new forms of media to spread the message. As early as 1926, Deputy Postmaster General Peter T. Coolican suggested to J. S. Scott, a leading member of the air lobby and holder of the first pilot's licence issued in Canada, that travelling film shows and radio talks be used to arouse public interest in flying; and, indeed, radio became one of the most effective means of reaching a wide audience. The Canadian National Railways Radio Department broadcast occasional lectures on aviation, the first being J. H. Parkin, one of the country's leading aeronautical engineers and later the director of Mechanical Engineering at the National Research Council, on civil aviation and the University of Toronto in January 1928. Weekly programs on flying were soon to follow.[15] *Airways Talks* was broadcast every Friday evening at 7 P.M. from radio stations in Winnipeg and Fleming, Manitoba; cards from listeners revealed that it was heard as far away as Cranbrook, British Columbia, and Hamilton, Ontario. It was later replaced by *Canadian Airways Half-Hour*, which broadcast Friday evenings from the Royal Alexandra Hotel in Winnipeg. This, in turn, eventually became *Over the Airlines*, which could be heard every Monday on Winnipeg radio. But things were not always as they seemed. In 1936, the CBC station in Edmonton broadcast a conversation between a pilot in the air and a man at the airfield. What listeners did not know was that both men were in fact in the hangar, and that sound effects had simulated aircraft noises.[16]

But all these initiatives, however successful, could only go so far. It was all very well for the public to read about flying in the daily newspaper and hear about it on the radio; but to promote air-mindedness, the air lobby had to take aviation and airplanes to the people. They knew that the barnstorming pilot drifting from town to town did not necessarily help the cause of aviation; but well-organized, carefully co-ordinated air displays, run with military precision by highly trained and experienced pilots, could show flying to its very best advantage. In the late 1920s and 1930s, the air show, more than the newspaper column or the radio address, became the air lobby's most potent weapon.

This new aviation event took two forms: the trade show and the flying display. The nascent aircraft industry in Canada used the trade show as a way to market itself, primarily to the business community. The first Canadian aircraft manufacturers' exhibition was held in Montreal's Craig Street Drill Hall in July 1928, and later that summer the Canadian National Exhibition in Toronto devoted an entire building to aircraft displays. "Now, for the first time," marvelled one aviation journalist, "will be unfolded before the eyes of Canadians the mysteries and wonders of the modern and future mode of travel—AVIATION."[17] But much more significant to the public were the air shows and air tours, the latter patterned after the goodwill automobile tours that had been so popular before the war. From the small-scale air shows mounted by the members of the local flying club to the huge national air tours, this was aviation's travelling road show, taking airplanes and pilots to eager crowds in villages, towns and cities.

In Alberta, the big draw was the air circus. Local pilots would organize eight or ten aircraft and fly from town to town putting on a show. Like the barnstorming shows of the early 1920s, they included all the standard tricks—parachute jumps, formation flying, stunting, air races and penny-a-pound rides. A typical gag was a pilot dressed up as an elderly woman who climbed into the aircraft for a closer look; of course, the airplane would then "accidentally" take off, much to the delight of the crowd. Usually, each town on the circus route would select an air queen for the day; at the end of the flying season, all air queens received a free trip to Calgary and a flight over the city. Air shows in other parts of the country offered the same mixture of entertainment and education, intended to reassure people that flying was neither mysterious nor magical.

Slightly more sophisticated were the regional air tours that became popular in the early 1930s, such as the All-Canadian Air Tour in Alberta and the Manitoba Goodwill Air Tour, first held in 1931 at the urging of the Young Men's Section of the Winnipeg Board of Trade. The tour was such a success that it was repeated the following year and extended to two weeks so more towns could enjoy the show. In many places attendance exceeded all expectations, and tickets sold out as soon as the aircraft arrived. "From Steinbach to Winnipeg," trumpeted *Canadian Aviation*, "the gospel of aviation was preached."[18] The same year, aviation boosters in Atlantic Canada got together to organize the first Maritime Air Tour in August 1932. The tour was followed by the gala Maritime Air Pageant in Charlottetown, which the province's air-minded lieutenant-governor recommended "not only as a means of entertainment, but as a practical demonstration of the value of the airplane as a safe means of transportation." He confidently predicted that it would not be long before every farmer on the island would own an airplane.[19]

These immensely popular regional air tours were themselves dwarfed by the Trans-Canada Air Pageant; it was modelled on the National Air Tour that criss-crossed the United States in the 1920s and 1930s and usually included a few Canadian stops. The Pageant was equal parts entertainment, education and marketing. Aircraft manufacturers had a significant presence, showcasing their newest products with demonstrations, flypasts and ground displays. There were segments that highlighted the speed and load-carrying capacity of aircraft and examples of aerobatics and precision formation flying, usually by an RCAF team of fighter biplanes; often a team from the U.S. Army Air Corps or the RAF also appeared. To lighten the mood, there was always a novelty act, frequently some variation on the senior-citizen-accidentally-flies-an-airplane routine. By all accounts, the Trans-Canada Air Pageant was a hit. The CFCA, which organized the event, estimated that the first tour drew more than 300,000 spectators in the twelve cities it visited; the crowds in subsequent years were even larger.

The air lobby was unanimous in its assessment of these events. "Through the Trans-Canada Air Pageant, we made thousands of friends equally for ourselves and for the government," wrote an official of the CFCA. "We sold aviation to the public that greatly exceeded all expectations." When J. A. Wilson toured the flying clubs of the Maritime provinces in 1931, he heard time and time again of the positive effect that the pageant had on public opinion. Officials of the Cape Breton Flying Club informed Wilson that the pageant's visit had drawn the largest crowd ever assembled at one time on Cape Breton.[20]

Unlike the air displays of the immediate post-war years, which were sometimes ill-organized, slapdash affairs that invariably promised hair-raising excitement from pilots cheating death, these shows featured military-style organization and displays demonstrating the utility, accessibility and respectability of aviation.

Spectators at the Trans-Canada Air Pageant, for example, knew precisely when each aircraft was to be expected overhead, and it was a rare day when the schedule was not adhered to. Absent were the death-defying stunts by daredevil pilots—they served no good purpose and could even be counterproductive. In their place were demonstrations of freight aircraft and formation flying, informative ground displays emphasizing the performance and practicability of private aircraft and dozens of friendly, knowledgeable and (according to contemporary photographs) well-dressed flying club members to answer questions—all intended to reassure the public about flying. The air show aimed to entertain but primarily offered flying as a business opportunity, a profession and a way of life.

, , ,

By the 1930s, the means the air lobby used to propagate the gospel of flight were omnipresent. There was an air show somewhere in Canada on virtually every weekend during the summer months. Guest speakers toured the country, promoting aviation to anyone who would listen. Hardly a week went by without a major magazine publishing a glowing article on the future of aviation. It occupied the front pages of Canada's newspapers and was a fixture of parliamentary debates. The air lobby was a relatively small group—in 1930, there were still only 539 licensed pilots in Canada—but they were remarkably successful in spreading the message.

A number of common themes ran through the campaign. The first was that flying was the safest way to travel, and that pilots were experienced, responsible professionals who put the security of their passengers above all other considerations. Allied to this was the notion that flying was just another form of transportation, like driving or taking the train, and that the pilot required no special skills. Flying was just another task that anyone could learn. Finally, the air lobby emphasized that young Canadians had none of the predispositions against aviation that older Canadians appeared to hold. Not for them the gloomy skepticism embodied by Susan in L. M. Montgomery's *Rilla of Ingleside*, who wondered solemnly "what the old folks down there in the graveyard would think if they could rise out of their graves for one moment and behold that sight [an airplane].... If the Almighty had meant us to fly he would have provided us with wings. Since He did not it is plain he meant us to stick to solid earth."[21] For young Canadians, flying was a natural part of life. And because the future lay with youth, the future of the nation lay with aviation.

But it all began with safety. "Air-mindedness," said one MP, "is a state of mind brought about through dismissal of fear, to a very great degree. Once a person has flown in a plane and realizes the convenience, comfort and safety of that method of transportation he becomes air-minded." Creating this impression was a not inconsiderable task. "There seems to be an idea imbued in the ordinary citizen's mind that flying is a mode of transportation that is to be feared," observed an Ontario newspaper in 1920.[22]

One way to address safety concerns was to create a regulatory regime to control aviation in Canada, something the Aero Club of Canada had long advocated. Since before the war, aviation boosters had regarded the absence of regulations governing pilots and aircraft as one of the main obstacles to progress. After the war, the availability of war-surplus aircraft gave a boost to aviation, but not all the machines were airworthy. Until an inspection process was put in place, thought some members of the air lobby, the government should place an embargo on second-hand aircraft and parts.[23] They were also concerned that there was no control over stunt-flying and argued that the public had to be protected from their own folly. "The public are quite aware of the dangers of flying and some people are too keen to enjoy these dangers and will take any nameable risk on their shoulders," Maj. R. H. B. Ker, a flying instructor in Canada during the war, told a meeting of aviation groups in Winnipeg. "I do not think this should be allowed." There was no great sympathy for the victims, many of whom were regarded as the architects of their own fate; but "if there are going to be accidents every few days in different parts of the country, it will put aviation back ten or fifteen years," maintained another delegate. "When you start killing the public, you kill flying."[24]

Because unlicensed pilots and unsafe equipment posed a danger not only to the public but to the very future of flying in Canada, the government moved promptly to bring some order to the air. On June 6, 1919, the federal government passed the Air Board Act, which created a seven-member board empowered to construct and maintain government airfields, determine air routes, study and recommend on matters of aviation law, control the licensing of pilots and other personnel, manage the inspection, certification and registration of aircraft and generally "to supervise all matters connected with aeronautics." The board held its first meeting later that month and agreed that its first task was to draw up air regulations to cover all aspects of flying. It acted with surprising dispatch: on December 31, 1919, Parliament passed legislation covering the operation of aircraft and on January 17, 1920, the air regulations became law. A significant provision required all pilots to hold a valid licence, whether for private or commercial flying; air engineers were also required to hold licences from the Air Board. Just seven days after the regulations came into force, the first private pilot's licence was issued; the first air engineer's licence was awarded in April 1920 and the first commercial pilot's licence in July 1920. With this, one of the major complaints about pre-war flying was addressed: there would be no more unqualified pilots flying in Canada.

However, it was one thing to create a regulatory regime; it was quite another to convince the public that it was safe to fly. Then as now, a single aircraft accident generated more press coverage than a thousand successful flights. Statistics published annually by the Air Board proved that flying was one of the safest forms of transportation. As the aviation sector expanded through the 1920s, so did the number of miles flown between accidents. In 1922, it was just over 26,000 aircraft miles per accident, but by 1931 it was more than 281,000 aircraft miles per accident. But cold statistics did not sell newspapers, nor did uneventful flights. The crash of a Loening air yacht in Muskoka in 1928, killing two passengers and injuring five others, on the other hand, allowed the journalist to write colourfully of the need to "add the airplane to the list of holiday hazards." Cottage country, noted Toronto's *Mail and Empire* archly, "experienced a new thrill of horror when it heard of the invasion of this new death." The two accidents during Hamilton airport's first three days of operation in 1929 interested the press more than the many uneventful takeoffs and landings.[25]

It was a constant source of frustration to the air lobby that a single sensational accident could undo weeks or months of careful educational work and cause the public to overlook all the successful flights. "All this crashing and glaring publicity had a detrimental effect on Commercial Aviation," wrote Norman Anderson, one of the CAF's first flying instructors, who pinned much of the blame on foolhardy pilots "with more nerve than common sense or flying experience." The commercial pilot J. D. Parkinson observed that the citizens of Regina grew skeptical about flying after two people were killed in separate air crashes: "Often because some poor fellow happens to kill himself in an aeroplane they immediately tend to shun the whole business, and yet religiously drive about in automobiles all day."[26]

As automobile use grew in North America and traffic deaths increased correspondingly, the air lobby returned ever more frequently to the argument that flying was much safer than driving or travelling by rail. Pointing out that traffic deaths had more than doubled between 1926 and 1931, one industry newsletter noted by way of contrast that Canadian Airways Limited had flown 410,629 miles for every fatal accident involving one of its aircraft. "Living may be dangerous," CAL claimed, "but Air Travel is safe." By 1936, calculated another aviation booster, the average motorist could fly 275 times as far as he could drive without having a fatal accident. "With the appalling increase in automobile accidents, and the great lessening of the accident hazard in aerial navigation during recent years, the probability is that the latter will continue to increase its margin of safety over the former until even the man on the street will be convinced it is safer to fly than to ride or walk upon the highway."[27] Air boosters were constantly playing up these statistics to soothe the public. Billy Bishop told a meeting of the Empire Club in 1936 that he felt safer in the air in good weather than driving along a main road (this from a man who accumulated dozens of citations for dangerous driving in the early 1920s). In his novel *The Flying Squad*, more a primer on aerodynamics and aerial etiquette than anything, the veteran flying instructor McIntyre tells his teenage pupils, "I want you to get it firmly fixed in your minds that flying in itself is by no means the dangerous pastime that some people would make out." In fact, proclaimed a Quebec newspaper, "an airworthy machine with a good qualified pilot at the controls is literally as safe as a baby carriage."[28]

One of the keys to proving this point was to emphasize the positive qualities of the pilots. The barnstormer persona had to be shed, as did the image of the long-distance pilot demigod. In their place would be a new kind of pilot—skilled and experienced but also prudent, reliable and, above all, safety conscious. While an advertisement for Willard's Willow Milk Chocolate characterized the Trans-Canada Air Pageant as the "supreme test of skill and aerial daring," aviation boosters were careful to point out that there was very little daring involved, given the skill and experience of the pilots. "The days of accidents are practically over," observed one journalist, "expert attention being directed to the examination of aircraft and their engines, while pilots have learned the value of safety, not only on their own account, but to further the advance of aviation." Air shows were not intended to be about danger and risk-taking. "Stunt flying, spectacular aeronautics and joy rides have no place in our programme," J. A. Wilson told a Victoria newspaper. "Our purpose is to advance aviation along sound, practical lines and ultimately make it a big and essential part of our commercial and industrial life."[29]

The bush pilots, who were already doing so much to demon-strate the utility of aircraft, were also keen to counteract press tales of their derring-do. Journalists were fond of lapsing into romantic prose when reporting the exploits of bush pilots—the Toronto *Daily Star*, for example, described Wop May and Vic Horner as "two knights, riding through cold and snow, their steed a shining aeroplane, their weapon a whirling propellor which lops off the miles one by one" as they raced north to Fort Vermilion, Alberta, to deliver diphtheria serum to an isolated settlement—but the aviators themselves disliked being referred to as "intrepid pilots" or "sky devils," both expressions popular with the press. According to an article in *Maclean's*, "Doc" Oaks, one of Canada's most famous bush pilots, regarded his flying as "all in a day's work"; he wasn't interested in stunting or publicity seeking, just in getting on with the task at hand.[30] There was no question that flying still required bravery, especially in the north country where a forced landing could have fatal consequences, but it was bravery of a dif-ferent kind. "Courage is no longer a matter of devil-may-care," observed an article on the flying Vachon brothers of Sainte-Marie-de-la-Beauce, Quebec, all of whom were active in aviation, "but is combined with the hard-headed business principles which count unnecessary risks as foolhardy." Few things seem to bother avia-tors more than the lurid tales of aviation that appeared in potboilers like *Wings of the West*, a gripping yarn featuring Jack McCaffrey of Canadian Flying Services, for such tales bore no resemblance to the work of real pilots.[31] Bernt Balchen, who made his name flying in the Canadian Arctic, was quoted in an Ottawa newspaper saying that "people should not get it into their heads that flying is a circus stunt, full of thrills, danger and excitement." When Floyd Banghart began the inaugural airmail flight linking Leamington, Ontario, with Pelee Island in 1927, a reporter asked if he was aiming for a record flight. Banghart, who had made his fair share of record attempts in the past, replied dismissively, "We are not out to make records. We want to play 100% safe."[32]

Underlying this emphasis on the prudence of the pilot was

another message: there was nothing magical about flying. "Aviation of itself is only the practical application of a knowledge of physics and mathematics," wrote one air booster in 1931. "It is by no means a mysterious or difficult subject and it does not require supermen for pilots, aerial navigators, or air engineers." Flying was just another way to get from place to place. It was merely transportation, "a quicker, cleaner and safer way of going places," wrote a correspondent to *Canadian Aviation* in 1929. "The spirit is no longer one of glamour, of taking chances, but something akin to the pride of the railwayman in his company's lines." Flying was different and had its own special problems, wrote Arnold Sandwell, but "so do railroading and the operation of bus-lines....Newcomers to aeronautics, thrilled by an experience that is an old story to some of us, are apt in their enthusiasm to overestimate the basic importance of artificial flight and seek to elevate it to a special pedestal."[33] Here was the crux: if flying was to progress, it had to be taken down off its pedestal.

A related pet theme of aviation boosters was that one day flying would be every bit as common as driving. Just as cars were starting to crowd the highways and city streets of Canada, so airplanes would crowd the skies. People would hop into their airplanes to fly to work or to visit friends, and children would think it normal to go everywhere by air. "The airplane within the next twenty years may do what the automobile has done in the last twenty," predicted a Maritime newspaper. "The next generation may see the world in the air instead of on wheels, with a safer means of transportation and with a machine which costs considerably less than the present motor car." Canadians would soon give up their obsession with good roads, thought J. A. Wilson in 1920; instead, they would be preoccupied with good aerodromes.[34]

This, of course, brings us to the holy grail of the air lobby—the personal aircraft or aerial flivver. Alexander Graham Bell had predicted its advent before the First World War, and in 1919 he told the Canadian Club of Saint John that there would soon come a time when people would call for an airplane just as they now called for a taxi. Ernest Stedman, too, told the Engineering Institute of Canada in Montreal of taxi airplanes that could be hired by the hour to run errands or "tootle about" the heavens. A Sydney, Nova Scotia, newspaper reported on a number of American designs for low-cost, simple flying machines with such exotic names as the Arrowbile that could be made "roadable." Some had detachable wings or wings that folded back so the airplane could be transformed into a "compact, streamlined three-wheeled automobile."[35] In 1936, Charles Woodsworth predicted in *The Beaver* that within a decade, the average businessman would be just as likely to fly his own airplane on business trips as take the train. In Montreal, a number of local aviators formed the Reid Aircraft Company to meet the demand for an easy-to-operate light airplane for private use at about the cost of a medium-priced car. One of the company's products was the Rambler, a two-person biplane with removable wings that was explicitly marketed as a commuter vehicle ("with wings folded,... an ordinary garage is your hangar"). Soon, the air lobby predicted, most Canadians would own such a flivver, and Wilson looked forward confidently to the day when factories produced ten thousand planes a year for domestic use alone.[36]

, , ,

The whole notion of the flivver was based on the assumption that flying required no special skill; anyone of sound mind and body, with a little instruction, could learn to pilot an airplane—even, the air lobby hastened to point out, a woman. Up to this point, flying had largely been a male preserve. The balloon age created Madame Carlotta and a few other female aeronauts, but their popularity rested on the very fact that they were so rare. A male balloonist could be seen anywhere, but a woman—now that was an attraction worth seeing. It was also customary for a balloonist to offer to take up a local lady in his balloon, a ploy to demonstrate the safety of the craft—after all, what balloonist would willingly endanger the life of a lady?

With the coming of the airplane, women became more active in aviation. The first time a woman flew in Canada was on April 24, 1912, when Billy Stark took his wife up on a flight at an air show in Vancouver. The first woman to pilot an airplane in Canada was the American Alys Bryant, who flew at a Vancouver exhibition on July 31, 1913; less than a week later, her husband, John Bryant, was killed in a flying accident in Victoria (the first fatal airplane accident in Canada), but Alys carried on. During the war, with most male pilots at the front or training new pilots, women took up the slack with flying exhibitions. The most popular display pilot in Canada during the war years was Katherine Stinson, a Texan who went on tour, often performing in second-hand or rebuilt aircraft, after her repeated attempts to enlist in the air force were rejected. Another popular personality was Ruth Law, a record-setting American aviator and later proprietor of Ruth Law's Flying Circus, a barnstorming troupe whose speciality was racing airplanes against cars or horses.

In the 1920s, more and more women were becoming interested in aviation, and the air lobby saw this as an opportunity. Contemporary gender assumptions being what they were, what better way to demonstrate the ease and safety of flying than with a woman pilot? How better to debunk the prevailing belief that flying was the preserve of a few remarkable and gifted super-humans? If a woman could do it, reasoned aviation boosters, anyone could learn to fly.

And women were proving that they could fly. The first to gain a private pilot's licence was Eileen Vollick of Hamilton, who received her licence on March 13, 1928, after only sixteen hours of instruction. Louise Jenkins, dubbed "Canada's best known avia-trix," was the first licensed woman pilot in Prince Edward Island. Considerably better known than her husband, the lieutenant-governor of the province and also an aviation booster, Jenkins convinced the government to register her Puss Moth airplane with the call letters CF-PEI in an effort to bring some publicity to flying on the Island. Nellie Carson went from the obscurity of an office in Yorkton, Saskatchewan, to become the province's first female pilot; she set an altitude record when she coaxed a Gipsy Moth to above sixteen thousand feet without oxygen. The success of women like Vollick, Jenkins and Carson was proof to many in the aviation community that "women have equal rights with men in the dominion of the air." There was no reason, wrote the First World War flying ace Roy Brown in 1928, "why a woman should not fly if she is the right type of woman and temperamentally adapted for it."[37]

Articles in praise of flying, with titles like "I Learn to Fly" and "Miss Canada Takes the Air," began to appear in women's magazines. Some played up gender stereotypes (Marjorie Elliott Wilkins emphasized the prettiness of female pilots and claimed that they were better suited to light aircraft[38]), but most were forward-looking and inclusive. Vancouver-born Elsie MacGill tackled head-on the suitability of women for flying. The first woman to graduate in electrical engineering from the University of Toronto and the first woman to take a master's degree in aeronautical engineering from the University of Michigan, MacGill held senior engineering posts with some of the biggest aircraft manufacturers in Canada; eventually she became the first woman to serve as technical adviser with the International Civil Aviation Organization. In 1931, in *Chatelaine*, she considered whether women were physically or temperamentally suited to flying. Her answer was unequivocal. Modern aircraft required less physical strength to fly—even large passenger and transport aircraft could be easily controlled by a woman pilot. As to temperament, MacGill was equally decisive. Temperament did not enter into flying; training was what mattered, and a woman could be trained to fly as easily as a man. In sum, MacGill concluded that women were coming into their own in the air: "Aviation and women are taking each other seriously. The foggy lighter-than-air mindedness that attended women's first flying ventures—the glaring headlines, frenzied publicity and overwhelming popularity of the pioneers— is dissipating. . . . Cross-country and transoceanic flying by the ladies now requires circumstances more startling than that bare fact to draw the spotlight of public interest."[39]

Regrettably, MacGill was a little optimistic, and even the fact that women pilots were useful in aviation propaganda could not fully overcome gender presumptions. Norman Yarrow, for example, was concerned that engine noise would be particularly distressing to women in the air. An article in *Saturday Night* conceded that a woman would be a capable pilot under normal circumstances, but "when it comes to meeting the unexpected she is far more likely to lose her head."[40] Even the regulations conspired against woman pilots. Men could earn a private pilot's licence at age seventeen, but women had to be nineteen; men who held commercial licences were to be re-examined every six months, women every three months. Moreover, the superintendent of Air Regulations for the Department of Transportation was on record as saying that women were not suitable to be commercial pilots.[41] Clearly, the air lobby was generally less interested in seeing women fly for their own sake than for the good of its cause.

Despite the air lobby's rhetoric of inclusivity, too many men involved in aviation firmly believed that the only proper role for a woman in the air was as a passenger. Besides, a much more useful symbol of the gospel of air-mindedness was the child. The lobby trafficked in the future, trying to sell Canadians on the impact that flight could have in the coming years, as the technology improved. With this in mind, what better way to demonstrate the future of flight than by converting the youth of Canada? "The present generation has, perhaps, an instinctive dread of travel by air," wrote one air booster in 1924, "but to our children who have seen aircraft in the skies since they can remember, there is nothing strange in flying. The rising generation will undoubtedly travel by air naturally and without hesitation."[42] By looking at the young, aviation boosters argued, one could get a glimpse of Canada in the future.

Children were unencumbered by adult reticence about a new technology and the ability of humans to move in three dimensions. "A new generation," observed J. A. Wilson in 1924, "is growing up to whom there is nothing strange in flying. They have seen aircraft in the sky since they were children. It stirs their youthful imaginations." For them, the airplane was little different from the automobile; it was simply a mode of transportation. For that reason, many air boosters argued, children would grow up wanting to learn to fly, just as they now wanted to learn to drive.[43]

Signs of a budding love affair between young people and flying were everywhere in the 1930s. McClelland and Stewart had sold a toy airplane called the Sail-Me in the early 1920s, and a decade later model-aircraft building was one of the most popular hobbies in the country. The Model Aircraft League of Canada came into being in 1930 and held its first national contest in Ottawa that summer, with J. H. Parkin and Ernest Stedman acting as judges. Model-aircraft leagues sprang up in dozens of cities, often affili-ated with or supported by the local flying club. The league in Hamilton, Ontario, for example, was launched in conjunction with the opening of the civic airport in 1929. Magazines regularly published plans for building balsa-wood airplanes, or kits could be purchased from a number of manufacturers. Canadian Model Aircraft of Shawbridge, Quebec, was established in 1926, its owner "endeavour[ing] to bring before the younger people of Canada a feeling of airmindedness." By the end of the 1930s, the Ontario Model Aircraft Company was producing more than a million kits a year. Its youthful owner drew praise from no less a figure than Billy Bishop, who credited him with "making other youthful Canadians more air-minded than their contemporaries in any other country in the world." As Bishop put it, "The builders of scale models will make tomorrow's airmen."[44]

Aviation also emerged as the most popular theme for young readers in the inter-war era. Flying had started to find its way into children's books during the First World War, with riveting tales of fighter pilots and pioneering aviators, but by the 1920s aviation writing had become a genre of its own. The American publisher A. L. Burt distributed the Aviator Series, aimed at young teenagers and written by H. H. Arnold, who would command the American air forces during the Second World War. Macmillan of Canada carried the British Air Adventure Series, which included novels such as *Seaplane Base*, *The Phantom Wing*, *The Air Dope-Hunters* and of course the obligatory *Flying with the Mounties*. There were the *Ted Scott Flying Stories*, *Kidnapped by Air* ("a rattling story, which throbs with action and the spirit of high adventure") by Dillon Wallace, the chronicler of Labrador, and the much-loved *Canadian Boys Annual*, printed from British page blocks and carrying a mix of fiction ("The Mystery Airman of Clanwood Manor") and non-fiction ("Airways of the Future"). Even established literary characters were put into airplanes. Fans of Tom Swift could read about their hero's aerial adventures in *Tom Swift and His Sky Racer* or *Tom Swift and His Aerial Warship*, and the Hardy Boys took to crime-solving by air in *The Great Airport Mystery* (1930). The Hardy Boys' author, Canadian Leslie McFarlane, lived as a child in Haileybury, Ontario, and would have appreciated the impact of the airplane on isolated settlements. Even Clarence Young's *Motor Boys* series, which first appeared in 1906 to capitalize on growing interest in automobiles, was increasingly putting the young heroes into airplanes and airships.

As publishers, manufacturers and the air lobby had realized, aviation had captured the imagination of the young generation, and if that enthusiasm could be built on, the future of flying in Canada was bright, for the adults of tomorrow would make the new technology part of their lives. As Samuel Morgan-Powell, the literary and drama critic for the Montreal *Star*, put it in a lyrical passage, "The whirling propellor's overwhelming roar is music to the ears of the youth of today. The sight of a graceful plane swooping, wheeling, darting, mounting up to the clouds or zooming down to earth will be a commonplace to the children of tomorrow...our children will live to greet the dawn in their airplanes just as we of this generation have been used to greet it at our casement windows."[45]

The rhetoric was inspiring, but there was a great irony in the education campaign mounted by the air lobby. By demonstrating the prudence of pilots, the safety of flying, its similarities to driving and the accessibility of flying, the campaign sought to dispel the very notions that had created the enthusiasm for aviation. The romance, danger, excitement and mystique had given flight a heady appeal, but they would all be undermined by the air lobby's campaign. For aviation boosters, there was no inherent contradiction: changing the attitudes that had drawn them to flying was part of the necessary evolution of flight. "The romantic phase of aviation may be expected steadily to decline as it passes into its practical work," observed one editor confidently. The newsletter of Western Canada Airways agreed, noting that "the leading air transport companies have succeeded today in eliminating the factor of 'adventure' from flying when considered as a method of transport."[46]

Not so many years in the future, many air-minded Canadians would have cause to regret flight's becoming a commonplace and the airplane just another kind of bus or taxi. But in the short term, the economic, political and social opportunities offered by the new technology were dependent on the Canadian people embracing flight as safe and practical. Once that occurred, Winnipeg South Centre MP W. W. Kennedy realized, an aerial revolution would sweep the nation: "Let us reach out and take our destined place among the nations. Opportunity is on tiptoe waiting to take off: let us give her wings.... Canada is on the Main street of the heavens. Would that I could splash it in letters of flame across the firmament! Would that it might stand out as a pillar of cloud by day and a pillar of fire by night, to lead Canada into her promised land!"[47]

· 5 ·

THE ANNIHILATION
OF TIME

IT WAS AUGUST 1937, AND DUNCAN MCLAREN WAS ON ANOTHER
flight over the northland on behalf of his employer, the Hudson's
Bay Company. He had been hired as aircrew not long after the company started to use aircraft to ply the territory between its far-flung
fur-trade posts, and by now the job was old hat to him. "Flying itself
is not very interesting," he wrote to his parents. "Rudy [Heiss, a
pilot for the company] often goes to sleep for a couple of hours
while I fly the kite." Nor did he find the scenery particularly inspiring: "The land is some of the most desolate and God-forsaken spots
I have ever seen, or hope to see," he wrote in another letter. "How
humans or animals can survive in such a country is beyond me.
Nothing but rock and a few small bushes as far as the eye can see."[1]
   What is striking about McLaren's letter is not so much its sour,
dismissive tone as the degree to which his sentiments were at vari-
ance with the rhetoric surrounding aviation. For McLaren, the
North was a barren wasteland, a desert with few redeeming

features.* For the aviation enthusiast, however, the North was something very different. Its forbidding aspect camouflaged untold riches; it was simply waiting to be made useful, according to European notions of utility. For this reason, the North elicited not McLaren's disdain but something that approached rapture: "Running the rapids of the air, the modern prospector looks on a marvelous panorama, his field of work, his world to open," mused a mining newspaper in 1929. "In a rush of air and a roar of sound, he rapidly surveys its salient features, plans his campaign, he and his machine a perfect combination of efficiency and mobility. Into this great arena throw the youth of this country and who, then, will deny Canada's claim to ownership of the treasure trove of the world?"[2]

Underlying this effusive prose was one of the main messages of the air lobby: if only people could be educated in its utility, the airplane could be used commercially for more than joyriding or dropping leaflets. It was not a paying proposition in the immediate post-war years, but it had immense potential to bring about an economic transformation in Canada, a nation tailor-made to be exploited by air. For centuries, explorers, trappers, merchants, settlers and politicians had struggled against the sheer distances involved. Now, those struggles were over. The airplane would shrink the country, collapsing time and space so that the remotest regions were accessible. Using the techniques of aerial mapping and photography, which had been brought to new levels of sophistication during the war, the resource wealth of the nation could be exploited by the lumberjack and the prospector. Aviation would allow Canada to realize its dream of opening the North, the last frontier. But this potential economic revolution carried with it an even more fundamental revolution. Not only would the

---

* Contemporary observers tended to be rather free with their use of the word "north." Typically, they used it to refer not to a specific geographic location but to any area more than a day's travel north of the railway line.

economy be changed, but the very nature of time and space would also be altered. New phrases in the vernacular—the devastation of distance, the annihilation of time—became watchwords of an era in which technology was redrawing the map.

, , ,

Even the most enthusiastic of aviation boosters in the early 1920s would not suggest that flying was a money-maker. "It is generally contended," observed Claire MacLaurin, the acting director of the Royal Canadian Naval Air Service, in a classic understatement, "that Aviation from a purely commercial point of view, at the present time, is not a perfectly sound business proposition." And with good reason. There were plenty of experienced pilots and cheap aircraft around, but the air services that emerged in the wake of the war rarely survived infancy. Thirty flying companies were registered in 1920, but only eight were in operation four years later; during the same period, the number of licensed commercial aircraft dropped from 111 to 32.[3] Not even notoriety could guarantee success. Bishop-Barker Aeroplanes Limited, founded by two of the country's greatest flying heroes, attempted to combine such prestigious services as a regular service linking the Toronto waterfront and Muskoka, aimed at wealthy cottage owners, with mundane tasks such as aerial photography.[4] Despite the well-known principals and influential shareholders, the company ceased operation in 1922, using a contract to paint Toronto streetcars to pay off its final debts. "Commercial flying will have great possibilities at some future time," predicted Edward L. Cousins of the Toronto Harbour Commission, one of the clients with which the Bishop-Barker line had attempted to do business, "but it would be many years before it could be put on a sound financial basis." Even into the 1930s, considerable skepticism prevailed. When an executive of Eastern Canada Air Lines asked the long-time Liberal cabinet minister J. L. Ralston for help floating a stock issue to finance the operation of feeder airlines in the Maritimes,

Ralston was pessimistic: "The air is literally filled with aviation projects just now....I wouldn't suggest to a friend of mine that he put a dollar in it."[5]

But the air lobby traded in dreams and the promise of the future. The failure of a few aviation companies was neither here nor there. They believed fervently in the potential of aviation to bring an economic miracle, because Canada had all the elements necessary to utilize flying to its fullest potential. The first essential was a skilled workforce, and in this regard Canada was richly blessed. One of the most significant obstacles to the development of aviation before 1914 was a shortage of skilled pilots and air mechanics. But the nation had contributed significantly to the Allied air war, not only in the flying aces but in the equally essential if less-heralded skilled workers, craftsmen and engine and airframe mechanics who built aircraft and kept them in the air. This experienced and air-minded group gave Canada a distinct advantage in the post-war world. As the editor of the Toronto *Daily Star* put it, "Canada is in the position of having more skilled and trained aviators in proportion to population than any other country in the world, and if flying is to become the new big business of the future the advantages which we possess ought to be turned to account."[6]

Canada was also geographically suited to a large and successful aviation sector; as air lobbyists were constantly reminding the public, the country had a virtually limitless supply of natural airfields. Barnstorming had been so popular in the West because airplanes could land almost anywhere. Given that the average biplanes of the time needed only about eighty yards to take off and land, they could operate in much of the country without specially groomed landing facilities. Furthermore, the war had produced a new kind of aircraft that would become critically important in Canada: the flying boat. Developed as a means to protect shipping lanes, flying boats were ideal for operations in the Canadian North, where the thousands of lakes and waterways could serve as airports. Later in the 1920s, aircraft were fitted with skis rather than wheels in the winter months, which meant that lakes and waterways could be used by flying boats or float planes in the summer and ski planes in the winter. Except for a few weeks during spring thaw and freeze-up, the north was open year-round to exploration and exploitation by air, with no need for expensive infrastructure.

But if Canada had the human resources and the landforms that could support a prospering aviation sector, it also had the need for a prospering aviation sector. In a sense, the country had both the means and the motive to become a world leader in flying, for if there is one constant in Canadian history, it is the challenge of the land. Since the earliest European presence, people have been at once awed by the potential wealth of the land and perplexed by the physical obstacles in the way of realizing it. Explorers, traders, merchants and settlers pushed into the wilderness in an attempt to exploit the potential of the land, but their success in developing the fur trade, lumbering, mining or agriculture was always tempered by the fact that there was so much more there, if only they could find a way to unlock it. For decades they moved westward, drawn first by the furs and later by the prairies that promised prosperity to the farmer or rancher. By the turn of the twentieth century, that promise was paying off—settlement, immigration and the completion of a transcontinental railway were fuelling a wheat economy that would bring boom times.

That left the North, a land more forbidding and isolated, to become the next stage on which the nation's quest for greatness would be played out. Before the war, it had utterly defeated all attempts to make it useful, in the European sense. Exploration by foot, dogsled or canoe required months of back-breaking work; it would take decades just to explore and evaluate even a fraction of the North. Pushing railways into the wilderness was out of the question, and ships could operate in northern waters for only a few months a year. Many Canadians, as fascinated as they were by the potential of the North, must have been equally convinced that it would not be accessible in their lifetimes.

But the air lobby had the solution: the airplane. It could be used for surveying, to create maps and photographic catalogues of its resources and to ferry in and out workers and materials so resources could be exploited. The way to prosperity was not along the ground but above it. "No country in the world has the enormous undeveloped natural resources that we have," declared the Ontario Minister of Lands and Forests, William Finlayson, "and it is therefore proper that we should direct our thoughts not to the spectacular flying but rather to useful flying in the development of Canada."[7] Stephen Leacock, writing as an economist rather than a humorist, agreed: "There is no country where aerial transport is destined to be a greater utility than with us in Canada. Our vast distances invite it. Our unexplored territory demands it. And our undiscovered mineral wealth warrants it and will pay for it." Again and again, air lobbyists argued that Canada was in a unique position to capitalize on the benefits of the air age. "Probably in no other country is commercial aviation making or is capable of making such a contribution to progress as in Canada," wrote J. H. Parkin in 1930. "Regions formerly regarded as inaccessible and otherwise doomed to remain forever undeveloped are now not only being explored, but are actually in the process of development wholly by means of aircraft."[8]

In this exploitation, the lessons learned during the war about the value of aerial reconnaissance were crucial. Just as an observation aircraft could bring back photographs of enemy trench works, enabling intelligence officers to create detailed maps of the front lines, so too could an airplane bring back photos of unexplored regions of Canada, as a first step to generating accurate maps. Indeed, the Air Board's photographic section was staffed by men who had honed their skills over the tortured landscapes of the Western Front. Here, the popular understanding that the occupants of an airplane saw the world in miniature, as on a map, was given practical application.[9]

As early as 1917, Gen. Willoughby Gwatkin, the chief of the General Staff, suggested that a Canadian air force should work with the Topographical Surveys, Geographers and Forestry branches of the Department of the Interior, but not until after the war did the department establish an air survey committee to make concrete plans. The committee elected to mount a test survey to see if techniques learned during the war could be fruitfully applied to peacetime aviation; Edouard Deville, the surveyor-general, proposed that the operation be flown in the Ottawa area, simply for administrative ease. (O. M. Biggar, who as a member of the Air Board should have been more optimistic, preferred a more remote location, to minimize the public relations damage should the operation fail.[10]) The experiment was a success, and the Air Board and the Canadian Air Force began mounting more ambitious operations. The first two years of surveys, in 1922–23 and 1923–24, were strictly experimental, carried out during the regular patrols by the CAF. The success of these operations convinced the Topographical Survey of Canada to turn the management of aerial surveying over to a separate agency, which would convene an interdepartmental meeting before each flying season to determine surveying priorities and the most efficient use of resources. In succeeding years the amount of territory covered by aerial survey flights grew dramatically: in 1924, the flights covered some 40,000 square miles; in 1925 nearly 50,000 squares miles; and 70,000 square miles in 1929.[11] Though operations were scaled back somewhat during the Great Depression, the Topographical and Air Survey Bureau achieved remarkable things with dwindling resources, covering a record 108,000 square miles during the 1935–36 fiscal year.

Surveying staff were delighted with the results, both in terms of efficiency and cost. They reported that aerial photography reduced by half the work that had to be done on the ground, and that aerial sketch mapping was fully 40 percent cheaper than traditional methods.[12] Even more significant than these impressive statistics, however, was the meaning with which they were endowed by contemporary observers. Aerial surveying meant much more than just taking pictures; it meant taking control of the landscape. "The aerial photograph is in effect a portion of the earth's surface," wrote one surveyor. To take a picture of the land, in essence, was to capture it; aerial photography allowed a person to "carry a given section of the country around in a pocket," as Lloyd Rochester, a pioneer in aerial prospecting, put it in 1936.[13] "'Veni! Vidi! Vici!'...How striking and pertinent can [those words] be to-day when applied to the work of the aeroplane," wrote A. M. Narraway, the chief aerial-surveys engineer of the Topographical Survey, in 1928. "It conquered and brought back what it saw. It subdued, as it were, the forests, the swamps, the watercourses, the rock exposures, and all the other associated data." Narraway described a flight over northern Manitoba in 1922; for most of the trip, he sketched a record of what he saw, but for the last fifty miles he used an aerial camera. "The photographs so simply taken in a brief half-hour laid bare, for all who wish to see, the features of that fifty miles which had from the beginning of time remained unobserved and unknown," he recalled. "That fifty miles of Canada's hinterland were truly conquered and a record was brought back good for all time to come. An infinitesimal fraction of time, a hundredth part of a second, was sufficient to do it, was sufficient to translate ignorance into knowledge, the unknown into the known."[14]

Narraway's comment reveals the degree to which land was valued only in so much as it could be made useful; the airplane made that possible. Using aerial surveying and photography, the country could be examined, charted and evaluated. "The day will come," predicted Robert Logan, a Canadian pilot who worked with Fairchild Aerial Surveys in New York, "when the whole of Canada will be mapped or rather photographed and the photos indexed."[15] This was imperialism plain and simple. The North was to be conquered. The surveyors and camera operators were the advance guard who would subdue the land with pencil and camera. In their wake, maps and photographs in hand, would come the armies of lumbermen and prospectors.

, , ,

Since the late eighteenth century, when the demands of the Royal Navy had transformed Canada into Great Britain's woodyard, trees had constituted an apparently inexhaustible natural resource. But by the early twentieth century, it was becoming clear to many people in the forest industry that the resource was not being exploited as efficiently as it might be. Timber stands were classified by a few foresters on foot (travelling "through the forest like an ant through a forest of grass," observed one forestry executive), supplemented by considerable guesswork. Parasite infestations were virtually impossible to stop and could destroy thousands of acres of prime timber. Much more devastating were forest fires, which could not be effectively fought, or even spotted, from the ground.[16] For each of these problems, the airplane offered a solution.

The classification of lumber resources proved to be remarkably simple. After all, noted one lumberman, anything would improve on the old method, "whereby we plow through the woods taking measurements at intervals and trusting to the good old standby 'law of averages' for results."[17] In the autumn of 1918, the federal Department of Naval Services and the Quebec Department of Lands and Forests agreed to mount an experimental forest survey, using naval flying boats operated by the St. Maurice Forest Protective Association, a consortium of Quebec lumber companies. In June 1919, after protracted negotiations between the two levels of government, Stuart Graham, an ex–Royal Naval Air Service pilot, made the first timber survey flight over the Lac-à-la-Tortue region of Quebec, and at the end of the season the St. Maurice forest manager Ellwood Wilson declared the experiment a complete success: a single two-hour flight could produce better data than two weeks of ground work, and ten men working on foot could cover in a month only a quarter of the territory recorded in one day of aerial photography flights.[18] An experienced "timber cruiser" could classify varieties of trees based on their colour and shape and determine both the density of timber and the ease with which it could be logged. Access routes could be mapped out, obstacles noted, burned over or swampy areas marked—all in one survey flight.

The forestry industry lost no time in harnessing the immense potential of the aircraft to maximize profit. Price Brothers was one of the first companies to establish a flying branch, and began air patrols over its holdings in the Lac-Saint-Jean area of Quebec in July 1920; in September 1922, Price Brothers' flying operations were taken over by the newly founded Dominion Aerial Explorations, under the management of Harry Quigley. The same year, Fairchild Aerial Surveys, a Canadian subsidiary of an American firm, set up shop at Grand'Mère, Quebec, to fly forest survey flights using the aerial cameras it had been developing. But Laurentide Air Service, established in 1921 by one of the partners in the St. Maurice consortium, emerged as the biggest player in the game, winning contracts from the Ontario government and private concerns to do forest reconnaissance flights from its base at Lac-à-la-Tortue. The company doubled its air fleet between 1922 and 1923 and established a larger headquarters at Trois-Rivières.[19] Though it ceased operations in 1925, Laurentide was one of the great success stories of post-war aviation in Canada.

But cataloguing forest resources was only part of the job; protecting them was just as important and certainly more challenging. The greatest threats to Canada's forests, then as now, were parasites and fire. The sawfly or hemlock looper could devastate timber stands; the federal Department of Agriculture estimated that a spruce budworm infestation in eastern Canada in the early 1920s destroyed as much as 150 million cords of pulpwood. Fire could be even more disastrous. Manned watchtowers covered only a tiny portion of Canada's forests, and a fire could burn for days or weeks before it was detected. Quite apart from the potential loss of life (the great Haileybury fire of 1922 killed forty-four people and burned two thousand square miles of forest), the loss of valuable timber was immense, averaging

900,000 acres a year in the five years up to 1924 and peaking at 2.2 million acres in 1923.[20] Faced with such losses, forest companies were willing to try almost anything to safeguard their assets.

Determining the spread of outbreaks of parasite infestation by air was simple: an aircraft survey to determine the spread of an outbreak of spruce budworm near Lake Abitibi in 1920 yielded "more information from the air in a day as to the extent of the outbreak than they could in a season from the ground," J. A. Wilson reported. On the West Coast, aircraft from the Jericho Beach flying boat station were used to trap white pine blister rust spores at different altitudes, so scientists could determine how the disease travelled to infect new areas.[21] Before long, governments and forestry companies discovered that outbreaks could be fought as well as monitored from the air. The techniques for fighting parasite infestation by air were relatively complicated and took some time to perfect, but the first aerial forest dusting occurred from June 18 to July 27, 1927, in Cape Breton. A decade later, when sawflys threatened forests in New Brunswick, the provincial Department of Lands and Mines used aircraft to transport sawfly parasites to the affected areas.[22] By the end of the 1930s, government and forestry officials had a whole new arsenal with which to fight parasite infestations.

The possibility of fighting forest fires from the air had been broached in 1917, when a naval lieutenant in Ottawa suggested using aircraft to patrol for forest fires and enforce fire laws. Experience at the front had convinced Ernest Potter that the smallest fires could be spotted from miles away. Emergency landing fields at regular intervals would increase the margin of safety for pilots; to help pay for the service, he recommended (with more imagination that common sense) that the airfields be planted with cash crops.[23] After the war, the federal Conservative leader, Arthur Meighen, suggested that the government of Canada acquire some war surplus airships. "A fair degree of efficiency in the fighting of forest fires may result from the bombing of fires with gas-producing material," he proposed to the cabinet minister George Perley. Meighen's idea was well intentioned but showed a limited appreciation for the technology, as a staff member in the Department of External Affairs pointed out. Airships would be useful only between the Great Lakes and the Rocky Mountains; the weather in eastern Canada was too unsettled, and the mountains made it difficult to operate small airships safely. They were also difficult to control and moved too slowly to cope with a sudden emergency. As well, the staffer suggested delicately, it was unwise to have a hydrogen-filled balloon drifting over a forest fire.[24]

But the premise was a good one, and the forestry companies quickly realized that their survey flights could double as forest fire patrols. The St. Maurice Forest Protective Association made forty flights in 1919; because the observer could see a distance of twenty miles in each direction, the flights covered 180,000 miles of forest that summer alone. The service's first success came on July 7, 1919, when Stuart Graham and Walter Kahre spotted and reported a forest fire while on a patrol. The following year, the federal and provincial governments established air stations at Jericho Beach, British Columbia, Morley (later High River), Alberta, and Roberval, Quebec, to provide forest fire patrols, but Ontario went a step further. In the early 1920s, it had contracted with Laurentide to fly forest patrols but in 1924, in a move that sealed Laurentide's fate, the cabinet decided to establish its own flying branch. And so was born the Ontario Provincial Air Service (OPAS), initially with thirteen flying boats purchased from Laurentide. Headed by Roy Maxwell, a swashbuckler with a blue Cadillac roadster and a weakness for high leather boots, the OPAS established its main headquarters at Sault Ste. Marie (with district bases at Sioux Lookout, Orient Bay and Sudbury) and for a few years was the largest aviation organization in Canada. In 1930, its thirty-three aircraft and seventy-nine flying personnel completed nearly twelve thousand flights over 875,000 miles and, despite later controversy over financial improprieties, achieved its primary goal of protecting the province's forests. By 1927, its aircraft were patrolling 125,000,000 acres of forest; losses that year were only

35,000 acres. The minister of Lands and Forests estimated that 90 percent of the province's forest fires never spread beyond 100 acres because of the OPAS's ability to deliver firefighting crews quickly and efficiently. In the words of the *Financial Post*, the province had created "an all-seeing eye that can nip forest fire, with all its appalling waste, in the bud."[25]

As the *Financial Post*'s lyrical rhetoric suggested, the forestry patrol was more than just an arm of the government or the timber industry; it was becoming an icon. The romanticism that pervaded the discourse at other levels is evident in F. V. Heakes's ode to the forest watcher:

> Over lake and pine-clad forest,
> Over river flashing by,
> Sails the white-winged forest watcher,
> Softly in a cloud-swept sky.
>
> Softly drones the distant engine,
> Over virgin timberland,
> Speaking peace unto the forest,
> Where the mighty giants stand.
>
> Onward then o'er tracts scarce charted,
> Over cataracts asweep,
> Over mountain, plain and valley,
> Over glades that lie asleep.
>
> Far into the western twilight,
> Flashing wings against the sun,
> Hums the softening song of engine,
> Throbbing until day is done.[26]

The overall impression is one of tranquility, of a machine that operates in harmony with nature. Despite the airplane's purpose—to ensure that the trees could be destroyed by lumbermen, rather than by fire or disease—it is represented as nature's friend. The softness of the engine, the notion of the airplane speaking peace, the white wings suggesting purity—all imply the benefi- cence of the new technology and the people who had mastered it.

In the public imagination, the miles flown or fires spotted were overshadowed by the personalities. The timber cruisers of the OPAS, Laurentide and other similar operations became legendary between the wars: Terry Tully and James Medcalf, OPAS employ- ees who would vanish in 1927 on a London-to-London flight across the North Atlantic; "Duke" Schiller, the American-born air racer and bon vivant who spent three years as a timber-cruiser and eventually lost his life flying out of Bermuda during the Second World War; Roméo Vachon, who flew with the Royal Canadian Naval Air Service before doing forestry patrols and, eventually, a mail run that would earn him the nickname "The Flying Postman"; and Fred Stevenson, a wartime ace who had ferried diplomats to the Paris Peace Conference and instructed pilots in the Soviet Union before joining the OPAS. These men transfixed a public already predisposed to idolize the aviator. Just like Lindbergh, they were object lessons to a society that needed inspi- ration: "the tale the north country discloses today of epic deeds and reckless jousting with death comes to a problem-weary world like a breath of fresh air. It brings its proof that out on the fron- tiers men are still engaged in battling nature in the raw in the same gay and gallant spirit as of old."[27] But they were not the only stars in the bush-flying firmament, nor was timber-cruising the only opportunity for the ambitious pilot; they could also open other new frontiers, by joining forces with a new generation of men who moiled for gold.

⁊ ⁊ ⁊

The old-fashioned prospector is one of the romantic figures from Canada's past. Carrying a season's worth of supplies and provi- sions, he canoed through the wilderness, scanning the shores for outcroppings that might hold a fortune in gold, silver or copper. Most of the season was taken up with getting to and from the potential sites; once they reached an area, the prospectors might have only a couple of weeks to look around before having to start the trek back to civilization again. Successful strikes were few and far between, so a promising discovery—or the rumour of one—would draw prospectors like a magnet, but in only a few places was there sufficient wealth to go around. Most grubstakers barely eked out an existence and had to supplement their income as hunters, trappers or labourers. But the reality of a prospector's life was overshadowed by the romanticized image of it, celebrated most famously by Robert W. Service and, later, by a legion of imitators. Service's paeans to figures like Dan McGrew and Sam McGee, "the men who moil for gold," fixed in the public imagination the figure of the prospector as a grizzled, independent fellow who revelled in the isolation of the North and the hardships of his vocation.

But romance was about to be overtaken by efficiency. As early as 1915, it had been suggested that aircraft offered a better way to discover and develop mineral resources, and in July 1920, Stuart Graham and Walter Kahre flew a prospector into a remote area of Quebec to stake the first mining claim by air.[28] In 1921, the geologist E. L. Bruce flew from Sioux Lookout to Lake St. Joseph in northern Ontario in a little over an hour, a distance that had taken him four days by canoe the previous summer. In the air, he spotted a number of significant features that he had been unable to see on his ground survey the previous year, and he was persuaded that the airplane could relieve the prospector or geologist of much time and effort. It could never replace the time-consuming practice of tramping through the bush with a hammer to gather samples, but it certainly made the getting in and out much easier. A prospecting party, instead of spending weeks canoeing and hiking, could be flown to any lake or river and begin work immediately. If the area proved a disappointment, they could easily be relocated; if prospects were good, the party could be supplied by air for the entire season and brought out in the fall. Moreover, a single air-craft could easily supply half a dozen prospecting parties.[29]

The mining boom was just what many struggling pilots and aviation companies were looking for. There was only so much timber-cruising work to go around, and there wasn't much call for aerial fisheries patrols in Ontario or Alberta; prospecting, typically a profession of big dreams, offered pilots virtually limitless growth potential. Laurentide, still reeling from the loss of its Ontario government contracts, filled its balance-sheet void by opening the first successful regularly scheduled service in Canada, to the gold fields of Rouyn, Quebec. Hundreds of miles to the west, an even bigger drama was about to be played out. On July 25, 1925, a party of four prospectors struck gold near the Manitoba-Ontario border. The Red Lake gold rush, the last classic gold rush of the twentieth century, was on.

But this one would be different. Jack Hammell, the Toronto mining promoter to whom the four prospectors looked for financing, knew that it was only a matter of time before word got out and eager grubstakers made perhaps more promising strikes. He needed to begin a surface exploration immediately, before the freeze-up, but there was not time to get a party in by foot. The only solution was the airplane. Hammell promptly chartered five flying boats from the OPAS, eventually taking in fifteen tons of supplies and seven workers to begin an assessment of the site. Hammell's haste was justified, because by early 1926 hopeful prospectors were coming to Red Lake from across North America. Mostly they came by dogsled, snowshoe and canoe, but Jack Elliott, a First World War pilot whose fledgling flying company had thus far given him more headaches than profit, sensed there was money to be made. He crated up a couple of Curtiss Jennys fitted with skis, sent them by rail to Hudson, Ontario, and was soon charging a dollar a pound to fly people in and out of Red Lake. At the same time, Doc Oaks and Tommy Thompson, with the blessing of their boss, had resigned from the OPAS to establish Patricia Airways Exploration Limited. In a modern odyssey

The members of the Aerial Experiment Association at Hammondsport, New York, 1908. Alexander Graham Bell is on the left. *National Film Board X-16336*

An unsuccessful flying display at Smiths Falls, Ontario, Dominion Day 1912. *J. J. Tallman Regional Collection, D. W. Weldon Library, The University of Western Ontario, Fred Hitchins Collection, IV-C-2*

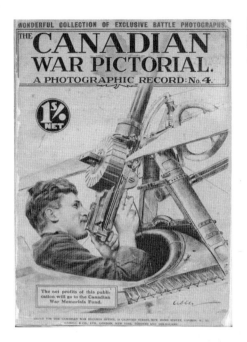

Billy Bishop with the tools of his trade. *D. B. Weldon Library, The University of Western Ontario*

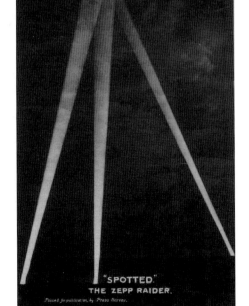

A fanciful postcard view of a German raider over London. *J. J. Tallman Regional Collection, D. W. Weldon Library, The University of Western Ontario, Hitchins Collection, IV- B-3*

"SPOTTED."
THE ZEPP RAIDER.

FROM GLOOM TO JOY

Relieved World—Three cheers for Hawker, Grieve and the

Jubilation as Harry Hawker and Kenneth Mackenzie Grieve are reported rescued. Border Cities Star *(Windsor, Ont.), 29 May 1919, p4*

John Alcock and Arthur Whitten-Brown lift off from Mount Pearl in their Vickers Vimy, June 1919. *J. J. Tallman Regional Collection, D. W. Weldon Library, The University of Western Ontario, Hitchins Collection, IV-E-1*

"He is more truly the god-man than anything I have ever seen": Charles Lindbergh (right). *J. J. Tallman Regional Collection, D. W. Weldon Library, The University of Western Ontario, Hitchins Collection, IV-E-4*

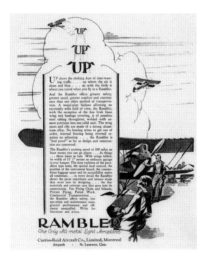

The contrast between air and ground is made explicit in this ad. Canadian *Aviation 2/6 (June 1929)*

This wartime ad captures both the child's fascination with flying and a faith in the ultimate benevolence of the technology. Maclean's, *15 Nov. 1943, p61*

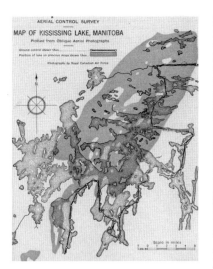

The miracles of aerial surveying. The dark, arrow-head shape is how Lake Kississing appeared on earlier maps. *Department of National Defence,* Report on Civil Aviation for the Year 1923 *(Ottawa: King's Printer, 1924), p44*

Prosperous businessmen ponder the best way of getting from place to place. Canadian Airways Ltd Bulletin *2/6 (15 Dec. 1930), p5*

Arthur Tylee, Mayor R. H. Gale and George Thompson after the first trans-Canada flight. *J. J. Tallman Regional Collection, D. W. Weldon Library, The University of Western Ontario, Hitchins Collection, IV-E-3*

CANADA
is only one day wide

Spanning the continent twice each day—T.C.A. has overcome the barriers of distance —shrunk the vast expanse of the Nation—until the shores of the Atlantic are but a day's distance from the shores of the Pacific. It speeds the men, materials and mails essential to Victory—104,446 passengers, 2,309,000 pounds of air mail and 363,000 pounds of air express last year.

In war as in peace, T.C.A. is an essential arm of the Nation's transport.

Daily Services

Transcontinental

Halifax · Moncton · Montreal
Ottawa · Toronto · North Bay
Winnipeg · Regina · Lethbridge
Vancouver

Inter-City

Montreal · Ottawa · Toronto
Toronto · London · Windsor (Detroit)
Halifax · Moncton · Montreal
Lethbridge · Calgary · Edmonton

International

Toronto · New York
Moncton · Sydney · Newfoundland

T.C.A. makes direct connections with the major U.S. Airlines

For information, reservations, etc., consult your nearest T.C.A. Traffic Office, or any C.N.R. passenger representative.

TRANS-CANADA *Air Lines*
CANADA'S NATIONAL AIR SERVICE
Air Mail · Passenger · Air Express

Trans-Canada Air Lines' ads often traded on the notion that the airplane could shrink the nation.
Maclean's, *15 May 1943, p52*

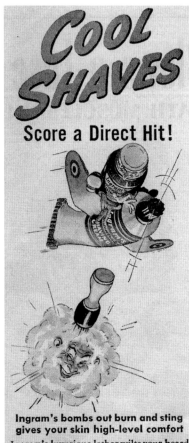

COOL SHAVES
Score a Direct Hit!

Ingram's bombs out burn and sting gives your skin high-level comfort

Ingram's luxurious lather wilts your beard so fast, your razor clips through like a propellor through fog. And Ingram's *coolness* helps condition your skin for shaving so your face feels fresh and invigorated long afterwards. Ask your druggist for Ingram's today. If you haven't an empty tube, you can get Ingram's jar for the same price!

INGRAM'S
SHAVING CREAM
in jar or tube

Bombing imagery was used to market many consumer products, including shaving cream. Maclean's, *1 Jan. 1943, p24*

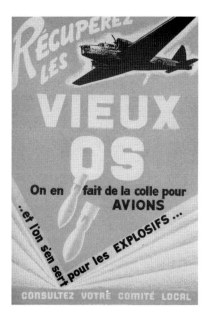

Bombing from the kitchen—save bones and contribute to the strategic bombing campaign. *National Archives of Canada C87545*

Modern business requires modern methods—a wartime ad for airmail services. Maclean's, *15 Jan. 1943, p29*

Technology tames the last frontier. Maclean's, *1 July 1943, p21*

carefully tracked by the press, Oaks and Thompson took nearly four weeks to get their brand-new Curtiss Lark from the factory in New Jersey to Red Lake, ready to handle passengers and freight.

The year 1926 marked the peak of the Red Lake gold rush. Prospectors came in droves, most staking claims that were never explored, and the two air services operated at capacity supplying the mining concerns working on the handful of productive claims. For a brief point in time, Red Lake even laid claim to being the busiest airport in the world, in the number of takeoffs and landings on a daily basis. Aviation boosters were fond of noting that the Red Lake and Rouyn runs were the world's only self-sustaining, regularly scheduled air routes. But more important, the mining boom would be the catalyst for the creation of other flying companies, including Canada's first great airline, Western Canada Airways.

James A. Richardson was a young, aggressive and visionary financier who was always on the lookout for new opportunities. After talking to a Curtiss flying boat operator at Minaki, Ontario, he became convinced that mining and aviation could be a profitable mix. On December 10, 1926, WCA came into being, with Richardson as president and Doc Oaks, who had resigned from Patricia Airways, as manager. In short order, WCA, which became Canadian Airways Limited in 1930, when it bought a number of eastern airlines, would grow from a modest operation serving the mining districts of northern Manitoba and Ontario into the leading air freight company in Canada and, arguably, the world. Five years after its foundation, it had become a complex network of air routes served by seventy-two aircraft—more than the Department of National Defence's Directorate of Civil Government Air Operations; CAL flew nearly 1.9 million miles, carrying over 1.1 million pounds of freight. Its operations were varied—air mail, passenger services, fisheries patrols, mercy flights, timber cruising, rescue missions, pilot instruction, charter services—but its staple was serving the prospecting and mining sectors. Other firms, with fabled names like Prospector Airways, Dominion Explorers and

Northern Aerial Minerals Exploration (NAME), would follow, but none would seriously challenge WCA's ascendancy.

WCA was adept at self-promotion, but even admitting the success of the airline's publicists, there is no denying that the public was fascinated by the role of aircraft in the drama being played out at Red Lake and other mineral finds. Magazine and newspaper articles focused on the personalities, while editorials attempted to assess the impact of the new technology. "The great development of our mines in the hinterland of the Dominion has been almost entirely due to the airplane," observed the London *Free Press* in 1936. "It has pushed forward the opening of the North Country by decades." Just what this process meant for the prospector was made clear in an anecdote related by the legendary bush pilot Walter Gilbert in 1930. He wrote of flying an old prospector to Teigen Lakes in northern B.C.; his passenger constantly peered over the side of the aircraft, intermittently saying "'There's a day!'—'And there's another day?' as the miles, which had so often meant to him weary days, streamed past us." For such men, noted the Hamilton *Spectator*, "no valuation can be placed on the service by air that has come with the march of progress. It is significant of the times that scientific development has reached into the innermost confines of undeveloped Canada."[30]

As the *Spectator* understood, the old ways were falling victim to progress. Harold Farrington's flights into Red Lake to supply the gold rush revealed that "the map that was rolled back by canvas and dog teams is going to be rolled still further back by wings. The paddle and the lash are going to yield first place to propellors and lashings." Indeed, this contrast between the old and the new became the most typical way to illustrate the impact of aviation. "Prospectors of the old school may now look heavenward as they plod under portage burden of pack and canoe and stand back amazed while their colleagues of the newer thought fly by them undaunted and untired," mused an article in a mining magazine in 1928. "The efficiency of field men will be doubled and in the next five years' time, more discoveries may be made than in the past fifty. This is the order of the newer day; and the elder has been overtaken by the Wings of Science."[31] A year later, a publicist for NAME made a similar point: "More development would result from the use of airplanes by experienced men in the next five years than had been accomplished in the last fifty years." James Montagnes, in one of his many pro-flying articles, predicted that "the airplane will bring the development of this country one hundred years ahead of where it would be if the airplane was not yet invented.... Within the next five years the mining development will nearly equal that of the last half century."[32]

, , ,

The numbers seem to have stuck, and it became a commonplace to state that the airplane had the power to accelerate tenfold the development of the mining industry. But the majority of Canadians conceived of the airplane's economic impact in much broader terms. Ignoring the statistics on air freight or troy ounces or board feet, they devoured stories of bush pilots traversing the northland, taming Canada's wilderness and turning it to good advantage. In 1957, John Diefenbaker would inspire Canadians with his vision of northern development, which would see the region populated by millions to become the economic engine of the continent. Perhaps as a young lawyer in western Canada, where WCA's propaganda was most pervasive, he had absorbed the rhetoric of the air lobby because, in the 1920s and 1930s, the vision of a vibrant and prosperous North emerged as the centrepiece of air-mindedness in Canada.

Aviation pioneers had been giving serious thought to conquering the North by air since the nineteenth century, but the First World War brought technological improvements that put the dream within reach. In 1915, Charles Camsell, the son of a Hudson's Bay Company factor in the Mackenzie district and later deputy minister of the Department of Mines and Resources and ex officio commissioner of the Northwest Territories, wondered if the federal government should acquire a number of flying boats for subarctic exploration. Two years later, the great Arctic explorer Vilhjalmur Stefansson urged Prime Minister Robert Borden to commission official studies on the possibility of establishing trans-polar air routes. In 1919, Alfred Thompson, the MP for Yukon, presented the House of Commons with an ambitious proposal for air services in the North, including aerial photography and sur-veys, ice and weather patrols flown over the Hudson Strait, and an airship service linking Edmonton, the Arctic Ocean, Dawson and Whitehorse. It had taken the prospectors of '98 eighteen months to travel from Edmonton to Dawson, Thompson informed the House; an airship could make the trip in eighteen hours.[33]

As it happened, the northward drive of aviation occurred much more incrementally than Thompson might have wished. The first flight into the North came in March 1921, when two Junkers monoplanes owned by Imperial Oil flew from Edmonton bound for Fort Norman in the Northwest Territories to assist in the development of the oil field there. (The flight is best known for its now-legendary bit of improvisation: a Fort Simpson car-penter and an Imperial Oil mechanic handcrafted a replacement propeller out of oak sleigh boards and moosehide glue.) Other pioneering flights, some unheralded, some highly publicized, soon followed. In 1925, an American expedition led by D. B. MacMillan made the first flights into the Arctic islands; one of the pilots was Richard Byrd, who would be the first person to fly to the North Pole, in 1926. No less significant was the first freight operation into the North: two aircraft from Western Canada Airways carried nearly eight tons of supplies, including drills, motors and eight hundred pounds of dynamite, to Churchill, Manitoba, for the construction of the rail line to Hudson Bay. The following winter, an RCAF detachment carried out aerial recon-naissance and photography over the Hudson Strait to determine how long the bay might be accessible to shipping in a season. In September 1929 came one of the great dramas of northern avia-tion, when two aircraft from Dominion Explorers force-landed on the south coast of Queen Maud Gulf. For the next six weeks, dozens of aircraft flew nearly thirty thousand miles searching for the missing prospectors, until they trudged into Cambridge Bay. The following year came what *The Beaver* magazine described as "the zenith of achievement in northern aviation" when Walter Gilbert flew Maj. L. T. Burwash of the Department of the Interior on a survey of King William Island and the north magnetic pole, a region that "gave one the impression of being the last created portion of the world, which, through a shortage of time or material, had necessarily been left uncompleted."[34]

These epic flights inspired innumerable press ruminations on the economic potential of the North once the airplane made it accessible. Perhaps not surprisingly, the rhetoric tended to duplicate the language that had characterized Canadian expansionism for centuries and had surrounded the new science of aerial photography; essentially, it was a discourse of imperialism. The northern frontier represented vast untapped potential; uninhabited (the First Nations peoples were irrelevant, except as contrast to the ultramodernity of the airplane), unexplored and uncatalogued, it had to be conquered and forced to yield up its riches. A new generation of aerial pioneers would bring progress to the North, and the region would never be the same.

This line of thinking took for granted that the North was the only remaining frontier in Canada and, perhaps, in North America. For centuries, the "promise of Eden," to use Doug Owram's phrase, had rested in the West; now, in the early twentieth century, it could be found in the North. "Nowhere in the world today lies there a land that offers such a challenge to the adventurous spirit of youth as those vast, gaping frontiers that sprawl across the roof of the North American continent," wrote a journalist in *The Beaver*. "No swifter moving, more dramatic quest has ever swayed the steps of visionary men than the epic empire building drama set in motion by the lure of untold wealth hidden in...North America's last great frontier." This land of "heretofore inaccessible riches" had long existed behind a "veil of ignorance." But now, the airplane could push back that veil.[35] "The coming of the aeroplane was civilization's last step in breaking down the age-long barriers of the North," wrote Philip Godsell, who had travelled across the North, mostly by canoe, scow and dogsled, as an employee of the Hudson's Bay Company. Aviation would set in train "a romance of progress," gushed the admittedly biased editor of *Canadian Aviation*.[36]

The meaning of progress was clearest in the contrast between the new North and the old. Visual images, from photographs to advertisements to airmail franks, frequently juxtaposed aircraft with older modes of transportation, such as dogsleds, or with native people. The latter were invariably portrayed as being initially terrified by the arrival of the Thunderbirds but eventually embracing the technological wonders brought by the white man. One of the great gifts brought to the Innu by the airplane was the miracle of catalogue shopping, wrote Godsell condescendingly. "Eskimos and Indians around the Hudson Bay in a few weeks will be gazing up into the sky at the coming of the real vanguard of the white man," predicted the Toronto *Daily Star*. "Humming over the bay this summer will be the greatest concentration of airplanes ever used in exploratory work in Canada." With this friendly invasion, the North was to be transformed forever, in a process that some people viewed with ambivalence. "The aeroplane has taken much of the romance from the Northland and its colourful people," observed a contributor to the *CAL Bulletin*; another aviation writer wondered if the coming of the airplane would destroy the humanities of the region. But for air lobbyists like Richard Finnie, an official with the Department of the Interior, the sacrifices were worthwhile. "It has been said that the airplane robbed the North of its romance," he wrote. "Certainly the airplane robbed the North of much of its terror and chill inaccessibility. But at the same time the airplane introduced a romance of its own—the romance of modern pioneering."[37]

That romance would soon give way to routine, as Finnie realized: "Annihilating distances, sweeping over immeasurably vast forests and barrens, in fair weather and foul, in summer and in winter, the aeroplanes of the Canadian north keep on schedule and perform miracles of modern pioneering with such frequency that they seldom make the front pages of the newspapers any more." In 1938, the legendary bush aviator Wop May told a CBC reporter that people in the North regarded the pilot "as a sort of fairy godfather"; but soon, he would be just a commonplace figure in the region.[38] As Finnie observed when recalling the winter of 1930–31, which he spent in Coronation Gulf on the Arctic coast, "I saw the beginnings of a new, accelerated tempo in the whole life of the country. . . . The isolation of that and many another Arctic district was conquered that year. . . . It was the dawn of a new era, when water, ice, and air would each be utilized to push back the last Canadian frontier." The settlements of the North would become hives of activity, more like the urban centres of the south. As a mining journal put it, "The remotest corners of continental Canada have been brought within easy reach of civilization." Dawson City, once weeks of back-breaking travel from Edmonton, was now a mere ten-hour flight away. "With the coming of the airplane," wrote one journalist, "the trail of '98 fades into the background of memory, and a younger Yukon looks forward with confidence to the development of new sources of wealth in that once fabulous land."[39] Keewatin and the northeastern Mackenzie would be transformed, thanks to the airplane, "the instrument which has brought this vast new empire within the economic orbit of Canada." Port Radium, Northwest Territories, which began life as a ragtag collection of tents, became a thriving resource town with electricity, running water, airmail service and radio stations, all thanks to the airplane. Fort McMurray would be the "air base for the vast empire of the north."[40] In 1957, John Diefenbaker spoke passionately about his Roads to Resources policy that would use highway development to create bustling urban centres in the North. Twenty years earlier, it was aerial highways that were to make a metropolis of places like Fort McMurray and Port Radium.

, , ,

But the economic impact of aviation carried with it another, more profound transformation. After predicting the metamorphosis of Fort McMurray, Lawrence Burpee in *Canadian Geographical Journal* pondered the deeper import of the process: "Man-power—steam—air. Transportation of a thousand years—of yesterday—of to-day. The first took a season to get from one trading post to another in the far north; the second, by rail and steamer, needs a fortnight; the last, from daybreak to dark."[41] Here, Burpee expressed what many people knew to be the real impact of aviation: it was changing the very nature of time and space.

Again, there is striking consistency in the rhetoric. In the past, "one estimated distance in miles. So many miles from here to there, and the time factor depended on the way luck favoured a variety of travel circumstances."[42] Measurement was static and unchanging; cities would always be the same number of miles apart. But this lack of dynamism hardly suited the modern age. The new measure of distance, more in keeping with the ethos of the twentieth century, was time: "minutes, not miles, [became] the standard of distance in a world that is shrinking rapidly." This practice could provide ongoing affirmation of the march of progress; improvements in technology meant that travel times would be reduced, and distances would shrink. In 1934, W. W. Kennedy, the MP for Winnipeg South Centre, told the House of Commons that "we should now think of Canada as not 3500 miles wide but as eighteen to twenty-four hours in width."[43] In a country so challenged by geography, this way of thinking could embody humanity's triumph over the land. In taking command of the skies, humans would shrink the earth.

The use of temporal rather than linear measurements to express distance also evidenced the centrality of speed to the modern era. In 1919, the Halifax *Herald* printed a graphic showing that in one hour, the average person on foot could cover four miles and the airplane a hundred miles. "As our forefathers crossed the Atlantic following the explorations of a fearless few to take possession of the wilderness lands, so the wing-trail-blazing pioneers of today are simply crowding into days and hours the perils which those brave men endured over months and years." It was the dawning of "an age in which the world's motto is 'Speed,'" read a letter on the occasion of the first airmail flight between Prince Edward Island and the mainland in 1919, "and the modern man requires modern methods."[44]

Because of the perceived connection between speed and success, advertisers constantly drew links between aviation and the prosperous businessman. "Travel by air should be the slogan of the busy business man," announced Winnipeg's *Mining and Industrial News* in 1927. "Time is Money," proclaimed another advertisement, directed at people wanting to share the wealth of the Red Lake gold rush. "Let the famous 'Lark' carry you to Red Lake with comfort, speed and safety." "In a hurry—why not fly?" asked an advertisement for Arrow Airways. An ad for aviation paint contrasted the plodding pace of the nineteenth century and the speed of the twentieth: "How a Forty-Niner would have gasped at the sight of a Duco-Finished Plane.... Gone are the sour-dough, and the desert canary!—today prospectors dash to the newest gold rush, at Red Lake, Ontario, in a Wright-motored Curtiss 'Lark.'"[45] We tend to think of our twenty-first-century obsession with speed—high-speed Internet connections, just-in-time delivery, instantaneous access to information—as a recent affliction, but clearly it has a long history.

In all this rhetoric, whether from airline publicists, editors or advertising agencies, we see a new face of imperialism. Space had always been the object of imperial expansion, but now it had been supplanted by time. By enabling people to leap over territory once all but impassable, the airplane "has virtually eliminated space," declared Samuel Morgan-Powell in 1928. "Each second devastates distances scarcely to be apprehended by human intelligence," observed an editorial in the northern Ontario Patricia *Herald*. But time could also be conquered by the airplane just as distance had been. A single recurring phrase expresses the faith that technology could bring time to heel. "This was an age of air," proclaimed one enthusiastic politician in 1931, that would witness "the annihilation of time."[46]

· 6 ·

WINGS FOR THE NATION

WERE IT NOT FOR THE DRIVING RAIN, THE CROWDS MIGHT WELL have been larger. As it was, only a small knot of people clustered at Brighouse Park racetrack, near Richmond, British Columbia, on the morning of October 17, 1920, waiting to see history being made. Ten days earlier, in Halifax, Basil Hobbs and Robert Leckie, both decorated aviators from the First World War, had climbed into a Fairey seaplane (the very aircraft that had been prepared to make the transatlantic hop in 1919) on the initial leg of the first airmail flight across Canada. Three aircraft and four crew changes later, pilot George Thompson and his passenger Arthur Tylee, commander of the Canadian Air Force, were approaching Vancouver after a refuelling stop at Agassiz, in the Fraser Valley.

Shortly before noon, their two-seater de Havilland appeared out of the clouds over Brighouse Park, and a cheer went up from the spectators. Thompson nimbly circled the field, apparently untroubled by the rain, and deposited the aircraft neatly on the grass.

He and Tylee climbed out to accept the congratulations of the waiting dignitaries and to pass on letters, addressed to the Vancouver mayor, R. H. Gale, that they had picked up along the way. One of the letters bore the frank of the Mayor's Office in Halifax, and brought greetings from the Maritimes. The flight, wrote the Halifax mayor, J. S. Parker, "may be the harbinger of a service by the air from one coast of Canada to the other, which will bind yet more closely together the cities of the Dominion, and in comparison with which the railway will seem as slow and antiquated as the mail coach now seems in comparison with the railway."[1]

As Parker fully appreciated, the benefits of aviation were not strictly economic. If the devastation of distance and the annihilation of time could make business more profitable, they could also improve the social and political life of the Dominion. No more would the West Coast be divided from the Maritimes by a week's travel; no more would mail and newspapers take days to pass between the major cities of the Dominion. With the airplane, mere hours separated the regions. By the 1930s, the trip from Montreal to Vancouver involved more than a hundred hours on the train, but just a third of that in the air. Even the governor general, the Duke of Devonshire, was taken by the possibilities, foreseeing a time when a person could breakfast in Montreal, have supper in Winnipeg and arrive in Vancouver the following morning. The day was not far off, predicted one aviation booster in 1932, when people could travel from Toronto to Winnipeg, or even British Columbia, "in the light of one day."[2] The airplane had the potential to complete the work of Confederation by transforming a nation of scattered provinces into a single community. The transcontinental airmail service, the construction of a chain of airfields from sea to sea, the establishment of a national airline—all these would help draw together the regions into the close-knit society that the nation's founders had long envisioned. Through the miracle of flight, Canada would realize its destiny.

, , ,

Such dreams were in the air even before flying came to Canada. In his 1883 futurist epic *The Dominion in 1983*, Ralph Centennius foretold the day when rocket-powered flying machines united the regions. He admitted that in his own time, differences in sentiment were inevitable when people three thousand miles apart were ruled by one government, but flight would change all that: fractiousness would be "replaced by a powerful unanimity that renders possible great social movements." Forty years later, the discourse had not changed dramatically. As Donald MacLaren put it in 1926, an integrated air transport system was essential to overcome the challenges of geography. Without such a system, Canada would remain "a country of tribes suspicious of each other, seldom venturing beyond their own preserves and a Nation would not be possible."[3]

But the realization of these dreams had thus far been blocked by the demands of commerce. As the Air Board reported in 1925, the regularly scheduled mail and passenger services that might unite the regions required a significant capital outlay and were unlikely to show a return for years; flying that could have immediate economic impact, in the forestry and mining sectors, took precedence. "Straight transportation work has been subsidiary" to timber-cruising and prospecting flights, admitted the Board, "and has been undertaken only when other modern facilities were lacking."[4] Faced with such inexorable logic, the air lobby had no choice but to use the dismal science of economics; the prosaic goal of finding a faster and more efficient means of moving the mails could be a first step to realizing this twentieth-century national dream.

In the major cities, the mail service was excellent, certainly better than it is today; the legend that it was possible to write a letter, receive a reply and send a response all in a single day is probably not too far from the truth. But between major cities or in rural areas, everything moved at the speed of the trains. When the train was delayed by weather or mechanical problems, or if there was no scheduled service that day, the mails did not arrive. Prince Edward Island was in a slightly different situation; mail deliveries from off the island were dependent on the weather in the Straits of

Northumberland, and the Charlottetown postmaster could recall a number of occasions when the province was cut off from the mainland for days at a time.[5] But such delays were minor compared with the obstacles to postal services outside the more settled parts of the country. Getting mail from Quebec City to the towns on the north shore of the St. Lawrence in winter can serve as an example. The train ran from Quebec to Murray Bay; from there the mail bags were transferred to horse cart for the trip to Betsiamites and to canoe for the next leg of the journey, to Pointe-des-Monts; from there, dogsleds carried mail to the various settlements. The entire process could take up to a month.[6]

But aviation would change all that. Equipped with either floats or skis, depending on the season, airplanes could bring remote settlements to within a few hours of the major cities. Regular mail delivery by air, predicted Claire MacLaurin in January 1919, "would bring settlements closer in touch with civilization and dampen the sense of isolation."[7] Airmail service would even encourage the spread of settlement, he thought, for homesteaders would be more likely to settle in remote locations if they knew they could stay in contact with the outside world.

South of the border, American aviation companies had already proved that airmail services were viable. The United States Postal Service began experimenting with airmail in 1917, and the following year instituted a service linking New York and San Francisco via Philadelphia, Washington, D.C., Cleveland, Chicago, Omaha and St. Louis. Its successful delivery rate of over 90 percent inspired Alexander Graham Bell, Lord Montagu, O. M. Biggar and others to recommend a similar experiment for Canada, but the Post Office Department would only give permission for the Aero Club of Canada to mount a number of experimental airmail flights between Toronto and Ottawa, using its own resources—and its own stamps.[8]

However, the Air Board was aware that it was only a matter of time before it received inquiries from companies interested in operating airmail routes, and at its second meeting it decided to draft specifications for a service linking Montreal, Toronto and Winnipeg, should one of the many new flying companies ask for information. Within months, the expected inquiries started coming in. One firm asked for the contract to fly the mails between Victoria and Vancouver, another between Prince Edward Island and the mainland. In November 1919, an Ontario business lobby group adopted a resolution that "every possible encouragement by subsidy or otherwise be given to Aviation for commercial and postal purposes by the Governments of Ontario and of the Dominion."[9]

The Post Office Department refused to be persuaded that airmail was anything more than a luxury. In a series of memos in the spring of 1920, Robert Leckie, the director of flying operations, suggested an experimental service between Moncton and Charlottetown, but Postmaster-General R. M. Coulter replied that "he had never known of Prince Edward Island to be in any hurry for mail." When a service between Winnipeg Beach and Rice Lake, in eastern Manitoba, was mentioned, Coulter observed that only the mining companies were interested, and if they were that keen, they should foot the bill. Leckie was forced to conclude that "the Post Office is extremely unwilling to even experiment in the direction of aerial mails and is rather skeptical of the entire project." Not only were postal officials put off by the potential costs and the projected 8.5 percent loss rate (which they regarded as unacceptably high), but they also made the point, not without foundation, that most of the interest had been shown not by the general public clamouring for speedier mail delivery but by aviation interests looking for employment.[10]

So it was left to the Air Board and the Canadian Air Force to organize and execute the October 1920 Halifax-Vancouver flight, if only to demonstrate that the Post Office Department had been myopic in its attitude. As Leckie said after the flight's successful conclusion, it had been "a demonstration of the feasibility of using the air route for the carriage of mails across Canada. The flying time will show that the trip can be made much more rapidly by air than any other way and succeeding trials will be even more successful."[11] Press coverage of the flight, however, was virtually non-existent, nor was the Post Office Department particularly impressed. It would give official sanction to airmail runs by private companies and permit the use of airmail stamps or stickers but declined either to initiate its own services or bear the costs or responsibility for the privately run services.

Not until 1927 did the Post Office change its policy, when it let a contract for an airmail service to pick up the mail from transatlantic liners off Rimouski and fly it on to Montreal at, it was hoped, a considerable saving in time. However, the first attempt, on September 9, 1927, was not a happy experience. The flying boat assigned to the run was damaged by heavy swells at Rimouski and crashed during takeoff. The five hundred pounds of mail from the liner *Empress of France*, which were supposed to reach Montreal a day before the ship docked, were salvaged from the wrecked airplane but not delivered until well after the *Empress* had reached Montreal. However, nine successful flights were made before the middle of November, both to incoming and outgoing liners, and in some cases the service shaved ninety-six hours from the delivery times of mail between Britain and Canadian cities. The Post Office was pleased enough with the results that in 1928 it tendered the contract again, eventually awarding it to Canadian Transcontinental Airways.

The Rimouski run was clearly oriented toward business and official correspondence, but three other contracts awarded in 1927 focused directly on reducing the isolation of certain settlements. They linked Leamington, Ontario, with Pelee Island, in Lake Erie, the southernmost settlement in Canada; Murray Bay, Seven Islands and Anticosti Island, in the Gulf of St. Lawrence; and Moncton and the Magdalen Islands. A fourth, connecting Rolling Portage with the Red Lake area, in northern Ontario, was intended to serve the booming gold fields. There is no denying the significance of these routes (and of other contracts let in subsequent years to service far-flung settlements) for the individuals involved. The Post Office admitted that the services had a strong humanitarian element, while a woman in Fort St. John, in northern British Columbia, wrote feelingly to the Air Board to request an airmail service for her community: "It would bring us into touch with the outside world; we are so isolated here after navigation closes." A not entirely objective article in the WCA newsletter agreed that the potential of the airplane for ending such isolation was significant: "The speed of the aeroplane has instilled into the minds of those who dwell in the northern posts a spirit of confidence and relief. The feeling of isolation and helplessness... has been dispelled by this latest method of transportation which reduces weeks to hours and thus transforms outposts into suburbs."[12] Aklavik was once a "place as distant as Teheran or Timbuctoo... [for] the lonely men who pioneered there," wrote one editor. Relatively accessible in the summer months, it was all but cut off in the winter, the only connection to the south being the one or two winter mail packets that made the 3,300-mile round trip from Fort McMurray by dogsled. But the airplane had changed all that. During the winter of 1929–30, WCA's weekly airmail service brought twenty-three winter mail packets; Aklavik was now in regular contact with the south. "Much in the same manner as British Columbia was more firmly united with other Canadian provinces through the establishment in 1886 of a transcontinental railway service," wrote J. Fergus Grant, "the Yukon need no longer be considered an outpost of Empire," for the airplane was ending the isolation of communities such as Dawson, Mayo and Stewart River. "No longer will the rest of Canada be 'outside' to them," he proclaimed.[13]

But regardless of its significance for local residents, airmail service to Aklavik or the Magdalen Islands was not terribly important to southern Canadians. It was the gradual creation of a coast-to-coast airmail service that really caught their imagination. The reluctance of the Post Office had not quelled the enthusiasm of the air lobby, and aviation companies continued to expand their airmail routes, using the small revenue generated by the sale

of airmail stickers to fund their operations. But this was no substitute for the system of subsidized airmail routes that had been
operating in the United States and Britain for years. Finally in
1928, after considerable lobbying, the Post Office agreed to
expand airmail services between urban centres. Canadian Airways
Limited* received the contract to operate the Montreal-Toronto
route (later extended to Detroit, to link up with the U.S. airmail
service), and the following year a Toronto-Buffalo run was added.
The Post Office also experimented with a number of other routes
in 1929—Moncton to Quebec; Montreal to Moncton via Saint
John; Montreal to Ottawa; Moncton to Charlottetown (replacing
a Saturday-only service instituted in the winter of 1927–28); and
Montreal to Halifax—with enough success that all services, except
the last, were maintained. There were further extensions in March
1930, when Western Canada Airways won the contracts for
Winnipeg-Regina-Calgary and Regina-Edmonton services; a
route to Lethbridge was added the following year. There was now
airmail service between Charlottetown and Edmonton.

Although the onset of the Depression pushed many companies
to the brink of collapse, there was still hope that the airmail project would enable them to weather the storm. But in January 1931
the Montreal-Quebec run, never particularly well used, was cancelled, and in March 1931 the Winnipeg *Free Press* revealed that
the new Conservative government of R. B. Bennett was contem-
plating deeper cuts to the airmail network. Bennett would tell the
House of Commons that "because of the crop failure in western
Canada, and with 300,000 of a population receiving some form of
relief, there was very little gratification in seeing an aeroplane passing day by day, when the unfortunate owner of the soil could
hardly see the aeroplane because his crop had gone up in dust." As
another cabinet minister told Fergus Grant, "with the farmers fac-

---

* Canadian Airways Limited, based in Montreal, was acquired by the parent
company of Western Canada Airways in 1930, with the new entity adopting
the name Canadian Airways Limited.

ing another bad season in the West, we cannot continue to flaunt aviation in their faces."[14] Frantic lobbying by airlines, their political allies, air-minded newspapers and pilots saved part of the system, but only at considerable cost: the suspension of the Montreal-Toronto section, the reduction of the prairie service from seven days a week to six, the replacement of the two prairies sections with a single Winnipeg-Edmonton run, and the elimination of the Toronto-Buffalo and Moncton-Montreal routes. Even this small victory was soon snatched away. In February 1932, the government announced the first of many cancellations that would ultimately see the Canadian airmail system reduced to a handful of scattered intercity routes and some services to isolated communities and resource areas. The main intercity routes would not be reinstated until later in the decade.

The cancellation of the airmail contracts provoked a storm of anger, particularly in western Canada, where the Winnipeg *Free Press* rapidly emerged as the stoutest defender of airmail and, not incidentally, the main airmail carrier, CAL. "By no other means could we so completely advertise ourselves to the world as a backward nation, without vision, courage or resources, as to announce that we are unable any longer to maintain the air mail," declared the paper in June 1931. The decision "may cost us every year many times the amount we shall save by our planned display of short-sighted national stinginess." The following week, it again hammered the Bennett government: "While every other country is paying more attention to aviation, would Canada be satisfied to go back to the rear of the procession?...If Canada, due to her youth and her resources, is to recover from the depression more quickly than any other country, she should not have such fits of pessimism as that which would wipe out the air mail service and place Canada among the most backward countries of the world."[15] The *Free Press* cartoonist Arch Dale had a field day with the cancellations, delighting readers with such images as an airmail plane crashing into a mountainous head of Bennett.

There was more to these criticisms than simple economics.

Newspapers, airline executives and politicians were concerned not only about job losses, but also about the fact that the airmail system had been more than just a way to move letters. Aside from one disgruntled MP who believed that "the air mail service is for the accommodation of the jazz element of the country who turn night into day" and L. M. Montgomery's observation that airmail would be wonderful "if the letters were any the sweeter or more vital thereby," most of the commentary generated by the expansion of the airmail system had a single theme: its ability to strengthen the ties that bound the provinces of Canada. Claire MacLaurin had predicted in 1919 that regular air services would do more than simply improve East-West communications; they "would tend to closer confederation of the provinces."[16] A decade later, this had become conventional wisdom in every region. The *Globe* thought the opening of the Toronto-Montreal run marked "a new era in Central Canadian transportation...the two leading Canadian cities put on terms of greater intimacy....Thus are the distances of this vast country cut down through the invention and initiative of man." Postmaster-General P. J. Veniot agreed, calling the service "another link in the bonne entente without which there can be no hope of actual, sound, reliable prosperity or progress with the people of the Dominion." The opening of the western airmail service occasioned similar sentiments. The Winnipeg *Free Press* observed that "the linking up of eight cities in a closer bond of union became an established fact" with the inauguration of the service. It marked "a new epoch in communication...the various parts of the expansive prairie country are being drawn closer together, and there will be an immediate and stimulating effect upon both business and social life."[17]

When the first Ottawa–Saint John airmail reached New Brunswick on January 28, 1929, it carried the greetings of Mackenzie King. The flight, announced the prime minister effusively, would "bring the Capital of the Dominion into closer relations with the great sea ports of Saint John and Halifax...[and] afford a further bond of union between the nine provinces of the

Dominion." For his part, Veniot promised that the airmail would "in a large measure cause to disappear the so-called isolation of the provinces by the Atlantic seaboard." The *Telegraph-Journal* promised to hold Veniot to his pledge that "no stones should be left unturned in placing the Maritime Provinces on an equal footing with the rest of Canada," and described the scene as the prime minister's message was handed to the mayor of Saint John and the premier of New Brunswick: "A deep impressive silence fell over the gathering, lasting for minutes, as men in silent thought pictured a vision of the Maritime provinces, flung far out into the Atlantic, being clasped closer to the industrial centre of Canada, in stronger unity with the industrial life of the Dominion, another vital step in the advancement of Maritime prosperity."[18]

Prince Edward Island was perhaps even more deeply affected by this rhetoric. As we have seen, the possibility of the flying machine fulfilling one of the terms of Confederation by providing year-round communication with the mainland had been bruited about for years, but came closer to reality on September 24, 1919, when Capt. Laurie Stevens and Lieut. Logan Barnhill made the first flight between Prince Edward Island and the mainland. Carrying a bundle of letters addressed to dignitaries and friends, Stevens and Barnhill flew a Canuck from Charlottetown to Truro, Nova Scotia. "I trust that this is the beginning of an interprovincial aerial traffic which will be far reaching in its advantages to the provinces by sea," wrote the mayor of Charlottetown to his opposite number in Truro. "This mode of communication brings us to realize as never before the nearness of our sister provinces." As the Charlottetown *Guardian* mused, "a new page in the history of PEI was written yesterday when for the first time the island was connected with the mainland by navigation via the clouds."[19]

For the next decade, a regularly scheduled air service, either for mail or passengers, became something of a cause célèbre for Islanders. Devere Aviation, the firm operated by Stevens and Barnhill, was quick to capitalize on the favourable publicity generated by their flight to suggest a regular service between Truro and Charlottetown, but the proposal never got beyond the talking stage. In March 1921, a delegation of Islanders resolved to petition the federal government for a flying service to the mainland, and the following January H. W. Wiltshire, representing Canadian Aerial Services, announced that he would request a federal subsidy to operate an airmail service between Charlottetown, Summerside and Moncton. Wiltshire and others with similar plans were regular visitors to PEI in subsequent years, and the Island's boards of trade occasionally forwarded petitions to Ottawa, emphasizing the difficulty in maintaining communications during the winter. "For a time saving mail and passenger service, no part of Canada would seem to have better claim upon the advantages which aircraft offer," said R. H. Cotton at a Board of Trade meeting in Charlottetown in January 1929.[20] Cotton may well have been right, for despite the Post Office's dismissive conclusion that Islanders were in no hurry for their mail, the Moncton-Charlottetown airmail service quickly became one of the most heavily used in the country.

These debates were only partly concerned with the quantities of letters and parcels that might be shipped by air; more fundamentally, they were about the twentieth century's national dream. In all these commentaries, we see broad acceptance of the argument that the Air Board had tried to make in 1919: the airmail service was more than just a business opportunity of benefit only to those who could afford it. It was a national project, identical in spirit and import to the construction of the transcontinental railway. As one editorial put it, "A transcontinental air mail is an all-Canadian project; the whole country is interested; the whole country will benefit."[21]

, , ,

There was a closer analogy to the transcontinental railway that was already under way: the trans-Canada airway, a chain of airfields stretching from coast to coast, the groundwork for a convenient, safe, modern system of air transport. The roots of the project lay with the Air Board, which in 1920 pledged to publish an air travel directory covering every civil and military air route and landing field. "There will be one vast highway across the Dominion," promised the Board. But instead of one highway, what evolved through the 1920s were disconnected routes that sprang up as enterprising aviation companies established local services based on municipal airports, private landing fields and bodies of water. There was no aerial highway spanning the country: some major cities were without municipal airports, and large stretches of terri-tory lacked even emergency landing fields. Indeed, a lack of ground facilities, as much as the intransigence of the Post Office, frequently stood in the way of extending airmail services. In 1919, the Air Board had advised cities, towns and even villages to equip themselves with landing facilities. "An urban municipality without an aerodrome," the Board warned, "will not be on the air map."[22]

By the late 1920s, the perceived consequences of being "off the air map" were becoming embarrassing. In Vancouver, the *Sun* warned that "if Vancouver is to keep pace with progressive cities to the south," the city must construct a proper airport. "Just as towns and cities held out inducements to railways twenty years ago, they must begin to hold out inducements to commercial flying today. No town in western Canada is too small to be fully equipped for the landing of airplanes and no town could make a better invest-ment than in such equipment." The following year, municipal boosters in Edmonton and Regina jockeyed to give their cities a head start in the airport race. One Alberta paper reminded read-ers that Edmonton was the first city in Canada to set aside land for a municipal airport, and that voters should endorse a bylaw that would provide money to get it into shape: "This is a chance to show the rest of the Dominion that Alberta's capital is awake to the rapid development now taking place." People in Saskatchewan's capital warned that unless the city began making concrete plans, "Regina will be passed up in the laying out of air routes and will stand to lose out in the competition which will inevitably develop in this rapidly expanding field of transportation."[23] In Winnipeg, too, there was a certain amount of desperation. When Northern Aerial Minerals Exploration moved its base from Winnipeg to Sioux Lookout because the Manitoba capital lacked a large enough airport, the *Tribune* urged the municipal authorities to address the issue. "Is this another case of short-sighted economy on the part of the City Council, or merely lack of interest and initiative?" it asked. Either way, the city had to construct an airport if it was to avoid being left behind. In Toronto, local businessmen and the city's Board of Trade warned municipal officials that an airfield would soon be as essential to a city's economic life as the railway or the docks, especially as Toronto was "the obvious starting-off point for flights into the North Country." The Board of Trade urged municipal officials to get moving: "the City would be looking to its future interests in providing such a site while it has the opportunity."[24]

Nowhere were these issues more contentious than in Halifax. Aviation had come early to the Nova Scotia capital, when the federal government established a seaplane base at Baker's Point, near Dartmouth, in the summer of 1918. In the absence of trained Canadian crews, American seaplanes of the U.S. Naval Air Service flew patrols from Baker's Point until January 1919, when it became the Dartmouth Air Station. In 1925, the base was closed for more than a year as a stringency measure, and thereafter was operated on a care-and-maintenance basis only. City authorities were aware that a seaplane base was no substitute for a proper airfield and formally requested the federal government to construct such a facility. The Air Board replied that it was up to municipalities to build their own airports, and the matter went no further until 1927, when the Civil Aviation Branch of the Department of National Defence offered technical assistance to cities constructing airport facilities. This time, municipal authorities got moving. In September 1928, a civil aviation inspector recommended a site at Bluebell Farm as the only suitable spot for an airfield, but it was far from ideal and would require substantial public money. The solution was a municipal plebiscite; on April 24, 1929, Haligonians would vote for or against permitting the municipal government to spend $150,000 of public money to develop the site.

An alliance of business leaders, aviation boosters and the city's major newspapers campaigned strongly in favour of the plebiscite, blanketing the city with editorials, mass mailers and shop-window displays. Since the beginning of time, proclaimed the *Evening Mail*, "Progress and Speed have matched strides. And then came the airplane!... It's the spirit of the times! It's modern! Enterprising businessmen and commercial houses are in the swing! Innovations follow one another with breath-taking rapidity—new ideas for bringing to you the latest merchandise, the latest news from all over the world. PROGRESS IS IN THE AIR IN HALIFAX." Halifax had always been a shipping centre; now it had a chance to become a hub of the newest form of transportation: "The world is on the eve of enormous aerial developments. Exploration, industry and wealth will follow in their train for cities that have vision." Fearing that logic might not be compelling enough, the pro-airport lobby also mobilized emotion, playing on the historic rivalry between Halifax and Saint John. Municipal authorities in Saint John had pursued the Department of National Defence relentlessly for assistance in building an airport, and by the spring of 1928 had selected a site near Millidgeville. Construction began immediately, and the airport was already in operation when Halifax's plebiscite campaign began. Clearly, civic pride was at stake. "Is Halifax to Play Second Place to Saint John?" read one article. "Saint John is ACTING—Halifax is TALKING," proclaimed another.[25] There was more to the airport than economics or airmail service; bragging rights were on the line.

Opponents of the plan were unimpressed by these arguments. According to the Halifax *Citizen*, a labour newspaper, an airport had nothing to do with civic pride or economics; it was nothing more than a "playground for military idlers." If the federal government was so keen on instituting airmail services, argued the

Citizen, it should pay for airport facilities. Besides, the North Common was a ready-made landing field; it could be used free, especially as the great airships of tomorrow would be able to come and go without large, expensive airports. The former alderman F. W. Bissett agreed that large airports were unnecessary because "in the near future means may be discovered by which airplanes can and will make perpendicular ascent and descent."[26]

But the weight of publicity mustered by the pro-airport lobby easily overwhelmed the dissenters; the plebiscite passed by better than two to one, and proponents waited confidently for the city to begin work. But it soon became clear that the Bluebell Farm site was not large enough for a first-class airport and would require considerably more work to bring it even to minimum standards. Indeed, engineers estimated that it would cost as much as $50,000 above the plebiscite amount to complete construction, but city council was not empowered to spend the extra money.[27]

As the politicians dithered, airport boosters grew more restive. City council was ignoring the will of the people, they charged, and transforming Halifax into a laughingstock. In Vancouver, rate-payers had approved the expenditure of $300,000 to establish an airport, and their city council got moving; in Halifax, they simply talked. "As the city of Saint John has shown sufficient enterprise to establish an airport adequately equipped for the air mail service, it will enjoy the benefit of being ahead of Halifax. Perhaps Saint John's initiative will spur the local authorities in Halifax into taking similar action."[28] Editors mocked the determination of certain city councillors to block the airport on the grounds that "the HUM of the motors overhead would keep residents of the North End awake" or that "aviation was only for sports and that an airport would only be used for sporting purposes." On the contrary, the Halifax postmaster D. A. King argued, "the lack of a landing place in Halifax places this city out of the service, and HANDICAPS BUSINESS TO AN EXTENT THAT CANNOT WELL BE CALCULATED; there is not only the loss in time of the faster mail communication, but also the widely advertised fact that there is no landing field. This information is not confined to Canada only but goes everywhere there is an air service, and that is practically world wide." Even some neighbouring cities joined the fray. In February 1930, Wolfville made public its "disgust [at] the belated and procrastinating policy of the City of Halifax with respect to the airport facility." In the absence of any initiative from the provincial capital, Wolfville's Chamber of Commerce has decided to "hitch its waggon to the stars" and establish a committee to investigate building an airport of its own.[29]

Finally, in late February 1930, city council voted 12–6 in favour of borrowing an extra $40,000 to build the airport. Construction began in June, and the airport received its operating licence in January 1931. Ironically after all that dithering, the airport had a relatively short lifespan. Since it did not have sufficient land to permit expansion, government officials decided in 1939 against undertaking further development of the Bluebell Farm site. Its licence was cancelled in October 1941, and all operations moved to RCAF Dartmouth, which served as Halifax's main airport until a new facility opened in 1960.

While municipal officials across Canada bickered over airport sites and funding formulae, the federal government was making considerable progress with its own construction efforts. According to the original plans, the trans-Canada airway would comprise nineteen main airports, twenty-four intermediate fields and forty-two emergency fields. Municipal authorities would be responsible for the costs of their facilities, but the federal government would contribute the bulk of the resources for the rest of the system: the intermediate and emergency fields; radio and meteorological services; and half the cost of improving lighting at municipal airports, so long as local authorities could secure the balance of the funding. The surveys began in 1928, with construction commencing the following year. The western section between Winnipeg and Edmonton was completed first, and by 1931 radio beam stations had been installed at Forrest, Manitoba, Regina, Maple Creek, Saskatchewan, Lethbridge and Red Deer. In the meantime, surveys continued through the Rocky Mountains in search of the best route to Vancouver. The Depression and the federal government's need to economize resulted in a suspension of construction work on the airway in the spring of 1932, although survey work in the Rockies and northern Ontario continued. But the Depression also proved to be the airway's salvation, for it provided the federal government with a ready source of cheap labour. Between October 8, 1932, and June 30, 1936, airfield construction in British Columbia, Ontario, Quebec and the Maritime provinces was done by unemployed men put to work under the federal government's relief scheme. When the government discontinued the scheme, the Civil Aviation Branch continued work by letting contracts, accelerating construction in 1937 to hasten completion. By the end of 1938, there were modern airports or intermediate and emergency landing fields, many fully equipped with radio facilities and lighting, at least every hundred miles between Vancouver and Montreal.

The construction of the trans-Canada airway, however, had already led to another pointed question: who would use the route? Airmail contracts had been let piecemeal, the Post Office believing that competition between carriers would keep bids low; as a result Canada had no national carrier analogous to the government-subsidized Imperial Airways in Britain. Many people saw this as a problem, for the spectre of American airlines loomed large. Some regions, observed J. A. Wilson in 1931, were clamouring for local passenger services and pressuring the federal government to act; American companies were already proposing to extend their services into Canada and to fly between Canadian cities. The government had always maintained that intercity services would be reserved for Canadian companies, but Wilson did not see how the government could refuse American and local requests if it was not willing to create a Canadian airline. "Until Canada has such a company [a national airline] which can deal directly with other national air operating companies and foreign Governments," he warned in a 1933 memo, "we shall be at a disadvantage."[30]

But how was that national airline to be created? One option was to use government subsidies to turn a regional carrier into a national one. Canadian Airways Limited seemed the natural choice, at least in the eyes of its very vocal supporters in the press. It was the largest airline in the country, with a presence in every region. It had flown most of the airmail routes, with a 93 percent completion rate, and employed some of Canada's most famous and experienced pilots. Even its supporters had to admit that CAL always seemed on the brink of financial collapse, but they blamed government parsimony in awarding airmail contracts. In their eyes, no company was better suited to become Canada's national carrier.

Unfortunately for Richardson and his allies, many people saw things differently. George Herring, chief superintendent of airmail services, deplored "the slip-shod method of operation which has been so characteristic of this Company" and thought CAL should confine its operations to bush flying. An interdepartmental committee agreed, noting that CAL would be an inappropriate choice for a national airline because its organization for controlling scattered bush operations did not suit transcontinental services.[31] Nor was the ill feeling confined to Ottawa. Roland Groome of the Regina Flying Club told Wilson that the western airmail service "is considered by many to be somewhat of a joke. The frequency with which the mail comes in late, or the next day, as shown by the air mail logs published in our newspapers has created anything but a favourable impression." He maintained that CAL's predecessor, WCA, had a poor record of carrying both passengers with mail, and that "the mail...has been neglected in order to allow Western Canada Airways to carry a few passengers—mainly company men and deadheads—in comfort." J. H. Parkin, Deputy Postmaster-General Peter T. Coolican and Chief of the General Staff Gen. Andrew MacNaughton agreed that airmail and passengers did not mix and that, at least until the service had been up and running for some time, one airline should not be providing both services.[32] The conclusion of these observers, one with which the federal government eventually concurred, was that a new corporation should be founded to serve as Canada's national airline.

The negotiations to create that airline were protracted. Various possibilities, including full government ownership, joint ownership by the CPR and CNR, or the expansion of CAL after hiving off its bush operations into a separate company, were discussed and rejected. Eventually, on March 22, 1937, minister of Transport C. D. Howe presented to the House of Commons the bill that would create Trans-Canada Air Lines. The company's operations would be confined to carrying mail, express packages and passengers on intercity routes; it would not compete with other carriers in bush flying. Perhaps the bill's most controversial clause, at least in the eyes of observers concerned about a repetition of "the railway problem," was that the new entity would be under the control of the Canadian National Railways (the Canadian Pacific Railway had pulled out before the legislation was presented to Parliament, and the CPR's own airline, CAL, had also declined to become involved). The new carrier took over its first route, the Vancouver-Seattle mail run, from CAL on September 1, 1937, using, much to Richardson's chagrin, CAL's brand-new Lockheeds (which he had just bought for the purpose), and on February 1, 1938, began flying between Winnipeg and Vancouver, in order to accelerate the training of ground and flight personnel. The success of those flights convinced the Post Office to begin including mail shipments, again on an experimental basis; this service was regularized on October 1, 1938. On April 1, 1939, TCA began its daily service between Montreal and Vancouver. At last, Canadians could cross the country by air, something that struck observers as highly significant: "When you know that you can board a plane in Montreal at nine o'clock at night and can be in Vancouver—across 2,411 miles of forest, lakes, prairies, foothills and mountains—in time for lunch next day, you realize what a change wings and propellers have wrought in the business and social life of the broad Canadian Dominion."[33]

, , ,

The construction of the trans-Canada airway and the creation of TCA occasioned spirited debate at the time and have continued to do so. Richardson and his airline have had many defenders, the most recent historian of the affair calling CAL's treatment by the federal government a double-cross. But beyond the debates over financing arrangements and management structures, Canadians found a more compelling subject to ponder: the ability of these two innovations to refashion the country.

If the country's huge distances had been an obstacle to economic development, they had also been an obstacle to political and social development. Simply put, the sheer size of Canada had stood in the way of integration. But no more. The air age was transforming a sprawling collection of regions into a tightly knit family of communities. "The essence of the whole matter," observed an article in *Canadian Aviation*, "is that a new map of the Dominion has been made, an air map in which the time factor had replaced distance. We shall think of the west coast as being not so many miles but so many hours away." The airplane could actually bring Canada's coasts closer together. An article with the suggestive title "Solving Canadian Geography" noted: "It's a pretty sound compact little country after all...it remains for the airplane, by taking businessmen as a matter of course from Toronto to Winnipeg (or even British Columbia) in the light of one day, to be the greatest agent in shortening those distances."[34]

In this discourse, the trans-Canada airway was more than just a series of landing fields; TCA was more than just an airline. As the Winnipeg *Free Press* noted, "The scope of the influence of this designed line of communication [the trans-Canada airway] and its studied corporate shape raise its significance high above that of any modern means to convey mail from one part of the country to another." They were both great national undertakings, of the order of Confederation or the transcontinental railway. Indeed, many writers pointed out that with these developments in aviation, the goals of Confederation were finally within reach. Together they constituted, in J. Fergus Grant's view, "another link in the chain of Confederation, which depends on an even closer union between the provinces for its strength... the peoples of all provinces [are] more closely united by the improved methods of inter-communication."[35]

It is hardly surprising, then, that the drawing together of Canada by air, with its connotations of progress and nation building, came to be described in the same romantic terms that characterized the rhetoric of Confederation, the transcontinental railway and western settlement. Frederick Watts, in *Canadian Magazine*, explicitly linked the trans-Canada airway to the great national efforts of the past: "Each trail that has been blazed across the Canadian West has been a trail of romance. The whisper of the voyageur's paddle, the creak of the Red River cart and the clang of the track-layer's sledge have been notes in a great national symphony of progress. It was an unfinished symphony, however, until the present year when the deep tones of the aeroplane motor were added with the completion of the last trail—a trail more blazing than blazed, and more romantic if anything than its predecessors." Another writer described TCA's first Montreal-Vancouver flight in equally rosy hues: "In the moonlight the shining silver wings gave off a radiance that was almost golden and seemed to express the glory of the thing which had come to pass, which was destined to bring such comfort and happiness to Canada, to bind the provinces closer together, and to make its citizens so much more easily known [to] each section intimately."[36] The airplane was making Canada a better place, and what it had done for the nation, it could do for the world.

· 7 ·

THE GREAT
HIGHWAY OF PEACE

IT WAS ONLY FITTING THAT IT SHOULD ARRIVE AT DAWN, AS THE
first streaks of light stretched over the airfield at St. Hubert, near
Montreal. After all, the dirigible R-100 was the precursor of a new
age, when British airships would link the great cities of the empire
and bind them in closer bonds of affection. She had been expected
at the mooring mast in the late afternoon of July 31, 1930, but
bad weather over the St. Lawrence had delayed its arrival, ironically to a more propitious time. "Nature had contrived," noted
one observer, "through the medium of this beautiful dawn, to
inspire a symbolic significance in the coincidence of the dawn of
the new era of transportation with the perfection of birth of a new
day and a new month. It seemed a happy augury for the future."

As many as thirty thousand people had camped out at St.
Hubert, some sleeping in their cars, others on the open ground, to
witness the arrival of a new era early on the first day of August.
When the R-100 was spotted, "indescribable pandemonium broke

loose on the ground. Hundreds of automobile horns honked and thousands of throats roared forth a lusty cheer of welcome."[1] The pandemonium persisted until the airship left Canada on August 13, after a circular flight over Quebec and Ontario. Some 800,000 spectators poured into St. Hubert to catch a glimpse of the leviathan (minor scuffles would break out when crewmen dropped some damaged pieces of the airship's canvas cover to the ground—everyone wanted a little piece of history), and as many as 1.5 million more saw it fly overhead on its goodwill flight. "A worthy successor to the stout ships of British oak which ruled the seas," she cruised over Parliament Hill "like a galleon of the air, some fairy boat of the Arabian nights" while the Peace Tower carillon played "Rule, Britannia" and "O Canada." When it was first sighted over Toronto before dawn, people dashed into the streets in their pyjamas to catch a glimpse of the airship, "impersonal, unreal, wraithlike as a dream yet strangely vivid."[2]

The Canadian visit of the R-100, the pinnacle of British airship design, was a seminal event in inter-war aviation, for it symbolized the potential of aviation to draw together not just the British Empire but the world. Everything that the flying machine could do for Canada—reducing regional isolation and creating stronger bonds of affection among the provinces—it could also do for the world. At the time of the R-100's visit, the rigid airship seemed to be the best hope for realizing that new age of amity. But those hopes would ultimately be reduced to ashes, passing the mantle to the airplane. By the mid-1930s, transatlantic flights in heavier-than-air flying machines were now a reasonable undertaking, and the airplane became the most tangible symbol of the ideology of peaceful co-operation. Despite the demonstration of air power's destructive capacity in the First World War and the predictions of futurists before 1914, aviation increasingly came to be seen as the progenitor of good. The air age, in the minds of many people, would be an age of peace.

, , ,

For many observers, the transatlantic flight of Alcock and Brown, remarkable though it was, highlighted the limitations of the technology. The intrepid pair had made it across, but it had been a near thing, and the setbacks that attended the other attempts in the summer of 1919 merely suggested that Alcock and Brown had succeeded mainly by luck. So, two decades before the establishment of Trans-Canada Air Lines and a decade before the trans-Canada airway was conceived as a way to facilitate airplane travel, many people set their sights on airships. Ignoring all the weaknesses that dirigibles demonstrated during the war—their relative fragility, difficulties with navigation, the instability of the hydrogen, problems of control and steering—they focused instead on their range and weight-carrying capacity, factors that made the airship, they believed, the vehicle of the future for long-distance transport.

Indeed, the Zeppelin company had planned to fly one of its airships across the Atlantic to the United States immediately after the war, but the Inter-Allied Armistice Commission squelched the idea, ordering that all German airships be turned over to the Allied governments. A number of British firms, including Cunard, Armstrong Whitworth and Beardmore, had already proposed a transatlantic airship service to the British government, subject to some demonstration of the airship's potential. In January 1919, Claire MacLaurin averred that the airship would soon be the vehicle of choice for transatlantic passenger services. Norman Yarrow, speaking in Victoria in 1921, agreed, arguing that the dirigible's range, safety and weight-carrying capacity made it a better option for long-distance flights than the airplane. The Ottawa *Citizen* was intrigued by the fact that Britain's airships, conceived as a means to destroy the enemy, might become the agent for rebuilding British commercial power and rejuvenating imperial communications.[3] Even Alexander Graham Bell, always skeptical about lighter-than-air flight, was susceptible to the lure of the airship. In March 1919, he told the Canadian Club of Saint John that airships would come into their own in peacetime because of their carrying capacity. Saint John would one day have airship masts in its harbour, he predicted, where people would board helium-filled dirigibles and be in Boston in a few hours. They were, he believed, models of efficiency. The engines would provide heating for passenger compartments and give the helium extra lift; hangars would be unnecessary because the airship, once moored to a mast, could weather any storm.[4]

By the time of Bell's talk, the British were already gearing up their post-war airship program. It had begun in 1908, but ended rather ignominiously in 1911 with H. M. Rigid Airship No. 1 (christened, somewhat unfortunately, the *Mayfly*) breaking its back near its shed at Barrow, in the north of England. But the apparent success of the German airship fleet sent the British government back to the drawing board, and in 1916 the program was restarted. The Germans provided more than just motivation, however; most of the design features of British dirigibles were taken from German airships, from photographs, plans smuggled out by spies or examinations of downed Zeppelins. Indeed, of the fourteen British rigid airships built between 1916 and 1921, only one, the R-80, was an original design. The most famous of the early British airships, the R-34, built for the Admiralty by Beardmore, was a copy of the German L-33, which had been forced down, largely undamaged, near Colchester in 1916. After much negotiating the Admiralty agreed to lend it to the Air Ministry for a transatlantic flight to New York. It would be publicized as a research flight to study weather conditions over the north Atlantic, and as a demonstration of the capabilities of the rigid airship for long-distance travel. A third goal was to forge a new "link of the air" between the United States and England.

Construction of the R-34 was completed in December of 1918, and the following March, it was ready for its maiden flight. The commander was Maj. G. H. Scott, one of the most experienced airshipmen in the world. Tough-minded, resolute and calm, Herbert Scott nevertheless seemed an indifferent pilot. Despite his experience, some wondered at his apparent inability to master the delicate touch required to pilot a big dirigible. In 1915, while under his command, H.M. Airship *Parseval* was badly damaged in a collision with its shed and never flew again. Six years later, a similar accident would result in the loss of the R-36; again in 1925, Scott would be at the helm when a third airship rammed its shed doors and was too severely damaged to be repaired.

But in 1919 Herbert Scott seemed the natural choice to command the R-34. Its initial tests went well, and in the early hours of July 2, 1919, the ship cast off from its base at East Fortune in Scotland. On board were three tons of water ballast, one ton of oil, official letters for American and Canadian dignitaries and a small packet of platinum for a New York jeweller. More than half of the ship's total weight, some sixteen tons, was fuel. Compared with the tribulations of the heavier-than-air pilots (not to mention the embarrassing fate of the U.S. Navy's dirigible, the C-5), the R-34 had a remarkably uneventful trip. After passing over Newfoundland and Nova Scotia, the dirigible reached New York on July 6, with only 140 gallons of fuel remaining. It began its return journey on July 9: three days, three hours and three minutes later, it moored in Norfolk after a journey that was, by any measure, an unqualified success.[5]

Not surprisingly, the public's response was effusive. "Who shall chant for them a worthy paean?" wrote James Lewis Milligan in an embarrassingly purple poem dedicated to the crew of the R-34:

> They who out-soared Olympus, made a path
> Above the clouds, charted the Empyrean,
>   Defied the lightning and the thunder's wrath,
> And spanned the heaving chasm of the sea—
> Where is the Homer for this Odyssey?[6]

Newspaper editors, eschewing the role of Homer, argued pragmatically that the flight of a large airship with the potential to carry either freight or passengers was much more significant than the flight of Alcock and Brown in their lowly converted bomber; their accomplishment, mused some journalists ungenerously, was more sporting than serious, for it would be years before the airplane would develop to the point at which it could make transatlantic flights with any useful purpose. The airship, on the other hand, was ready to go. The R-34 foreshadowed the day when, as Rudyard Kipling had predicted, the skies would be filled with airships. Indeed, carried on the R-34 was a copy of *Actions and Reactions*, the volume that included Kipling's futuristic story "With the Night Mail." It was autographed by all the crew members and presented to the author after the flight as a token of appreciation to the man who had seen the future of air travel.

After the flight of the R-34, other people began to see the same future, and the pressure for an expansion of airship services mounted. Public opinion and influential supporters in government and industry pressed for action. The press championed the dirigible, and prominent pilots showed themselves to be converts to the cause. All around the world, governments began to make plans to expand their airship services, to avoid being left behind.[7]

When the Inter-Allied Armistice Commission ordered Germany to turn over its airship fleet, three of them went to the government of France: two entered service immediately, and the third was broken up for scrap. The more successful of the two was the *Dixmude*, which began life as the L72. It made a world-record endurance flight of 118 hours in 1923, and that December was dispatched from its base near Toulon to make a survey flight over the Sahara. The French navy received transmissions from the airship stating that it was approaching heavy weather; then the *Dixmude* vanished. An intensive search failed to turn up any trace of the giant dirigible, and not until the commander's body was found by a Sicilian fisherman did the French government get some clue of what might have happened. The fisherman reported seeing a glare on the horizon early in the morning of the airship's last flight, and French officials concluded that the ship had broken up in the storm and been destroyed in an explosion. A decade later, the discovery of the wreckage of the *Dixmude* in the Mediterranean confirmed these fears. By then, the French government had already quietly shut down its airship program.

Italy, too, received three German airships and also launched its own design, the *Roma*, manufactured in Italy but assembled and tested in the United States. In February 1922, while undergoing high-speed tests, the *Roma* broke up over Hampton Roads, Virginia, and crashed, killing thirty-four of the forty-five people on board. More successful was the *Norge*, which, despite its name, was designed by the Italian aviator Umberto Nobile. In May 1926, Nobile and the Norwegian explorer Roald Amundsen completed the first air flight over the North Pole. But they quibbled over the credit, so Nobile returned to Italy in a huff and began building another airship, the *Italia*, which left Milan in April 1928, also bound for the North Pole. The *Italia* completed a very successful survey flight over the Arctic and reached the Pole, but on the way home the crew became lost in stormy weather. While cruising gingerly through the murk, the dirigible struck an ice ridge and the control car was torn off; the balloon, relieved of most of its weight, shot back up into the sky, carrying with it six crewmen, no trace of whom was ever found. Nobile and seven other survivors from the control car were eventually saved after a massive rescue effort that, ironically, claimed the life of Amundsen and five other airmen. Nobile was unfairly blamed for the loss of the *Italia*; his reputation was left in tatters and, with it, the Italian airship program.

But the French and Italian programs were minuscule compared with those of the big airship powers—the United States, Germany and Britain. During the Great War, the U.S. government had devoted most of its attention to blimps, but in August 1919 the navy approved a plan to build a large rigid airship based on the German dirigible L49. The ZR1, christened the *Shenandoah*, had its maiden voyage on September 4, 1923, and a year later embarked on an immensely successful transcontinental flight. But on September 5, 1925, the airship was caught in a storm over Byesville, Ohio, and broke up in mid-air, killing fourteen crew members. By this time, the navy had a second airship in service, the *Los Angeles*, built by the Zeppelin company as part of its reparations payments. Launched in September 1924, it flew to New York the following month and eventually made many successful test flights between its base in Lakehurst, New Jersey, and the Caribbean. It was such a success that in 1926, the U.S. Navy announced that it would construct two airships that would be the largest the world had ever seen: 6.5 million cubic feet, and nearly eight hundred feet long. The Americans had thrown down the gauntlet.

Germany was more than willing to take up the challenge. The undisputed leaders in airship technology, German firms were quick to restart passenger services after the war, announcing plans to link Berlin and Stockholm. The seizure of the airship fleet for war reparations was a setback, but in building the *Los Angeles*, the Zeppelin company turned things to its advantage. The success of that ship gave Dr. Hugo Eckener, the legendary German airship pilot who headed the Zeppelin company, both the funds and the public profile to build an airship to rival those planned by the Americans. That ship, the LZ127, was launched on July 8, 1928, and christened the *Graf Zeppelin*. It would become the most successful airship in history, flying more than a million miles without an accident and capturing the imagination of a generation in 1929 with the only round-the-world flight ever completed by an airship. This odyssey, for many people, was the realization of the predictions of Kipling, Jules Verne and a dozen other futurists. It was, wrote one passenger on the flight, like the "undying epics of ancient Greece and Rome" and the voyages of Columbus and Magellan: "Man has conquered the air—not in solitary stealth, but boldly—challenging the jealous elements to refuse him in numbers. We harnessed the sullen wind gods to our silver chariot... blazed a trail through Death's own kingdom of desolation.... We have lived a dream, savored a lifetime of romance, emotion and spiritual experience... sixty human products of this skeptical, scientific analytical era, found what savages instinctively know to be there—God. God of Miracles, of Nature, beauty, truth."[8]

Taking keen interest in the successes and failures of the American and German airship programs were the brains behind Britain's airship scheme, who were determined to surpass the achievements of the great Eckener. After the flight of the R-34, the Air Ministry had taken over the British airship program from the Admiralty, and in September 1919 proposed a regular service to India, using three airships that were about to enter service.[9] The government rejected the plan as too costly, and it became clear to many airship boosters that the Liberal government of David Lloyd George was losing interest in lighter-than-air flight. Indeed, in the summer of 1920, the cabinet informed the Air Ministry that because of financial constraints, it should cease all airship work, except to complete construction of the R-38, which was to be sold to the U.S. Navy. Its maiden flight in June 1921 revealed a number of serious control problems, and efforts to correct them were unsuccessful. On August 23, 1921, the R-38 broke in half during manoeuvring and plunged into the Humber River; only five of the forty-nine crewmen on board survived.

The crash of the R-38 put paid to Britain's military airship plans, at least for the time being; shortly after the tragedy, the Air Ministry announced that its Airship Section would be disbanded. This, however, did nothing to diminish the enthusiasm that was growing for commercial airship schemes, which the government promised would be unaffected by the Air Ministry's announcement. Indeed, those plans were generating increasing interest in the empire. In 1922, an ambitious proposal was put forward by Dennistoun Burney, a charismatic financier who had made a reputation (and a small fortune) during the war by inventing the minesweeping paravane, a device that prevented ships from striking mines. Burney knew nothing about airships, but he knew a good opportunity when he saw one. He proposed that a private organization, to be linked to the Zeppelin company, take over the Air Ministry's airship assets and establish a passenger and mail service linking Britain with India and eventually Australia. The company would build five new airships, each with a capacity of five million cubic feet, a length of approximately 760 feet, a range of three thousand miles and a speed of eighty miles an hour.

Burney's scheme was, in many ways, a microcosm of the airship mystique. On the one hand, it was almost breathtaking in its technical ignorance. Burney was not an engineer, and there was no proof that it was even possible to construct an airship with the performance characteristics that he promised. No dirigible of that size had ever been constructed or even designed; the most advanced German airships from the First World War were only about 2.4 million cubic feet and considerably shorter and thinner than Burney's leviathans. Nor was there any indication of sufficient demand, either for passengers or freight, for a twice-weekly service to India. Furthermore, the reliability of the airship was anything but proved. By the end of 1923, the major powers had built and flown 154 airships, 104 of which had been lost. Granted, 39 fell to enemy action, but the figures still represented one life lost for every sixty-five hours of flying time.[10]

Supporters of dirigibles argued that it was unfair to judge the technology based on the experience of the war. Without the pressures of military necessity, the technology could be improved at a safer pace, with more time for development work and testing. Already (and this point was indisputable), the airship offered better possibilities in terms of range, endurance, comfort, quiet and load-carrying capability than any heavier-than-air machine yet built. But Burney, like so many other aviation promoters of his day, was selling a dream, the potential of a largely unproved technology.

His vision appealed to the Admiralty, the Air Ministry and the Committee of Imperial Defence, but the government was soon swept from office and Burney's scheme was lost in the shuffle. Not until May 1924 did the new prime minister in Britain's first Labour government, Ramsay MacDonald, announce that Burney's program was unacceptable, as it would create a virtual private monopoly. Instead, MacDonald announced that the Air Ministry would undertake a massive research-and-development program to build both a brand-new, five-million-cubic-foot airship and mooring masts in England and India. As a sop to Burney, his new firm, the Airship Guarantee Company, would receive a contract to build a second airship to the same specifications. The press quickly seized on this distinction, dubbing Burney's R-100 the capitalist airship, and the Air Ministry's R-101 the socialist airship.

Construction of both ships began in the summer of 1926, the R-100 at Howden in Yorkshire, and the R-101 at Cardington. The process was not unlike assembling an immense child's toy. The skeleton of each airship consisted of huge rings of stainless steel and aluminum girders and tubes, joined by longitudinal ribs. The luxurious passenger compartment was located in the belly of the airship, surrounded by the immense gasbags. Made of cotton lined with goldbeater's skin, a thin membrane obtained from the intestines of cattle, the R-100's fifteen gasbags had a total area of more than ten acres. Once the frame had been assembled and the bags mounted, the entire airship was covered with strong linen, pre-doped to make it watertight. The outer skin gave the airships a simple, elegant look that belied the complicated web of girders, tubes and wires underneath.

Although the two airships looked similar, there were significant differences. The R-100's design team relied on tried-and-true construction methods wherever possible, including the use of standardized parts in the frame and variants of the gasoline engines that had powered British dirigibles since the First World War. The R-101 team chose revolutionary methods of design and construction to create the most advanced airship in the world. It would be powered by specially designed diesel engines and would feature a revolutionary steering mechanism. The engineers had developed a system of bolted joints to speed the assembly process, and the frame was to contain a much greater proportion of stainless-steel pieces than did other airships. Finally, the hull was as close as possible to a perfect streamlined shape; many other airships were essentially tubes with rounded ends. The Cardington team was supremely confident in R-101's design, insisting it would be the strongest airship ever built and occasionally making invidious comparisons with the more conventional elements of the R-100.

As construction proceeded, empire politicians were trying to hammer out a co-ordinated air policy at the 1926 Imperial Conference in London. Sir Samuel Hoare, Britain's secretary of state for Air, opened the deliberations on October 28 with a stirring summary of imperial aviation efforts and prospects for the future. Land and sea transportation, he observed, was unlikely to improve enough to make any appreciable difference in travelling time around the empire; it took sixty days for the Australian and New Zealand delegations to reach London, and "they are likely to continue to take sixty days for many Conferences to come"—unless the empire embraced the air. In the not too distant future, the farthest reaches of the empire would be days, not weeks, away from the mother country. Airplanes will be used on shorter routes, he believed, but "airships will carry out the long-distance non-stop air journeys of the future," cruising between the great cities of the empire and uniting the dominions like never before. But the airship would bring more than imperial unity, thought Hoare: "Hitherto the air has been the scene of glorious though terrible conflicts; it has been the background from which death and destruction have been hurled upon camps and cities. The purest of the elements was not intended for the destruction of civilisation by high explosive or poison gas. The invention of the flying machine, which the pioneers of successive centuries strove to achieve, was meant for something better than an instrument of concentrated frightfulness. With the horror of the last war in our memories and the limitless terror of any future war in our minds, let us make the air a highway of peace."[11]

Mackenzie King professed to being thrilled by Hoare's romantic vision. He promptly agreed that Canada would provide both the mooring mast and meteorological information necessary for a transatlantic flight of one of the new airships to Canada and invited the delegates to Ottawa for an imperial air conference. Having taken the decision, the Canadian government set about developing the required infrastructure. In April 1927, Herbert Scott travelled to Canada to inspect possible sites for the mooring mast. After spending nearly two months checking locations in Nova Scotia, New Brunswick, Quebec and Ontario, Scott and his committee advised that a site near St. Hubert, outside Montreal, offered the most advantages. It was a triangular parcel of nearly six hundred acres of flat land that was well served by road and rail. Water and hydroelectric power were readily available, and there were no hills, trees or power lines in the vicinity to obstruct an incoming or outgoing airship. Ignoring the lobbying of municipal officials from Toronto, Halifax and Ottawa, who desperately wanted to host the R-100, the federal government promptly acquired the St. Hubert site for $143,000 and ordered the mast and fittings from an English manufacturer.

The government expected that the R-100's arrival would draw a large crowd, so in October 1928, Ernest Stedman, now chief aeronautical engineer at the Department of National Defence, and R. de B. Corriveau, assistant chief engineer of the Department of Public Works, travelled to Lakehurst, New Jersey, to watch the arrival of the *Graf Zeppelin* and get a sense of the logistical obstacles involved. The landing was a shambles. Determined not to miss the momentous moment, tens of thousands of people had converged on Lakehurst, and before long there were fifteen-mile-long traffic jams around the airport. Food quickly ran out, and it was soon impossible to get a snack anywhere nearby. Furthermore, because the Zeppelin company had an exclusive contract with the Hearst news organization, the airship's captain refused to give the ground crew at Lakehurst a precise time of arrival, and tempers flared as the crowds waited for hours for the airship. Stedman and Corriveau returned to Canada knowing exactly what they had to do to avoid a similar fiasco.

Meanwhile, construction of the R-100 had been proceeding on schedule, and on Armistice Day 1929 the airship was turned over to its flight crew for trials. Seven test flights were completed before the end of November, and in December and January the dirigible flew another set of trials, including a series of five flights totalling nearly ninety hours. So far, everything had gone almost without a hitch, but on April 24, 1930, while the airship was being walked out of its shed, a gust of wind blew it against the shed door, damaging one of the tail fins and necessitating repairs. Then, the Canadian government requested that the flight be postponed until after the federal election, set for July 28, 1930. Finally, there was the question of command. Scott was to make the flight, but there was concern that his skill and judgment, always a bit suspect, had declined in recent years owing to illness and drink. It was therefore decided that R. B. E. Colmore, the director of Airship Development at the Air Ministry, would be the "only individual empowered to speak officially [for the Air Ministry and the] ... sole authority for deciding any questions which may arise during the course of the flight." Scott would fly as a consultant with no command function over the ship or its crew.[12]

If there was confusion over the flight specifics, the physical arrangements on the ground were coming together admirably. The CNR would run special trains every fifteen minutes from downtown Montreal to the airport in hopes of reducing vehicular traffic; local officials also carefully laid out a one-way road network around St. Hubert so cars could circulate with relative ease. To avoid confusion around the mast, no spectators would be allowed onto the airport grounds until the R-100 had actually moored, and even then they would be kept well back of the mooring apparatus by a detachment of the Royal Canadian Dragoons. Meanwhile, to ensure that the crowds were kept informed, no exclusive radio arrangements were permitted. Instead, the Department of National Defence hired French and English broadcasters to cover the arrival; their stories would be relayed to the Bell Telephone switchboard in Montreal, where any station could pick them up. Communication with the ship itself was also established, so people on the ground could hear on-board conversations "while viewing the silvery ship in the starry heavens."[13] The CNR Radio Department opted to do its own broadcasts and put together a fifteen-station, coast-to-coast live hookup to follow the R-100 up the St. Lawrence to St. Hubert. A third live national broadcast was provided by the Toronto *Daily Star* and the CFCA radio chain, using Foster Hewitt, the voice of *Hockey Night in Canada*.

All these arrangements were tested after the R-100 left Cardington on the afternoon of July 29, 1930. The flight across the Atlantic went almost without incident, the ship passing over Belle Isle, Newfoundland, on the evening of July 30. Everything was in order for the airship to reach Montreal the following afternoon, but over the mouth of the Saguenay River, the R-100 passed through a brief squall. It lasted only a few minutes, but it was enough to cause tears (one larger than a double-decker bus) in the outer cover of the tail. The crew had no choice but to attempt repairs as the ship cruised slowly up the St. Lawrence. It offered a stirring sight to the forty thousand people who had packed Quebec City's Dufferin Terrace and Battlefield Park (fortunately the torn fin faced away from the crowd), but at Trois-Rivières heavy cloud surrounded the dirigible as it fought its way west against strong headwinds. Reports of these difficulties were transmitted to the crowds waiting at St. Hubert, so there were no disturbances such as the ones Stedman and Corriveau had witnessed at Lakehurst, only intense excitement that peaked as the R-100 was sighted over Montreal around 2:30 A.M. on August 1. For the next three hours it drifted slowly toward St. Hubert. At 5:37 A.M., after nearly seventy-nine hours in the air, the ship was secured to the mooring mast.

For the next thirteen days, the R-100's visit was *the* story in Canada. The ship's crew was feted in banquets and receptions, and some three thousand dignitaries, including MPs, industry leaders and aviation personalities, were given a tour of the airship. The hundreds of thousands of spectators who converged on St. Hubert had to be content with watching from a distance, but it was enough. They came by train, car, airplane, bicycle and on foot, waiting patiently to file into the viewing area.

On the evening of August 10, the R-100 began a triumphal

tour of Quebec and Ontario. With eighteen Canadian military and press officials as passengers and before an estimated crowd of 200,000, the airship slowly pulled away from the mooring mast at St. Hubert and sailed regally toward the setting sun. It reached Ottawa a little before 10 P.M., to the cheers of 20,000 spectators on Parliament Hill and tens of thousands more who filled nearby vantage points. Then it was on to Carleton Place, Smiths Falls, Kingston, Belleville and Peterborough. Toronto was next, just before dawn, a *Globe* reporter describing it as "a delicate silver fish against the deep rich blue of the sky, with the coloured port and starboard lights like rubies and emeralds amid the scintillating diamonds of the stars." For the rest of the day, it cruised majestically over eastern and southern Ontario, causing a flurry of excitement in each town it passed over, before returning to Montreal. In it wake, it left a host of souvenirs: poems and songs, postcards and commemorative magazines, advertisements ("All of us can't be airmen, and lots of us will never experience the thrill of an ocean crossing in the air; but everyone can experience the genuine pleasure that Kraft adds to any meal," read one ad, reminding consumers that they could enjoy the same cheese as the crew of the R-100), ribbons and scale models, even the R-100 Restaurant in Toronto.[14]

And then it was gone, slipping the mast at St. Hubert on the evening of August 13, with a party of journalists and government officials as passengers. On the return voyage to Britain, they debated the possibilities of a future airship service—about fixed mooring masts (one reporter suggested that Moncton would be the next city to receive a mast) or "floating service stations of concrete, moored in the Atlantic or maintained in position by powerful tugs." The ever-optimistic Dennistoun Burney spoke of bringing Prime Minister R. B. Bennett to London by airship for the next imperial conference. He was already looking ahead to bigger ships that could travel at speeds of eighty-five knots and carry a hundred passengers across the Atlantic in just forty-eight hours.[15]

But few people were interested in the technicalities; they were much more taken with the R-100 as a symbol of hope and faith in the ultimate good of humankind's use of technology. That faith was captured by an amateur poet in Toronto:

> Silver majestic giant of the air,
> In humbled silence here below we dare
> To stretch our vision to thy lofty height
> To catch the exultation of thy flight.
>
> The very birds must envy thee thy grace,
> The sun thy beauty, awe-inspiring lark:
> Yet once thou wert a dream, a flimsy thread,
> A fairy finger beckoning in the dark.
>
> Oh man of little faith, back to thy tools;
> Thy dreams will live, the scorners are but fools.
> "Impossible"—how piteous weak the cry,
> While thou, grand eagle, soarest through the sky.

R-100's flight was "stranger than the fantasy of the floating island in Gulliver's Travels," wrote the Vancouver *Sun*. "Truth has a way of surpassing the imagination. For in man's ingenuity, imagination is the only starting point for fact."[16] The *Canadian Forum* was clearly smitten: "On her western course she passed by low at night, vast, majestic, gold-washed by the moonlight against a serene dark sky, her lights as steady and assuring as those of a liner at sea...as much at home in her element and as beautiful as a full-rigged ship on blue water.... There may be a hundred reasons why these ships of the air cannot be a commercial success: what does that matter! The machine age, which has filled our lives with noise and stinks and soul-cramping ugliness, can also give us things as poetically romantic as the R-100. Whether we can afford them or not, let us have all of them we can get."[17]

For those on board, the experience was so effortless, trouble-free and perhaps even a little dull. "While transatlantic flights are still a hazardous peril for airplanes, the airship has made a voyage as unexciting as a trip on a great lake," wrote one observer. "The future of ocean travel lies in the air. All discomforts of sea voyages are missing.... The fear of vertigo, nervousness about great heights, and temerity about travelling in the air...gave place to a feeling of absolute security." When a correspondent for *Canadian Aviation* wrote that "flying over the Atlantic was simple, boring and monotonous," he was not being critical, but merely trying to underline the significance of an achievement that had made the impossible seem so easy.[18]

If the R-100 seemed to confirm the dawning of "a new era of progress, one in which time and distance are annihilated and the world leaps forward to meet her glorious destiny,"[19] it also seemed to fulfil the promise that the British Empire, crippled by war and a decade of social, political and economic turmoil, would return to her former station as the greatest empire the world had ever seen. The British airship program had always been explicitly about improving imperial communications and therefore the empire. Lord Thomson of Cardington, the British air minister, had written in October 1926 that the scheme's aim was "to give a unity to widely scattered peoples, unattainable hitherto; to create a new spirit, or, maybe, to revive an old spirit which was drooping and to inculcate a conception of the common destiny and mission of our race."[20] Once the R-100's flight demonstrated the feasibility of the scheme, politicians, journalists, aviation boosters, even advertisements all trumpeted the R-100 voyage as opening a new chapter in imperial unity. Dennistoun Burney took every opportunity to impress upon Canadian audiences the new imperial age. "We must superimpose upon our existing structures," he told the Canadian Club of Toronto, "a method of transport which will allow great statesmen, great business men and leaders to travel from one end of the Empire to the other with little delay in a short time." Once that structure was in place, the empire would be transformed. "It would affect the British Empire not only economically but socially and politically," he said. "Air transport would affect our civilization, and the present generation would live to see great changes in the economic structure of the world." He envisioned a day when fourteen-hundred-foot-long airships would carry a hundred passengers and ten tons of cargo across the Atlantic in perfect safety and comfort, in an all-British, twice-weekly service between Canada and England. It was an opportunity no one could afford to pass up: "The pioneer spirit of Canada should associate itself with this enterprise, and send us back to England with the word, 'If you do not see it, we do.'"[21]

Burney was hardly an impartial observer, but countless people were drawn to the vision of imperial unity. Mackenzie King announced that it was the "consummation of the combined efforts of the British and Canadian governments to provide, by air navigation, yet another avenue of trade and commerce between this country and the old land." R. B. Bennett proclaimed that the airship's visit "will bring us closer to the motherland."[22] The mayor of Toronto regarded the voyage as "not merely a trans-Atlantic flight but the first step in a far-sighted plan to bind together the distant parts of the Empire, to expedite a more rapid service which will not only serve in a commercial sense but will rouse all people to the realization that they are being brought into closer contact by regular air routes throughout the world." In newspapers, magazines, aviation journals, even advertisements for cheese and cigarettes, the same future was conjured: "Leviathan of the air...looming gigantic in the heavens...annihilating space... spanning oceans...droning out its message of empire unity... cruising majestically with goodwill as freight...thrilling millions in that Empire upon which the sun never sets."[23]

Amid this wave of euphoria, a few skeptics dared to question the potential of the giant dirigible. In 1928, Stephen Leacock had dismissed the airship as being of little moment: "It is not likely that people will rush in airships to linger in slow trains," he wrote acerbically. The Toronto *Daily Star* noted that the record of the airship was not encouraging.[24] Even the Edmonton *Journal*, usually so optimistic about advances in aviation, was not convinced that the R-100 was anything more than an experiment; it was unlikely that the craft could be used on a commercial basis, decided the editor. John Nelson was more pessimistic still. He marvelled at the size of the R-101 (the *Graf Zeppelin* could fit inside it), but was concerned because recent tragedies had proved the vulnerability of airships. "Authorities agree," he observed, "that should a disaster such as overtook the *Shenandoah*, the R-38 or the *Dixmude* befall the R-101 or R-100, it is unlikely that any more work will be undertaken on airships in Great Britain." J. Fergus Grant, the aviation editor of the Montreal *Gazette*, admitted that travel by airship could not be matched for speed or enjoyment but counselled the engineers to "beware too much speed in pushing to completion plans still in the embryonic state."[25] It was September 23, 1930, and Grant was about to be revealed as more prescient than he could possibly have imagined.

, , ,

On the day that Grant's article appeared in the *Gazette*, the R-101's engineers at Cardington were grappling with the latest in a string of troubling discoveries that had begun a year earlier, when the ship was first fully inflated. The R-101 was radically different in structure from all previous airships, but in embodying everything the British knew about airship design, it also revealed how much they didn't know. In short, it was clear that the craft would perform far below the original estimates. The diesel engines, modified from engines designed for Canadian railways, were twice as heavy as projected, and the frame and passenger areas were also overweight. When it was fully inflated, R-101's useful lift had dropped to thirty-eight tons, well below the sixty-three tons called for. The only ways to increase the useful lift were to reduce the weight of the ship or to increase its gas capacity. A few minor modifications saved some weight but had little impact on the overall calculations. The only option was to increase the gas capacity.

The designers began by rearranging the wiring that supported the gasbags. This allowed each bag to be inflated with more gas, thereby increasing the overall lift of the ship but at the cost of another potential problem: the fatter bags now rubbed against the internal structure of the airship. When the bags were deflated after the September tests, they were found to have hundreds of holes through which the hydrogen had been escaping. Designers created a complicated system of pads and buffers to protect the bags, but Frederick McWade, Britain's most capable and experienced airship inspector and a member of the R-100 flight crew, was adamant that the pads be only a temporary expedient; until a permanent solution was found, he would not recommend extending the R-101's permit to fly. In another modification intended to boost lift, the engineers chopped the airship in half and added another bay of framing, which increased the ship's length by forty-five feet and allowed for an extra gasbag to provide greater lift. But this, too, revealed a potentially fatal flaw: the ship's outer skin had so deteriorated that in places one could put a fist through it. The designers came up with another expedient: the worst spots would be patched and the entire airship wrapped in wide canvas straps to hold down the skin in the event of a tear.

By mid-September 1930, the extra bay was in place, the canvas had been repaired, and the re-inflation of the ship was about to begin. But on the twenty-third, McWade made another alarming discovery: the rubber cement used to attach the patches had reacted with the original cover, making the canvas brittle and crumbly. The only safe course was to replace the original outer skin, but the very pressures that Fergus Grant feared were coming to bear: Lord Thomson had already decided to take the R-101 to India in the first week of October, and although he insisted that his schedule not compromise safety there was no question that the engineers felt that the repairs were being rushed past the point of prudence. McWade's concerns about the outer skin were overruled, just as his warnings about the pads had been. The airship design-ers decided that the most brittle areas would be repatched, but that the rest of the cover would easily manage a flight to India and back.

The risks involved might have been reduced had the flying crew had adequate time to put the R-101 through her paces. Given that the heavily modified airship was essentially a new craft, the crew wanted seventy-two hours of test flying, including twenty-four hours in bad weather. However, Colmore and Scott suggested that this time could be reduced if the initial stages of the test flight went well. In the end, the test time was reduced to less than seventeen hours. The ship experienced no major problems (except for an engine that gave out), but the weather had been clear and calm with little turbulence; the crew had no idea how the R-101 would perform in heavy rain or stiff winds.

Those were precisely the conditions that the R-101 encountered on its maiden flight to India, which began with much hoopla on the evening of October 4, 1930. Gusting winds whipped the rain into lashes as thunder rumbled through the heavy clouds and flashes of lightning lit up the countryside. As the crew battled the elements on their way to the first stop, Ismailia, in Egypt, the airship's flaws were becoming apparent. Barely thirty-five miles out, one of the heavy and troublesome engines gave out; nearly four hours passed before the crew fixed the engine and returned the ship to full power. The craft also felt very unstable. Noel Atherstone, the R-101's first officer, had reported soon after the first test flights that the R-100 was much easier to control than the sister ship; the R-101 seemed poorly balanced, tending to be either stern- or bow-heavy, depending on conditions. On this flight, the crew had difficulty keeping the nose up, and the ship frequently went into sharp dives for no apparent reason. Only the quick reaction of the crew prevented it from coming to grief over southern England.

But more worrying was that despite the modifications, the R-101 did not have enough useful lift. Even with the pads and buffers, the fatter gasbags still rubbed against the frames, and it was not long before gas was escaping through dozens of holes. With each mile, the R-101 became less buoyant—and heavier. The crew had not been happy to see all the trappings that accompanied Lord Thomson, including two cases of Champagne and an expensive Persian carpet (so he could exit the airship in style). Now they were growing increasingly concerned that the outer skin was not sufficiently impermeable; instead of the rain running off, it soaked into the fabric, adding to the weight and putting a tremendous strain on the aluminum frames.

As the giant dirigible lurched over the Pas de Calais, its situation was desperate. Just after 1 A.M. on October 5, it passed over Poix, in northern France, sailing into the teeth of fifty-mile-an-hour winds that drove rain into the fragile skin. Worse, the ship had been unable to regain altitude lost in the dizzying dives. The manager of Poix airfield estimated that the R-101 was less than three hundred feet off the ground as it passed. By 2 A.M., the ship had reached Beauvais, the next town along the rail line to Paris, where a poacher watched in fascination as it lurched toward him. The R-101 dipped lower and lower, and then, at five minutes past the hour, its nose struck a small hillock and exploded. Two more explosions followed, and within seconds the giant ship was a raging inferno. Six crew members clambered from the wreckage; everyone else on board, including Lord Thomson, Major Scott, Colmore, Atherstone and seven others who had been on the R-100's Canadian tour, perished.

What happened in those few minutes remains a matter of conjecture. Evidence suggests that the immense stress on the frame created by the strong winds and the soaked envelope caused an aluminum girder to twist, tearing a large hole in the already weakened outer skin. The headwinds whipped through the hole, pummeling the gasbags, causing dozens of leaks and forcing the nose of the ship down. As it struck the ground, the escaping hydrogen was ignited, either by a backfire from one of the troublesome diesel engines or by flares stored in the control car; the two subsequent blasts finished the work of destruction. In the cold dawn, the field at Beauvais revealed the remains of the once-proud airship: a shattered jumble of blackened girders, with a Royal Air Force flag fluttering bravely from the nearly intact tail section.

Amid the wreckage lay the imperial airship dream. A few observers tried to put on a brave face; *Saturday Night* believed that the setback was terrible but not irretrievable, and C. H. J. Snider of the Toronto *Evening Telegram*, one of the passengers on the R-100's return flight from Canada, lamented the loss of public confidence caused by the crash but insisted that transatlantic airship service would one day be a reality.[26] But the crash killed many of Britain's most experienced airshipmen; even if there had been the will to go on, it is not clear whether there was sufficient expertise remaining. The imperial airship scheme did indeed die at Beauvais. The R-100 was immediately taken out of service, and in December 1931, just eighteen months after her triumphant tour of Canada, it was dismantled and sold as scrap for a few hundred pounds. The mast at St. Hubert stood until 1938, when it was removed as a risk to aerial navigation; built at a cost of $376,000, it had been used only once. Virtually all that remains today of the scheme are the two huge sheds at Cardington.

There were other airship disasters in the 1930s, although none stirred the same emotion in Canada as the loss of the R-101. The first of the U.S. Navy's new generation of dirigibles, the *Akron*, made its maiden flight on September 23, 1931 (it later set a world record for carrying 270 passengers), but on April 4, 1933, it foundered in a storm over the Atlantic; only three of the seventy-six crewmen were saved. Three weeks later her sister ship, the *Macon*, began her maiden flight, but her career was no happier. On February 11, 1935, while it was on manoeuvres with the fleet over the Pacific, the ship's tail fin broke away, taking part of the hull with it. This time, all but two of the eighty-three crewmen were saved; one of the survivors was Comdr. Herbert Wiley, who had also survived the *Akron* tragedy. And then, on May 6, 1937, the *Hindenburg*, the successor to the *Graf Zeppelin* and pride of Germany's airship program, burst into flames as it came in to land at Lakehurst, New Jersey. When Herb Morrison captured on live radio the last, tortured moments of the *Hindenburg*'s life, he was also capturing the end of the airship age.

, , ,

The dirigible's loss, of course, was the airplane's gain. Despite the clear dominance of airships in the 1920s, the dreams of transoceanic airplane services had never died. Confident aviation boosters viewed Alcock and Brown's flight as the precursor to regularly scheduled transatlantic passenger services. "From their non-stop flight in a two-seater biplane," predicted the Manitoba *Free Press*, "there will stretch out the great future systems of transatlantic air flight, with great fleets of giant aircraft which have not yet even been dreamed of." In the view of many commentators, this would mark "the beginning of a new era of inter-empire communications that offers possibilities as yet undreamed of... there would seem to be no good reason why every empire dominion in the seven seas should not be in airplane touch with the motherland and each other before many years have passed." Even greater was the potential impact on the world, for the airplane held the promise of ushering in a new age of amity. "Are artificial barriers not also to be broken down with the barrier of distance?" mused the Ottawa *Journal*. "Will the word foreigner remain at all when the peoples of all countries are within a few hours of one another?"[27]

A decade later, these predictions were still being aired, the air lobby arguing that pioneering long-distance flights did have practical utility. J. A. Wilson admitted that their commercial value was nil but stressed that they foreshadowed future developments. When Richard Byrd became the first man to fly to the North Pole, journalists took pains to point out that such flights were not mere "'dashes' into 'the unknown,'" as the Ottawa *Citizen* put it. "They will be voyages of investigation and experiment, each bringing nearer the day when flying to Europe will be a regular thing." The Toronto pilot Errol Boyd made the same point as he prepared for the flight that would make him the first Canadian to fly the Atlantic. "This is no reckless stunt," he told a Charlottetown newspaper. "It is no hit or miss adventure. We will endeavour to do our bit to show the practicability of aviation, when conducted along scientific lines."[28]

By the mid-1930s, transoceanic flying was indeed becoming increasingly practicable. Aircraft, particularly the flying boat that would become the mainstay of transoceanic aviation in the 1930s, became more stable and reliable and gained increased range with improved engines and airframe design. A new long-range direction-finding apparatus solved many of the navigational problems that had beset pilots, and improved meteorological instruments meant that weather conditions could be gauged and predicted more accurately. Finally, the failure of airships, at least in Britain, freed up money and technical expertise that could be turned to heavier-than-air flying machines.

Indeed, the fiery demise of the imperial airship scheme renewed the dream of a transatlantic airplane service. J. A. Wilson held it to be the most important trade route in the world, and in July 1933 a remarkable flight by the Italian pilot and air minister, Italo Balbo, and twenty-five flying boats ("men of flesh and hearts of steel," the Saint John *Telegraph-Journal* called them) to the Century of Progress Fair in Chicago proved that the ocean had surrendered to aerial navigation.[29] "A new armada swept today," wrote the Nova Scotia journalist and poet Charles Bruce, "sworn not to the conquest of men but to Victory over nature's barriers. Stockades of Alp and ocean which hold the nations apart were ignored again as General Italo Balbo..." But others saw darker motives in the flight: Canadians "hear of fleets of Italians crossing the Atlantic, but should not be fooled into thinking that is merely a brave show. It is part of the international fight for air supremacy."[30]

However, it was not so much the Balbo flight as the attitude of Pan American Airways, the aggressive and well-financed American carrier, and its legendary president, Juan Trippe, that spurred the governments of Britain and the Dominions to join the fight for aerial supremacy. Since its creation in 1927, PanAm had been developing services on routes in central and South America, China and the Pacific, and by the mid-1930s, it was also seeking a monopoly in transatlantic passenger services. At a conference in Ottawa in November 1935, government delegates from Canada, Britain, Ireland and Newfoundland came together to establish the Committee on Trans-Atlantic Air Services. Wilson realized that action was imperative: PanAm was attempting to extend its operations into Alaska, the Arctic and Newfoundland, and Canada could not afford to be complacent. "A situation under which Canada takes no action and will permit no development by foreign interests, cannot succeed in the long run and is not in the best interests of international amity or world progress in aviation."[31] The delegates eventually struck a deal that they hoped would forestall PanAm's ambitions: Imperial Airways, Britain's national airline, would get a fifteen-year monopoly on landing rights in Newfoundland, a prerequisite if Imperial was to begin a transatlantic service. To ensure Canada's co-operation, the privilege would be extended to Canada's yet-to-be created national airline.

The agreement was a major victory for Canadian negotiators, but no one was under any illusions about Imperial's chances in a head-to-head battle with PanAm. Thus, it was imperative that Trippe's airline be brought into the deal, to avoid ruinous competition. In November 1935, at the Ottawa Conference on Trans-Atlantic Air Services, Commonwealth delegates agreed to present PanAm with a two-stage proposal: preliminary experimental flights, to be followed by two regular flights a week for three months. If it was successful, a regularly scheduled service with mandatory stops in Canada and Ireland would begin. The following month, the Commonwealth delegates took their plan to Washington and convinced American negotiators that PanAm and the Empire consortium should have reciprocal privileges on each other's routes; the American and British services would begin simultaneously to ensure that neither side got a head start. But when it came time to implement the agreement, there was a hitch. The Commonwealth governments had agreed that Montreal was to be the Canadian terminus, but PanAm demurred, insisting on

Shediac, New Brunswick, as its stopover between New York and Botwood, Newfoundland.

This was a nasty shock for Ottawa, because the choice of a Canadian terminus had already been a contentious matter as various cities tried to position themselves at the centre of the world's aviation map. Winnipeg had urged the Canadian government to support a subarctic airway over Iceland, Greenland and the Canadian north, with Winnipeg as its North American terminus. An article in *Saturday Night* suggested that Quebec City would be a better choice for a route from London to Canada via Scotland, the Faroes, Iceland, Greenland, Godhavn, Pangnirtung, Lake Harbour and Baffin Island; it could be used 365 days a year, as long as the way stations were properly maintained, and "it is perfectly feasible to link this route with existing Empire air routes to Australia, India and Africa, and thus circumnavigate the globe under the Civil Air Ensign." Sydney, Nova Scotia, reasoned that as it was the closest Canadian city to England, it should become the North American terminus. A local entrepreneur even acquired a nine-hundred-acre site just outside the city, and convinced Mayor S. E. Muggah to head a committee to effect a liaison with an Irish company claiming to be ready to inaugurate an air service between Cape Breton and Londonderry.[32]

Halifax was in an even stronger position. In 1926, a Halifax newspaper had confidently predicted that the city "will undoubtedly be the first 'station' on the Imperial air route from London.... [It] promises to be...a place of great strategic importance." The opening of PanAm's scheduled service between Halifax and Boston in the summer of 1931 was taken as a positive sign: "A giant plane swept out of the western skies," wrote one journalist lyrically of PanAm's inaugural flight, "described a graceful arc and dipped to a perfect landing on a field that has placed the Nova Scotia capital on the air map as the broad, straight channel and deep waters have given her port pre-eminence on mariners' charts."[33] More than a quarter of the flights that first season had to be cancelled because of bad weather, yet observers confidently predicted that "it won't be long before the old city comes into its own again and prosperity of other years returns." Buoyed by a visit by Charles Lindbergh, retained by PanAm as a technical expert, municipal politicians pressed the city's case forcefully in Ottawa. In January 1934, the mayor urged the federal government to undertake improvements to Halifax airport as part of the national public works scheme. "Due to our geographical position and other conditions," he argued, "Halifax would be the natural Canadian terminus of any Trans-oceanic or Trans-Canada Air lines."[34]

But Halifax's claim was being challenged by Shediac, which had been the first North American city to greet Balbo's goodwill flight. "Without doubt a great future lies in store for Shediac as a terminal for trans-Atlantic air-craft," trumpeted the souvenir brochure prepared for the occasion. As there were no dangerous tides or water currents, little fog, and low land around the bay eliminated dangerous air currents, it was a natural choice for PanAm's North American terminus. "With aviation circles convinced that the flying boat is not soon to be superseded by ocean-jumping landplanes," wrote a later observer, "rabidly air-minded Shediac residents are certain that their harbor is to be the great landing place on this side of the water for planes from Britain and the European continent.... The inhabitants of Shediac are, perhaps, more familiar with ocean aerial activities than the people of any town on this continent.... Shediac basks in the glory of her aeronautical glory."[35]

The Canadian government found itself in a dilemma. PanAm was determined to support Shediac's claims expressly to prevent Montreal from becoming a transatlantic air terminus to rival New York, but Ottawa was equally determined to back Montreal, for the same reason.[36] In the end, Ottawa blinked. After protracted discussions, Canadian officials concluded that an insistence on Montreal could wreck the entire agreement; Canada should strongly encourage PanAm to use Montreal, but would give it the necessary permission to use Shediac.

Little of this wrangling was apparent to the Canadian public, which was overtaken by enthusiasm as the transatlantic air services came closer to fruition. That enthusiasm received a boost when Britain's new long-range flying boats took to the air in early 1937. The first two aircraft, the *Caledonia* and the *Cambria*, were to be used on Imperial Airways' north Atlantic run; PanAm would use the Boeing 314 *Clipper*. According to the terms of the 1935 agreement, the two experimental flights were to begin simultaneously, so on July 5, 1937, as PanAm's *Clipper* was leaving its base in Port Washington, New York, the *Caledonia* departed from Foynes, Ireland, bound for Botwood and Montreal. It carried no passengers or freight; every non-essential, even the floorboards, had been stripped out to save weight. The *Caledonia* and the *Cambria* would make five round-trip Atlantic flights that summer, creating a sensation in Canada similar to that caused by the arrival of the R-100. When the *Caledonia* first landed in Montreal on July 8, 1937, "business practically ceased for about 15 minutes as thousands rushed to windows, roofs and streets." In September, the *Cambria* embarked on a tour of southern Ontario, including stops in Ottawa, Toronto, Windsor and Hamilton. In Toronto, "the populace were warned of the arrival by blasts of factory whistles, also by flash broadcasts over local radio broadcast stations, given during the flight from Ottawa"; as many as twenty thousand people crammed the CNE waterfront to watch the flying boat's arrival. It was the same wherever the *Cambria* and the *Caledonia* appeared; government officials estimated that 3.5 million people saw the aircraft on their demonstration flights.[37]

Imperial Airways mounted further test flights in 1938, although the program was curtailed by the Munich crisis and the diversion of resources to the Royal Air Force. The following year, problems with new equipment delayed the flights yet again, and PanAm was first out of the gate, beginning regularly scheduled transatlantic service in June 1939. Carrying a full complement of luminaries, including senators, congressmen, officials of the Civil Aeronautics Authority and Juan Trippe himself, the *Yankee*

Clipper left Port Washington at 1:21 in the afternoon on June 24. On June 28, after a three-day layover in Shediac and twenty-six hours in the air, the flying boat touched down on Southampton Water. The PanAm service was everything aviation boosters, journalists, politicians and futurists had hoped: speedy, reliable, safe and, above all, opulent. For sheer comfort, the transatlantic flying boats came close to rivalling the R-100. The passengers' quarters were less spacious, but white-coated stewards served gourmet meals at tables set with crisp linen, fine china and fresh flowers. Beverley Baxter, the former editor of London's *Daily Express* and a columnist for *Maclean's*, likened the rarified experience to "a yachting party in the air." A journalist writing in *National Home Monthly* was even more effusive: "To any person who has never before 'flown' this is more than 'travel'; it is an amazing experience, a thrill eclipsing all others that life has given us."[38]

, , ,

The opening of regular air service between North America and Europe was the culmination of a decade of rhetoric about the impact of aviation on international relations, but the rhetoric was no longer that of imperial unity. A few commentators still longed for a day when the airways would knit the British Empire more closely, but increasingly observers took a different tack. Disputes over routes were not struggles for political or economic power, but the re-fashioning of international relations. The transatlantic airline was not simply a money-making route but "the tangible pledge of friendship." The expansion of international air routes was both dependent on and productive of international goodwill. As the Montreal *Gazette* put it, "This girdling of the earth, then, because effected largely in virtue of greater international amiability, inevitably will be for the world's good."[39] The destination of the air route was not simply to imperial unity but world peace.

Of course, this was not a new idea. As early as 1908, the Baddeck aviation community quoted Maj. George Squier, who would command the American air service during the First World War, that "the use of balloons and aeroplanes for military purposes will deter nations from going to war and go towards bringing about universal peace." In 1926, the American aviation engineer William B. Stout, speaking to the Canadian Club of Toronto, conjured up a vision of a new world made more peaceful by the airplane: "As we are beginning to know each other better we are finding that all the hearsay stories are not true and that a lot of good things are true and that everybody else is not such a bad fellow after all.... You have no boundaries; you are all one nation... we are coming to a brotherhood in Europe through the mechanical missionaries which the engineers are sending into that part... and brotherhood of man will be close behind."[40]

But it was Charles Lindbergh who made the world think of the aviator as an emissary of peace. Mackenzie King's praise of Lindbergh as "a young god from the skies, bringing anew the message of peace and goodwill," was entirely in keeping with contemporary perceptions of his flight. First, the world could find unity in admiring his achievement. As the *Globe* put it, "There is no greater kinship known to the race than the latent principle of admiration that exists in all people for a brave man and a courageous deed."[41] But more important, Lindbergh had demonstrated that the pilot had the power to bring distant peoples into closer contact. He had "shown that the nations are after all neighbors in the real sense of the term... daily contact is what will help bring better understanding between nations and peoples as well as individuals.... [His flight] will tend to hasten the day when war shall be no more and when peoples shall dwell together in unity." A contributor to *Canadian Aviation*, wrote, "Regarded as a weapon of destruction during the war, the aeroplane is now an agent in promoting goodwill between different countries. Lindbergh's name at once looms up when the subject is mentioned, and undoubtedly he has been the greatest ambassador of goodwill, made possible through his plane, in the last decade. As an agent of peace, the aeroplane has done much, and will do more in the future."[42]

In the wake of Lindbergh's flight, similar feats were interpreted in the same terms. The odyssey of the *Bremen*, which landed on an isolated island near the Quebec-Labrador border after a non-stop flight from Baldonnel in Ireland, was a major news story around the world in the spring of 1928, in part because the partnership of two old enemies, the former Royal Flying Corps pilot James Fitzmaurice and the former German ace Hermann Koehl (not to mention their curious passenger, the eccentric Baron von Huenefeld), was interpreted as a sign that old animosities had been forgotten. As Mackenzie King observed in his message to the trio, "Your achievement marks a distinct and notable advance in the development of aviation as a means of bridging the oceans and of making possible closer relations and friendships among the nations of the world."[43] Transatlantic travel came closer to realization, and the rhetoric grew ever more optimistic, paralleling the discourse that had seen aviation as the solution to provincial or regional antipathies within Canada. Conflict was the product of ignorance. Vast distances allowed nations to become isolated from one another, and that isolation bred misconceptions as they attributed nefarious motives to their neighbours. Those misconceptions in turn fostered suspicion and mistrust, which paved the way for conflict.

In the air age, everything would be different. Herbert Hollick-Kenyon, a long-time employee of WCA who took part in the first flight across the Antarctic in 1935, pointed out that isolation would be impossible in the air age: "With the shortening of distances should come an increasing intercourse and a better understanding with our neighbors...a well-developed community of interest should be able to influence world opinion toward peace." In removing isolation, observed the *Globe*, "one obstacle to a fresh and more reasoned approach to world affairs" would disappear. Once neighbours were brought into regular contact, the result would be greater knowledge and understanding of other nations and their interests. Once the airplane banished ignorance, the world would be a more peaceful place. "Today all the great natural barriers are overcome by aerial transportation," wrote the Winnipeg postmaster T. T. Bowers, "and with them go many of the disharmonies of race and blood that have so often disturbed the peace of the world...all nations shall be drawn closer and closer together by aerial transit; men will lose their local national outlook and become internationalists—citizens of the world."[44]

But the new age of amity would rest not only on the practical impact of flight. The fact that flight was a spiritual journey would give it immense power. Since the nineteenth century, the air had been perceived as a realm where earthly concerns mattered little. To fly was more than just to leave the ground; it was to escape from the confusion and malaise of life, to be elevated to a higher plane of existence, where one has "a sense of complete detachment from mundane affairs, of being transposed for the time being to a more spiritual, peaceful existence."[45] Because the air was "the place of vision, or speed and freedom of movement," wrote J. Fergus Grant in 1937, the air age would be a time of vision and freedom, when individuals and nations would not be distracted by petty quarrels and when more enduring values would be evident. "What we of this generation are witnessing is a process whereby the air shall come into its own," said J. A. Wilson. "It will become a great highway for the traffic of peace." Because flying was infinitely superior to life on the ground, the air age would be infinitely superior to the age that preceded it, thanks to the airplane, the "herald of a new and more peaceful age when planes of all nations may go scudding through the air, passing in flight with a salute of friendship and a whirr of freedom."[46]

To the discerning eye, signs of that new, more peaceful age were evident everywhere in Canada, even in something as prosaic as the air show. Before the First World War, air displays had invariably featured an exhibition of bombing, using bags filled with flour or sawdust to simulate explosions. In the 1920s, mock dogfights were the order of the day, and crowds flocked to see the great air aces of the Western Front re-enact their life-and-death battles in the clouds. By the late 1920s, such warlike exhibitions had been largely replaced by goodwill visits; indeed, no air show worth its salt could be without a goodwill visit of aircraft from another country. In 1927 the Italian aviator Francesco de Pinedo arrived in Montreal from Chicago as part of his three-month air voyage to spread goodwill. Not even the presence in the cheering crowd of "Fascisti in black shirts and fez," as the *Gazette* put it, could spoil the amity that de Pinedo's visit symbolized. In 1929, the Toronto Flying Club brought in a delegation of U.S. Army aircraft for the CNE air show. The visit would "do much to cement international goodwill," thought the editor of *Canadian Aviation*, "and exchanges of goodwill visits should be more frequent." Indeed, they became so in the early 1930s. When ten American bombers visited Winnipeg's Stevenson Field in 1934, it was hailed as a triumph of neighbourliness. Only the *WCA Bulletin* added a sour note: "Even the fact that they carried no 'eggs' and were on an essentially peaceful mission did little to assuage the peculiar mental reaction to their presence. From their aerial vantage they dominated all, and the impotence of the man in the street in face of aerial attack was obvious."[47]

But few others were as pessimistic, and in their ideology of goodwill, the stereotypes of the First World War were inverted. In 1916, at the height of the German air offensive against English cities, the Vancouver *Sun* had proclaimed bitterly that "the Zeppelin stands for Germany and Germany's vicious militarism." Ten years later, and for the rest of the inter-war era, the Zeppelin was a symbol of peaceful relations between nations. When the airship LZ126 was renamed the *Los Angeles* after being sold to the U.S. Navy in 1924, the ceremony included a release of white doves as a mark of friendship between Germany and the United States; the Secretary of the Navy announced that the name *Los Angeles* had been chosen because the airship "has come from overseas like an angel of peace." The flight of the *Graf Zeppelin*, too, came to symbolize peaceful coexistence between former enemies, one passenger observing that the voyagers found "mirrored in themselves the shining reflection of loyalty, comradeship and courageous cooperation of their cosmopolitan fellow travellers."[48]

Just as potent in symbolic terms were the great flying aces of the First World War. During the war, pilots had argued against the suggestion that aerial combat was somehow purer and nobler than the war on the ground, pointing out that enemy pilots were their bitter enemies. For them, the chivalry of the skies was simply propaganda; in the real air war, the only rule was "kill or be killed." Between the wars, however, the notion that air combat had been governed by codes of chivalry took on a life of its own, and the aces came to personify amity.

In 1918, Billy Bishop's best-selling memoir *Winged Warfare* had described his delight at seeing an enemy aircraft go down in flames, and his speeches rarely failed to remind society matrons and local worthies that the way to win a dogfight was to shoot at the opposing pilot's head or body. But by the 1930s, Bishop the calculating killer had been replaced by Bishop the knight of the air, who piously laid a wreath on the tomb of Manfred von Richthofen, the Red Baron, while on a business trip to Berlin in 1928. He was feted by the German Ace Association at the Berlin Aero Club and socialized with his former foes, including Hermann Göring and Ernst Udet, who would soon rise to prominence in Hitler's air force. Bishop returned the hospitality by hosting his one-time enemies in London, and though he was personally wary of their motives, his public statements made much of the bond between aces and the example it could set for world affairs. "The bitterness and hatred between the Armies and Navies engaged in the War, as well as the intense feeling of the civilians, was not present in the Air Forces of the countries involved," he wrote in a 1931 magazine article. "In its place was a healthy respect for and interest in the opposing flying men...there were no sordid points of contact between the opposing pilots, such as surrounded the troops on the ground. They met in the cold, clear air...free from animosity of any kind, a game more than a war." Seven years later, on the eve of the next war, he would reiterate that pilots had been most active in "drawing the world closer together in peace."[49]

Nor was Billy Bishop the only one to subscribe to the notion that there was a unique bond between pilots that transcended political disputes. "All pilots belong to the fraternity," Sydney Cleverley told his Toronto Flying Club. "There is a common bond which, by its very existence, established an interest, a comradeship, even a love between men." Roy Maxwell, head of the OPAS, evinced similar sentiments in a letter to the father of a dead employee: "All aviators face a common danger, and it is this which binds us together in friendship not known outside the realm of aviation."[50] This bond made it entirely appropriate that the knights of wartime should come together to serve higher ideals. In 1923, Walter Gilbert, the legendary arctic pilot who learned to fly with the RFC, became first president of Vancouver's International Air Force Club, where ex-pilots from both sides came together "to retain the common bond which had been established during the Great War." The Ottawa *Journal* was entirely in favour of this kind of reconciliation: "Colonel Bishop's breaking of bread with his old foes is an example to us all," the editor opined, and concluded that such displays of amity were much wiser than sabre-rattling. In 1936, George Drew, an artilleryman who joined the ranks of aviation boosters with his best-selling *Canada's Fighting Airmen* (1930), quoted a German aviator: "Bigger than the national fame that these heroes, friend and foe alike, won as patriots to conflicting causes, is the growing international recognition of their achievements, not as partisans but as men who gave to the world new and unprecedented examples of the highest form of physical and moral courage. Respect for human qualities of this high order knows no frontiers."[51]

Then there is the curious correspondence of Roy Brown, who for decades was credited with bringing down von Richthofen. One of Brown's souvenirs of that fight was a black cross cut from the fuselage of Richthofen's aircraft after the crash. For some years after the war that cross weighed heavily on Brown's mind. He did not want his children to look on it as proof that their father had been another man's killer, nor did he want to see it in a museum "as a trophy of war, as hunters mount the antlers of a deer or the skin of a wolf." The more he thought about it, the more the cross came to symbolize the tragedy and pointlessness of war as a way to solve disputes. As a sign of reconciliation with and "to show that any enmity I had, if I ever had any, against Germany and the Germans, is gone," Brown proposed to return the cross to von Richthofen's family in Germany.[52] It was to be a symbol that the bitterest enemies of the war had become the emissaries of reconciliation, living testament to the power of the air to purify and elevate international relations.

Clearly, by the mid-1930s, aviation had been largely rehabilitated in the eyes of the world. Intercontinental flight had transformed the flying machine into an emissary of peace, while the camaraderie and chivalry of the skies had re-emerged, albeit in propaganda more than reality. In the view of its strongest proponents, aviation had the power to make new friends of old enemies and to lead the world to a new age of co-operation, friendship and peace. The alarmists of the pre-1914 era had been proved wrong; humanity could be trusted to make the most of the new technology. And then came Guernica.

· 8 ·

FLAMING CHARIOTS OF WAR

THE FIRST SIGN OF ANYTHING UNUSUAL WAS THE RINGING OF THE bell in the church of Santa María in the centre of Guernica, the thriving town in northern Spain that was the spiritual centre of the Basque nation. It was Monday afternoon, market day, and the people clustered in the square did not immediately comprehend what the bell meant. Minutes later, voices carried above the noises of the street: *"Avión! Avión!"* German aircraft, sent to Spain by the Nazi government to support the Spanish Fascists, were approaching. Were they headed for Bilbao, to the west? Toward the Republican forces retreating to the east? When a lone bomber came into view, there was no doubt: the city itself was the target. A few people rushed to find sanctuary in churches or cellars, but most did not have time to clear the streets.

The first bombs landed around the town's railway station. One blasted away the front of the Julián Hotel, burying a group of children who had been playing in the street. Another crashed into the station, where dozens of passengers were waiting to board the train to Bilbao. As the dust cleared, rescuers began to dig out the wounded and collect the dead. Fifteen minutes later, a second wave of three bombers came. Their high explosives tore into factories, shops and homes, while incendiaries set fire to the wooden stalls that packed the marketplace. Terrified survivors ran through the town, many falling to the fighter aircraft that machine-gunned the streets. They would continue to strafe Guernica long after the bombers had departed.

But the worst was yet to come. Just after 6 P.M., the main attack force, made up of twenty-three Junkers Ju 52 three-engine bombers—the civilian variant of which had been operating in Canada's north since 1931 and been celebrated in an article in *The Beaver* just a year earlier[1]—approached Guernica from the north-east. Each trio of aircraft rained nearly ten thousand pounds of high explosives and incendiaries on the town. One cluster of bombs hit the town hall, trapping dozens of people in the shelter beneath it; nine hit the convent of La Merced. The Bank of Vizcaya, the Residencia Calzada (home to the elderly, orphans, nuns and wounded soldiers), the Church of San Juan, the monastery of the Augustine Fathers were all reduced to rubble.

By 8 P.M. the skies above Guernica were clear of aircraft, but it would be sixteen hours before the last of the flames were doused. Rubble clogged the streets, and the bodies of the dead and dying lay scattered throughout the ruins. The stench of burning flesh hung in the air as dazed survivors picked through the remains of the town, searching for survivors or possessions. Three-quarters of the buildings in Guernica had been destroyed; nearly seventeen hundred people were dead and more than eight hundred were wounded.[2]

In the early 1920s, the bombing raids on England had been fresh in the minds of the public. The Zeppelin and Gotha raids were icons of popular culture, but more and more they were subsumed into the ideology of aviation as a vehicle of universal amity: German flying machines and airships like the *Graf Zeppelin* and the *Bremen* were idolized and old enemies made into new comrades. Two decades of propaganda by the air lobby, combined with the undeniable economic advantages of aircraft, had affirmed the positive value of aviation.

The bombing of Guernica on April 27, 1937, by the German Condor Legion, directed by Wolfram von Richthofen, a gallant ace of the Great War and cousin of the Red Baron, dashed those hopes. In the ensuing years, dozens of cities would undergo the same ordeal, and the popular perceptions of aviation would be fundamentally altered. The prophets of a terrifying new age of aerial bombardment, for years drowned out by the proponents of the airplane as a messenger of peace, were vindicated by the bombing raids of the late 1930s and early 1940s. The airplane, so recently seen as the pinnacle of human achievement, was evolving into a sinister killing machine capable of spreading destruction. The sound of an airplane engine had once sent people dashing outside to catch a glimpse of the aerial wonder; now it was as likely to send them scurrying for shelter.

The air raids of the late 1930s revitalized the simple morality play that had coloured the bombing raids of the Great War, but with a twist. No longer an unspeakable evil to which only the basest of enemies would stoop, indiscriminate bombing was now a legitimate, justified act of vengeance. Revulsion at the use of bombers against unarmed civilians became pride that the Allies could hit enemy cities harder and more often than ever before. Irrespective of its tactical or strategic necessity, the bombing campaign of the Second World War marked a turning point in public perceptions of aviation.

, , ,

In the years immediately following the First World War, one did not have to look far to find reminders of the bombing campaign against English cities. In the summer of 1919, the newest film to hit Victoria, British Columbia, was *Boots*, starring Dorothy Gish. It was a "drama of London life during Hun Zeppelin raids," which recreated "those trying times when the Huns swept over the city and dropped their tons of death on a fear-stricken population." Crowds lining up for the Canadian war trophies exhibition in Hamilton, Ontario, looked forward to examining a Gotha bomber, described in the catalogue as the "Giant German Bombing Plane used by the Hun for bombing London and Paris." People who saw the show at Toronto's Canadian National Exhibition could inspect a twelve-foot-long aerial bomb ("prepared for the attack on Berlin just prior to the Armistice"), a German bomb recovered after a raid on London and pieces of wreckage from the first Zeppelin brought down over England. Also on display was a collection of official war photographs, including one showing a dugout at a German airfield, colourfully captioned "Baby Killers' Funk-Hole."[3]

The mark of the Zeppelin raids on the public consciousness was also evident in the futurist literature of the immediate postwar period. Douglas Hallam, in a 1919 memoir of his years in a flying boat squadron patrolling the English Channel, envisioned a war in 1929 that breaks out when "a pushing Island People made a snatch at Australia and the islands in the Pacific." In response, the Royal Navy mobilized twenty massive flying boats, each carrying a one-ton aerial torpedo, and unleashed them on the enemy navy. The ships were quickly sunk, but the enemy "was a stiff-necked and brave people, so we had to smash up a few of his coast towns before he surrendered."[4] Hilda Glynn-Ward, in her bitterly racist novel *The Writing on the Wall* (1921), went further. In her apocalypse, the Japanese, bent on conquering British Columbia, assembled and tested aircraft at secret bases on the Queen Charlotte Islands. Then, as representatives of the white population were meeting to organize their defences, one fellow heard a sound: "There was no mistaking the sound that grew louder and louder; it was the same sinister sound that had driven many out of their minds when the Germans raided England—the droning buzz of an aeroplane, *of a fleet of aeroplanes.*" In Vancouver, Victoria and Nanaimo, poison-gas bombs crashed to the ground, and before long "the street was a hideous chaos of death and disaster; the living ones, who ran about among the piles of corpses in an attempt to find their friends, wailed and shouted in a frenzy of despair and disorder." Ubald Paquin's *La Cité dans le fer* (1925) also brought the air war close to home, as dirigibles and aircraft laid waste to Quebec City and Montreal in a Canadian civil war.[5]

But it was not just the novelists who deduced that Canada was open to aerial attack. Robert Logan, while investigating possibilities for aviation in the Arctic archipelago, was struck by the ease with which Canada could be attacked over the North Pole: "Much has been said of the possibilities of future hordes of Slavs overrunning Europe and the great uses of aircraft which would be certain in such an event. Aircraft operated from Arctic or sub-Arctic bases could swoop down and leave trails of destruction throughout the rest of the world." In the House of Commons, Jacques Bureau, the minister of Customs and Excise, warned that the Dominion Arsenal at Lindsay was vulnerable to aerial bombing; and Ian Mackenzie, the minister of National Defence, predicted that any future attack on Canada would most likely come from the air. Bombers from European nations could use aircraft carriers to reach Canadian soil with impunity, with the result that "an air raid on Canadian territory could do more damage than a sea raid."[6] Jean François Pouliot, the member for Témiscouata, agreed, warning that any enemy nation could use commercial aircraft to rain bombs upon cities and towns. Even as the R-100 was drawing thousands of curious onlookers and inspiring in people the possibilities of aerial travel, at least one correspondent offered a reminder of a different time: "Talking of airships, I remember the time in the old country when we used to make for the cellar, not the roof, when we heard the unique drone through the moonless night. Their greetings were anti-aircraft guns and aeroplanes dropping bombs."[7]

But such warnings were most noteworthy for their infrequency. Canadians remained fascinated by stories of wartime atrocities, but there is every indication that they were relatively quick to forgive and forget the air raids that had stirred such ire in 1917 and 1918. By the late 1920s, the R-100, the *Graf Zeppelin*, the new friendships between Great War aces—these were heralds of a new age of amity. Certainly aircraft had been used for war, but the years of peace had demonstrated that the ultimate impact of aviation must be for good. This comforting certainty would persist until the bombing of Guernica in the spring of 1937.

⸰ ⸰ ⸰

The western democracies might have been unwilling to marshal tangible support for the Spanish loyalists—one correspondent remarked on the outpouring of press sympathy for a dog hit by a car, wondering, "Is the life of a dog of more value than the lives of thousands of our fellow creatures who are being hurled to eternity by the bombs and bullets of Italian and German airman?"[8]—but they were generous with their righteous indignation. Canadian newspapers were horrified by the bombing of Guernica and by similar air raids on Bilbao and Madrid, trumpeting their disgust in headline after headline in late April 1937: "Horror at Rebel Murder of Defenceless Spaniards," "Warplanes Pour Bombs on Defenceless Civilians," "Indescribable Horrors of Bombardment of Basque Town." The Ottawa *Citizen* called Guernica "the Devil's work" and "the worst atrocity of the Spanish Civil War.... [The bombing] shocked every democratic country in Europe...the moral is drawn that as the perpetrators were chiefly German airmen this is what nations may expect in the next war in which Germany is engaged.... [Guernica's] destruction can only be put down to a renewed outbreak of that frightfulness which

characterized German methods of fighting during the Great War."
The use of the term "frightfulness" is instructive, for what is most
striking about the press accounts is the ease with which they
slipped back into wartime rhetoric. Indeed, many commentaries
from April 1937 might have been written twenty years earlier:
"The bombing of defenceless towns is frightful under any circumstances, but when the fugitive people are first driven
underground to escape from the machine guns of low-flying aircraft, only to be buried alive or burnt by incendiary bombs,
modern war has sunk to a new depth of inhuman villainy.... It has
been more or less openly stated by British authorities that about
the only effective answer to an air raid from an enemy abroad
would be to retaliate by bombing the enemy's towns."[9]

Journalists might have seen Guernica in the context of the air
raids of the Great War, but some poets saw it as something entirely
different. For Frank Scott, the tragedy of Guernica was not simply
the destruction of a single town; it was a universal tragedy that
reached far beyond Spain:

> For these we too are bleeding: the homes burning,
> The schools broken and ended, the vision thwarted,
> The youths, their backs to the wall, awaiting the
>   volley,
> The child staring at a huddled form.
> And Guernica, more real than our daily bread.[10]

Raymond Souster, who joined the RCAF in 1941 but never saw
action, was at once fascinated and repelled by accounts of the air
raids on Madrid:

> Bombs have laid these houses
> open to the sky. The dead face the sun
> directly from their stretchers, no fear now
> in the eyes, nothing there but blackness
> where once life sparkled, love swelled.

More important, he recognized that the raids had altered the character of aviation, transforming the airplane into a loathsome creature that defecates death:

> High above, still gloating, the hate-crossed vultures
> sniff the smell of blood, the smoke of ruin.
> They hum with fresh purpose,
> their black wings glistening in the morning air,
> as other slick droppings of murder
> fall shrieking from their stinking bowels.[11]

Other poets took up the same theme, although with less-brutal imagery. They, too, were struck by the contrast between what aviation used to be and what it had become. They remembered the promise of flight as an agent of good, the simple joy of a youngster seeing an airplane fly overhead and lamented that those days had passed. For the Victoria poet Doris Ferne, this loss of innocence was painful:

> He picks the wild salmon-berry,
> Bees point the silence here, until
> In sharp staccato over head
> A silver hooded Army plane
> Goes droning by. A sudden dread
> Links his heart with ruined Spain.

In the aptly titled "Ever Since Spain," Elsie Fry Laurence of Edson, Alberta, was just as pessimistic:

> Ever since Spain,
> Our hearts have contracted
> Again and yet again,
> As a child ran out
> To look at an aeroplane.[12]

For Ferne and Laurence, the implications were clear and tragic: the world had changed because of Spain, and no one would look at an airplane in quite the same way again.

Guernica was only the first of many cities destroyed from the air. Later in 1937 Shanghai and Nanking were bombed by the Japanese during their campaign in China. The air battle of Shanghai began on August 12, 1937, with a horrific example of friendly fire: Chinese aircraft missed the targeted Japanese warship and bombed a number of hotels in the International Settlement, killing and maiming hundreds of civilians. The Japanese continued the air raids in succeeding weeks, and Shanghai, which had already been bombed during the Japanese invasion of 1932, suffered more than two thousand civilian casualties. From August 15, 1937, until the fall of the city four months later, Nanking was subjected to dozens of indiscriminate aerial attacks that destroyed hospitals, schools, government buildings, commercial establishments and warehouses. These raids and the plight of non-combatants moved the poet Edna Jaques:

> An old woman crouches by the curb,
>   And rocks herself in wordless agony,
> A little girl clings to a broken doll
>   And leans against her sobbing mother's knee.
> A few men hunt amid the shattered walls,
>   Dreading to find what they are looking for—
> Blood-spattered faces search the midnight skies
>   To find the flaming chariots of war.

"The Tranquil Hour" by Sara Carsley begins with an idyllic scene: the poet sitting peacefully before a fire. But then she turns on the radio and hears of a new wave of air raids: "Eastward, in air the thundering squadrons go, / Blasting the crystal skies with murderous rain; / The pitiless dawn awakes in doomed Shanghai."[13]

Poems like "The Tranquil Hour" reflect the fear that had lurked beneath the promise of flight since the earliest days: that humanity's greatest technological achievement would be used for destructive purposes. The poet Verna Loveday Harden asked the painful question:

> ... With a fatal skill
> We mould the smooth torpedo...
> And stronger planes in which to storm the skies
> And rain destruction on our cowering kind.
> Can this be progress, this the shining goal
> To which the growing wisdom of the years
> Has led our pilgrim feet...?

But the realization was perhaps most painful for the pioneers of flight. In May 1938, Matthew Halton interviewed Sir John Moore-Brabazon, then credited with making the first airplane flight in Great Britain. Moore-Brabazon spoke with weary disillusionment. When he first flew in 1909, he recalled, he dreamed "that the age of world peace and internationalism was on the horizon." But now, those dreams lay in ruin: "It is bitter to reflect that when I took up an aeroplane for the first time I brought nearer the dark ages of the 20th century."[14]

For many people, Guernica, Shanghai and Nanking proved that Canada, too, was in danger of aerial attack. Through 1938 and 1939, ever more alarming stories appeared in Canadian magazines and newspapers—noiseless aircraft that could bomb a city with impunity; an aerial fleet that could drop more bombs in a single day than were dropped in the entire First World War; air raids that could kill twenty thousand civilians in a single month.[15] All these possibilities demanded that Canada devote more attention to air-raid precautions, and indeed in March 1938 the federal government struck an interdepartmental committee to consider the matter. The committee eventually decided that the Department of Pensions and National Health should be responsible for air-raid precautions. Officials busied themselves with printing bulletins, perfecting blackout techniques and pricing gas

masks, often making decisions on incomplete information. Dr.
F. S. Parney of Pensions and National Health admitted that no
one on the committee had any direct experience of air raids; they
relied almost exclusively on British government accounts of events
in Spain and China or, as a last resort, on the daily press.[16]

Members of Parliament also jumped into the fray. Toronto
MP Tommy Church, never a stranger to hyperbole, treated the
House of Commons to the spectre of air attacks on Canada:
"These raids will be the chief source of danger in all future
wars...a fleet of aircraft could pass up the Ottawa river without
a moment's notice and blow up these buildings, the Chateau
Laurier, the railway station and other large buildings...the
enemy's aircraft would be upon us before you could say 'O
Canada,' or sing 'God Save the King'...large quantities of poison gas could easily be spread over a large area...these attacks
would not only bring ruin to our cities and towns but break the
morale of our people and prevent us from developing a proper
defence and mobilizing our man power and armaments." The
York South MP J. E. Lawson told the House that Canada was
particularly vulnerable to air attack, and that "a few well-placed
bombs in this country might create havoc, not merely where
they were dropped but upon our industrial fabric throughout
the length and breadth of this country." Even Ian Mackenzie,
who as minister of National Defence should have had a better
grasp of the technology, was alarmist, warning that enemy aircraft could take off in Europe, drop their bombs in Canada and
fly back again without landing.[17] The journalist Fraser Hunter
was just as dire in an article subtly titled "Canada Must Fly or
Die": "In recent years an entirely new and revolutionary principle for the application of armed force has been evolved in the
form of air power (and by this is meant massed air bombers)....
Air power in the next war will not fight rival air power....Its
complete duty is the destruction of its target....Air power has
no barriers. Gone are frontiers, seas, rivers, fortifications, mountains, marshes or forests...air power does its dirty work and

returns safely home." As Billy Bishop put it in October 1938, "It is no longer possible to shield the heart of a country with its army. An army can no longer stop an air attack than a suit of mail can stop a rifle bullet. Aviation has, I believe, created the most fundamental change ever made in war.... We can no longer protect our families with an army."[18]

, , ,

Less than a year later, Canadians were to learn just how right Bishop had been. On the first day of September 1939, German troops rolled across the border into Poland, supported by waves of dive-bombers. Within days, the Polish armies were in full retreat, and remnants of units streamed into Warsaw. Impressed by the work of his Condor Legion in Spain, Wolfram von Richthofen ordered a series of incendiary raids to destroy the Polish capital and break the nation's will. The most devastating raid came on September 25, when Ju 52s released more than six hundred tons of high explosives and incendiaries on Warsaw. Two days later, its baroque palaces, cathedrals, the Royal Castle and the old walled town in ruins, the city capitulated.

Canadians seemed to have little interest in Poland as a state, but they were moved by the fate of Warsaw. "Hourly the bombers came in wave on wave," wrote Audrey Alexandra Brown in a poem inspired by the fact that the city's air-raid defences consisted of loudspeakers playing Chopin. "The folk of Warsaw died in square and street; / Their blood was dabbled on the passing feet, / A common bed had they, the common grave." Robert W. Service, from his estate in the south of France, added his own lament:

> I was in Warsaw when the first bomb fell;
> I was in Warsaw when the Terror came—
> Havoc and horror, famine, fear and flame,
> Blasting from loveliness a living hell.

Like Guernica, Warsaw was inverting the meaning of aviation. In the popular imagination, the pilot who had once approached the divine was now one of the four horsemen of the Apocalypse who "ride with Death . . . / Shatt'ring our prayers with Bombs!"[19]

Warsaw was not uppermost in the minds of Nazi leaders when they turned their attention to Britain after the fall of France in June 1940. Realizing that air superiority was essential if the invasion of England was to succeed—and that bombing civilian targets in London would do nothing to achieve command of the air—Hermann Göring, who had been elevated to the command of the Luftwaffe since his dinner with Billy Bishop in Berlin, put the English capital off limits, directing his crews to concentrate on destroying the Royal Air Force and its airfields. In July and August 1940, the Luftwaffe came very close to achieving that goal, as pilot losses and damage to Britain's communications network and airfields almost crippled the RAF. But on August 24, two German bombers assigned to bomb aircraft factories and oil storage tanks east of London lost their way. Unable to locate their targets and harried by anti-aircraft fire, they jettisoned their bombs over central and northeast London. It was the first air raid on the city since May 1918, and the British prime minister, Winston Churchill, was quick to order a retaliatory strike on Berlin. Neither raid caused significant damage, but the exchange shifted the focus of the German air offensive. Angered by the attack on Berlin and exasperated by the Luftwaffe's apparent inability to neutralize the RAF, Hitler ordered the air effort away from Fighter Command and to London.

On September 7, 1940, the Blitz began in earnest. The city would endure fifty-seven consecutive nights of bombing before Göring widened the attack to industrial centres, ports and historic cities. On November 14, 1940, ten hours of bombing left the centre of Coventry ablaze, its cathedral a ruin, its transportation and utilities infrastructure shattered. Its large aircraft factories made Coventry a legitimate military target, but public outrage at the damage to the historic city was heightened by German boasts that the Luftwaffe could "Coventrize" any target it wished. Attacks on English cities would continue until the spring of 1941, when the Luftwaffe withdrew its bomber force for the invasion of Russia. Some forty thousand civilians had been killed and a million homes destroyed, but the bombing had failed to achieve a decisive result. Britain was still in the war and was ready to carry the battle to Germany.

It would be difficult to overestimate the impact of the Blitz on Canadian opinion. It dominated newspapers beginning in the fall of 1940 with banner headlines, accounts from the Canadian Press and other wire services, photographs, line drawings, maps and eyewitness accounts. Precise statements of damage and civilian casualties were not permitted, but large and small papers included as many different kinds of human interest stories as they could. In early 1941, Hugh Templin of the Fergus *News-Record* was dispatched to Britain by the Canadian Weekly Newspaper Association to do a series of articles on the impact of the war in England. His eighteen-part series eventually appeared in more than five hundred weekly newspapers across Canada.[20] *Saturday Night* and *Maclean's* covered the Blitz extensively, with opinion pieces and first-hand accounts such as "This Was My First Air Raid" and "Democratic Bombs"; even specialist publications like the *Canadian Banker* ("Mass Attack in the Air") and the *Royal Bank Magazine* ("Christmas Under the Blitz") covered the bombing raids.

Perhaps more important was the CBC, which provided a direct link to the bomb-stricken cities. The announcers Bob Bowman and Rooney Pelletier provided on-the-spot reports from the heart of the Blitz; the soundman Art Holmes, a pioneer in recording news events, made dozens of recordings of bomb blasts and anti-aircraft guns for broadcast in Canada. There was also a wide range of speciality programs that covered the bombing. The radio program *We Have Been There* allowed Canadians to hear first-hand stories of the Blitz from people such as Brig. Maurice Pope, the assistant chief of the General Staff; Lester Pearson, then an assistant at the Canadian High Commission in London; the *Saturday Night* editor B. K. Sandwell; and Grattan O'Leary, the editor of the Ottawa *Journal*. The series was such a success that the CBC transcribed it and had sold more than twenty-five thousand printed copies of the text by the spring of 1942. Just as popular was R. S. Lambert's *Old Country Mail*, excerpts from letters from people across England; not surprisingly, most were devoted to accounts of the Blitz from the fall of 1940 to mid-1941. There was even a radio soap opera titled *Front Line Family*, which featured the residents of 88 Ashleigh Road, "an ordinary, common little semi-detached house, like thousands of other homes in England." The brainchild of E. L. Bushnell, the CBC's general supervisor of programs, it followed the Robinson family as they lived through the Blitz and became hugely popular not only in Canada but in Britain and the United States as well.[21]

In all these varied accounts of the Blitz, a number of common themes stand out. The public was fascinated by the resistance of the British civilians, particularly what the RCAF officer George Creed called "the Little Folk of London, / Of all but courage shorn, / Who stand beside their bomb-rent homes / And laugh the Hun to scorn."[22] Accounts of the Blitz tended to be built on a cast of standard characters: the genial Cockney matron brewing tea in the wreckage of her east-London home; the stoic constable, unruffled by the destruction around him; the upper-class Londoner, cheerfully cursing the Hun for destroying his club; and the children playing happily amid the rubble of their neighbourhood. The reality, of course, was rather different. The bombing exacerbated class tensions, particularly in east London, where decades of grinding poverty had long since convinced Cockneys that the British establishment had little regard for their well-being. For them, the propaganda of cheerfully pulling together for a common cause rang hollow, knowing that the tonier districts of Chelsea and Mayfair were suffering little damage while their neighbourhoods in industrial London were being flattened. But this reality was never allowed to compromise the myth of

Londoners, bloodied but not bowed, shaking a collective fist at the German bombers and perhaps enjoying the experience. "The people are not only existing, they seem to be living normally, in fact happily," the Montreal *Standard*'s Davidson Dunton told CBC listeners in May 1941. "You hear them talking cheerily to one another. They chat about the latest bombing and prospects of more, as we would about the weather." Account after account paid tribute to their courage under fire and their determination to ensure that it was business as usual. "The ordinary Englishman, the man on the street, gets tougher and tougher," wrote the Canadian army officer John Douglas Macbeth in *Somewhere in England*. "Magnificent is a pretty weak word. Everyone carries on, and just grins."[23] Even the Canadian High Commission staffer Charles Ritchie, never taken in by such rosy propaganda, admitted to being impressed by the determination of the British people: "Their stolidity was unshaken. Their retort was the Englishman's immemorial reply to danger—irony.... They were not afraid but they did want one thing—'a cup of tea.'" Their homes might be demolished, their possessions burned, wrote the Manitoba poet Donald Aiken, but "impregnable, untouched, alone, / This Britain's soul, unbroken yet, / Enshrined within her humbler folk, / Stands fierce and firm."[24]

Also implicit in the press coverage was a deep attachment to the historic buildings of England, which came to stand as tangible symbols of the people's spirit. "They shall not bomb our Abbey," thundered George Creed. "The bomb that lays in dust a nation's Shrine / But brings to whiter heat the wrath Divine." Particularly loathsome in this regard were the so-called Baedeker raids, which targeted English cities of historical or architectural, rather than military, significance. "They selected gentle cathedral towns, those spots where U.S. and Canadian tourists find their way with eager feet and loving hearts," observed Beverley Baxter in a *Maclean's* column carefully written to tug the reader's heartstrings. "Exeter, where you lunch and do the cathedral before motoring on to the rugged joys of the coast of Devon, and York, where the Romans struck their camp. Norwich came under Hitler's lash, too, and quaint old Bath with its hill, its pump room and its memories of Mr Pickwick."[25] But more significant were images of landmarks surviving amid destruction. The photograph of St. Paul's Cathedral, ringed in the smoke of an air raid, became one of the most famous images of the war, inspiring journalists and poets alike. It carried the same message as Louis Keene's watercolour of a night raid on London, painted for the Canadian government's war art program, which used Nelson's Column as a focal point, the survival of the monument through many attacks symbolizing the ultimate impotence of the German air offensive.

Underlying this confidence that the English spirit was impervious to aerial attack, however, was the more general concern that had emerged in the wake of Guernica: "Mankind has gleefully discovered that it is possible to divert the beneficent powers of aviation towards the dealing of death and destruction," wrote the journalist Arnold Sandwell, "to make of the aeroplane...a presentiment of doom whose very approach drives men, women and children underground."[26] In "Airplanes in the Evening," Dorothy Trail sketched a scene that could be drawn from an aviation poem of the early 1930s:

> There hums a plane
> far in the peaceful grey,
> one with the gulls that curve on the river,
> one with wings and pulsing throat,
> one with throbbing freedom and scorn of earth,
> one with the winding sheet of clouds.

All the standard elements are there—the emphasis on peace, the bond between the airplane and the natural world, the notion of freedom, the superiority of the air. But the poem appeared in the summer of 1940, after the bombing of Warsaw and on the eve of the Blitz. The idyllic scene is a chimera, the tranquil natural images mere illusions; the airplane is a bomber that holds "hissing death in its entrails."[27] There was a time when Edna Jaques had "dreamed of swift winged messengers, / Passing along starry roads of night, / Angels of mercy running on the wind, / Along the aisles of light." But Guernica, Warsaw and the Blitz had changed all that:

> ... now I am afraid of wings that gleam
>   Above the towns where people cringe in fear,
> Running to hide in burrows of the earth,
>   When evil wings are near.

> The cruel glint of them when moonlight makes
>   A silver mantle o'er the quiet town,
> Spawning their death into the summer air,
>   Like blossoms drifting down.

Clara Bernhardt drew the same contrast in her poem "Summer Resort," which begins with holidaymakers lying on the beach, "remote from all the carnage of those lands / Which fall beneath invading tank and gun." But suddenly a formation of training aircraft from a nearby base swoops overhead, "blotting out the sunlight" and transforming the tranquil scene: "they vanish into space, / And peace has vanished likewise from this place."[28]

In this rhetoric, the powerful symbols of air-mindedness were transmuted to emphasize the new character of aviation. The connection between airplanes and birds, the theory of the ornithopter, the characterization of aviators as birdmen, the use of natural symbolism to describe aircraft—all affirmed the unity of birds and the machines constructed to imitate them. But with the advent of strategic bombing in the 1930s and 1940s, the man-made bird was increasingly perceived as evil or malicious, as in Maurice Huot's poem "Le Bombardier." It begins with natural images to describe the aircraft, which is immediately transformed into a terrifying bird of prey as it begins its bombing run:

Soudain, vertigineux, il plonge vers l'abîme.

Effrayant des oiseaux qui s'enfuient affolés,
Croyant voir en ce monstre, un aigle tourmenté,
Prêt à fondre sur eux comme le sombre orage.

Mais la bombe a quitté la moderne nacelle,
Et fait jaillir du sol qu'elle mine et ravage,
Une masse de chair, fleur étrange et cruelle.[29]

In other visions, the airplane as "natural" was replaced by the notion that it was a machine, soulless and amoral. Murray Bonnycastle's "Plane Formations," published in December 1944, was clearly inspired by the huge formations of silver American bombers winging their way to targets in Germany:

> These are the icy angels of death and fire;
> they alone can shiningly face the sun
> and pierce the ineffable and unwalked space
> without love and without fear.[30]

The "angels of mercy" that Jaques recalled are now "angels of death and fire," no longer one with the elements. They insolently stare down the sun as they conquer the skies; unmoved by love, unaffected by fear, aircraft have become cold, heartless agents of destruction. Patrick Anderson's poem "Bombing Berlin" is representative of this shift:

> Tonight some boys were history
> moved together in a cloud of disaster
> and one released with prim precision aim
> his vertical verdict:
> below smiles burst, anger became senile
> and the houses fell down on their knees
> and made for their inhabitants a surrealist prayer.[31]

In Anderson's vision, there is no man-made bird, only a machine that operated coldly, killing without remorse or concern.

Nor was this the only notion to be subverted by the bombing campaign. The airplane, once the means of a spiritual journey toward the divine, was transformed in the popular imagination into a demonstration of the impotence of the divine. The Calgary poet Elizabeth Garbutt found little comfort in Robert Browning's epithet "God's in his heaven—/ All's right with the world" after the bombing raids of 1939 and 1940:

> To-day, men, cowering
> In blind shelters,
> Hear the vicious heavens
> Spitting death,
> And ask the whereabouts
> Of God.[32]

There was no better proof that the airplane could vanquish God than the churches and cathedrals, humanity's monuments to a faith, reduced to rubble by enemy air raids. Indeed, the bombed-out church became a symbol not only of the enemy's perfidy but also of the aircraft's power to overcome the forces of good. "So many a church they've toppled down," wrote Audrey Alexandra Brown in a poem that linked the destruction of English cities with the meaning of Christmas. Edna Jaques, too, found in the bombed church a powerful symbol, her poem "Airkrieg" turning on the destruction of a village church by German bombs.[33] For the Saskatchewan poet John Nixon, the fate of Coventry cathedral was more than the destruction of an English landmark; it was the dawn of a new dark age:

> Faith and piety and trust
>   Raise me heavenward from dust
> Poised my tapering spire on high,
> Man and God to glorify.

Dark the age that saw me rise
(Is your own more fair and wise?)
Man, who could in love create,
Hurls me down in lust and hate![34]

Just as the airplane as the path to divinity had been replaced by
the airplane as the destroyer of the divine, so the relationship
between aviation and children had been corrupted. A few years
earlier, children had represented the future of aviation, and young
people were among flight's most passionate supporters. The
Winnipeg poet Helen Ross wrote that the sky used to be a place
for kites, birds and cloud watching, a place of joy and wonder.
Now, "children have lost their sky / ... Their stricken eyes / Have
looked on Hell effacing Paradise." In Mary Quayle Innis's novel
Stand on a Rainbow, little Miles and his sister Sheila play with airplanes. No longer do they simply guide them through loops and
turns as they once might have done; now the airplanes are armed
with tiny tissue bags filled with flour to bomb their stuffed animals. "We're blitzing the bears. Blitzing the bears," Miles and
Sheila chant.[35] Later in the war, shops would sell the Victory
Bomber target game and Captain Marvel's Buzz Bomb, with
which children like Miles and Sheila could duplicate the air war.
As well, the child as air-raid victim became as common an image
as the child as air lobbyist of the 1930s. There are many poems
like Dorothy Dumbrille's elegy to the dead children of
Coventry—

They shall play all day without harm,
Nor fear the terror by night;
They shall be happy and warm
In a place of Eternal Light,
Nor crouch in the earth any more,
To wait for the moan on the air,
As Death goes shrieking by—;

or Wynne Bunning's "If This Were Our Little Son," a harrowing poem in which a young boy clutches his three-year-old sister and begs God to stop the bombing, which has already killed his mother.[36] Nor were the victims all on one side. H. A. C. Mason's "Easter, 1942" recognizes that children in every country were dying under the bombs:

> Little Gretchen Kinderkin lies dying in the rubble,
> Lies dying in the rubbish where the British bomb
>   exploded,
> Twisted, torn, and flung to die
> Pinned beneath the broken brickwork.
>   She is lucky, she is dying
> Free from pain and free from terror
> After that first shrieking instant,
> That bright brief shrieking instant,
> Not again to hear the bombers, not again to bear
>   the bombings,
> Not again to shrink and shiver
> And to hear the children cry.[37]

But there was little sympathy for Gretchen Kinderkin, at least as far as Charles Ritchie could sense. During the height of the Blitz, he had wondered if Berliners could imagine what Londoners were enduring; but in November 1941, when Allied bombers began to hit the German capital, he knew the answer: "Now I feel quite sure that they never did. We never stop to think that they [Berliners] are now having just the same terrifying experience. We shut our eyes to that fact and only think how many bombers we have lost. The capacity for sympathizing with other people's troubles seems to have completely dried up."[38] It is impossible to gauge whether civilians were as hard-hearted as Ritchie suggests, but clearly a belief in the beneficence of aircraft had been replaced not simply by a fear of their potential but also by a desire to use the airplane as an agent of retribution. This had been an element of the rhetoric during the First World War; now the Allies had the equipment to do the job.

, , ,

The raid on Berlin that had been the catalyst for the Blitz did not do a great deal of damage, nor did most of the other bombing raids executed by the RAF in 1940 and 1941. Britain's bombers, the majority of them two-engine machines in service since the mid-1930s, were slow, ungainly and carried only small bomb loads. More significantly, navigational and bomb-aiming aids were so primitive that hitting a specific target depended almost entirely on luck. Indeed, a 1941 report presented to the British War Cabinet revealed that when attacking Germany's industrial Ruhr Valley, only one in ten aircraft was able to get within five miles of the target. There was little hope of achieving a decisive result with those odds.

But in February 1942, Bomber Command was shaken up. Richard Pierse, the commander, was shuttled off to Southeast Asia (where he would undo what little good he had done for his career while at Bomber Command by running off with the wife of another senior commander). In his place was appointed Arthur Harris, a big, gregarious Rhodesian utterly convinced that the bomber could win the war. Harris had a number of advantages over Pierse. The big four-engine bombers, the Stirling, the Halifax and the Lancaster, were becoming available in large numbers, giving Harris the increased bomb-carrying capacity he so desired. New navigational and bomb-aiming aids would permit aircrews virtual pinpoint accuracy. The American Eighth Air Force was building up strength after its first raid (fittingly, on the fourth of July 1942), allowing Harris to look forward to the day when Allied bombers could hit German cities around the clock. Finally, unlike Pierse, Harris had an aggressive, stubborn personality, which would ensure that his will would be done.

Harris's first big raids, on Lübeck and Rostock in March and

April 1942, were mere preludes to what he perceived to be the real opening of his campaign: a thousand-plane raid on Germany. On May 30–31, 1942, he scraped together every available aircraft in the British Isles and sent 1,043 two- and four-engine bombers to Cologne for Operation Millennium. From Harris's point of view, the raid was a complete success; six hundred acres of the city were burned and more than eighteen thousand buildings destroyed, rendering sixty thousand people homeless and vindicating Harris's faith in bombing. The British government, having almost no other means to strike at the Nazis, gave him virtual carte blanche to bring Germany to its knees.

Over the next three years, the air offensive would demonstrate the immense destructive capacity of the airplane to a degree that made Guernica, Warsaw and even the Blitz appear inconsequential. In July and August 1943, the city of Hamburg was subjected to four nights of bombing that left the city centre a charred ruin and killed as many as fifty thousand people—most during the raid of July 27–28, when high explosives and incendiaries created the first man-made firestorm. Harris then sent nearly ten thousand heavy bombers to Berlin between November 1943 and March 1944, but the results were inconclusive. Not so the last big raid of the European war, on Dresden between February 13 and 15, 1945. The fabled medieval city had escaped damage thus far, but in three successive raids, thirteen hundred aircraft of Bomber Command and the Eighth Air Force again used the deadly combination of high explosives and incendiaries to set the city alight, killing as many as sixty thousand civilians. Three weeks later, American B-29 Superfortresses opened the fire-raid offensive against Japan with an attack that devastated Tokyo, killing eighty thousand people and rendering a million homeless. Over the next six months, the B-29s would destroy Japan's six principal industrial cities and many smaller ones in attacks far more horrifying than anything the pre-war futurist writers could have imagined.

The strategic bombing offensive remains one of the most controversial campaigns of the Second World War. The fire raids on

Japan clearly had a significant impact on civilian morale and industrial output, and therefore on shortening the war, but the effect on the German war effort is less clear. Morale did not collapse entirely, as Harris predicted it would, nor was German industry crippled. The ethics of strategic bombing has been even more contentious. Since the war, the legitimacy of targeting civilian areas has been hotly debated. This is as true in Canada as anywhere else, in large part due to the 1992 CBC documentary *The Valour and the Horror*, which argued that Allied civilians, and even the bomber crews themselves, were misled as to the nature and extent of the bombing offensive. The implication was that had average Canadians known of the campaign against the German civilian population, they would have been outraged.

However, the evidence suggests that neither of these propositions is valid. Not only were Canadians fully aware of what was happening in German cities, but they also seem to have had few reservations about the propriety of the strategic bombing offensive. The bombing of German cities was front-page news, especially in 1942 and 1943. The press coverage was graphic, and though it did not state explicitly that civilians were being targeted it certainly left little doubt about the impact of the bombing. Headlines often told the story: "Smell of death rank in bombed Nazi cities," "Bombs leave Berlin flaming sea of fire," "Hamburg ceases to exist." But the articles, essays and opinion pieces were even more forthright, outlining the Allied strategy and giving it wholehearted approval. "The defeat of Germany can only be brought about by killing Germans," wrote B. K. Sandwell, the editor of *Saturday Night*. "If the object of these raids [is] to kill Germans...it is a perfectly proper object." The Toronto *Evening Telegram* admitted that the campaign would visit misery and death on the Axis peoples, but argued that "it is better that they should be blotted out entirely than that the world should be subject to the rulers they have tolerated for so long." A year later, a wire service account of an August 1943 raid on Düsseldorf reported with evident satisfaction that the official civilian death toll should be multiplied by a factor of three or four, "since only victims recognized during the most urgent salvage work are listed officially as dead. The stench in the streets is proof that many are never found and never listed."[39]

Two of Canada's most widely read journalists were also two of the strongest supporters of area bombing. When the RAF's "avenging bombers" hit Augsburg in May 1942, Beverley Baxter could barely contain his glee: "And into Augsburg, flying the whole way just above the ground, come British bombers. There is an inferno of destruction. Bombers circle about with angry droning engines. Take that for Coventry! Take that for Plymouth! Take that for Southampton!" Baxter had no moral qualms, no need to claim that attacks on civilian targets were navigational errors. "There is no use pretending that our bombers sought only the bull's-eye of their target," he wrote of a raid on Lübeck. "They let the whole place have it until the centre of the town was a heap of rubble and hundreds of people were fleeing terror-stricken into the hinterland." The attacks on Augsburg, Lübeck and Rostock, he wrote, were "extermination raids," pure and simple. These cities were not vital to the German war machine; the plan was simply that such "towns were to be effaced from the map as far as normal habitation was concerned." For Baxter, this was only just and right. "What a change from those halcyon days when brave Luftwaffe pilots bombed defenseless towns in Spain," he concluded.[40] Wilson Woodside, a long-time Canadian commentator on international affairs, also argued the justice of retaliatory raids. "I personally think that we shall have to come to this," he wrote of indiscriminate bombing in May 1941, "and that it may be the only way we can stop the Germans from destroying such historic monuments as the Abbey, Westminster Hall and St. Paul's." He was delighted that in the summer of 1941, German civilian casualties from air raids were increasing, and the following year opined that direct attacks on civilians had to continue, to depress morale by keeping them "worrying and sleepless in their cold basement shelters." Precision raids were no substitute for "the simple blotting out of important cities."[41]

Whether journalists were leading or expressing public opinion is an open question, but Canadians seem to have had few qualms about targeting civilians. A public opinion poll in late 1942 revealed that 57 percent of respondents approved of bombing the German civilian population (62 percent approved when Japan was the target). Many of them probably agreed with Mackenzie King, who had little sympathy for German civilians because "it was Hitler who started total war and [the] killing of women and children." Poets also embraced the retributive air power. The Toronto poet Robina Monkman called the Royal Air Force the Eagles of Death, an epithet more frequently applied to the German Luftwaffe, and made it clear that Allied airmen were birds of revenge: "Wings, wings, wings, beating a steady song, / A song of retribution that shakes the stars apart." In Helen Middleton's "Scroll of Honor," one of the heroes is a bomber pilot who drops his bombs on Berlin "with a twisted grin" (another description typically applied to the enemy) to secure vengeance for the Blitz. Robert Main, in a poem dedicated to his son, who died in 1943 while serving with the RCAF, celebrated the ability of the Allies to bomb German targets and observed that "the biggest thrill of Dick, Tom and Bill / Is the bomb, bomb, bomb on Berlin."[42] Fiction writers, too, found an appealing figure in the pilot who enlisted in the bomber force to seek revenge on the enemy. In Jack Paterson's "Green Geese," Gil Tucker joined the RCAF to avenge the bombing of Plymouth, the birthplace of his grandfather. "Some Go in Darkness," by W. E. Johns, tells the story of a pilot who transferred to bombers after his sister was killed in an air raid. ("Death flamed in Berlin skies but revenge burned brighter in the bomber pilot's heart," read the display copy accompanying the story.) He taped a photograph of his sister to his instrument panel, and it seemed to smile every time his crew began their bomb run.[43]

But taking revenge by air was not the exclusive preserve of the aviator. Commercial and government advertising often traded on the notion that every Canadian could play a part in the bombing campaign—by purchasing the right products. An advertisement for Goodyear reminded consumers that they could ride on the very tires that equipped Allied bombers. "*Thousand-Plane* Raids Need *Thousands* of Tires!" declared the text. Studebaker of Canada bragged that the expertise that went into their vehicles also went into the manufacture of engines for B-17 bombers, "America's invincible dreadnaught of the skies." Canadian Pacific Air Lines made much of the company's role in training bomber crews: "'German cities blasted…planes return safely.' Next time you see a headline like that, remember that back of the smooth proficiency of a bomber's crew are many months of difficult training," perhaps at one of the six Air Observer Schools run by the airline.[44] Even something as prosaic as saving bones allowed civilians to partake in the bombing campaign: "*On en fait de la colle pour avions…et l'on s'en sert pour les explosifs.*"

The notion that average Canadians could vicariously join the bomber force was explicit in the Victory Bond drives, which played on the suggestion that by purchasing bonds, everyone could contribute to the destruction of German cities. "Back the Attack," a ditty written for the fourth Victory Loan campaign, reminded contributors that their money would buy "tons of explosives that blast to smithereens." "Your Bond may buy This Bomb!" trumpeted an ad for the fifth Victory Loan. "Put your money in bonds to bomb the Axis. Put your dollars to work smashing 'Festung Europa.'" The theme returned in the following year's campaign: "Their Target—Berlin!" proclaimed an advertisement picturing a Lancaster crew and implying that every Canadian could join them by buying Victory Bonds. Another advertisement depicted a smiling munitions worker, with the slogan "*Je fabrique des bombes et j'achète des obligations.*" Not everyone could drop bombs, or even make them, but everyone could take part in the bombing campaign by purchasing Victory Bonds. In an ad for a cereal company, Joe Smith pondered how he might help his son, a Lancaster pilot. The solution?—buy Victory Bonds equalling the cost of one bomb.[45] In these ads, we see how far public opinion had travelled since the heady days of the 1920s. Then, the dream of the air lobby was for every person to fly, for only then could the airplane work its potential magic. Scarcely a decade later, the dream was for every person to bomb.

, , ,

By this time, it was increasingly clear that not only did the airplane have immense destructive capacity but also that aviation itself had the potential to create competition and discord. "Because of the rapid development of aviation during the war, the international rivalries which would develop in the future after the conclusion of hostilities would be even sharper than those of the past unless some improvement is effected," C. D. Howe warned the House of Commons in 1944. Trevor Lloyd wrote in *Maclean's* in 1943 that "the plane's conquest of time and space is giving new meaning to global geography and is radically changing the pattern of international relations."[46] A decade earlier, it would have been understood that the change was for the better, but no longer.

Now it was widely conceded that the air had to be controlled in some way to prevent it from becoming just another forum for disputes. Politicians, journalists, pilots, airline executives—all realized that aviation policy would be critical to world peace in the future. "One field wherein intense rivalry will be the rule is undoubtedly that of aviation," wrote D. M. LeBourdais in *Canadian Forum*. "It is not beyond the bounds of possibility that the precipitating cause of another great war will result from that rivalry." Unless the great powers came to agreements on the use of the skies, the novelist and political commentator Leslie Roberts argued, conflicts over air space would mean that "we shall soon be getting ready for World War III."[47]

The crux was whether the skies should be open or closed. Should there be complete freedom of the air, or should the world's aerial highways be tightly controlled by an international body? The open-skies lobby believed that only complete freedom of access could bring peace. "Aviation is making the world into a neighborhood," wrote Parker Van Zandt, turning the traditional argument of the air lobby on its head, "but making people closer neighbors does not automatically make them friends." The only way to ensure amicable relations, in his view, was to guarantee that everyone had access to the airways. "If we sincerely want a better world we shall not fail to promote the freest possible development of world air transport."[48]

Others were bitterly opposed to this future, believing it would ensure that only strong governments and aviation companies had access to the skies. As the American aviation authority Theodore Wright told the 1944 Chicago air conference, "completely wide-open competition might well result in injustice and in damage to amicable relations to an extent out of all proportion to the expected gain in air transport expansion that might result." The proper course of action was regulation of air routes by an international body, "as a means of ensuring world peace as well as the sound development of air transport," wrote the journalist S. G. Cameron in 1944.[49] Canadians seemed to agree that international regulation was necessary if aviation was to become an instrument for co-operation rather than discord. A July 1943 public opinion survey revealed that fully half of respondents believed that all airlines should be government run; fewer than 20 percent favoured free competition among private companies. The following month, a survey showed that nearly two-thirds of respondents favoured joint, co-operative regulation of international air routes, rather than open competition.[50]

Perhaps the most eloquent plea, however, came from Billy Bishop, still the most famous flier in Canada. Exhausted by his public responsibilities and plagued by ill health, he nevertheless found the energy to write *Winged Peace*, a summary of his "hopes and fears as our civilization takes up the tasks of the Air Age." With characteristic forthrightness, Bishop laid out what he understood to be the choice facing humanity: "Aviation is the greatest single force which can ensure an enduring peace, or, on the other hand, will be the most destructive weapon man has produced in his history." The history of flight, in which he had been so intimately involved, pointed in both directions, and he pleaded with the public to think seriously about the lessons of the Second World War: "All the people in the world have to be awakened to the implications of this behemoth of the skies. I am at a loss to understand how the true impact of air-power can have failed to impress them ... the press and radio drummed into our eyes and ears stories of thousands of tons of bombs which inexorably and mercilessly were reducing Nazidom's capital and many of its great industrial centers to rubble." In Bishop's view, the only possible course was for the air to be directed co-operatively, by a recognized international body that would hold "under closest control the means to destruction inherent in aviation." Realizing that aviation had passed to younger hands, he could only warn, "The Air Age faces mankind with a sharp choice—the choice between Winged Peace or Winged Death. It's up to you."[51]

, , ,

But the question of open or closed skies would not be resolved at the Chicago conference or by Billy Bishop; it remains one of the most contentious aspects of aviation policy. What was clear, however, was that the Second World War had dramatically altered perceptions of flight. The dream of aviation producing a new age of amity was gone; the air merely provided a new realm in which nations would struggle. This had the positive consequence of providing impetus for co-operation in civil aviation, but it also revealed the degree to which the dreams of the air lobby had been subverted. Even the poets had to agree that the future of aviation looked very different in 1945 than it had in 1939, and the change was not entirely for the better. For the poet Mary Matheson, it was a change that humanity did not yet fully appreciate:

Somewhere tonight beneath a quiet sky
Death rides on wings that men have perfected
To slay mankind, and having slain have sped
Back to their base nor think of hosts that die
Within their wake of fire; while far on high
Oblivious to all this shattered world
They coolly tabulate the bombs they hurled
Nor heed the echoes of earth's anguished cry.

Each star looks down, a calm cathedral light,
Serene, unchanging, on a world of change.
Who knows in future what shall be the range
Of winged squadrons—or to what great height
They shall ascend—and what their purpose when
That future writes their epitaph again?[52]

, 9 ,

THE EVERLASTING
ARMS OF SCIENCE

First to arrive were the surveyors, armed with transits and tape measures and wooden stakes of various colours. Next came the bulldozers, even though the land was flat, and a convoy of trucks carrying building materials—water pipes, electrical cable, sections of prefabricated huts, pumps, telephone poles, generators, lumber, shingles, corrugated iron, fencing. Soon the buildings began to take shape along the roads that the surveyors had laid out, and work crews began to pave the three wide, smooth double runways and the aprons. Before long, the buildings were completed, the gravel paths laid, new sod put down and flower beds planted. Great excitement greeted the arrival of the aircraft—powerful and handsome Harvards, painted a glorious bright yellow. What had once been a field northeast of Aylmer, in Ontario's tobacco country, was now #14 Elementary Flying Training School, a 515-acre airport with five double hangars, fifty-odd other buildings, as many as 1,228 cadets, instructors, and military and civilian staff members (with a new batch of keen students arriving every four weeks) and 177 of the most modern training aircraft available.[1]

What happened in Aylmer was more than just the transformation of a community; it was symbolic of the changing times. The Second World War and the proliferation of strategic bombing robbed aviation of its potential to act as an agent of world peace, but the war had other, equally far-reaching consequences. As the people of Aylmer realized, aviation changed quantitatively during the war. Passenger airlines expanded, as did the aircraft manufacturing industry and the Royal Canadian Air Force—more people and more aircraft in more communities were involved than ever before. But aviation also changed qualitatively. As it touched the lives of more and more Canadians, flight began to lose some of its romance and mystique. This, combined with the increasing technological sophistication of aircraft, altered the character of the pilot and indeed the nature of flying. In the process, the war achieved what the air lobby had been unable to do: it made flying part of everyday life.

, , ,

In July 1917, a local newspaper in the Toronto area reported a most singular incident: "About half-past seven on Monday morning, the residents of Pickering were treated to a novel sight, one which was never seen in this vicinity before. Their attention was first directed to the objects of interest by the continuous hum of the machinery, and the noise of the gasoline motor boats. At first the sound was supposed to come from approaching autos, but in a few moments scores of eyes were directed heavenward to three aeroplanes. When first seen they were coming from the west along the lake shore and then when south west of the village they turned northwards and passing over the village westwards again presumably on their return trip to the aviation school at Long Branch, west of Toronto. They were at considerable height, but were plainly visible. We believe the time is not far distant when the passing of an aeroplane over our heads will excite but little interest."[2] Since 1919, the air lobby had been working assiduously toward that very end, but by the late 1930s the consensus seemed to be that Canada was even less air-minded than it had been a decade earlier. Editorials with provocative titles such as "What Is Our Air Policy?" "Canada's Air Problem" and "Ignoring Commercial Flying" assailed the government for its failure to develop a consistent, forward-thinking air policy and accused the country's leaders of squandering a golden opportunity. All the building blocks had been in place after 1918—inexpensive aircraft, experienced pilots and mechanics, limitless opportunities, a sympathetic public—but the nation had "allowed itself to get into a backwater in the matter of air transportation," lamented *Saturday Night* in an editorial that summed up the conventional wisdom. While other countries had been moving forward to the air age, Canada was slipping back, "inexplicably blind to her own opportunities." Many aviation writers concluded sadly that the term "air-minded" could not yet be applied to Canada.[3] Despite the extensive education campaign mounted by the air lobby, the advent of air-mindedness in Canada had little to do with their efforts. Rather, it was the Second World War that brought aviation into the lives of so many Canadians. By increasing the demands placed on aircraft and by accelerating the pace of technological change that made flying safer and more practical, the Second World War took aviation to new levels of acceptance.

This was particularly true with respect to passenger services, which grew dramatically during the war years. By September 1939, Trans-Canada Air Lines had only the beginnings of a national service. The company had inaugurated its Montreal-to-Vancouver run on April Fool's Day 1939, but the "transcontinental" service did not yet fly to the Maritime provinces, as a Nova Scotia newspaper was quick to point out: "This Pioneer Province is the most shamefully located of all areas in the field of commercial aviation in this dominion. We make that statement deliberately; the neglect of the province by the public authorities in this field is both shameful and disgraceful."[4] TCA flew more than three million miles in 1939, but carried fewer than twenty-two thousand paying passengers, at fares that only the well-off could afford. After six years of war, the airline was transformed. Its workforce exploded, from fewer than five hundred in 1939 to more than thirty-two hundred in 1945; in the last year of the war it carried more than 180,000 passengers and flew some 11½ million miles. The fleet, which began with two Lockheed Electras, sleek, ten-passenger aircraft that were the last word in airliners in 1937, grew to twenty-eight aircraft, including bigger, more modern machines such as the Lockheed Lodestar and the DC-3. New routes had been added—Moncton in 1940, Halifax in 1941, Sydney and St. John's in 1942 and Victoria in 1943. This expansion, combined with the opening in 1940 of a second daily transcontinental service, allowed TCA to legitimize its advertising claim of flying from sea to sea: "Canada is only one day wide. Spanning the continent twice each day—Trans-Canada Air Lines has overcome the barriers of distance—shrunk the vast expanse of the Nation—until the shores of the Atlantic are but a day's distance from the shores of the Pacific."[5]

But TCA was not the only player. The Canadian Pacific Railway, still smarting from being squeezed out of the national airline business by TCA and the federal government in 1937, had retained an interest in aviation through its partial ownership of Canadian Airways Limited, and the railway recognized that wartime conditions created an opportunity to increase its involvement. The untimely death of James A. Richardson, CAL's founder and driving force, in 1939 made the CPR's decision easier. Beginning in 1940, the railway aggressively acquired aviation companies operating in the Canadian north, and in May 1942 the

CPR amalgamated its new acquisitions, as well as CAL and its affiliates, into the new Canadian Pacific Air Lines. A year later, the new carrier was flying eighteen thousand miles a day, deriving fully 60 percent of its revenue from passenger fares. CPAL had one major intercity route, a daily service between Montreal and Quebec City; the bulk of its flying was in the northwest, from its hubs at Edmonton and Winnipeg. The airline's advertisements made much of the fact that it complemented rather than competed with TCA, and that together the two airlines gave Canada a passenger and freight system second to none.

Most of this expansion was made possible, and indeed essential, by the war. Speed, which had become a watchword of business in the 1930s, had become even more critical, for neither the nation's leaders nor captains of industry could afford to waste time in the fight against the enemy. As an article in *Saturday Night* put it, "Speed is more than ever becoming the essence of modern travel. . . . Millions of people have taken to the air in their quest for speed and still more speed, for . . . more business hours." Moreover, Canadians came to rely on aircraft not only to get from place to place quickly but to transport mail and freight. The men and women of Canada's armed forces who were separated from their families placed ever-growing demands on the Post Office, more than quadrupling the total weight of airmail carried during the war years. And increasing wartime wages meant that Canadians had more disposable income to spend on airmail and, when seats were not being taken up by priority passengers, vacation flights. "In a brief fortnight's holiday you can now do things you've dreamed of," mused a TCA advertisement in the spring of 1940, a few weeks before the German invasion of France. "Distance no longer prevents you from enjoying the tang of Atlantic breezes in the Maritime Provinces, Quebec's quaint charm, Ontario's lake-dotted Highlands, the magnificent Canadian Rockies, or the rugged forests of British Columbia."[6]

While passenger services within Canada were expanding, international services were also experiencing modest but significant growth, again due to the demands of the war. PanAm's flying boat service to Portugal continued through the war, albeit under military direction, but the Canadian government had limited access to these flights, either for mail or passengers. With Canadian troops in England growing increasingly restive over slow mail delivery, the Canadian government opted to establish its own transatlantic air service. Initially hampered by a lack of suitable aircraft, the government eventually acquired a Lancaster bomber, which was converted to a passenger carrier and inaugurated the Canadian Government Trans-Atlantic Service (CGTAS) on July 22, 1943; within a year, it and two other Lancastrians (as the aircraft were renamed) were making three return trips to England each week. In its first eighteen months, the CGTAS carried more than one million pounds of mail and two thousand passengers, considerably more than had flown the Atlantic between the R-34's flight in 1919 and the opening of PanAm's scheduled service in 1939.

But the Lancastrians were not the only aircraft regularly crossing the Atlantic. Even before the war, the British Air Ministry had used North American manufacturers to build up its squadron strength, and British orders increased dramatically through 1939 and 1940. But it was not clear how those aircraft—twenty-six thousand on order by the summer of 1940—would get to Britain. Taking them apart for transport by sea was time-consuming and wasteful, as they had just been put together in the factories. Air Cmdre. Norman Anderson, a long-time air booster who was now head of the RCAF's Eastern Air Command, pointed out the self-evident: they were airplanes—why not fly them over? The British Air Ministry thought the plan was suicidal, given the recent history of transatlantic flying, but it appealed to Lord Beaverbrook, the Canadian-born minister of Aircraft Production. Ignoring the Air Ministry, he struck a deal among the Canadian Pacific Railway (which would provide ground logistical support), G. E. Woods Humphery, the former managing director of Imperial Airways, and his own ministry, which would supply the flying personnel and pick up the tab. In November 1940, three months after

Beaverbrook concluded the agreement, seven Lockheed Hudson medium bombers made the first successful ferry flight.

Although the first few months were marred by a number of tragedies, the most serious a February 1941 crash that killed Nobel Prize–winning scientist Sir Frederick Banting, the proportion of completed flights was so encouraging that the program was expanded, although without the CPR (it dropped out in May 1941). The number of aircraft ferried across the Atlantic increased dramatically—more than nineteen hundred in 1942, nearly twice that two years later. The stream of aircraft, flying either singly or in small groups, left the main North American base of Ferry Command in Montreal, bound for Prestwick in Scotland, via either Gander or Goose Bay and Reykjavik. By 1944, an average of ten aircraft left Ferry Command bases each day to cross the Atlantic.

The flight was not always a pleasant one, for the weather conditions that had challenged the long-distance pioneers of the 1920s also confronted the pilots of Ferry Command. Yet the loss rate was remarkably low—just 2 percent, fewer than two hundred of the nearly ten thousand aircraft flown across the Atlantic by Ferry Command. (Interestingly, only about a third of the lost aircraft went down in mid-ocean; the majority crashed over land, many of them on takeoff or landing.) The success rate of Ferry Command vindicated Beaverbrook's faith in the idea and demonstrated the exceptional skill of the crews who routinely retraced the route of Alcock and Brown, Lindbergh, and Nungesser and Coli. Without their deliveries, the Allied air forces would soon have been starved of equipment.

If Ferry Command's impact on the Allied war effort was significant, its effect on perceptions of aviation was even greater. For decades, conquering the North Atlantic had been the greatest prize in aviation. The adulation of the transatlantic flying heroes was born of the realization that humans had finally overcome the barrier separating the old world from the new. PanAm's transatlantic services had not yet had time to affect the public's perceptions in any meaningful way; the fascination with flying boats was still built on the fact that these flights were so remarkable and exceptional. But with the establishment of the CGTAS and Ferry Command, the North Atlantic was flown every day and not just by legendary pilots. Soldiers, politicians, civil servants, businessmen—all crossed the Atlantic by air with relative ease. In one well-publicized flight in 1941, cabinet ministers "Chubby" Power and Ian Mackenzie had breakfast in Scotland and dinner in Canada, and newspapers lauded the Duke of Kent for being the first member of the royal family to cross the Atlantic by airplane.[7] Even Mackenzie King made the flight, in a Liberator bomber in August 1941, albeit after consulting the spirit world and receiving encouraging omens through numerology. King intimated to his diary that he felt no fear or foreboding, although the crashes of two fully loaded Ferry Command Liberators, with a loss of forty-four lives, just days before his scheduled departure convinced the ever-cautious prime minister to write his will. He enjoyed the flight immensely and interpreted it, typically, in religious terms: "The words that kept coming to my mind were: terrestrial and celestial; seeing a new heaven and a new earth . . . every impression I had was very clear and I could feel the nearness of spiritual beings."[8] King's wonder, however, was becoming increasingly rare. "The lone planes of the peacetime trans-oceanic airlines have become a cloud of war planes ferried by the R.A.F. and the A.A.F. ferry command," wrote one young aviation enthusiast in 1942. Crossing the ocean by air was, by the middle of the war, an everyday occurrence. "Royal Air Force Ferry Command Makes a Pond of the Atlantic," declared a headline in *Saturday Night* in 1942— one of the most daunting flights in aviation had become a commonplace.[9]

A significant number of the warplanes that crossed the Atlantic were manufactured in Canadian factories, as the aircraft industry also experienced extraordinary growth during the war. Between 1919 and 1939, a total of 678 aircraft of all types were manufactured in Canada, by a small number of specialized firms—Fleet

Aircraft of Canada, a tiny operation in Fort Erie, Ontario, with a full-time staff that could fit in one of TCA's Lockheeds, and the larger Noorduyn Aircraft of Montreal, which produced the legendary Norseman bush plane—and a few big concerns— Canadian Car and Foundry; National Steel Car in Hamilton; and the Ottawa Car Manufacturing Company, which manufactured British-designed aircraft as a sideline. But the industrial capacity was there, and when demands for military aircraft skyrocketed Canadian manufacturers were quick to increase production. By 1944, the aircraft industry had become a major employer, with more than 116,000 workers at plants across the country. In Fort William, Ontario, and Verdun, Quebec, CCF manufactured Hurricane fighters and the Hampden, a medium bomber adored by its crews despite being obsolete, on an assembly line that was the brainchild of Elsie MacGill. Victory Aircraft in Malton, Ontario, was running two nine-hour shifts six days a week to turn out fifty Lancasters a month. Just down the highway, de Havilland in Downsview produced the Tiger Moth, a graceful and much-loved training biplane, and the Mosquito, a revolutionary high-performance medium bomber constructed primarily of wood. Canadian Vickers at Cartierville, Quebec, and Boeing's Canadian plant in Vancouver built Canso flying boats, a variant of the American Catalina that were used for anti-submarine patrols over Canada's coasts. By the end of the war, Canadian workers had built some 16,400 aircraft.

The Canadian-built Mosquitos, Lancasters and Hampdens were bound for operational squadrons in England, but the Ansons and Tiger Moths produced in Canadian factories became part of the British Commonwealth Air Training Plan, one of Canada's greatest contributions to the Allied war effort. Training Commonwealth aviators in Canada had been proposed as early as 1936, but intermittent negotiations failed to produce an agreement. Mackenzie King, always leery of British designs on Canada's human resources in time of war, feared that such a scheme might be misinterpreted as a promise that Canada would participate in a future European war. British officials, for their part, were desperate to take advantage of Canada's wide-open spaces for training pilots but not desperate enough to be very flexible in the discussions. The coming of war, however, had a salutary effect on both sides. The British made a new formal proposal on September 6, 1939, before Canada entered the war, and King responded with an enthusiastic pledge to expand training facilities for airmen. The prime minister welcomed the prospect of Canada serving as a training ground: training airmen was essential but immeasurably safer than a large infantry commitment.

Although the plan fitted admirably into King's notion of a limited liability war, that did not prevent Canadian negotiators from driving a hard bargain with their British counterparts. For more than six weeks, the two sides haggled, mostly over the financial arrangements for the $600 million cost, but on December 17, 1939, King and Lord Riverdale, Britain's lead negotiator, finally signed the agreement for the British Commonwealth Air Training Plan. Intended to produce 1,464 pilots, observers and wireless operators/air gunners each month, the scheme would require an immense infrastructure: initial estimates (which turned out to be very low) put the requirements at thirty-five hundred aircraft (more than ten times as many as the RCAF had when the war began), thirty-three thousand servicemen and -women, six thousand civilian employees and more than a hundred airfields. After an exhaustive survey of Canada's 153 registered airfields, officials calculated that twenty-four of them were ready or could be made so in fairly short order; another dozen required extensive upgrading; and the remaining seventy-five would have to be built from scratch. These airfields would be instrumental in spreading airmindedness across Canada.

The American president, Franklin Delano Roosevelt, called Canada "the aerodrome of democracy" (a phrase apparently coined by Lester Pearson), and the figures are indeed impressive: nearly 132,000 graduates from more than one hundred training establishments employing tens of thousands of military and civilian personnel. But as one pilot expressed it, "More impressive than any cold list of establishments...is the daily sight of training aeroplanes in the sky here in Canada, the thousands of boys in air force blue on the streets of our cities, in the trains and in the restaurants."[10] Here lay the real impact of the BCATP in spreading the gospel of flight in Canada: the friendly invasion of air-minded men and women who descended on hundreds of communities across the country. Nowhere is this clearer than in rural areas, where the airmen and base employees often outnumbered the townspeople. For example, Gimli, Manitoba, with a population of 853 in 1941, was the site of #18 Service Flying Training School, which eventually had a peak strength of 1,337 all ranks. A newspaper in Yorkton, Saskatchewan, the home of #11 SFTS, predicted that on any given night, as many as six hundred airmen would be in town on leave from the base. Such communities enthusiastically adopted their bases and their staff, and successive classes of airmen-in-training became part of the social fabric. The townspeople developed a deep interest in and attachment to their bases—lists of graduating aviators appeared prominently in the local paper, and any loss in training accidents was deeply felt. Thousands of locals attended base open houses; the units' magazines were of sufficient interest to the citizens to be sold at newsstands; base bands were a fixture at social events; and sporting teams from the bases squared off against local sides. As the Weyburn *Review* suggested, the local base achieved what decades of propaganda by the air lobby had failed to do: "People in Weyburn who a few months ago found it difficult to sleep because of the unfamiliar drone of training planes overhead, are like the child accustomed to being rocked to sleep—they now find it difficult to get to sleep without the familiar purr of engines in the sky."[11]

The growth of the BCATP was part of a remarkable expansion of the RCAF during the Second World War. From a minuscule service of 270 aircraft and 3,048 all ranks in 1939, the RCAF emerged in 1945 as the fourth-largest air force in the world:

249,662 men and women (roughly two-thirds of whom served in Canada) had worn the air force blue, and at its peak strength in January 1944, the RCAF boasted seventy-eight squadrons, thirty-five of them overseas. For the first time, young Canadians were able to get involved in flying in unprecedented numbers. The Air Cadets of Canada boasted 138 squadrons and nearly sixteen thousand personnel when it came under RCAF control in November 1941; its commander, Russell Frost, predicted that the force would soon grow to four hundred squadrons and more than fifty thousand all ranks. "Yours is the first of history's generation to receive the wonderful heritage of aviation," he told the cadets; "you are the first to whom the age-old dream of riding the skies is passed as reality that henceforth all may share."[12] When the RCAF ballooned from a few thousand members in 1939 to a quarter of a million six years later, it fundamentally changed the relationship between aviation and the general population. During the First World War, only a select few Canadian families could boast an airman in their ranks; by 1945, hundreds of thousands of families had members in the air force or air cadets.

, , ,

The extraordinary expansion of the military and civilian air services and of the aircraft industry during the Second World War meant that for the first time, the public was deeply and, in many cases, personally interested in aviation. Flight became ubiquitous—it was in newspapers, magazines and books, on radio and in movie houses, in advertisements and children's toys. During the First World War, pilots and their exploits garnered coverage because they were exceptional and far from the experience of the public. During the Second World War, aviation was everywhere in popular culture because it touched everyone's life, either personally or through a close relative or friend.

As a result, the press devoted considerable space to the air war. Coverage was largely conventional and not particularly revealing—letters of a local boy in the RCAF, descriptions of newly designed aircraft, accounts of air operations in various theatres—in other words, nothing that would have been out of place in a Canadian newspaper in 1917. What is striking, though, is the amount and variety of coverage. The fighter pilots who had dominated press coverage during the First World War continued to enjoy a high profile, but they no longer stole the limelight. Articles in mass-circulation magazines, such as *Maclean's* and *National Home Monthly*, documented every conceivable aspect of the air effort, from the ferrying of bombers to Alaska to the assembly of Harvard trainers for the BCATP to the development of special pants for pilots. In January 1942, the broadcast journalist Peter Stursberg wrote a series of articles for the Vancouver *Province* on reconnaissance flights from RCAF Jericho Beach in British Columbia. The aircrews of Jericho Beach never encountered an enemy vessel, but Stursberg hastened to point out that "the inspection of shipping was one of our most important jobs in guarding the BC coast."[13]

For more in-depth accounts, publishers were ready with books about the air war. There were the concise and, it must be said, somewhat tedious official histories, such as the three-volume *The RCAF Overseas* and D. F. Griffin's rather less dry *First Steps to Tokyo: The Royal Canadian Air Force in the Aleutians*. Readers who wanted a little more colour could turn to first-person accounts, such as D. A. MacMillan's *Only the Stars Know* and Alec McAlister's *Hi-Sky!: The Ups and Downs of a Pinfeather Pilot*. Like Billy Bishop, George "Buzz" Beurling, Canada's greatest ace of the Second World War, published his memoirs, the highly successful *Malta Spitfire*. (It was ghost-written by the journalist Leslie Roberts over nineteen days, when the two were hospitalized together.) There were such memorial volumes celebrating the lives and sacrifice of fallen airmen as *The Diary of a Canadian Fighter Pilot*, a tribute to Flying Officer W. S. Large of Camrose, Alberta, who went missing on operations over Malta in 1943, and *Jacques Chevrier, Chef d'Escadrille*, about a native of Saint-Lambert,

Quebec, who was lost on an anti-submarine flight in 1942. There were collections of poetry, sensitive and well-crafted fiction such as Irene Baird's epistolary novel *He Rides the Sky*, and such potboilers and thrillers as Frank Sheridan's *Paid in Full*. ("To his family he was irresponsible and devil-may-care...but to the Chinese he was a fabulous hero.")

Children's books with aviation themes were also popular. Some were American imports, such as Al Avery's *A Yankee Flier on a Rescue Mission*, but there were plenty of homegrown flying aces to be found in the pages of the Montreal-published *Canadian Heroes*. An issue of True Comics celebrated the achievements of Elsie MacGill, the "Queen of the Hurricanes," and Triumph Comics published Jerry Lazare's *Air Woman*, which followed the adventures of the fictitious Sally Dunlop as she talked down a crippled bomber to a safe landing. Other comics focused on the air war—*The Camera Commando* by E. T. Legault, about a newsreel cameraman, Jimmy Corrigan, filming the RCAF in action; *The Invisible Commando* by Leo Bachle, starring the dashing young RCAF office Lee Pierce, who discovered a substance that made him invisible; and Ohrt and James's *Spanner Preston*, a Canadian in the RAF who went undercover to find a missing spy. And what Canadian child did not thrill to the adventures of Johnny Canuck, the pilot and secret agent who, more than once, fought Adolf Hitler with his bare hands?

But Canadians could do more than just read about airmen in action; thanks to an organized and highly efficient propaganda network organized by the RCAF's Directorate of Public Relations, they could hear and see them. Billy Bishop proved a tireless ambassador, making personal appearances and giving speeches across the country, and the RCAF dispatched a legion of tour-expired airmen to talk to Canadian communities about flying. Even Buzz Beurling made a cross-country patriotic tour in February and March 1943, but the morose and troubled man from Verdun, Quebec, was entirely unsuited to the task. He was ill at ease in a crowd and uncomfortable speaking in public:

"During the whole interview, he did not utter two consecutive sentences," observed the Montreal *Daily Star*.[14] Bishop was comfortable talking about his exploits, but Beurling appeared cold and aloof, uncommunicative and vaguely threatening. This air of danger and mystery made Beurling a huge draw with women, but he was a dismal failure as a propaganda tool.

Radio also emerged as a powerful tool for spreading the word about Canada's air effort. Such regular features as *Flying for Freedom: The RCAF in Action* were supplemented by reports from correspondents attached to units of the air force, many of whom got as close to the action as possible. John Kannawin and Art Holmes of the CBC were interviewing the crews at an RCAF Coastal Command base in Northern Ireland when Kannawin was invited to join an anti-submarine patrol. Sixteen and a half hours later, he stumbled off the Short Sunderland flying boat with a story that was broadcast across North America and Britain. The CBC reporter Harold Wadsworth and Ray Mackness, an RCAF public relations officer, flew on the first mission of the first Lancaster to roll off the Victory Aircraft production line. The aircraft failed to reached Berlin, turning back and eventually crash-landing with engine trouble, but listeners got a great story. The Vancouver announcer Bill Herbert went to Normandy with the first Canadian fighter squadrons to follow the invasion forces. The former CBC farm commentator Don Fairbairn, who joined the RCAF in 1942 as a radio mechanic and transferred to the RCAF Information Unit, hitched a ride in a B-25 Mitchell medium bomber that flew one of the pre-dawn raids on the morning of the D-Day landings. These broadcasts brought the air war to Canadians in a very immediate way; listeners came to appreciate both the immense variety of aircraft tasks and the sheer scale of the air effort. In one compelling broadcast, describing the aerial armada that was to drop Allied paratroopers on Arnhem in September 1944, Fairbairn sketched a scene that could have come straight from a futurist novel: "That roar which you hear is from hundreds of our transport planes passing overhead, carrying airborne troops to be dropped in an offensive against Germany.... On all sides of these transport planes are fighters.... These fighters now are coming in from all directions. The sky is literally full of aircraft.... The fighters are still coming. Wherever I look, all the way around us here, are fighters."[15]

At the same time, the National Film Board brought Canadians powerful visual images of the air war, with such documentary films as *Target—Berlin*, which told the story of the first Canadian-made Lancaster bombers to see action, and *Train Busters*, an account of the Allied air campaign against the German rail system. But it wasn't just the men at the sharp end who got noticed, for the NFB made every effort to cover the breadth of the story. *Wings on Her Shoulder* told the story of the RCAF Women's Division ("they serve that men may fly"), and *Trees That Reach the Sky* followed a Sitka spruce as it was transformed into a Mosquito medium bomber. *Flight 6* took viewers along on TCA's nightly flight from Vancouver to Montreal, and *Wings Over Canada* showed them the mysteries behind the nation's airmail system. The Air Cadets of Canada were the subject of a documentary, and there were even two films about the RCAF's use of homing pigeons to locate downed airmen.

With the British and American feature film industries gearing up as de facto propaganda arms of government, it was a foregone conclusion that Canadian cinema-goers would be treated to stirring aviation epics. Most of these were about American (*Flying Tigers*) or British (*One of Our Aircraft Is Missing*) airmen or both (*Eagle Squadron*), but there were a few pictures with Canadian themes. The best known was *Captains of the Clouds*, in which Jimmy Cagney and his mates join the RCAF as a lark ("a quartet of bush pilots—rough and ready, greedy for action against the bloodthirsty Hitler"), but come up trumps when their mettle is tested. Filmed at BCATP bases with the encouragement of the RCAF and using cadets as extras, the movie even featured Billy Bishop in a cameo and drew glowing reviews from the press. The Ottawa *Citizen* judged it to be "magnificently produced and pulsating with a vibrant timeliness that will grip the motion picture world with its dramatic tension ... breathtaking in its loveliness, flawlessness and ease of direction and presentation."[16]

Aviation also became familiar to Canadians through its connection to consumer goods, a link made explicit by many advertisers. The 1942 De Soto was as "advanced in styling ... advanced in engineering" as the fighter plane that soared above it in the advertisement. The Chrysler's Spitfire engine, fluid drive and Simplimatic transmission gave it the power and flexibility of "a plane with variable-pitch propellers." Of course, both these cars could be even better, simply by installing Champion spark plugs, the very plugs that helped the RAF vanquish the Luftwaffe during the Battle of Britain. At home, the RCA Victor Globe Trotter radio enabled the discerning consumer, by taking the advice of the good-looking airman pictured beside his aircraft, to "command the airways of the world."[17] Barrett roll roofing was "as modern as a Spitfire ... and as dependable," while HP steak sauce had the blessing of the air force—"the 'bomber' boys know a good sauce when they taste it." And for the fashion-conscious woman, there was Peggy Sage's new Flying Colours line of nail polish, with shades that will "send your spirits—and his thoughts—into the stratosphere."[18]

Even children became involved in aviation in wartime Canada. Model aircraft making grew in popularity, and young model makers could feel an extra swell of patriotic pride in the knowledge that some of their models were used by airmen in training for aircraft recognition exercises. Major corporations such as Eaton's continued to sponsor national model aircraft contests, and aviation-related toys proliferated. Billy Bishop endorsed the board game Be an Airman ("a splendid gift for an air-minded boy"); and fifteen cents and two box tops from Quaker Oats would get the budding pilot Captain Sparks' Big Training Cockpit, a cardboard instrument panel with stick and rudder pedals. There were cigarette cards and jigsaw puzzles, birthday cards and crayons, all adorned with the birds of war.

These toys and ephemera, no less than the rhetoric that surrounded Ferry Command and the BCATP, evidenced the high profile of aviation during the Second World War. In the 1930s, despite the best efforts of the air lobby, there were still a good many Canadians who were uninformed or uninterested or both about advances in flying, but in the 1940s it is difficult to imagine that this could have been true. Aviation was everywhere, and Canadians were better informed about airplanes and pilots than ever. This growing familiarity reduced much of aviation's mystique, something the air lobby had been trying to do for years, and the image of the pilot in Canadian culture was being refashioned. But not before the traditional image had its most eloquent retelling, by an airman-poet already dead when his work became famous.

, , ,

The Spitfire and the Oxford came together at around two thousand feet, almost certainly because of poor visibility. The wreckage of the twin-engine Oxford fluttered to the earth not far from Roxholm Hall in Lincolnshire, the body of its pilot—a young cadet just days away from winning his wings—still strapped in the seat. The Spitfire also came down in pieces, the engine and port wing having been torn away from the fuselage. Its pilot, nineteen-year-old John Gillespie Magee, had struggled free of the cockpit but was too close to the ground to deploy his parachute. His body was found deeply embedded in a farmer's field about fifty yards from his aircraft. Magee never got much chance to meet the enemy he was so keen to fight, but he left a more enduring legacy—a poem that would, like John McCrae's "In Flanders Fields," inspire the Allied nations:

> Oh, I have slipped the surly bonds of earth,
> And danced the skies on laughter-silvered wings;
> Sunward I've climbed and joined the tumbling mirth
> Of sun-split clouds—and done a hundred things

You have not dreamed of—wheeled and soared and
   swung
High in the sunlit silence. Hov'ring there,
I've chased the shouting wind along and flung
My eager craft through footless halls of air.
Up, up the long delirious, burning blue
I've topped the wind-swept heights with easy grace,
Where never lark, or even eagle, flew;
And, while with silent, lifting mind I've trod
The high untrespassed sanctity of space,
Put out my hand, and touched the face of God.[19]

Canadians have long claimed "High Flight" for their own, and indeed the RCAF even adopted it as its official poem. Yet its author was not Canadian, it was not written in Canada, nor was its subject matter Canadian. Magee was an American citizen, born in Shanghai of missionary parents, although he seems to have considered himself more English than American. His connection with Canada was relatively slight: he joined the RCAF in October 1940, trained at Toronto and Ottawa and was posted overseas in July 1941. In September he was assigned to 412 Squadron RCAF and flew with the unit for two months until his fatal crash on December 11.[20] Contrary to the oft-repeated tale, the poem was not found on Magee's body after the crash, nor was it written when the young pilot was topping the windswept heights in his Spitfire. That it was probably written in the officers' mess, the barracks or a pub in no way lessens its dramatic effect.

The symbolic flight that the poem describes is an evocative summation of the meaning of aviation as it evolved in Canadian culture, a fourteen-line character sketch of the pilot as a cultural icon. Magee had many imitators in the months and years following the publication of "High Flight" in 1941. Poets, pilots and journalists took up his image of the pilot as able to break free of the constraints of earth and experience a world closed to the non-flier. Three years after Magee's death, Alex Sutherland echoed him in a poem that bore more than a passing resemblance to "High Flight": "Free from the sordid trammelings of earth, / On shining silver wings I mount and fly / Scorning the lowly bondage of my birth." Other poets underlined the exceptional nature of the pilot, remarking that "we earthbound men are envious, for the earth's ties hold us fast. / But you shall fly forever with a glory that will last." One young airman's first flight was very much like the ascent described by Magee: "The range of vision widened breathtakingly! Higher and higher we climbed until...a world, hitherto in the imagination, had opened before my eyes. Life was suddenly richer and fuller....I felt like a bird who had escaped from a cage." Magee's conclusion, that having slipped the surly bonds of earth, the pilot entered into a union with God, retained its resonance. "We are alone on a floating throne, / All alone in the hand of God," wrote one airman-poet. Others found it easy to imagine the aviator "riding the sky-lanes close to God" or flying "up, up through the limitless blue, there to commune with God." "When I was up in the air I felt as if I was just that much closer to God," wrote the very devout Ted Gray as he trained to be a fighter pilot in 1941.[21]

Despite the popularity of Magee's poem, it signalled the end of the very image it celebrated, for the individualism, uniqueness and divinity of the aviator that he had described so beautifully could not be sustained in the huge expansion of aviation after 1939. There were simply too many people involved in flying either for pilots to be a chosen elite or to maintain that such a common act had a spiritual dimension. These icons had been tailor-made for the Great War, when the fighter pilot was the epitome of the romantic individualist. Whatever the reality of the air war, in the public mind the pilot was a lone wolf and the author of his fate. But in the 1940s, the notion of heroism being displayed in individual combat was out of date. If the First World War demanded a hero who could stand out from the masses in the trenches and who attained a measure of divinity in the process, the Second World War demanded a representative Everyman who could symbolize the unity of a nation fighting for a common cause. No longer was individualism valued so highly; now it was teamwork that mattered.

This emphasis on teamwork altered the image of the pilot. First, the pilot came to share the spotlight with the ground crew, the men and women who kept the aircraft flying. They came to occupy a larger place in the public mind primarily because there were more of them, in both relative and absolute terms. During the First World War, of the roughly 16,600 Canadians who enlisted in the flying services, only about 7,400 served as the mechanics, riggers and fitters who kept the planes airworthy.[22] They wrote no best-sellers, rarely found their way into the daily papers and were ignored by poets, songwriters and painters. In Canada's art of the First World War, there are only a handful of depictions of the people who prepared the aircraft. Even Franz Johnston, who recorded life on Canadian training airfields in dozens of works, devoted only a passing reference to the ground crew.

In the Second World War, the more sophisticated aircraft required more people on the ground. After early 1943, there were always more ground crew than aircrew serving with the RCAF overseas, and the ratios were even larger when the Home War Establishment was taken into account.[23] This statistical reality was also a cultural reality. Dozens of war artists recorded the behind-the-scenes work—mechanics dismantling bent propellers, parachute packers, riggers and fitters repairing aircraft, engine mechanics at work, armourers cleaning machine guns. A booklet distributed to all graduates of the BCATP included short sketches of Canada's great aces of the First World War but asked the next generation of aviators to remember the "thousands of loyal men whose work is on the ground, who give untiring and ungrudging service." Patriotic posters, like one titled "Teamwork—Thanks Pal!" recognized the essential unity between the man who flew the airplane and those who maintained it, and journalists and public speakers were careful to pay equal tribute to the ground crews. Don Fairbairn's broadcasts from RCAF bases in northwest

Europe frequently lauded the work of the mechanics and armourers, and pilots on speaking tours invariably stressed that the average pilot "would almost sooner lose his right hand than part with a good fitter or rigger."[24] There were even poetic tributes written to "the boys whose work and skill / Keep you up in the sky, / They are the boys who groom your ship / And make it safe to fly." The ground crewman Vic Hopwood's paean to his fellow mechanics is representative:

> Oh, I have pandered to your heart,
> Washed away all grease, all dirt,
> Noted with love the working measurements,
> Checked zealously the safety of each part...
> I have pushed the throttle to the gate,
> Checked your perfection on the instruments,
> Felt your body trembling for the sky;
> And then I've throttled back, climbed out,
> Pulled chocks, and watched another fly.[25]

The new cultural reality was that the pilot was just one component of a team. In 1940, Frederick Edwards of *Maclean's* repeated the old air force maxim that it took ten men on the ground to keep one in the air. During the First World War, this truism had been appreciated only by men in the flying corps; during the Second World War, the public was constantly being reminded that the ground crews "do the actual work and the pilot is only their field representative."[26]

But if teamwork on the ground was important, so too was teamwork in the air. During the First World War, much of the air war's appeal to the imagination lay in the fact that it allowed for the expression of individualism. By the Second World War, however, the individual had been subordinated to the collectivity, and the air war expressed unity, co-operation and solidarity. In the Great War, the airplane had stood apart from the war machine; thirty years later, it became a powerful symbol of that machine.

The *Air Force Review* expressed this in terms repeated in any number of other publications: "One requisite qualification for service in the Air Force to-day is the faculty of team play. The pilot to-day must be able to co-ordinate to the full with his fellow pilots. The days of individual exploits are largely a thing of the past. Not that individuality is non-existent in the Air Force, but it must be the individuality of a great hockey or rugby player whose stellar performance is the result of close understanding with the team." In recruiting posters such as "Join the Team!...Royal Canadian Air Force," budding airmen were reminded that they were enlisting not to be individuals but to be part of a team. "Down you go, Hun...you don't score on my team," proclaimed a recruiting ad for RCAF aircrew. Even commercial advertisements, such as a 1943 ad for the Hudson's Bay Company, played up this theme: "The pilot falls behind, a vulnerable target for enemy fire! The leader snaps an order and his team-mates rush to his rescue. Today, Canada's Air Cadets are learning team-work, assuring their competence in battle—tomorrow."[27]

Even the fighter squadron, once the preserve of the ultimate individualist, was transformed into a band of brothers whose very survival depended on teamwork and co-operation. Ernie McNab was the first RCAF pilot credited with an aerial victory in the Second World War, but he was careful to stress that he was fighting a different kind of air war than his predecessors: "Now the individual counts for nothing. As a matter of fact he dare not sally forth alone. Team play is the whole thing in air combat today."[28] *Wings Abroad*, the official newspaper of the RCAF, reminded readers in 1942 that "to-day flying is to a large extent a matter of team work—even in fighter aircraft. In this respect it differs from the last war when it was largely a matter of the individual." It was important for the public to understand this change, because this war would produce a different kind of air hero. "If there are no legendary heroes with enormous individual scores...that is because air war is a team business in these days," announced the newspaper in April 1942.[29] Even Buzz Beurling, the ultimate individualist and throwback to the lone-wolf fighter pilots of the Great War, was given a makeover. Leslie Roberts tried mightily to suggest that Beurling had started to feel the team spirit while at the Initial Training Wing, and that he became the unofficial field captain of his squadron team. This, of course, was nonsense; however, the fact that Roberts and the propagandists who organized Beurling's 1943 speaking tour tried so hard to transform the intractable ace into a poster child for the team spirit shows the importance attached to the concept.

Gradually, the image of the lone airman taking off at dawn to meet the Hun over the trenches in single combat faded and was replaced by other cultural motifs better suited to the times. The wings parade, when newly minted pilots assembled to receive their flying badges, emerged as a popular motif for poets ("You shall inherit the earth, who march today / Rank upon rank beneath the summer sun," wrote Gloria Lauriston in 1942[30]) and for artists, who found the lines of young men in air force blue a powerful metaphor for the nation's unity and resolve. The wings parade became a staple photograph in Canadian newspapers, particularly in towns that hosted BCATP training establishments, and could be found on RCAF recruiting posters. Aircrew gathering to await the call to operations was another popular theme. Paintings by official Canadian war artists such as Edwin Holgate (*Dispersal Hut*) and the Briton William Dring (*Zero Hour*) implicitly acknowledged that the group was more important than the individual.

The emphasis on teamwork also reflected the expansion of the air forces. During the First World War, most Canadians who joined the Royal Flying Corps served as aircrew; because most operational aircraft required only a one- or two-man crew, the greatest need was for pilots. In November 1918, the RFC Canada had on strength nearly ten times as many pilot cadets as observer cadets.[31] During the Second World War, the RCAF still flew single-engine aircraft requiring only a pilot, but many more squadrons flew two- and four-engine aircraft with up to eleven-member crews. As a result, a much smaller percentage of aircrew in the RCAF were pilots. Among the members of the RCAF who graduated from the BCATP, there were nearly twice as many navigators, bomb-aimers, wireless operators, air gunners and air engineers as pilots.

Billy Bishop, the ultimate individualist during the Great War, was sensitive to the changing times. As he told the Canadian Clubs of Quebec in 1940, "The day when the pilot got all the credit is most definitely, and rightly, gone"; the observer, the gunner, the wireless operator were now "the most important people on that aircraft." In 1921, Charles Grey, influential editor of the British journal *The Aeroplane*, wrote to J. A. Wilson that "a pilot is no longer a heroic aviator but merely a kind of superior chauffeur who has to go and do a job of work in the air instead of on the road."[32] Few would have accepted Grey's characterization in the early 1920s, but by the early 1940s it was strongly rooted in the popular imagination. In Frank Bunce's short story "Wings of Hazard," an airline pilot says, "This looks like a pretty good job, and most of the time I think it is. But sometimes—well, the other day a passenger set me to thinking. One of these tactless guys jerked at my sleeve as I was going through the cabin, and started off a question with: 'Say, driver...!'" Willie McKnight, an Albertan who spent two years in the RAF and was killed in action in January 1941, chafed at being transferred from fighters to bombers: "I'm only a bloody taxi driver for the rest of them," he told a friend.[33]

But this transformation was often cast not as a pilot's lament on the diminution of his status but in a growing sense of pride surrounding the other trades involved in the air war. The war artists Paul Goranson and Carl Schaefer executed striking depictions of the various members of a bomber crew, the technical detail in their work underlining the increasing sophistication of aircraft and the need for expertise in specific elements of the airplane's operation. Airmen-poets celebrated their specialties in verse. An anonymous poem titled "The Wireless Boy" jokes that "the pilot guy / Is but a chauffeur who can fly," an expression of pride in the trade of the wireless operator. Strikingly similar is another piece of air force doggerel, "Air Gunner's Song": "The pilot's just a chauffeur, / It's his job to fly the plane. / But it's WE who do the fighting / Though we may not share the fame." Even the bomb-aimer was the subject of a poetic tribute:

> Let others plot the trackless night
>   That lies around us icy, stark—
> Let others steer the great bird's flight
>   With eyes and ears that pierce the dark—
> We topple thrones! We sow revolt!
> For lo—we hold the thunderbolt.[34]

It may not be a masterpiece, but it does reflect a significant cultural shift away from the pilot.

This emphasis on the collectivity, whether it be the crew, the squadron or the air force as a whole, reduced the significance of the pilot in cultural terms. No longer sole master of his fate, he became estranged from his machine. Technology took over many of his tasks; as modern devices came to replace human skill and intuition, flying became more a technical exercise than an exercise of the spirit.

The transformation, of course, did not happen overnight. The creation of the trans-Canada airway, which aimed to provide groomed landing facilities, radio navigation aids and meteorological information to pilots across the country, was instrumental, as was the establishment of TCA. As the successful operation of a passenger and mail service demanded safety and punctuality, any mechanical means to achieve those goals were embraced. As a 1937 report argued, "In the past the pilot always thought himself better than his machine; his only fear was that his engine might let him down, or one of many structural or mechanical failings might happen. Science has changed all this—practically every modern transport accident can be traced either wholly or in part to pilot error. The machine is now better than the man, and the sooner we realize this, the farther ahead we shall be."[35]

The war brought new devices into the cockpit, all designed to enhance the efficiency and effectiveness of aircraft. The Air Position Indicator and the Ground Position Indicator, both primitive versions of the currently effective Global Positioning System (GPS), allowed a navigator to plot, with reasonable accuracy depending on wind conditions, the aircraft's exact position. Oboe, Gee, H2S and G-H were navigational aids that relied on either ground-based radio beams or airborne radar sets. An automatic pilot system, known as George, maintained an aircraft in straight and level flight virtually indefinitely. These devices made aircraft safer and more efficient, but they also reduced the role of the pilot in the operation of the airplane. In doing so, they seemed to support the argument of the 1937 memorandum: far from being divine, pilots were fallible and should be replaced as much as possible by machines.

Some saw this development as entirely positive. In a 1943 report, J. A. Wilson wrote favourably about the construction of a modern airway communication network, "a complicated but closely integrated system using radio and land-lines, voice and key each in its most efficient field," and about the meteorological services, which sent hourly reports to all airports and stations, making them available to all aircraft operators. All these innovations, concluded Wilson, took the guesswork out of flying. The journalist Ronald Keith, in an enthusiastic article in *Maclean's*, agreed that modern aviation required a new kind of pilot: "With the radio beam, 'seat-of-the-pants' flying is going out of style, even in the Yukon."[36] For Frank Scott, the growing sophistication of aircraft engendered admiration of the human ingenuity:

> The plane, our planet,
> Travels on roads that are not seen or laid
> But sound in instruments on pilots' ears
> While underneath,
> The sure wings
> Are the everlasting arms of science.[37]

Other writers were not so sure that progress was entirely positive, for taking the guesswork out of flying meant devaluing the
pilot's intuition. There were probably more than a few pilots like
Frank Bunce's fictional Arvin Gayle, the quintessential lone aviator who looks askance at what flying has become: "This was no
careless adventure of one man across uncertain country, into an
uncertain sky. It was a timed collaboration of specialists and scientists," he remarks sourly about a flight on a passenger aircraft.
He was impressed by the ease with which "the great ship slid down
the smooth groove of its radio beam; dipping, unobtrusively, to
brush earth at Medford, Portland, Tacoma; delivering him, with
the timed efficiency of an assembly line, at Seattle to a Canadian
plane, which in turn deposited him on the scheduled minute at
Vancouver. It was magnificent. It was a stupefying, almost incredible demonstration of man's mastery of a medium that for all but
the most recent tick of time had been denied to him." Yet he was
also saddened, because it was so unlike the flying that he loved:
"On established air lanes you could fly according to a careful plan,
providing against almost any conceivable emergency; in the
North, no such procedure was possible. You took off into an enig-
matic sky; even your route might be unknown, not alone to you
but to the map-makers. As weather formed, you watched it coolly,
unhurriedly deciding whether to try to fly through or over or
around it, or to descend to some smooth sheet of ice or water. He
liked that; using up each instant to itself, without reference to the
next. He thought it a fair rough-rule for living."[38]

, , ,

As Gayle noted, nowhere was the transformation more evident
than in the North. In the 1930s, people like Richard Finnie and
Philip Godsell had described the airplane as throwing back the
"veil of ignorance" that had long lain over the North. During the
Second World War, the North's immense strategic value was made
clear by the ever more ambitious American designs on the region.

Therefore, the drive to extend dominion northward took on new urgency, if not in the Canadian government, then in a group that one historian has called the "northern nationalists."[39] Ruminations had stressed the potential mineral wealth that might be discovered, but attention was increasingly focused on the North's geopolitical significance. Editorials and articles with such suggestive titles as "Canada: Mainstreet of the Air" and "Canada's Aerial Destiny" made much of the fact that Canada lay astride the northern route both to Europe and the Far East. The North "is our front door to the air world of the future," wrote the journalist Trevor Lloyd in *Maclean's*. Canada's geography and mastery in wilderness flying gave the nation "a place in world affairs out of all proportion to its population and wealth." If Canadians jumped at the opportunity, predicted Lloyd, they would occupy a prime place "on the shore of the Mediterranean of tomorrow."[40]

Lloyd might have been a little optimistic in his prediction of the future of the Arctic Ocean, but the war certainly brought a new level of development to the region, especially in the northwest: the Canol pipelines, which brought oil from the Northwest Territories and Alaska; the Alaska Highway, linking Fairbanks and Edmonton through northern Alberta, British Columbia and Yukon; and the North West Staging Route (NWSR), a string of airfields that followed the highway and transported American aircraft, personnel and supplies to Alaska. These projects were bigger than anything the Canadian North had ever seen, and it was clear that the bush planes of the 1920s and 1930s were not sufficient for them. The large modern transport aircraft needed to supply the projects, and the American fighters and bombers to be ferried along the route for transfer to Soviet pilots, required modern airports with radio and meteorological equipment and artificial lighting for use in darkness or inclement weather. The situation demanded not just a lake on which airplanes could take off and land but a modern, urban airport carved out of the wilderness.

In early 1941, the government began to construct the NWSR's main airports at Grande Prairie, Fort St. John, Fort Nelson,

Watson Lake and Whitehorse, as well as intermediate fields along the route. The airfields were fairly basic, even by contemporary standards, but unlike anything else in the North. Fort Nelson and Watson Lake, once accessible only to float- or ski-planes, had 4,400-foot paved runways and radio-location facilities; Fort Nelson also had a 20,000-square-foot hangar, twenty other buildings and a projected strength of 308 officers and men, considerably more people than the settlement had ever had before.[41] The war was transforming both the North and northern aviation, as the public eagerly looked on. National Film Board documentaries such as *Northwest by Air* and *Look to the North* documented the impact of aviation on the North, and writers lauded the changes. "The outer spaces of Canada, of Newfoundland, of Labrador have donned the majestic mantle of tomorrow," wrote the journalist Harold Albert in *National Home Monthly*. "There in the barren northlands you already find not mere spruce-waste and lonely muskeg but...the concrete vistas and flashing flarepaths that denote the dawning of mid-century."[42]

The transformation of the airfield might serve as a metaphor for the changes in aviation during the Second World War. In the 1930s, the airplane had offered a way to get in touch with nature; even when it was used to exploit natural resources, the rhetoric confirmed the essential unity between the bush plane and the natural world. But now, such harmony was replaced by concrete runways and electrification that made the lonely wastes useful. It was the same in the southern parts of the country. There, the airfield had once been a verdant utopia used by birdmen. As the artists of the Great War portrayed them, they were essentially benign—a field of green, a few buildings or tents, the ubiquitous windsock. In the Second World War, they became full-blown military installations with jumbles of buildings, cement runways and aprons and aircraft packed in cheek by jowl. Nature was effectively banished, and the airfield had become, in the view of at least one poet, a modernist nightmare:

Flat wastes of ugliness,
Desolate in the moonlight,
Spewn from the lips of hell;
Terrain arid and hot,
Treeless and forsaken of beauty...
Stagnant pools of oily water glisten in chasm-like
    ditches,
And crater-deep holes leap from the darkness
Along the treacherous, newly-cut road
Leading to barracks.
Light shines from bleak buildings.[43]

What Clara Bernhardt saw in an airfield under construction might be applied to aviation as a whole. Flying had always been sold as the last word in modernity, but during the Second World War the rhetoric and the reality finally merged. The last vestiges of aviation's romance and excitement were jettisoned. The pilot, once the ultimate individualist, had become simply one small cog in a very large machine. Knightly birdmen in craft that were mere extensions of their own bodies were now technocrats sharing the controls of increasingly complex machines. Flying as a spiritual act that allowed the aviator to approach the divine was now a technical exercise best left to machines. Once carrying high hopes for the future, flight was now burdened with grave concerns of the past. No more would people see aviation as a promised land; now, wrote one astute observer in 1943, "we see the future of the aeroplane through the telescope of thousands of Spitfires and Hurricanes and Mosquitos and Lancasters blasting the air."[44]

EPILOGUE

IN 1937, GORDON MCGREGOR CUT OUT A NEWSPAPER EDITORIAL that was inspired by the conjunction of two incidents emblematic of where aviation had been and where it was going. On July 5, 1937, both PanAm and Imperial Airways began experimental flights that would lead to regularly scheduled passenger services across the Atlantic. Three days earlier, on the other side of the world, Amelia Earhart and her navigator, Fred Noonan, disappeared over the Pacific Ocean, probably not far from Howland Island, a tiny speck that was to have been the next stop on their round-the-world flight. For the editor, there was a striking connection between these two events: "The old eras and the new, in ocean flying, thus overlapped very neatly." Earhart was the "last of the free-lance trail blazers...she stood for the old era in ocean flying—the era of high adventure, danger and high-hearted romance." The transatlantic services were very different. "They are the fruits of years of research...their object is not to take risks but to avoid them; not to show what one man in a plane can do, but to demonstrate that the cooperation of many men, prepared as carefully as the operations of a railroad are prepared, can span the ocean with regular, passenger-carrying commercial service that will be safe and unexciting enough to pay its own way."[1]

McGregor had been interested in airplanes since childhood, when he attended Canada's first international air show in

Montreal in 1910. He had taken up flying in 1931 and three times won the Webster Trophy, awarded to the best amateur pilot in Canada. He would go on to be a leading fighter pilot during the Second World War and president of TCA for twenty years, overseeing its transformation to Air Canada. Even in 1937, however, McGregor might have been intrigued by three notions raised in the editorial: that aviation must pay its own way, the comparison of airlines and railways, and that flying should be unexciting. Each contains ironies that cannot fail to strike an observer looking back over many years.

No one in the air lobby ever denied that aviation could, and should, pay its own way, but the consequences of becoming a self-supporting industry might have brought about an unforeseen end. That running a successful flying company required the same business acumen as any other pursuit did not always impress itself on people in the flying world. Many post-1918 flying companies, such as Bishop-Barker Aeroplanes, failed not simply because of limited demand for their services but because their owners were better pilots than business managers. True, when a flying operation was small, it was possible to succeed despite limited business skills—a bush pilot with a good aircraft, a capable mechanic and a bit of money for emergencies could eke out a living. Being able to nurse down a flying boat with an unco-operative engine was more important than correct ledger entries. When operations began to expand, however, the situation changed. More and more, the aviation companies that prospered were those run by businessmen, not pilots. As Douglas Hallam wrote in 1928, "As time goes on, the actual pilot of a plane will become a less important person, and the man who knows the technical end and the business end will be the man who will make a commercial success out of flying."[2] J. S. Scott, who had been involved in aviation in Canada from the earliest days, wrote to the committee studying trans-Canada air services that good flying equipment and personnel were less important than ground organization—terminals, landing facilities, shops, freight and passenger agents, ticket offices, a ground communications system. He calculated that the relative importance of these factors to flying equipment and personnel was roughly in a 7:3 ratio, so it made sense (and Scott was certainly not alone in thinking this) for the railways, which had all of these services in place, to run airlines. Canadian-born aviation investor Clement M. Keys was both blunter and less precise. "Ten percent of aviation is in the air and ninety percent is on the ground."[3]

The notion that what happened on the ground, rather than in the air, was critical to the success of an aviation company was a real departure from past thinking, and a powerful irony. For decades aviation boosters had attempted to show that flying was superior to all other forms of transportation, including rail. In many ways, air-mindedness was based on invidious comparisons between the sordid, dirty ground and the clean, pure air. But by the 1930s, leading members of the air lobby were suggesting that flying companies had to become more like railways if they were to survive. This, of course, is precisely what happened. By the early 1940s, the major air routes in Canada were virtually controlled by the rail companies, and the airlines had come to resemble the railways in almost every respect.

As aviation expanded and became more like other forms of travel, much of its mystique evaporated. The more people flew, the more difficult it became to suggest that sailing through the clouds in an airplane had a spiritual dimension or that flying somehow made you a better person. In some sense, with the expansion of aviation in the 1940s, flying became less special. In 1932, the Hamilton *Spectator* had predicted that "travel by air will never become prosaic";[4] in fact, flying did become prosaic, and not just because the air lobby set out to demonstrate that flying *was* unexciting. Ultimately, people connected with commercial aviation would make a virtue of necessity and transform the commonness of flying into a selling point.

Of course, private flying was less affected by corporatization. But of all the air lobby's dreams, none proved more elusive than the goal that everyone would one day fly his or her own airplane. The number of private pilots in this country has certainly grown since the 1920s, when there were only a few hundred, but despite the confident predictions of the air lobby, only a small proportion of the population currently holds a pilot's licence. Many more people do indeed fly, but for most, flying has long meant being a passenger, probably on a commercial aircraft. Even in the 1930s, members of the air lobby were tacitly admitting that passengers on a commercial aircraft might just as well be on a bus or a train.

There was another transformation, one in which Gordon McGregor was also intimately involved. If flying became merely a common means of getting from place to place rather than a magical feat performed by superhumans, it was also diminished by the airplane's use as a weapon. The achievement of mechanical flight, the fulfilment of one of humanity's most ancient and enduring wishes, fell from grace during wartime. As one poet put it,

> The wings I gave that search among the stars;
> Secrets, for ages hidden, now unlocked,—
> Passion's intrigues enlist all this for Mars,
> 'Till old securities with fear are rocked.
> Reason, be with him! Or what man has learned,
> Shall to his own destruction soon be turned.[5]

Herein lies another irony. Both world wars were responsible for accelerating the improvement of technology; without the impetus of war, it is difficult to imagine how long it would have taken to reach the technological sophistication, or level of acceptance, that aviation reached by 1945, just four decades after the Wright brothers' flight. But the realization that war had been very good for aviation technology and for popularizing flying could not disguise a note of sadness that it had also taken much of the bloom off flight. Many observers regretted that humanity had taken a great gift and corrupted it for destructive purposes.

I have tried to argue that 1945 closed one chapter in the

history of the idea of flight. In the post-war world and up to the present day, very different ideas coloured the aviation debate. Sadly, no one uses the term "air-mindedness" any more. Articles in praise of flying no longer dominate our newspapers and magazines, and we rarely read poetic tributes to the airplane or pilot. Instead, we read of takeovers and accusations of unfair trade practices, maintenance problems and airport gridlock, lost luggage and cancelled flights. And yet there remains something very special about flying in this country. Perhaps it is because as a people we have taken to heart at least one assumption of the air lobby: that aviation, in its early days, meant more to Canada than it did to most other countries. For all the air lobby's dashed hopes and failed predictions, Canada retains a deep, almost elemental, connection to flying. How else to explain the storms of anger whipped up by an announcement that the much-loved Snowbirds aerial display team might fall victim to government budget cuts? What else can account for our persistent efforts to lay claim to John Gillespie Magee's poem "High Flight"? And the Avro Arrow? If it had been a revolutionary battle tank or a state-of-the-art submarine, it would long ago have been forgotten. But because it was an airplane, it lives on in our national psyche.

Perhaps for all its modernity and technological sophistication, flying still has the ability to take people back to the heady days of the 1920s, when aviation in its infancy exerted a powerful pull on the imagination. The sound of an airplane flying low overhead can still send children dashing into the backyard to catch a glimpse. There is still magic in looking down at tiny cars and trains crawling across a toy landscape. A float plane taking off from a northern lake, no trace of its presence existing after the ripples have subsided, can still fill one with a sense of awe for aviation pioneers. At times like these, the inconveniences of modern air travel are forgotten, leaving only the wonder of an earlier age. At times like these, we can sense what the first generation of Canadians to fly sensed—that there was something special in the air.

NOTES

Prologue

1. Stephen Leacock, "The Man in Asbestos," in *Nonsense Novels* (London: J. Lane, 1919), 214, 221; "Rural Urbanity" and "The Last of the Rubber Necks," in *The Iron Man and the Tin Woman, and Other Such Futurities: A Book of Little Sketches of To-day and To-morrow* (Toronto: Macmillan, 1929), 24–30, 158.

1. Balloonatics and Aeronaunts

1. New Brunswick *Courier*, 15 August 1840, 2; George A. Fuller, "The First Aerial Voyage in Canada," *CAHS Journal* 19, no. 1 (spring 1981).

2. Matilda Edgar, ed., *Ten Years of Upper Canada in Peace and War, 1805–1815* (Toronto: William Briggs, 1890), 53, 60; Jeremiah Milbank Jr., *The First Century of Flight in America* (Princeton, NJ: Princeton University Press, 1943), 34.

3. Quebec *Mercury*, 5 September 1820, 1.

4. *The Nova Scotian, or Colonial Herald*, 26 October 1836, 1; 6 September 1837, 285.

5. Montreal *Gazette*, 16 October 1834, 1; 25 August 1836, 2; G. A. Fuller, J. A. Griffin, and K. M. Molson, *125 Years of Canadian Aeronautics: A Chronology, 1840–1965* (Willowdale, Ont.: Canadian Aviation Historical Society, 1983), 1.

6. St. Catharines *Journal*, 25 September 1850, 2; quoted in Geoff Rowe, "Early Flying in Ottawa," *CAHS Journal*, no. 4 (winter 1968): 114; Hamilton *Evening Times*, 23 July 1862, 3.

7. Ottawa *Daily Citizen*, 13 September 1877, 4.

8. "Ballooning," Toronto *Globe*, 26 June 1875, 4.

9. Quoted in F. H. Hitchins, "Aerial Daredevils of 1888," *CAHS Journal* 3, no. 3 (fall 1965): 76; editorial, "Ballooning Extraordinary," Sherbrooke *Daily Record*, 8 July 1908, 3.

10. London *Free Press*, 14 September 1909, 9; Sherbrooke *Daily Record*, 5 September 1907, 1.

11. Victoria *Colonist*, 23 September 1909, 1–2; 24 September 1909, 4; 25 September 1909, 1.

12. Rowe, "Early Flying in Ottawa," 117–18; "Fatal Fall from a Balloon at Ottawa," *Dominion Illustrated*, 13 October 1888, 230.

13. Calgary *Herald*, 6 July 1908, 1; Geoff Rowe, "Early Flying in Ottawa," part 2, *CAHS Journal* 7, no. 1 (spring 1969): 17.

14. Nena C. Rickerson, *The Banker's Grandchildren* (Saint John: George W. Day, 1876), 11; James De Mille, *A Comedy of Terrors* (Boston: James R. Osgood and Company, 1872), 89; John Charles Dent, *The Gerrard Street Mystery and Other Weird Tales* (Toronto: Rose Publishing, 1888), 134.

15. Brockville *Recorder*, 9 July 1874, 2; Ottawa *Daily Citizen*, 27 September 1884, 3.

16. London *Free Press*, 18 July 1889, 1; W. C. Way, "The Problems of Aerial Navigation," *Queen's Quarterly* 16, no. 3 (January–February–March 1909), 262.

17. Charlottetown *Daily Patriot*, 22 July 1908, 1; Patricia A. Myers, *Sky Riders: An Illustrated History of Aviation in Alberta, 1906–1945* (Saskatoon: Fifth House Publishers, 1995), 17.

18. Rudyard Kipling, "With the Night Mail," in *Actions and Reactions* (1909), reprinted in *The Collected Works of Rudyard Kipling*, vol. 8 (New York: AMS Press, 1970), 401–42.

19. PEI Public Archives and Records Office (PEIPARO): Earl Taylor Collection, accession 3523/123, Charlottetown *Island Patriot*, 27 September 1912.

20. Charlottetown *Daily Patriot*, 25 March 1909, 4; 26 March 1909, 4.

21. Calgary *Herald*, 3 August 1909, 4; editorials, Victoria *Colonist*, 29 June 1910, 4, and 19 October 1910, 4; editorial, Calgary *Herald*, 3 July 1912, 6.

22. A.L.C., "Flight," *Queen's Quarterly* 16, no. 4 (April–May–June 1909): 320.

23. Halifax *Herald*, 30 September 1907, 1.

24. Alexander Graham Bell Papers [AGBP], Alexander Graham Bell National Historic Site: Home Notes, vol. 58, pp. 147–52, Bell at Canadian Club of Ottawa, 27 March 1909.

25. "The Means of Flying," *Canadian Illustrated News*, 7 February 1863: 148; "A Flying Spaniard," *Canadian Illustrated News*, 18 April 1863: 271.

26. AGBP: Home Notes, vol. 11, pp. 2–6, 29 March 1894. Emphasis in original.

27. AGBP: *Beinn Bhreagh Recorder*, vol. 4, 14 April 1910, "The Flying-Machine of the Future; as conceived in 1892"; Robert V. Bruce, *Bell: Alexander Graham Bell and the Conquest of Solitude* (Ithaca, NY: Cornell University Press, 1973), 362.

28. Toronto *Daily Star*, 18 December 1903, 1; London *Advertiser*, 18 December 1903, 1.

29. This account is drawn from Mabel Bell's description of the founding of the Aerial Experiment Association, written in 1909, in AGBP: Laboratory Books, vol. 107, pp. 64–71.

30. AGBP: Laboratory Books, vol. 30, p. 38, resolution dated 24 February 1909; vol. 30, p. 43; House of Commons, Debates, 11 March 1909, 2383.

31. AGBP: *Beinn Bhreagh Recorder*, vol. 3, pp. 451–54, 18 March 1910.

32. Quoted in Halifax *Chronicle*, 23 March 1910, in AGBP: *Beinn Bhreagh Recorder*, vol. 4, p. 30, 25 March 1910.

33. Bell at Canadian Club of Ottawa, 27 March 1909.

34. Baldwin at University of Toronto, 27 February 1909, in AGBP: *AEA Bulletin* 33 (22 February 1909), 11; Norman Patterson, "Why, Casey Baldwin?" in *Canadian Courier, The Weekly* 7, no. 23 (7 May 1910): 16.

35. Edmonton *Journal*, 27 April 1911, 1; 1 May 1911, 9; K. M. Molson, "Montreal to Ottawa by Air, 1913," *CAHS Journal* 11, no. 4 (winter 1973): 120–25; Montreal *Gazette*, 8 December 1913, 11.

36. Montreal *Gazette*, 27 June 1910, 12.

37. Calgary *Herald*, 7 July 1911, 7; quoted in Lloyd M. Bungey, *Pioneer Aviation in the West: As Told by the Pioneers* (Surrey, BC: Hancock House, 1992), 14.

38. Montreal *Gazette*, 16 September 1912, 7; 24 September 1912, 3.

39. F. H. Hitchins, "Dominion Day 1912," *CAHS Journal* 6, no. 3 (fall 1968): 76–77.

40. Montreal *Gazette*, 27 June 1910, 12; Calgary *Herald*, 18 October 1911, 1.

41. Montreal *Gazette*, 27 June 1910, 12; 28 June 1910, 5; editorial, Calgary *Herald*, 17 October 1910, 6; "Auto History Instructive to Aeroplane Designers," Calgary *Herald*, 4 July 1911, 13.

42. F. O. Willhofft, "Aviation," *Queen's Quarterly* 18, no. 3 (January–February–March 1911): 233.

43. "One More Death to Make an American Holiday," Edmonton *Journal*, 21 October 1911, 4; *New York Times*, 8 August 1913, 3.

44. AGBP: *Beinn Bhreagh Recorder*, vol. 10, p. 94, 6 May 1912; Ottawa *Citizen*, 25 June 1910, 6.

45. Gerardine Macpherson, *Memoirs of the Life of Anna Jameson* (London: Longmans, Green, and Co., 1878), 212; M. H. Nickerson, "The Wish, A Lydian Legend," in *Carols of the Coast: A Collections of Songs, Ballads and Legends* (Halifax: Nova Scotia Printing Company, 1895).

46. Peter Corley-Smith, *Barnstorming to Bush Flying: British Columbia's Aviation Pioneers, 1910–1930* (Victoria: Sono Nis Press, 1989), 21; Canadian Literature Scrapbooks, vol. 1, p. 86, *Canadian Courier*, 18 October 1913.

47. Quoted in Ramsay Cook, "Landscape Painting and National Sentiment in Canada," in *The Maple Leaf Forever: Essays on Nationalism and*

Politics in Canada (Toronto: Macmillan, 1977), 168; Taylor Collection, accession 3523/123, Charlottetown *Island Patriot*, 27 September 1912.

48. Halifax *Herald*, 5 July 1913, in AGBP: Home Notes, vol. 78, pp. 138–39, 9 July 1913; Halifax *Herald*, 17 September 1911, 8.

49. De Mille, *A Comedy of Terrors*, 89, 96–97.

50. Quoted in "Aviation in the Niagara Peninsula, 1911–1914," *CAHS Journal* 10, no. 3 (fall 1972): 75.

51. "Paris from a Balloon," *Canadian Methodist Magazine* 16, no. 3 (September 1882): 208.

52. Toronto *Mail*, 15 September 1885, 2; Grace E. Denison, *A Happy Holiday* (Toronto: private, 1890), unpaginated; London *Free Press*, 28 June 1875, 2.

53. Edward Allen Talbot, *Five Years' Residence in the Canadas: Including a Tour through Part of the United States of America in the Year 1823*, vol. 1 (London: Longman, Hurst, Rees, Orme, Brown and Green, 1824), 154.

54. Alonzo Cinq-Mars, "Aviation," in *De L'Aube au Midi* (Quebec: Societé des Poètes, 1924); Mrs. Dick-Lauder et al., *Wentworth Landmarks* (Hamilton: Spectator Printing Company, 1897), unpaginated.

55. Notes and Comment, Calgary *Herald*, 2 August 1909, 4; London *Free Press*, 19 October 1910, 4; Calgary *Herald*, 3 July 1911, 3.

56. Vancouver *Daily Province*, 19 May 1910, in AGBP: Home Notes, vol. 66, p. 63, 19 May 1910; Charlottetown *Daily Patriot*, 7 July 1908, 3; Calgary *Herald*, 16 August 1909, 4.

57. Hamilton *Times*, 19 May 1909; H. Percy Blanchard, *After the Cataclysm: A Romance of the Age to Come* (New York: Cochrane Publishing, 1909).

58. Frederick Nelson, *Toronto in 1928 A.D.* (Toronto: National Business Method and Publishing Company, 1908).

59. Hugh Pedley, *Looking Forward: The Strange Experience of the Rev. Fergus McCheyne* (Toronto: William Briggs, 1913).

60. Ralph Centennius, *The Dominion in 1983* (Peterborough: Tober & Co., 1883), 13.

61. Editorial, Charlottetown *Daily Patriot*, 15 November 1909, 4.

62. D. B. Weldon Library, University of Western Ontario, Fred Hitchins Papers, II-A-4, J. A. Wilson, "The Influence of Civil Aviation in the Development of Canada's Air Power," 3 November 1943; Willis W. Cunningham, "Evolution of a Century," in *Anvil Whispers* (private, n.d.).

2. Soon Shall the Sky Be Ours

1. Bill Lambert, *Combat Report* (London: William Kimber, 1973), 52–53.

2. Editorial "The Mastery of the Air," Regina *Morning Leader*, 17 May 1911, 4.

3. Annie Elizabeth Mellish, *Our Boys Under Fire, or New Brunswick and Prince Edward Island Volunteers in South Africa* (Charlottetown: Examiner,

1900), 23; S. F. Wise, *Canadian Airmen and the First World War* (Toronto: University of Toronto Press, 1980), 342.

4. Hamilton *Times*, 19 May 1909.

5. Lee B. Kennett, *The First Air War* (Toronto: Collier Macmillan, 1991), 21.

6. Hitchins Papers, II-A-4: J. A. Wilson, "The Influence of Civil Aviation in the Development of Canada's Air Power," 3 November 1943; http://www.canadiangeographic.ca/Magazine/SO00/aviation_quotes.html

7. Montreal *Witness*, 24 June 1910; London *Free Press*, 20 July 1912, 17.

8. Winnipeg *Telegram*, 14 May 1910; House of Commons, Debates, 16 February 1910, 3701.

9. W. H. C. Lawrence, *The Storm of '92: A Grandfather's Tale Told in 1932* (Toronto: Sheppard Publishing, 1889), 66; Percy Blanchard, *After the Cataclysm: A Romance of the Age to Come* (New York: Cochrane Publishing, 1909), 46.

10. Lt.-Col. J. R. Wilkinson, "Armageddon," in *Canadian Battlefields and Other Poems* (Toronto: William Briggs, 1899).

11. Wise, *Canadian Airmen and the First World War*, 27–29, 335; Kennett, *The First Air War*, 30.

12. Kennett, *The First Air War*, 38; Jack Turner, "The Aeroplane," in *Buddy's Blighty and Other Verses from the Trenches* (Boston: Small, Maynard and Company, 1918).

13. W. A. Bishop, *Winged Warfare: Hunting the Huns in the Air* (Toronto: Hodder & Stoughton, 1918), 57; AGBP: Home Notes, vol. 96, pp. 146–51, 28 June 1916.

14. Coningsby Dawson, *Carry On: Letters in War-Time* (Toronto: S. B. Gundy, 1917), 50–51.

15. Diary entry of 11 August 1915, in Mary F. Gaudet, ed., *From a Stretcher Handle: The World War I Journal and Poems of Pte. Frank Walker* (Charlottetown: Institute of Island Studies, 2000), 75.

16. Anon., *More Letters from Billy* (Toronto: McClelland, Goodchild & Stewart, 1917), 93–94; Stuart Ramsay Tompkins, *A Canadian's Road to Russia: Letters from the Great War Decade*, ed. Doris H. Pieroth (Edmonton: University of Alberta Press, 1989), 275.

17. "Up in the Air," words and music by Morris Manley (Toronto: Morris Manley, 1918); Jesse Edgar Middleton, "To the Absent" and "The American Aviator," in *Sea Dogs and Men at Arms: A Canadian Book of Songs* (New York: G. P. Putnam's Sons, 1918).

18. Randolph Carlyle, "The Royal Flying Corps in Canada," *Canadian Magazine* 49 (1917): 334; Ward Maclennan, "A Flying Officer's Training," *Queen's Quarterly* 26, no. 1 (July 1918), 88; Bishop, *Winged Warfare*, 1–2.

19. Hartley Munro Thomas, *Songs of an Airman and Other Poems* (Toronto: McClelland, Goodchild & Stewart, 1918), 12.

20. Maclennan, "A Flying Officer's Training," 88.

21. Quoted in Oliver Hezzlewood, ed., *Trinity War Book: A Recital of Service and Sacrifice in the Great War* (Toronto: Ontario Press, 1921), 60; Frederick George Scott, *The Great War as I Saw It* (Toronto: F. D. Goodchild, 1922), 262.

22. Bishop, *Winged Warfare*, 94–96; letter dated 6 September 1917, in Harry Quigley Papers (private collection).

23. Bishop, *Winged Warfare*, 18, 118; Maclennan, "A Flying Officer's Training," 77.

24. T. A. Browne, "The Aviators," in *The Belgian Mother and Ballads of Battle Time* (Toronto: Macmillan, 1917); diary entry of 21 August 1915, in Deborah Cowley, ed., *Georges Vanier: Soldier. The Wartime Letter and Diaries, 1915–1919* (Toronto: Dundurn Press, 2000), 50.

25. Thomas, "The Canadian Airman," "Above the Clouds," "Children of the Air," and "The Song of the Contact Patrol," in *Songs of an Airman*.

26. Jack Turner, "The Aeroplane," in *Buddy's Blighty*; George C. Bidlake, ed., *The Last Year of the Great War as Seen by Gunner Temple Sutherland* (Fredericton: Royal Canadian Legion Branch #44, n.d.), 11; diary entry of 19 October 1915, in Cowley, *Georges Vanier*, 80.

27. Norah M. Holland, "The Air-Men," in *Spun-Yarn and Spindrift* (Toronto: J. M. Dent & Sons, 1918).

28. Thomas, "Above the Clouds," in *Songs of an Airman*; Kim Beattie, "Broken Wings," in *And You!* (Toronto: Macmillan, 1929).

29. Scott, *The Great War As I Saw It*, 263; Len Richardson, "My Overseas Will," in *Pilot's Log: The Flying Log, Diaries, Letters Home and Verse of Lt. Leonard Atwood Richardson, Royal Flying Corps, WWI, 1917–1918* (St. Catharines, Ont.: private, 1998), 135; diary entry of 15 March 1917, in Brereton Greenhous, ed., *A Rattle of Pebbles: The First World War Diaries of Two Canadian Airmen* (Ottawa: Department of National Defence, 1981).

30. Diary entry of 28 December 1915, in Greenhous, ed., *A Rattle of Pebbles*.

31. Carlyle, "The Royal Flying Corps in Canada," 335; C. G. Grey, "Canadians as Aviators in the R.F.C.," in *Canadian War Pictorial* 4 (1918): 7; Lord Montagu, "Aeronautics," in *Addresses Delivered before the Canadian Club of Ottawa, 1917–1918* (Ottawa: Dadson-Merrill Press, 1918), 106.

32. John H. Morrow Jr., "The War in the Air," in *World War I: A History*, Hew Strachan, ed. (New York: Oxford University Press, 1998), 276.

33. Lord Montagu, "War and Aviation," in *Addresses Delivered before the Canadian Club of Toronto, Season of 1917–1918* (Toronto: Warwick Bros. & Rutter, 1918), 112; Kim Beattie, "Dawn Patrol," in *And You!*

34. Diary entry of 11 September 1916, in Gaudet, *From a Stretcher Handle*, 101.

35. Thomas, "The Canadian Airman," "Children of the Air," and "Chivalry of the Air," in *Songs of an Airman*; quoted in George Drew, *Canada's Fighting Airmen* (Toronto: MacLean, 1930), 233.

36. Halifax *Herald*, 17 July 1915; AGBP: Home Notes, vol. 96, pp. 146–51, 28 June 1916.

37. National Aviation Museum [NAM]: J. A. D. McCurdy scrapbook, vol. 2, unidentified clipping; W. A. Bishop, "Aircraft," in *Addresses Delivered before the Canadian Club of Montreal, Season 1917–1918* (n.c.: n.p., n.d.), 176–77; Lord Montagu, "Aircraft in the War," in *Addresses Delivered to the Canadian Club of Montreal, Season 1917–1918* (n.c.: n.p., n.d.), 124.

38. Manitoba *Free Press*, 3 July 1917, 9; editorial "The Air Forces of War," in Toronto *Daily Star*, 1 April 1918, 10.

39. Vancouver *Sun*, 8 September 1915, 1; 13 September 1915, 1; Toronto *Daily Star*, 7 July 1917, 1; Regina *Leader-Post*, 28 May 1917, 1.

40. Editorial "The Long-Awaited Air Raid," Manitoba *Free Press*, 1 January 1915, 9; editorial "Reprisals for Raids," Ottawa *Citizen*, 10 July 1917, 12; editorial "A Canadian V.C.," Vancouver *Sun*, 9 June 1915, 4; editorial "German Zeppelin Crews Worse than Sitting Bull's Scalping Parties," Toronto *Evening Telegram*, 7 February 1916, 10; editorial "More 'Frightfulness,'" Vancouver *Sun*, 2 February 1916, 4.

41. Toronto *Daily Star*, 2 June 1915, 1.

42. James L. Hughes, "An English Volunteer," in *Rainbows on War Clouds* (Syracuse, NY: C. W. Bardeen, 1919).

43. Jesse Edgar Middleton, "The Zeppelin," in *Sea Dogs and Men at Arms*; Walter Brindle, "Air Raid," in *France and Flanders: Four Years' Experience Told in Poem and Story* (Saint John, NB: S. K. Smith, 1919).

44. Montagu, "Aeronautics," 110; Montagu, "War and Aviation," 108; editorial "The Air Forces of War," Toronto *Daily Star*, 1 April 1918, 10.

45. McCurdy scrapbook, vol. 2, "Giant aircraft to Tackle Teuton— Toronto to Turn Out Nemesis for Baby-Killers?" n.d.; Toronto *Globe*, 5 July 1915; George Palmer, "Air Reprisals," in *Stand To* (Calgary: S. A. Hynd, 1919).

46. Mary Josephine Benson, "The North Sea's Emptiness," in *My Pocket Beryl* (Toronto: McClelland & Stewart, 1921); H. G. Castle, *Fire Over England: The German Air Raids of World War I* (London: Secker and Warburg, 1982), 106–7; editorial "Left Baby Butchers to Die," Toronto *Evening Telegram*, 5 February 1916, 22.

47. Editorial "What the Aeroplane Can Do," Ottawa *Citizen*, 9 June 1915, 12.

48. Manitoba *Free Press*, 8 June 1915, 9; "What Time the Morning Stars Arise," in *Jean Blewett's Poems* (Toronto: McClelland & Stewart, 1922).

49. Castle, *Fire Over England*, 71; Ottawa *Citizen*, 8 June 1915, 1; 9 June 1915, 2.

50. "The Avenging Angel," in *The Poetical Works of Wilfred Campbell* (Toronto: Hodder and Stoughton, 1923).

51. National Archives of Canada (NAC): George Kendall Lucas Papers, journal, n.d., pp.113–14; John H. Morrow Jr. and Earl Rogers, eds., *A Yankee*

Ace in the RAF: The World War I Letters of Captain Bogart Rogers (Lawrence: University Press of Kansas, 1996), 176; quoted in Elizabeth O'Kiely, *Gentleman Air Ace: The Duncan Bell-Irving Story* (Madeira Park, BC: Harbour Publishing, 1992), 48.

52. London *Advertiser*, 27 October 1917, 1; Bishop, *Winged Warfare*, 101, 104–5, 139, 260; Raymond Collishaw, "War Flying and Commercial Flying," in *Addresses Delivered before the Canadian Club of Toronto, Season of 1918–19* (Toronto: Warwick Bros. & Rutter, 1920), 282.

3. The World at Your Feet
1. Toronto *Evening Telegram*, 31 August 1920, 16; Toronto *Globe*, 30 August 1920, 16.

2. Wayne Ralph, *Barker VC: William Barker, Canada's Most Decorated War Hero* (Toronto: Doubleday, 1997),189.

3. NAC: Department of National Defence [DND] Records, vol. 3577, f. HQ 866-1-53, pt. 1, J. A. Wilson, "Progress in Aviation," 12 February 1920.

4. Toronto *Globe*, 14 May 1919, 5.

5. Harry Fitzsimmons, "Barnstorming Days," in *Alberta Historical Review* 18, no. 2 (spring 1970): 22.

6. René Bélanger, *Conquering the North Shore by Air: Development of Aviation on the North Shore, 1919–1954* (Quebec: Éditions la Liberté, 1978), 18–20; Toronto *Globe*, 15 May 1919, 9; Victoria *Daily Colonist*, 10 June 1919, 12; 11 June 1919.

7. Ottawa *Citizen*, 30 May 1919, 1; Fitzsimmons, "Barnstorming Days."

8. NAC: Russell M. Smith Papers, NAC MG30 E409, circular letter dated 1 February 1920.

9. Regina *Leader*, 26 May 1919, 5, 9; Calgary *Herald*, 8 August 1919, 16.

10. Hitchins Papers, II-A-4, J. A. Wilson, "The Influence of Civil Aviation in the Development of Canada's Air Power," 3 November 1943.

11. Toronto *Daily Star*, 7 May 1927, 19.

12. Hitchins Papers, aviation scrapbook vol. 1, unidentified clipping; Percy Rowe, *The Great Atlantic Air Race* (Toronto: McClelland and Stewart, 1977), 82–83.

13. Notes and Comment, Calgary *Herald*, 29 May 1919, 8; editorial "Aerial Achievement," Toronto *Globe*, 28 May 1919, 6.

14. Ottawa *Journal*, 29 May 1919, 4.

15. Editorial "Well Done, Hawker and Grieve," Toronto *Globe*, 20 May 1919, 5; editorial "Hawker and Grieve," Toronto *Daily Star*, 20 May 1919, 6.

16. Editorial "The World Rejoices," *Border Cities Star*, 27 May 1919, 4; editorial "Hawker and Grieve," Toronto *Globe*, 26 May 1919, 6; Rowe, *The Great Atlantic Air Race*, 177.

17. Editorial "The Atlantic Bridged," Ottawa *Journal*, 17 June 1919, 6; editorial "The Trans-Atlantic Flight," Regina *Morning Leader*, 17 June 1919, 4.

18. Editorial "The Atlantic Flight," Toronto *Globe*, 16 June 1919, 6;

Notes and Comments, Toronto *Globe*, 16 June 1919, 6; editorial "Cook's of the Air," Toronto *Globe*, 17 June 1919, 6; editorial "The Trans-Atlantic Flight," Victoria *Daily Colonist*, 17 June 1919, 4.

19. Toronto *Daily Star*, 7 May 1927, 19.

20. Editorial "From Toronto to Winnipeg," Toronto *Daily Star*, 11 May 1927, 6.

21. Toronto *Daily Star*, 14 May 1927, 19.

22. Toronto *Daily Star*, 20 May 1927, 1, 16.

23. Toronto *Daily Star*, 21 May 1927, 1.

24. For the best account of Lindbergh's impact, see Modris Eksteins, *Rites of Spring: The Great War and the Birth of the Modern Age* (Toronto: Lester & Orpen Dennys, 1989), ch. 8.

25. Edmund Vance Cooke, "The Hero," in *The Spirit of St. Louis*, Charles Vale, ed. (New York: George H. Doran, 1927).

26. Editorial "Lindbergh's Triumph," Montreal *Gazette*, 23 May 1927, 12; editorial "The Triumph of the 'Flying Fool,'" Regina *Leader*, 23 May 1927, 4.

27. Editorial "Captain Lindbergh's Feat," Ottawa *Citizen*, 23 May 1927, 18; editorial "Lindbergh's Triumph," Ottawa *Journal*, 24 May 1927, 4.

28. Editorial "Adventure Spirit Still Lives," Calgary *Herald*, 23 May 1927; editorial "Long-Distance Flying," Toronto *Globe*, 21 May 1927, 4; Joseph Cook, "Lindbergh," in Toronto *Globe,* 24 May 1927, 1.

29. Bliss Carman, "Youth in the Air," in Vale, ed., *The Spirit of St. Louis: One Hundred Poems*.

30. King Diary, 21 and 23 May, 2 and 3 July 1927.

31. Claude-Henri Grignon, *Le Secret de Lindbergh* (Montréal: Éditions de la Porte d'Or, 1928).

32. Editorial "Lindbergh," Ottawa *Citizen*, 4 July 1927, 20.

33. NAM: Western Canada Airways [WCA] scrapbooks, Winnipeg *Free Press*, 3 March 1930; Canadian Literature scrapbooks, vol. 1, p. 357, Agnes Laut, "Canadian Woman Flies Far North," Toronto *Star Weekly*, 15 February 1921.

34. J. H. Parkin, *Aeronautical Research in Canada, 1917–1957: Memoirs of J. H. Parkin,* vol. 1 (Ottawa: National Research Council, 1983), 268; "The Magic of Flight," in *CAL Bulletin* 6, no. 11 (August 1936): 28.

35. Jack Paterson, "Canada Flies," *Maclean's*, 1 June 1939: 11; cf. Peter Fritzsche, *A Nation of Fliers: German Aviation and the Popular Imagination* (Cambridge: Harvard University Press, 1992), 154.

36. Advertisement in *Canadian Aviation* 2, no. 6 (June 1929); Isabell C. Crawford, "The Airman," in *The Redman's Prayer and Other Poems* (Kamloops: private, 1929).

37. Annie Charlotte Dalton, "To an Airman," in *Lilies and Leopards* (Toronto: Ryerson Press, 1935); J. Fergus Grant, "Trans-Canada Airway," in *Canadian Geographical Journal* 14, no. 2 (February 1937): 117; George B.

Foster, "The Air Cadets of Canada," in *Canadian Air Cadet* 1, no. 1 (October 1941): 7. Cf. Laurence Goldstein, *The Flying Machine and Modern Literature* (Bloomington: Indiana University Press, 1986).

38. "Flying," words and music by Will J. Whyte (Toronto: Musgrave Brothers, 1918).

39. T. D. Hallam, "To My Old Bus," in *The Spider Web: The Romance of a Flying-Boat War Flight* (London: William Blackwood & Sons, 1919), 27–28; "A Toast to Flying," in *Canadian Aviation* 5, no. 6 (June 1932): 4; Archives of Ontario (AO): Frank E. Davison Papers, MU823, scrapbook #1, editorial from Patricia *Herald*, undated.

40. Arnold H. Sandwell, "The Camera Takes to the Air," in *Canadian Geographical Journal* 1, no. 1 (May 1930): 61; letter of 28 May 1933 in Henry Borden, ed., *Letters to Limbo by the Right Honourable Sir Robert Laird Borden, PC, GCMG, KC, Prime Minister of Canada, 1911–1920* (Toronto: University of Toronto Press, 1971), 33; W. A. Bishop and R. Stuart Wortley, *The Flying Squad* (London: George G. Harrap, 1928), 31.

41. Wilfrid Gibson, "Earth-Bound," in *WCA Bulletin* 2, no. 5 (15 November 1930): 13; WCA scrapbooks, D. R. P. Coats, "Up in the Air," 1 September 1927.

42. L. M. Montgomery, *Rilla of Ingleside* (Toronto: McClelland & Stewart, 1920), 286; Hallam, *The Spider Web*, 114.

43. A. M. Stephen, "Lords of the Air," in *Lords of the Air: Poems of the Present War* (Vancouver: privately published, n.d. [1940?]); Herbert J. Brooks, "Wings," in *Alberta Poetry Year Book, 1936–1937* (Edmonton: Canadian Authors' Association, 1937).

44. Edna Jaques, "A Housewife Salutes a Flier," in *Beside Still Waters* (Toronto: Thomas Allen, 1941); Eva Phillips Boyd, "By Air," in *Dalhousie Review* 12 (1932–33): 24.

45. Clara Hopper, "The Aviators," in *Canadian Forum* 12, no. 139 (April 1932): 267.

46. Callisthenes, "Why Don't You Learn to Fly?" in *Canadian Aviation* 4, no. 9 (September 1931): 26; Paterson, "Canada Flies," 41; *Canadian Aviation* 5, no. 7 (July 1932): 2.

47. F. M. Delafosse, "Oh, Lord of Hosts: A Hymn for Airmen," in *Verses Grave and Gay* (Peterborough, Ont.: private, 1937); Marie Sylvia, "En Avion: Ottawa–Toronto," in *Reflets d'Opale* (Montreal: private, 1945).

48. McCurdy scrapbooks, vol. 3, Stewart McCawley, "Baddeck and That Sort of Thing" (16 July 1934); Frances Beatrice Taylor, "Evolution," in Vale, *The Spirit of St. Louis*.

49. Joseph J. Corn, *The Winged Gospel: America's Romance with Aviation, 1900–1950* (New York: Oxford University Press, 1983), 74.

50. Alonzo Cinq-Mars, "Excelsior!" in *De L'Aube au Midi* (Quebec City: Societé des Poètes, 1924).

4. An Air-Minded People

1. Editorial "Let Us All Fly," Sault *Daily Star*, 23 May 1927.

2. Quoted in Margaret Mattson, "The Growth and Protection of Canadian Civil and Commercial Aviation, 1918–1930" (Ph.D., University of Western Ontario, 1979), 3; DND Records, vol. 3577, f. 866-1-53, Wilson to Clayton-Kennedy, 12 July 1919.

3. J. A. Wilson, "Civil Aviation To-day," in *Canadian Defence Quarterly* 1, no. 3 (April 1924): 22; DND Records, vol. 2928, f. 866-1-13, pt. 1, D. R. MacLaren, "Development and Control of Civil Aviation in Canada," n.d. [April 1926].

4. Stephen Leacock, "The Economic Aspect of Aviation," in *Transactions of the Royal Society of Canada*, 3rd series, vol. 22 (1928), 213; DND Records, vol. 3577, f. HQ 866-1-53, pt. 2, memorandum, "Civil Aviation in Canada," n.d. [1924].

5. Senate Debates, 7 June 1934, 471; W. A. Bishop, "What Aviation Means to Canada," in Empire Club of Canada, *Addresses Delivered to the Members during the Year 1935–36* (Toronto: Warwick Bros. & Rutter, 1936), 247–48.

6. DND Records, vol. 2928, f. 866-1-13, pt. 1, Norman Yarrow, "Commercial Aviation in Canada," April 1921.

7. DND Records, vol. 3564, f. HQ1011-1-15, D. R. MacLaren, "Suggested Scheme of Aeronautical Propaganda in Canada," 5 May 1920.

8. MacLaren, "Development and Control of Civil Aviation in Canada."

9. NAC: W. A. Steel Papers, vol. 5, f. 22, Air Ministry, "The Progress of Imperial Air Communications," September 1930.

10. AO: RG1 Ser. JAII-2 b3, f. Reports–Newspaper Clippings, *Canadian Aviation* to OPAS, 16 April 1928.

11. DND Records, vol. 3564, f. HQ1011-1-15, O. M. Biggar to Clayton-Kennedy, 27 February 1920.

12. DND Records, vol. 3564, f. HQ1011-1-15, Wakeman to CAF, 22 November 1919.

13. *Canadian Aviation* 1, no. 1 (June 1928): 1.

14. Montreal *Gazette*, 10 January 1927, 7.

15. DND Records, vol. 2929, f. 866-8-1, pt. 2, Coolican to J. S. Scott, 18 December 1926; Parkin, *Aeronautical Research in Canada*, vol. 1, 256.

16. William Paul Ferguson, *Snowbird Decades: Western Canada's Pioneer Aviation Companies* (Vancouver: Butterworth and Co., 1979), 53.

17. AO: RG1 Ser. JAII-2 b3, f. Reports–Newspaper Clippings, Toronto *Daily Star* to OPAS, 27 June 1928.

18. "A Matter of Education," in *CAL Bulletin* 4, no. 2 (15 August 1932): 18–19; *Canadian Aviation* 5, no. 9 (September 1932): 22.

19. Charlottetown *Patriot*, 1 September 1932, 1.

20. NAC: J. A. Wilson Papers, vol. 2, H. H. Richards, CFCA, to Manion,

24 February 1932; DND Records, vol. 2928, f. 409-1-3, J. A. Wilson, memorandum on inspection of Maritime provinces, 24 November 1931.

21. L. M. Montgomery, *Rilla of Ingleside* (Toronto: McClelland & Stewart, 1920), 283–84.

22. House of Commons, Debates, 1 April 1937, 2455; Hamilton *Spectator*, 5 April 1920.

23. Edmonton *Journal*, 6 December 1919, 1.

24. Public Archives of Nova Scotia (PANS): Minutes of meeting of delegates of Provincial Executive Committees of Canadian Air Force Association, Winnipeg, 3 July 1920, H2.

25. WCA scrapbooks, vol. 1, Toronto *Mail and Empire*, 10 August 1928; Toronto *Globe*, 10 June 1929; Hamilton *Herald*, 10 June 1929.

26. DND Records, vol. 2928, f. 866-1-13, pt. 1, Norman Anderson, "Commercial Aviation in Western Canada," July 1922; J. D. Parkinson, "The Story of the First Aerial Trans-Canada Tour," in *Canadian Air Review* 3, no. 1 (March 1930): 25.

27. "Air Travel Is Safe," in *The Bulletin* (Western Canada Airways Ltd.) 4, no. 12 (15 June 1933): 15–16; Dalton Little, "Aviation to Stimulate All Canadian Industry," in *Saturday Night*, 20 August 1938: 24.

28. Bishop, "What Aviation Means to Canada," 250; Bishop and Wortley, *The Flying Squad*, 114; PANS: MG9 v100 aviation scrapbook, article from Granby, PQ.

29. Montreal *Gazette*, 15 August 1931, 5; 17 August 1931, 5; DND Records, vol. 3577, f. 866-1-53, Victoria *Daily Colonist*, 18 August 1921.

30. Toronto *Daily Star*, 4 January 1929; William R. Campbell, "It's Easy to Learn to Fly," in *Canadian Aviation* 2, no. 9 (September 1929): 18; Clare Ward Farrell, "Flying Frontiersmen," in *Maclean's*, 15 January 1929: 55.

31. Robert Leslie, "The Flying Vachons," in *Canadian Magazine*, February 1930: 10; W. B. Burchall, "Fact and Fiction," in *The Bulletin* (Western Canada Airways Ltd.) 2, no. 1 (15 July 1930): 15.

32. Hamilton *Spectator*, 28 July 1927, 6; London *Advertiser*, 15 December 1927.

33. DND Records, vol. 3577, f. HQ866-1-53, pt. 2, "Aviation as a Vocation," February 1931; Charles Evans, letter to *Canadian Aviation* 2, no. 5 (May 1929): 28; A. H. Sandwell, "Does Canada Need an Air Ministry?" in *Saturday Night*, 2 March 1940: 3.

34. Callisthenes, "Why Don't You Learn to Fly?" in *Canadian Aviation* 4, no. 9 (September 1931): 26; PANS: MG9 vol. 101, aviation scrapbook, editorial dated February 1930; DND Records, vol. 3577, f. HQ866-1-53, pt. 1, J. A. Wilson, "Progress in Aviation," 12 February 1920.

35. Saint John *Evening Times-Globe*, 21 March 1919; NAC: Ernest Stedman Papers, vol. 1, scrapbooks, Montreal *Gazette*, 27 November 1925; Sydney *Post-Record*, 13 July 1936, 9; Corn, *The Winged Gospel*, ch. 5.

36. Charles J. Woodsworth, "Canada's Flying Future," in *The Beaver*,

March 1936: 9; E. L. Chicanot, "Canada's Aircraft Independence," in *Saturday Night*, 11 August 1928: 19; *Canadian Aviation* 2, no. 6 (June 1929); Hitchins Papers, II-A-4, J. A. Wilson, "The Influence of Civil Aviation in the Development of Canada's Air Power," 3 November 1943.

37. *Canadian Air Review*, 1, no. 2 (April 1928): 23.

38. Marjorie Elliott Wilkins, "Miss Canada Takes the Air," in *Canadian Magazine*, November 1929.

39. Elsie Gregory MacGill, "Women on the Wing," in *Chatelaine*, August 1931.

40. Yarrow, "Commercial Aviation in Canada," 6; quoted in Joyce Spring, *Daring Lady Flyers: Canadian Women in the Early Years of Aviation* (Porter's Lake, NS: Pottersfield Press, 1994), 7.

41. Shirley Render, *No Place for a Lady: The Story of Canadian Women Pilots, 1928–92* (Winnipeg: Portage and Main Press, 1992), 13, 23; Spring, *Daring Lady Flyers*, 55.

42. DND Records, vol. 3577, f. HQ866-1-53, pt. 2, "Civil Aviation in Canada," n.d. [1924].

43. Wilson, "Civil Aviation To-day," 23; Wilson, "The Influence of Civil Aviation in the Development of Canada's Air Power."

44. NAC: R. B. Bennett Papers, vol. 831, reel M1471, R. P. Young to Bennett, 16 November 1936; Arthur Lowe, "Kindergarten of the Air," in *Maclean's*, 1 May 1940: 32.

45. WCA scrapbooks, Montreal *Daily Star*, 7 July 1928.

46. PANS: MG9 vol. 100, aviation scrapbook, unidentified editorial, 5 May 1928; *The Bulletin* 6, no. 11 (August 1936): 2.

47. House of Commons, Debates, 14 May 1934, 3043.

5. The Annihilation of Time

1. Hudson's Bay Company Archives: Duncan McLaren papers, E66/4/1, McLaren to parents, 28 August and 23 September 1937.

2. *Northern Miner*, 28 February 1929, 17.

3. DND Records, vol. 3525, f. HQ886-25-8, "Memorandum regarding formation of National Canadian Air Service," 28 January 1919; J. A. Wilson, "Civil Aviation in Canada," in *Queen's Quarterly* 36, no. 2 (spring 1929): 300, 305.

4. Muskoka *Herald*, 15 July 1920, 4; Wayne Ralph, *Barker VC*, chs. 10 and 11.

5. Quoted in *Royal Commission on the Future of the Toronto Waterfront, Toronto Island Airport 50, 1939–1989* (1989); NAC: J. L. Ralston Papers, series 11, vol. 15, f. Aviation 1935, letter 27 November 1935.

6. Editorial "A Canadian Air Force," Toronto *Daily Star,* 15 May 1919, 6.

7. William H. Finlayson, "The Utilization of Aircraft in Canada," in *Addresses Delivered before the Canadian Club of Toronto, Session of 1928–29* (Toronto: Warwick Bros. & Rutter, 1929), 88.

8. Stephen Leacock, "The Economic Aspect of Aviation," in *Transactions of the Royal Society of Canada*, 3rd series, vol. 22 (1928), 224–25; J. H. Parkin, "Solving the Problems of Aviation in Canada," in *Industrial Canada* 30, no. 9 (January 1930): 118.

9. Arnold H. Sandwell, "The Camera Takes to the Air," in *Canadian Geographical Journal* 1, no. 1 (May 1930): 61–74.

10. NAC: Arthur Sifton Papers, vol. 8, f. 1, meeting of Air Board #3, 2 July 1919.

11. Department of National Defence, *Report on Civil Aviation for the Year 1924* (Ottawa: King's Printer, 1925), 15; Department of National Defence, *Report on Civil Aviation for the Year 1925* (Ottawa: King's Printer, 1926), 48; "Aerial Mapping Activities in 1930," in *Canadian Mining Journal* 51, no. 50 (12 December 1930): 1,196.

12. Department of National Defence, *Report on Civil Aviation for the Year 1923* (Ottawa: King's Printer, 1924), 48; Department of National Defence, *Report on Civil Aviation for the Year 1924*, 49.

13. R. C. Purser, "Use of Aerial Camera in Mapping," in *Canadian Mining Journal* 50, no. 5 (1 February 1929): 96; NAC: Lloyd Rochester Papers, vol. 18, "A Few Observations on Prospecting, Aircraft and the Mining Industry," given to the Canadian Institute of Surveying, 6 February 1936.

14. A. M. Narraway, "A Challenge to the Canadian Pilot," in *Canadian Aviation* July 1928: 18–19.

15. Wilson Papers, vol. 1, f. 2, Logan to Wilson, 31 October 1924.

16. Department of National Defence, *Report on Civil Aviation for the Year 1926* (Ottawa: King's Printer, 1927), 83; James Montagnes, "Firemen of the Air," in *Canadian Magazine*, October 1929: 12–13.

17. Department of National Defence, *Report on Civil Aviation for the Year 1926*, 83.

18. William J. McAndrew, "The Evolution of Canadian Aviation Policy Following the First World War," in *Journal of Canadian Studies* 16, nos. 3 and 4 (autumn–winter 1981): 92.

19. Department of National Defence, *Report on Civil Aviation for the Year 1923* (Ottawa: King's Printer, 1924), 14–15.

20. Bruce West, *The Firebirds: How Bush Flying Won Its Wings* (Toronto: Ministry of Natural Resources, 1974), 18–20.

21. DND Records, vol. 3577, f. 866-1-53, Wilson to Charles Grey, 10 September 1920; Department of National Defence, *Report on Civil Aviation for the Year 1923*, 28.

22. Frank Ellis, *Canada's Flying Heritage* (Toronto: University of Toronto Press, 1954), 129; Public Archives of New Brunswick (PANB): Department of Lands and Mines Records, *77th Annual Report of the Department of Lands and Mines, Year Ending 31 October 1937*, 21.

23. NAC: Robert Borden Papers, reel C272, f. 411 Canadian Flying Service, Potter to Borden, 26 May 1917.

24. NAC: Department of External Affairs (DEA) Records, series B1b, vol. 203, f. I43/84, Meighen to Perley, 21 December 1918; B. Thomson, "Small airships for forest fire patrol," 28 June 1919.

25. Quoted in Finlayson, "The Utilization of Aircraft in Canada," 90; "Canada's Future in the Air," in *Saturday Night*, 7 July 1928: 11; E. W. Stedman, "Aviation and Modern Engineering Practice," in *Engineering Journal* 9, no. 6 (June 1926): 291; quoted in West, *The Firebirds*, 138.

26. Quoted in Chris Weicht, *Jericho Beach and the West Coast Flying Boat Stations* (Chemainus, BC: MCW Enterprises, 1997), 33.

27. Editorial "Heroes of the North," Winnipeg *Tribune*, 16 January 1933.

28. NAC: H. A. Oaks Papers, vol. 2, f. 10, staff of Northern Aerial Minerals Exploration Ltd., "Aerial Exploration," in *Canadian Mining & Metallurgical Bulletin*, March 1929, 8.

29. Morris Zaslow, *The Northward Expansion of Canada, 1914–1968* (Toronto: McClelland and Stewart, 1988), 104–5.

30. Bennett Papers, vol. 143, reel M4490, editorial, London *Free Press*, 1 October 1936; W. E. Gilbert, "BC's Newest North," in *WCA Bulletin*, 16 June 1930: 13; Hamilton *Spectator*, 4 March 1926.

31. WCA scrapbooks, Toronto *Star Weekly*, 1 May 1926, 2; Oaks Papers, vol. 2, f. 12, *News from the Mines*, 16 March 1928.

32. Staff of Northern Aerial Minerals Exploration Ltd., "Aerial Exploration," 3; James Montagnes, "The Modern Prospector Flies," in *Canadian Magazine*, August 1928: 13, 42.

33. Richard Finnie, *Canada Moves North* (Toronto: Macmillan, 1948), 92–93; House of Commons, Debates, 7 March 1919, 303–5.

34. E. Green, "Wings Over the Magnetic Pole," in *The Beaver*, March 1936: 46–50, 66; Kathleen Shackleton, *Arctic Pilot: Life and Work on Northern Canadian Air Routes* (London: T. Nelson, 1940), 118.

35. Sandy A. F. Macdonald, "Famous Flights of the North," in *The Beaver*, March 1936, 52; PANS: MG9 vol. 101, aviation scrapbook, unidentified editorial reproducing ad from Edmonton *Journal*; Montreal *Gazette*, 17 February 1934.

36. Philip H. Godsell, *Arctic Trader: The Account of Twenty Years with the Hudson's Bay Company* (New York: G. P. Putnam's Sons, 1932), 307; *Canadian Aviation* 4, no. 1 (January 1931): 5.

37. Godsell, *Arctic Trader*, 308; Toronto *Daily Star*, 7 May 1927, 2; Allen Bill, "The High North Is Living," in *CAL Bulletin* 4, no. 11 (15 May 1933), 4; J. Fergus Grant, "North to the Yukon by Air," in *Canadian Geographical Journal* 15, no. 2 (August 1937): 84; Finnie, *Canada Moves North*, 102.

38. Richard Finnie, "Romance and Routine," in *WCA Bulletin* 6, no. 2 (February 1935), 3; NAC: W. R. May Papers, interview at Edmonton airport, 13 December 1938.

39. Finnie, *Canada Moves North*, 99; "Sound Position of Canadian Aviation," in *Canadian Mining Journal* 51, no. 38 (19 September 1930): 914;

D. M. LeBourdais, "Flying the Trail of '98," in *Maclean's*, 1 November 1939: 38.

40. WCA scrapbooks, editorial "Canada's New Empire," in Winnipeg *Tribune*, 6 May 1931; *Arctic Pilot*, 130; Lawrence J. Burpee, "Where Rail and Airway Meet," in *Canadian Geographical Journal* 10, no. 5 (May 1935).

41 Burpee, "Where Rail and Airway Meet," 239.

42. J. P. de Wet, "Commercial Flying in Canada," in *Canadian Geographical Journal* 13, no. 6 (October 1936): 317.

43. DND Records, vol. 3577, f. HQ866-1-53, pt. 2, Toronto *Evening Telegram*, 20 April 1937; House of Commons, Debates, 14 May 1934, 3,043.

44. Halifax *Herald*, 19 October 1919, 6; Taylor Collection, accession 3523/2, letter from Stevenson to Harold Pickard.

45. These advertisements can be found in a number of locations, particularly the Frank E. Davison Papers at the Archives of Ontario, the Western Canada Aviation Museum and the WCA scrapbooks at the National Aviation Museum.

46. Montreal *Daily Star*, 7 July 1928; Davison Papers, MU823, scrapbook #1; Charlottetown *Guardian*, 1 September 1931, 7.

6. Wings for the Nation

1. PANS: MG100 vol. 101, #3, reel 15158, Mayor of Halifax to Mayor of Vancouver, 23 September 1920. For the full story of the flight, see Frank Ellis, "Wings Across Canada," in *The Beaver*, December 1947, 38–42.

2. DND Records, vol. 3577, f. H866-1-53, pt. 1, J. A. Wilson, "Progress in Aviation," 12 February 1920; Geoff O'Brian, "Solving Canadian Geography," in *Canadian Aviation* 5, no. 12 (December 1932): 9.

3. Ralph Centennius, *The Dominion in 1983*, 10; DND Records, vol. 2928, f. 866-1-13, pt. 1, D. R. MacLaren, "Development and Control of Civil Aviation in Canada," April 1926.

4. Department of National Defence, *Report on Civil Aviation for the Year 1923* (Ottawa: King's Printer, 1924), 12.

5. Taylor Collection, accession 3523/42, J. McCarey, Charlottetown postmaster, to F. Smith, Truro postmaster, 29 September 1919.

6. Bélanger, *Conquering the North Shore by Air*, 53.

7. DND Records, vol. 3525, f. HQ886-25-8, "Memorandum Regarding Formation of National Canadian Air Service," 8 January 1919.

8. Lord Montagu, "War and Aviation," in *Addresses Delivered before the Canadian Club of Toronto, Season of 1917–1918* (Toronto: Warwick Bros. & Rutter, 1918); Bell to Canadian Club of Saint John, in Saint John *Evening Times-Globe*, 21 March 1919; Borden Papers, reel C268, f. 329 Air, W. M. Merritt to Borden, 26 August 1918.

9. Sifton Papers, vol. 8, f. 1, minutes of Air Board meeting #2, 27 June 1919; report to Air Board by Biggar, November 1919; DND Records, vol.

2929, f. 866-8-1, pt. 1, Ontario Associated Boards of Trade and Chambers of Commerce to Wilson, 28 April 1920.

10. DND Records, vol. 2929, f. 866-8-1, pt. 1, memo by Leckie "Aerial Mail," 4 March 1920; memo from Post Office, 15 March 1920.

11. Quoted in Ellis, "Wings Across Canada," 42.

12. Department of National Defence, *Report on Civil Aviation for the Year 1927–28* (Ottawa: King's Printer, 1928), 5; DND Records, vol. 2929, f. 866-8-1, pt. 1, Emily Crawford to Biggar; WBB, "Aerial Transportation in the North," in *WCA Bulletin*, 16 December 1929.

13. WCA scrapbooks, unidentified clipping, September 1929; Zaslow, *The Northward Expansion of Canada*, 177; J. Fergus Grant, "North to the Yukon by Air," in *Canadian Geographical Journal* 15, no. 2 (August 1937).

14. Peter Pigott, *Flying Colours: A History of Commercial Aviation in Canada* (Vancouver: Douglas & McIntyre, 1997), 63; J. Fergus Grant, "Trans-Canada Airway," in *Canadian Geographical Journal* 14, no. 2 (February 1937): 99.

15. WCA scrapbooks, editorial "Air Mail Contracts Cancelled," Winnipeg *Free Press*, 18 June 1931; editorial "What Would Canada Look Like?" Winnipeg *Free Press*, 24 June 1931.

16. House of Commons, Debates, 3 May 1929, 2220; diary entry of 14 February 1928. I am grateful to Mary Rubio for this reference; DND Records, vol. 3525, f. HQ886-25-8, "Memorandum Regarding Formation of National Canadian Air Service," 8 January 1919.

17. Editorial "By Air to Montreal," Toronto *Globe*, 1 October 1928, 4; "Montreal Is Mecca for Postal Airmen," in Toronto *Globe*, 2 October 1928, 5; NAC: Alex D. McLean scrapbook, reel M2982, *Manitoba Free Press*, 4 March 1930; editorial "An Epoch in Western Communication," Winnipeg *Free Press*, 4 March 1930.

18. McLean scrapbook, Saint John *Evening Times-Globe*, 28 January 1929; Saint John *Telegraph-Journal*, 29 January 1929.

19. PEIPARO: accession 3523/131, Mayor of Charlottetown to Mayor of Truro, 30 September 1919; accession 3523/127, Charlottetown *Guardian*, 25 September 1919, 9.

20. Quoted in Lana Isenor, "Upton Airport, Charlottetown, PEI" (1976), 4 in PEIPARO.

21. DND Records, vol. 2929, f. 866-8-1, pt. 4, unidentified editorial.

22. Muskoka *Herald*, 19 August 1920; DND Records, vol. 3564, f. HQ1011-1-15, "Air Administration in Canada."

23. Editorial "Wanted—A Landing Field," in Vancouver *Sun*, 21 May 1927, 6; editorial "Aviation Equipment Needed," in Vancouver *Sun*, 26 May 1927, 8; WCA scrapbooks, unidentified editorial "Keep Edmonton on the Air Map," December 1928; editorial "Regina and a Suitable Airport," in Regina *Morning Leader*, 11 July 1928, 4.

24. Editorial "A Municipal Air Port," in Winnipeg *Tribune*, 1 February

1929; editorial "Air Port for Winnipeg," in Winnipeg *Tribune*, 1 May 1929; De Havilland of Canada to Langton, 12 February 1929, and Board of Trade to Mayor Wemp, 1930, both quoted in *Royal Commission on the Future of the Toronto Waterfront, Toronto Island Airport 50, 1939–1989* (1989).

25. All these articles are taken from the aviation scrapbooks in PANS: MG9 vol. 100 and 101.

26. PANS: MG9 vol. 101, aviation scrapbook, editorial, Halifax *Citizen*, 23 November 1928, 5 April 1929; letter to *Evening Mail*, n.d.

27. WCA scrapbooks, vol. 2, Halifax *Daily Star*, 14 February 1930.

28. DND Records, vol. 2929, f. 866-8-1, pt. 4, editorial, Ottawa *Citizen*, 1 December 1929.

29. PANS: MG9 vol. 101, aviation scrapbook.

30. DND Records, vol. 2928, f. 409-1-3, memo "Airway Development, Maritime provinces—Montreal," 27 November 1931 by Wilson; DEA Records, vol. 1646, f. 72-F, memo "Trans-Pacific Airway," 9 November 1933.

31. DEA Records, vol. 1646, f. 72-M, pt. 1, Herring to Coolican, 26 December 1933; Report on Interdepartmental Committee on the Trans-Canada Airway.

32. DND Records, vol. 2929, f. 866-8-1, pt. 4, Groome to Wilson, 8 April 1931; see also J. H. Parkin, "Aviation in Canada and the National Research Laboratories," in *Engineering Journal* 14, no. 11 (November 1931): 564; NAC: A. G. L. MacNaughton Papers, series II, vol. 101, f. Interdepartmental Committee on Trans-Canada Airway, vol. 1, minutes of meeting, 11 July 1933.

33. Robert Ayre, "Flying with 'T.C.A.,'" in *Canadian Nurse* 35, no. 11 (November 1939): 623.

34. *Canadian Aviation*, April 1939, quoted in David H. Collins, *Wings Across Time: The Story of Air Canada* (Toronto: Griffin House, 1978), 14; Geoff O'Brian, "Solving Canadian Geography," in *Canadian Aviation* 5, no. 12 (December 32): 9.

35. Editorial "Canada's Air Expansion," Winnipeg *Free Press*, 3 February 1934; J. Fergus Grant, "Three-Hour Passenger Service to Maritimes by Plane Now Planned," in Montreal *Gazette*, 3 November 1930.

36. Frederick Watts, "The New Prairie Schooner," in *Canadian Magazine*, July 1930, 10; E. E. W. Rhodes, "Trans-Canada Air Lines," in *Caduceus* 20, no. 3 (July 1939): 13.

7. The Great Highway of Peace

1. William R. Campbell, "An Epic of Aerial Progress," in *Canadian Aviation* 3, no. 9 (September 1930): 17.

2. "The Story of the R-100," in *Canadian Geographical Journal* 1, no. 6 (October 1930); Bennett Papers, reel M-4490, vol. 1043, Ottawa *Morning Journal*, 11 August 1930; Toronto *Daily Star*, 11 August 1930, 1–2.

3. DND Records, vol. 3525, f. HQ 886-5-8, "Memorandum Regarding

Formation of National Canadian Air Service," 28 January 1919; vol 2928, f. 866-1-13, pt. 1, Norman Yarrow, "Commercial Aviation in Canada"; E.M.R., "R33 as a Commercial Carrier," Ottawa *Citizen*, 10 May 1919, 22.

4. AGBP: Laboratory Books, vol. 3, pp. 24–28, *Evening Times-Globe*, 21 March 1919.

5. Patrick Abbott, *Airship: The Story of the R.34 and the First East-West Crossing of the Atlantic by Air* (New York: Charles Scribner's Sons, 1973).

6. James Lewis Milligan, "The New Olympians," in *The Beckoning Skyline and Other Poems* (Toronto: McClelland & Stewart, 1920).

7. Robert Jackson, *Airships: A Popular History of Dirigibles, Zeppelins, Blimps, and Other Lighter-than-Air Craft* (Garden City, NY: Doubleday, 1973), 138–39; Basil Collier, *The Airship: A History* (London: Hart-Davis, MacGibbon, 1974).

8. Lady Hay Drummond-Hay, "Aboard the Graf Zeppelin," in *Western Home Monthly*, February 1930.

9. For the British airship scheme, see the document "Imperial Air Communications," dated 8 September 1930, submitted to the Imperial Economic Conference, Bennett Papers, vol. 155, reel M-997, pp.104,181 ff.

10. Peter G. Masefield, *To Ride the Storm: The Story of Airship R.100* (London: Kimber, 1982), 447–49.

11. Statement by Sir Samuel Hoare, 28 October 1926, in *Imperial Conference, 1926: Appendices to the Summary of Proceedings* (Ottawa: King's Printer, 1927), 155–56.

12. Bennett Papers, vol. 76, reel M-950, p. 50,796, Thomson to Ralston, 23 July 1930; Masefield, *To Ride the Storm*, 242.

13. Bob Sinclair, "Adieu, R-100," in *Canadian Aviation* 3, no. 9 (September 1930): 13–14.

14. Barry Countryman, *R100 in Canada* (Erin, Ont.: Boston Mills Press, 1982), 87; ad for Kraft cheese, Calgary *Herald*, 31 July 1930, 23.

15. Calgary *Herald*, 11 August 1930, 1; C. H. J. Snider, "Across in R-100," in *Queen's Quarterly* 38, no. 3 (summer 1931): 422.

16. Kathleen Purdy, "To the R100," in Toronto *Daily Star*, 13 August 1930, 6; Vancouver *Sun*, 6 August 1930, 6.

17. *Canadian Forum*, September 1930, quoted in Countryman, *R100 in Canada*, 87–92.

18. NAC: Ernest Stedman Papers, vol. 1, scrapbooks, "Viking of the Storm and Wind, R-100 Rides to Home Mooring Mast"; Sinclair, "Adieu, R-100," 13–14.

19. Ad for Ten-Test fibre-board, Toronto *Daily Star*, 1 August 1930, 11.

20. Quoted in Masefield, *To Ride the Storm*, 7.

21. Dennistoun Burney, "Aviation and the Empire," in *Addresses Delivered before the Canadian Club of Toronto, Season of 1930–31* (Toronto: Warwick Bros. & Rutter, 1931), 11; Ian Shaw, "Future Atlantic Airship Services as

Visualized by Sir Dennistoun Burney," in *Canadian Aviation* 3, no. 9 (September 1930): 20.

22. Toronto *Daily Star*, 1 August 1930, 15; 11 August 1930, 3.

23. Burney, "Aviation and the Empire," 4–5; ad for Buckingham's cigarettes, Vancouver *Sun*, 29 July 1930, 11.

24. Stephen Leacock, "The Economic Aspect of Aviation," in *Transactions of the Royal Society of Canada*, 3rd series, vol. 22 (1928), 218; editorial "A Transatlantic Air Service," Toronto *Daily Star*, 10 October 1928, 6.

25. Editorial "R-100 for Business," Edmonton *Journal*, 30 July 1930, 4; John C. Nelson, "Britain's Air Liner," in *Canadian Magazine*, January 1930: 15; NAC: W.A. Steel Papers, vol. 5, f. 23, J. Fergus Grant, "Atlantic Flown by Airships on 11 Attempted Flights," in Montreal *Gazette*, 23 September 1930.

26. "Disaster to Dirigible R-101," in *Saturday Night*, 11 October 1930, 1; Snider, "Across in R-100," 421–23.

27. Editorial "The Atlantic Flight," Manitoba *Free Press*, 17 June 1919, 11; editorial "Accomplished," Calgary *Herald*, 16 June 1919, 8; editorial "The Atlantic Bridged," Ottawa *Journal*, 17 June 1919, 6.

28. DND Records, vol. 2928, f. 409-1-3, memorandum "Airway Development, Maritime Provinces—Montreal," 27 November 1931; editorial "Byrd's Great Flight," Ottawa *Citizen*, 5 July 1927, 18; Charlottetown *Evening Patriot*, 15 September 1930, 4.

29. WCA scrapbooks vol. 3, Saint John *Telegraph-Journal*, 13 July 1933; David MacKenzie, *Canada and International Civil Aviation, 1932–1948* (Toronto: University of Toronto Press, 1898), 23.

30. Ottawa *Morning Citizen*, 14 July 1933; editorial "Our Pitiful Air Effort," Winnipeg *Free Press*, 24 July 1933.

31. DEA Records, vol. 1646, f. 72-F, Wilson, "PanAm Airways," 23 January 1933.

32. Editorial "Pre-empting an Airway," Winnipeg *Free Press*, 9 August 1932; J. D. M. Gray, "The Northern Air Route," in *Saturday Night*, 10 September 1932, 5; Montreal *Gazette*, 21 October 1935.

33. PANS: MG9 vol. 100 scrapbook aviation clippings, Halifax editorial, 20 November 1926; PANS: MG100 vol. 41, #85, reel 9241, scrapbook Halifax airport, unidentified article, 1 August 1931.

34. PANS: MG100 vol. 41, #85, reel 9241, scrapbook Halifax airport, report from Logan to PanAm, Boston, 20 October 1931; PANS: RG35-102 3B.1.1, Mayor to D. M. Sutherland, 30 January 1934.

35. NAC: Stuart Graham Papers, "Official Souvenir program of the landing at Shediac of the Italian Air Armada, July 1933"; J. E. Belliveau, "Sky Sailors' Port," in *Maclean's*, 15 November 1939, 22–24.

36. DEA Records, series G1 vol. 1766, f. 72-M, pt. 2, J. A. Wilson, "Trans-Atlantic Air Service," 17 August 1936; pt. 3, Wrong to Beaudry, 7 October 1936.

37. DEA Records, series G1, vol. 1767, f. 72-M, pt. 6, Trans-Atlantic Service Progress Reports, 31 August 1937 and 31 October 1937.

38. Beverley Baxter, "By Clipper," in *Maclean's*, 15 October 1941, 49–50; W. G. Fitz-Gerald, "Empire Airways Girdle the Globe," in *National Home Monthly*, March 1939: 12.

39. Bennett Papers, p. 50,385, M. H. Nickerson to Bennett, 24 March 1935; "Gives Canada Place on Air Map," Montreal *Gazette*, 3 August 1936.

40. *AEA Bulletin* 24 (21 December 1908): 37; William B. Stout, "Serving Industry by Air," in *Addresses Delivered before the Canadian Club of Toronto, Season of 1925–26* (Toronto: Warwick Bros. & Rutter, 1926), 166–67.

41. Editorial "The Tie That Binds," in Toronto *Globe*, 24 May 1927, 4.

42. Editorial "Captain Lindbergh's Feat," in Ottawa *Citizen*, 23 May 1927, 18; *Canadian Aviation* 2, no. 10 (October 29): 1.

43. NAC: W. L. M. King Papers, series J6, vol. 68, f. 17, Ottawa *Citizen*, 14 April 1928.

44. H. Hollick-Kenyon, "29,000 Miles Over the Arctic," in *Maclean's*, 1 July 1938, 34; Bennett Papers, vol. 1043, reel M4490, Toronto *Globe*, 1 May 1936; WCA scrapbook, Winnipeg *Free Press*, 3 March 1930.

45. "The Magic of Flight," in *CAL Bulletin* 6, no. 11 (August 1936): 28.

46. J. Fergus Grant, "Trans-Canada Airway," in *Canadian Geographical Journal* 14, no. 2 (February 1937): 117; AO: Frank E. Davison Papers, MU818, unidentified article on Wilson's talk to Empire Club; Belliveau, "Sky Sailor's Port," 24.

47. Montreal *Gazette*, 18 May 1927, 1; editorial, *Canadian Aviation* 2, no. 8 (August 1929): 1; *WCA Bulletin* 5, no. 11 (August 1934): 7.

48. Editorial "More 'Frightfulness,'" Vancouver *Sun*, 2 February 1916, 4; Collier, *The Airship*, 159; Lady Hay Drummond-Hay, "Aboard the Graf Zeppelin," in *Western Home Monthly*, February 1930, 55.

49. NAC: W. A. Bishop Papers, vol. 1, f. clippings, unidentified cutting; W. A. Bishop, "Chivalry in the Air," in *Liberty*, 24 January 1931, 17–22; W. A. Bishop, "Canada's Air Position" in *Addresses Delivered before the Canadian Club of Toronto, Season of 1938–39* (Toronto: Warwick Bros. & Rutter, 1939), 98.

50 Quoted in West, *Firebirds*, ix, 136.

51. Shackleton, *Arctic Pilot*, 22; Arthur Bishop, *The Courage of the Early Morning* (Toronto: McClelland and Stewart, 1965), 175; Bishop, "What Aviation Means to Canada," 237.

52. King Papers, reel C-4288, Brown to Otto Schneider, Lauenberg, 15 October 1935.

8. Flaming Chariots of War

1. Charles J. Woodsworth, "Canada's Flying Future," in *The Beaver*, March 1936.

2. This account is taken from Gordon Thomas and Max Morgan Witts,

Guernica: The Crucible of World War II (New York: Stein and Day, 1975); and Hugh Thomas, *The Spanish Civil War* (London: Eyre & Spottiswoode, 1961).

3. Victoria *Daily Colonist*, 12 June 1919, 11; Hamilton *Spectator*, 1 November 1919, 35; *Catalogue of Canadian War Trophies, National Exhibition, Toronto, August 23–September 6, 1919*.

4. Hallam, *The Spider Web*, 273–74.

5. Hilda Glynn-Ward, *The Writing on the Wall* (Toronto: University of Toronto Press, 1974 [1921]), 140–43. Italics in original; Ubald Paquin, *La Cité dans le Fer* (Montréal: Editions Edouard Garand, 1925).

6. Hitchins Papers, II-E-12, R. A. Logan, "Report of Investigations on Aviation in the Arctic Archipelago carried out in the summer of 1922"; House of Commons, Debates, 22 May 1922, 2087; Ian Mackenzie's Warriors' Day speech, quoted in Toronto *Evening Telegram*, 19 September 1936.

7. House of Commons, Debates, 5 April 1935, 2496; Toronto *Daily Star*, 13 August 1930, 6.

8. Letter from D. C. Maddox, Ottawa *Citizen*, 30 April 1937, 31.

9. Editorial "Samaritan Work in Spain," in Ottawa *Citizen*, 28 April 1937, 22; article by A. C. Cummings, Ottawa *Citizen*, 28 April 1937, 2; editorial "Frightfulness" in Ottawa *Citizen*, 29 April 1937, 30.

10. "Spain 1937," in *The Collected Poems of F. R. Scott* (Toronto: McClelland and Stewart, 1981).

11. "Air Raid (Madrid 1937)," in *Collected Poems of Raymond Souster*, vol. 1, *1940–55* (n.c.: Oberon Press, 1980).

12. Doris Ferne, "Unease," in *Ebb Tide* (Toronto: Ryerson Press, 1941); Elsie Fry Laurence, "Ever Since Spain," in *Rearguard and Other Poems* (Toronto: Ryerson Press, 1944).

13. Edna Jaques, "China...at Night," in *Beside Still Waters* (Toronto: Thomas Allen, 1941); Sara E. Carsley, "The Tranquil Hour," in *Canadian Poems* (Calgary: Canadian Authors' Association, 1937).

14. Verna Loveday Harden, "All Valiant Dust," in *Crucible* 5, no. 4 (December 1938): 4; M. H. Halton, "Has Canada the Key to Britain's Destiny?" in *Star Weekly*, 21 May 1938: 6.

15. "Silent Planes," in *Maclean's*, 15 April 1939, 24–26; B. H. Liddell Hart, "Civilization in Danger," in *Maclean's*, 15 April 1939, 8, 62–63; Montreal *Gazette*, 8 November 1938.

16. NAC: Ian Mackenzie Papers, vol. 15, f. 8-H, Parney to Minister of Pensions and National Health, 5 December 1938.

17. House of Commons, Debates, 24 March 1938, 1662–63; 31 March 1939, 2473; 26 April 1939, 3236.

18. Bennett Papers, vol. 1043, reel M4490, Fraser Hunter, "Canada Must Fly or Die," in Toronto *Globe*, n.d.; W. A. Bishop, "Canada's Air Position," in *Addresses Delivered before the Canadian Club of Toronto, Season of 1938–39* (Toronto: Warwick Bros. & Rutter, 1939), 98.

19. Audrey Alexandra Brown, "To Chopin," in *Challenge to Time and Death* (Toronto: Macmillan, 1943); Robert W. Service, "Warsaw," in *Collected Poems of Robert Service* (New York: Dodd, Mead & Co., 1963); Anson Bailey Cutts, "September Third," in *Canadian Poetry Magazine* 4, no. 2 (October 1939), 43.

20. Hugh Templin, *Assignment to Britain* (Fergus, Ont.: News-Record, 1941).

21. A. E. Powley, *Broadcast from the Front: Canadian Radio Overseas in the Second World War* (Toronto: Hakkert/Canadian War Museum, 1975), 25–27.

22. G. L. Creed, "The Little Folk of London," in *For Freedom* (Toronto: J. M. Dent, 1942), 11.

23. Broadcast of 4 May 1941, in *We Have Been There* (Toronto: CBC Publications Branch, 1941), 12–13; John Douglas Macbeth, *Somewhere in England: War Letters of a Canadian Officer on Overseas Service* (Toronto: Macmillan, 1941), 28.

24. Charles Ritchie, *The Siren Years: A Canadian Diplomat Abroad, 1937–1945* (Toronto: McClelland & Stewart, 2001 [1974]), 66; Donald Aiken, "Britain," in *Saturday Night*, 26 October 1940: 7.

25. G. L. Creed, "They Shall Not..." in *For Freedom*; Beverley Baxter, "Can the R.A.F. Break Germany?" in *Maclean's*, 1 June 1942, 37.

26. A. H. Sandwell, "Does Canada Need an Air Ministry?" in *Saturday Night*, 2 March 1940: 3.

27. Dorothy Trail, "Airplanes in the Evening," in *Canadian Forum* 20, no. 235 (August 1940): 150.

28. Edna Jaques, "Wings," in *Beside Still Waters* (Toronto: Thomas Allen, 1941); Clara Bernhardt, "Summer Resort," in *Far Horizon* (Preston, Ont.: private, 1941).

29. Maurice Huot, "Le Bombardier," in *Poèmes et Satires* (Montréal: Éditions Fernand Pilon, 1946).

30. Murray Bonnycastle, "Plane Formations," in *Canadian Forum* 24, no. 287 (December 1944): 204.

31. Patrick Anderson, "Bombing Berlin," in *The White Centre* (Toronto: Ryerson Press, 1946).

32. Elizabeth Garbutt, "Air Raid," in *Alberta Poetry Year Book, 1939–40* (Edmonton: Canadian Authors' Association, 1940).

33. Audrey Alexandra Brown, "A Modern Carol," in *Challenge to Time and Death* (Toronto: Macmillan, 1943); Edna Jaques, "Airkrieg," in Toronto *Daily Star*, 23 August 1940.

34. John E. Nixon, "Coventry Cathedral," in *Selected Poems* (Regina: private, 1945).

35. Helen E. Ross, "Lost Sky," in *Alberta Poetry Year Book, 1940–41* (Edmonton: Canadian Authors' Association, 1941); Mary Quayle Innis, *Stand on a Rainbow* (Toronto: Collins, 1943), 112–13.

36. Dorothy Dumbrille, "Children of Coventry," in *We Come! We Come!*

(Toronto: Carillon Poetry Chap-Book, 1941); Wynne Bunning, "If This Were Our Little Son," in *Dear Mom* (Blenheim, Ont.: private, 1945).

37. H. A. C. Mason, "Easter, 1942," in *Three Things Only…* (Toronto: Thomas Nelson & Sons, n.d.).

38. Ritchie, *The Siren Years*, 131.

39. Brereton Greenhous et al., *The Crucible of War, 1939–45* (Toronto: University of Toronto Press, 1994), 727–28.

40. Beverley Baxter, "Can the R.A.F. Break Germany?" 8.

41. "The Air War in 1941," in *Saturday Night*, 24 May 1941: 12; "The Hitler War," in *Saturday Night*, 19 July 1941: 11; "Something Goebbels Can't Explain Away," in *Saturday Night*, 23 January 1943: 12; "The Great Question: Will Bombing Beat Germany?" in *Saturday Night*, 19 September 1942: 12.

42. Robina Monkman, "Eagles of Death (To the RAF)," in *Alberta Poetry Year Book, 1940–41* (Edmonton: Canadian Authors' Association, 1941); Helen E. Middleton, "Scroll of Honor," in *Drumbeats through Your Dreams* (Montreal: private, n.d.); "The Boys of the R.A.F.," in *Poems by Robert Main* (private, n.p., [1945?]).

43. Jack Paterson, "Green Geese," in *Maclean's*, 1 June 1942: 24; W. E. Johns, "Some Go in Darkness," in *Maclean's*, 15 February 1942: 17.

44. *Maclean's*, 15 August and 1 September 1942; *The Honker* 6, no. 3 (March 1944): back cover.

45. "Back the Attack," words and music by J. M. Gibbon and Murray Adaskin (Toronto: Gordon V. Thompson, 1943); *The Gander* (RCAF Gander) August–September 1943: back cover; ad for Kellogg's, Montreal *Star*, 2 November 1942, 8.

46. House of Commons, Debates, 17 March 1944; Trevor Lloyd, "Canada: Mainstreet of the Air," in *Maclean's*, 1 July 1943: 31.

47. D. M. LeBourdais, "The Coming Struggle for Air Control," in *Canadian Forum* 24, no. 279 (April 1944): 8; Leslie Roberts, "Assets for an Air Age," in *Maclean's*, 1 July 1943: 8.

48. J. Parker Van Zandt, "Air Transportation and World Understanding," in *Public Affairs* 9, no. 2 (winter 1946).

49. Quoted in J. A. Wilson, "Canada in World Aviation," in *Public Affairs* 9, no. 1 (December 1945): 4; S. G. Cameron, "International Air Transport," in *Canadian Forum* 24, no. 285 (October 1944): 155.

50. King Papers, vol. 71, f16, Vancouver *Province*, 31 July 1943; Hadley Cantril, ed., *Public Opinion, 1935–46* (Princeton: Princeton University Press, 1951), 9.

51. William A. Bishop, *Winged Peace: The Story of the Air Age* (Toronto: Macmillan, 1944), xi, xiii, 175.

52. Mary Matheson, "In England, 1940," in *The Moving Finger and Other Poems* (Vancouver: Clarke and Stuart, 1944), 9.

9. The Everlasting Arms of Science

1. M. L. McIntyre, "The Aylmer Story: No. 14 SFTS," in *I'll Never Forget…: Canadian Aviation in the Second World War* (Toronto: Canadian Aviation Historical Society, 1979), 67–86.

2. Uxbridge *Journal*, 26 July 1917, 1. I am grateful to Mary Rubio for this reference.

3. Editorial "Canada Begins to Fly," in *Saturday Night*, 22 October 1938: 1; John Thompson, "Skyways and Byways," in Winnipeg *Evening Tribune*, 2/ March 1937: 2; Dalton Little, "Aviation to Stimulate All Canadian Industry," in *Saturday Night*, 20 August 1938: 17.

4. Halifax *Mail*, quoted in Tim Stephens, "The Development of Commercial Aviation in the Atlantic Provinces, 1909–72" (Dalhousie University, 1972), 10.

5. Philip Smith, *It Seems Like Only Yesterday: Air Canada, the First 50 Years* (Toronto: McClelland and Stewart, 1986), 83, 114; ad for TCA in *Canadian Air Cadet* 2, no. 8 (May 1943): 25.

6. Leslie Collins, "The Flying Forties," in *Saturday Night*, 22 June 1940: 20; PEIPARO: accession 3523/14, TCA schedule, 28 April 1940.

7. NAC: Harold Edwards Papers, f. 2, Port Arthur *News-Chronicle*, 25 July 1941; Ottawa *Journal*, 29 July 1941.

8. Mackenzie King Diary, 17, 19, 20 August 1941.

9. Wilfred Womersley, "Canada and Aviation," in *Canadian Banker* 50 (1943): 129; *Saturday Night*, 21 March 1942: 4–5.

10. NAC: Clayton Knight Papers, reel M-5509, file 46, talk by Fl/Lt W. J. Bundy, n.d.

11. Weyburn *Review*, 18 June 1942, quoted in Brereton Greenhous and Norman Hillmer, "The Impact of the Commonwealth Air Training Plan on Western Canada: Some Saskatchewan Case Studies," in *Journal of Canadian Studies* 16, nos. 3 and 4 (fall-winter 1981): 142.

12. NAC: Russell Frost Papers, vol. 2, Administration of Air Cadets of Canada, Report and Recommendation, February 1942; R. W. Frost, "Air-Borne," in *Canadian Air Cadet* 1, no. 2 (November 1941): 5.

13. Article of 6 January 1942 quoted in Weicht, *Jericho Beach and the West Coast Flying Boat Stations*, 201.

14. Montreal *Daily Star*, 10 November 1942, 5.

15. Powley, *Broadcast from the Front*, 125–26.

16. Ottawa *Citizen*, 13 February 1942, 20.

17. *Saturday Night*, 25 October 1941: 89; *Maclean's*, 15 August 1941: 53; 15 June 1943: 57; 15 November 1940: 21.

18. *Country Guide and Nor'west Farmer* 61, no. 8 (August 1942): 32; Victoria *Daily Colonist*, 3 March 1943, 7; *Saturday Night*, 12 October 1940: 24.

19. John Gillespie Magee Jr., "High Flight," in John Robert Colombo and

Michael Richardson, eds., *We Stand on Guard: Poems and Songs of Canadians in Battle* (Toronto: Doubleday, 1985), 171.

20. See Andy Saunders, "John Gillespie Magee," in *After the Battle* 63 (1989): 43–54.

21. Alex H. Sutherland, "Flight," in *Canadian Poetry Magazine* 7, no. 3 (March 1944): 23; North Atlantic Aviation Museum #996.05.288, N.V., "Night Flight," in *The Gander* (mid-winter 1945); Fl/Sgt E. G. C. Richards, "Everlasting Wings," at http://web.mala.bc.ca/davies/letters.images/ E.Richards/_collection.htm>; Alec McAlister, *Hi-Sky!: The Ups and Downs of a Pinfeather Pilot* (Toronto: Ryerson Press, 1944), 52; Ethel Stewart Southcott, "Sky-Lanes," in *Rainbows of Promise* (London, Ont.: private, 1946); letter of 15 September 1941, in Edwin Gray, *In All Thy Ways: Letters from a Canadian Flying Officer in Training in Canada and England and in Action in North Africa* (Toronto: Oxford University Press, n.d. [1944]), 3.

22. Wise, *Canadian Airmen and the First World War*, appendix C; Alan Sullivan, *Aviation in Canada, 1917–1918* (Toronto: Rous and Mann, 1919), 146.

23. Greenhous et al., *The Crucible of War*, 48.

24. *Canada's Air Heritage* (Ottawa, 1941); Knight Papers, reel M-5509, file 46, talk by Sq/Ldr Hanna, 25 March 1941.

25. NAC: Earle Briggs Papers, vol. 1, "The Boys of the Hangar Crew," in J. G. Wilson, *Rhymes Anew of Class 42 at #6 EFTS* (Prince Albert, SK: private, 1941); LAC Vic Hopwood, "Ground Crew," in *Contemporary Verse: A Canadian Quarterly* 14 (July 1945): 4.

26. Frederick Edwards, "Canada's Fighting Forces: In the Air," in *Maclean's*, 1 January 1940: 8; William L. White, "Fighter Type," in *Maclean's*, 15 September 1941: 10.

27. Comrades of the Royal Air Forces Association statement of policy, *Air Force Review* [Toronto] 1, no. 2 (August 1940): 27; Toronto *Daily Star*, 9 November 1942, 15; *Canadian Air Cadet* 2, no. 8 (May 1943): 21.

28. Quoted in Regina *Leader-Post*, 5 May 1941, 19.

29. *Wings Abroad*, editorials, 1, no. 10 (24 June 1942): 2; and 1, no. 2 (29 April 1942): 2.

30. Gloria Lauriston, "Wings Presentation," in *National Home Monthly*, March 1942: 38.

31. Sullivan, *Aviation in Canada*, 151.

32. Bishop Papers, vol. 2, f. Speeches, W. A. Bishop, "Winged Warfare over Britain"; DND Records, vol. 3577, f. 866-1-53, Grey to Wilson, 11 January 1921.

33. Frank Bunce, "Wings of Hazard," in *Maclean's*, 1 January 1940: 32; NAC: W. L. McKnight Papers, letter from #6 Flying Training School, Little Rissington, 3 May 1939.

34. North Atlantic Aviation Museum, Gander: #996.05.287, "The Wireless Boy," in *The Gander*, March-April 1944: 13; quoted in Weicht,

Jericho Beach and the West Coast Flying Boat Stations, 206; A. J. G. Walters, "The Air Bomber," in *Wings: Log of the RCAF* 1, no. 4 (May 1943): 10.

35. DND Records, vol. 3577, f. HQ866-1-53, pt. 2, "The Technique of Scheduled Air Transportation in Canada," 28 April 1937.

36. Hitchins Papers, II-A-4, J. A. Wilson, "The Influence of Civil Aviation in the Development of Canada's Air Power," 3 November 1943; Ronald A. Keith, "Preview Flight," in *Maclean's*, 1 January 1942, 16.

37. F. R. Scott, "Trans Canada," in *Preview* 18 (February 1944): 6.

38. Frank Bunce, "Wings of Hazard."

39. Shelagh Grant, "The Northern Nationalists: Crusaders and Supporters of a New North, 1940–1960," paper presented to CHA annual meeting, Ottawa, 1982.

40. Trevor Lloyd, "Canada: Mainstreet of the Air," in *Maclean's*, 1 July 1943: 48.

41. Zaslow, *The Northward Expansion of Canada*, 212; K. S. Coates and W. R. Morrison, *The Alaska Highway in World War II: The U.S. Army of Occupation in Canada's Northwest* (Norman: University of Oklahoma Press, 1992), 43.

42. Harold Albert, "Grand Centrals of Tomorrow," in *National Home Monthly*, November 1943: 8.

43. Bernhardt, "Air Field Under Construction," in *Far Horizon* (Preston, Ont.: private, 1941).

44. Gilbert Layton, "Post-War Air Plans Should Be Agreed on Now," in *Saturday Night*, 2 October 1943: 32.

Epilogue
1. NAC: Gordon McGregor Papers, vol. 3, f. clippings, unidentified editorial, "Closing the Period of Ocean Pioneers."

2. Douglas Hallam, "Boys: Learn How to Build Model Aircraft and Fly Them," in *Canadian Aviation* 1, no. 1 (June 1928): 30.

3. MacNaughton Papers, ser. II, vol. 101, f. Interdepartmental Committee on Trans-Canada Airway, pt. 2, J. Stanley Scott, "Air Transportation in Relation to Airways"; House of Commons, Debates, 25 March 1937, 2216; quoted in Robert Daley, *An American Saga: Juan Trippe and his PanAm Empire* (New York: Random House, 1980), 117.

4. Editorial "It's Still News," Hamilton *Spectator*, 25 January 1932.

5. Alexander Louis Fraser, "The Plaint of Science," in *Ruth and Other Poems* (Toronto: Carillon Poetry Chap Book, 1946).

READINGS

In the interests of brevity, I have confined the chapter reference notes to archival and primary sources. My aim in this section is to suggest sources that were both especially useful to me and fairly widely available.

Because *High Flight* is a history of the idea of aviation, I begin with some general studies in this vein, primarily written by historians of Europe and the United States. Laurence Goldstein's *The Flying Machine and Modern Literature* (Bloomington: Indiana University Press, 1986) and Michael Paris's *From the Wright Brothers to Top Gun: Aviation, Nationalism and Popular Cinema* (Manchester: Manchester University Press, 1995) examine the impact of aviation on two different elements of culture, while Robert Wohl's *A Passion for Wings: Aviation and the Western Imagination, 1908–1918* (Yale University Press, 1994) takes a broader look at the relationship between flight and ideas, as does Peter Fritzsche's *A Nation of Fliers: German Aviation and the Popular Imagination* (Cambridge, MA: Harvard University Press, 1992). Joseph J. Corn's *The Winged Gospel: America's Romance with Aviation, 1900–1950* (New York: Oxford University Press, 1983) beautifully captures the evangelical fervour with which flight was promoted by its supporters, and Roger E. Bilstein's *Flight Patterns: Trends of Aeronautical Development in the United States, 1918–1929* (Athens: University of Georgia Press, 1983) effectively combines a technological with a cultural examination of flying. Guillaume de Syon's *Zeppelin: Germany and the Airship* (Baltimore: Johns Hopkins University Press, 2002) uses the same approach to study the nation that led the world in airship technology. Two of the best studies of these matters in the context of the First World War are John H. Morrow Jr.'s essay "The War in the Air," in *World War I: A History*, edited by Hew Strachan (New York: Oxford University Press, 1998), and Dominick Pisano's *Legend, Memory and the Great War in the Air* (Washington: University of Washington Press, 1992). Just as interesting as many of these scholarly works is Billy Bishop's *Winged Peace: The Story of the Air Age* (Toronto: Macmillan, 1944), a fascinating reflection addressing many of the issues that these historians have dealt with, but forty or more years earlier.

From the beginning of this project, I came to rely heavily on some of the excellent general histories of Canadian aviation. Nearly fifty years ago, Frank Ellis, one of the country's aviation pioneers, wrote *Canada's Flying Heritage* (Toronto: University of Toronto Press, 1954), a detailed and personal account of flight in Canada from the earliest days. His later book, *In Canadian Skies: 50 Years of Adventure and Progress* (Toronto: Ryerson Press, 1959), is a concise survey published to mark the fiftieth anniversary of the flight of the *Silver Dart*. J. R. K. Main's *Voyageurs of the Air: A History of Civil Aviation in Canada* (Ottawa: Queen's Printer, 1967) is another concise account that was written as a Centennial project. For the past twenty years, the standard general history has been Larry Milberry's *Aviation in Canada* (Toronto: McGraw-Hill Ryerson, 1979), a book that is still difficult to top. As a reference guide, G. A. Fuller, J. A. Griffin and K. M. Molson's *125 Years of Canadian Aeronautics: A Chronology, 1840–1965* (Willowdale, Ont.: Canadian Aviation Historical Society, 1983) is indispensable.

There are also a number of good regional histories of Canadian aviation that were particularly useful to me. Eugenie Louise Myles's *Airborne from Edmonton* (Toronto: Ryerson Press, 1983) is dated but still provides a good account of how aviation transformed the Alberta capital. More recent is Patricia A. Myers, *Sky Riders: An Illustrated History of Aviation in Alberta, 1906–1945* (Saskatoon: Fifth House, 1995). A model of regional aviation history is Peter Corley-Smith's multi-volume series on British Columbia, published by Sono Nis Press in Victoria: *Barnstorming to Bush Flying: British Columbia's Aviation Pioneers, 1910–1930* (1989); *Bush Flying to Blind Flying* (1993); and *Pilots to Presidents: British Columbia Aviation Pioneers and Leaders, 1930–1960* (2001).

For the origins of aviation, Clive Hart's *The Prehistory of Flight* (Berkeley: University of California Press, 1985) is still difficult to improve on, although Charles H. Gibb-Smith's *Aviation: An Historical Survey from Its Origins to the End of World War II* (London: HMSO, 1970) is also good. Tom D. Crouch has written a number of excellent books on early pioneers of flight, including *The Eagle Aloft: Two Centuries of Ballooning in America* (Washington: Smithsonian Institution Press, 1983) and *The Bishop's Boys: A Life of Wilbur and Orville Wright* (New York: W. W. Norton, 1989). A more recent account of the drama at Kitty Hawk, North Carolina, is Spencer Dunmore, Fred E. C. Culick and Peter Christopher's *On Great White Wings: The Wright Brothers and the Race for Flight* (Hyperion, 2001). On the Canadian side, J. H. Parkin's *Bell and Baldwin: Their Development of Aerodromes and Hydrodromes at Baddeck, Nova Scotia* (Toronto: University of Toronto Press, 1964) is a comprehensive and technically detailed study of the work of the Aerial Experiment Association. It should be read in conjunction with Robert V. Bruce's fine biography *Bell: Alexander Graham Bell and the Conquest of Silence* (Ithaca, NY: Cornell University Press, 1973). For a short biography of one of the key members of the

AEA, see H. Gordon Green's *The Silver Dart: The Authentic Story of the Hon. J. A. D. McCurdy, Canada's First Pilot* (Fredericton: Atlantic Advocate, n.d.).

As I have suggested, the bush pilot has long fascinated the popular imagination and the historian too. Philip H. Godsell's *Pilots of the Purple Twilight: The Story of Canada's Early Bush Flyers* (Toronto: Ryerson Press, 1958) and Margaret Mason Shaw's *Canadian Portraits: Bush Pilots* (Toronto: Clarke, Irwin, 1962) are early surveys that captured the public's fascination with the subject. J. A. Foster's *The Bush Pilots: A Pictorial History of a Canadian Phenomenon* (Toronto: McClelland & Stewart, 1990) is a more recent, illustrated history of wilderness flying, while William J. Wheeler's *Skippers of the Sky: The Early Years of Bush Flying* (Calgary: Fifth House, 1999) is more anecdotal in character. Bruce West's *The Firebirds: How Bush Flying Won Its Wings* (Toronto: Ministry of Natural Resources, 1974) is an institutional history of the Ontario Provincial Air Service. The first full account of aerial photography in Canada has been written by S. Bernard Shaw, *Photographing Canada from Flying Canoes* (Burnstown, Ont.: General Store, 2001). Georgette Vachon provided an early history of airmail services in *Goggles, Helmets and Air Mail Stamps* (Toronto: Clarke, Irwin, 1974); a more recent illustrated history that covers airmail is Chantal Amyot, Bianca Gendreau and John Willis's *Special Delivery: Canada's Postal Heritage* (Fredericton: Goose Lane Editions, 2000).

Canada's airlines are the subjects of a number of good studies. The earlier histories of Trans-Canada Air Lines and its successor, Air Canada, such as David H. Collins's *Wings Across Time: The Story of Air Canada* (Toronto: Griffin House, 1978) and Philip Smith's *It Seems Like Only Yesterday: Air Canada, the First 50 Years* (Toronto: McClelland and Stewart, 1986), have largely been superseded by Peter Pigott's new, more comprehensive account, *National Treasure: The History of Trans Canada Air Lines* (Madeira Park, B.C.: Harbour Publishing, 2001). D. M. Bain's *Canadian Pacific Air Lines: Its History and Aircraft* (Calgary: Kishorn Publications, 1987) is a brief, illustrated account of TCA's early rival; Peter Pigott's *Wingwalkers: A History of Canadian Airlines International* (Madeira Park, B.C.: Harbour Publishing, 1998) is more comprehensive and balanced. Another essential study is Shirley Render's fascinating book *Double Cross: James A. Richardson and Canadian Airways* (Vancouver: Douglas and McIntyre, 1999), which argues that Richardson and his company were unfairly treated by the government. Only a few of Canada's smaller airlines of the pre-1945 period have been chronicled (Larry Milberry's *Austin Airways: Canada's Oldest Airline* [Toronto: Canav Books, 1985] is a good example), but there are a number of excellent general histories of commercial aviation in Canada: K. M. Molson's *Pioneering in Canadian Air Transport* (Winnipeg: James Richardson and Sons, 1974); Peter Pigott's *Flying Colours: A History of Commercial Aviation in Canada* (Vancouver: Douglas & McIntyre, 1997); and Larry Milberry's *Air Transport in Canada* (Toronto: CANAV Books, 1997). A related work is T. M. McGrath's *History of Canadian*

Airports (Toronto: Lugus, 1992), a useful reference source on the development of the aviation infrastructure.

Aviation historians continue to be fascinated by the personalities involved in flying, and there are many good collections of short biographical sketches of famous fliers. Peter Pigott's *Flying Canucks* series, which has just published its third volume, covers many of the big names, while Shirley Render's *No Place for a Lady: The Story of Canadian Women Pilots, 1928–92* (Winnipeg: Portage and Main Press, 1992) and Joyce Spring's *Daring Lady Flyers: Canadian Women in the Early Years of Aviation* (Porter's Lake, N.S.: Pottersfield Press, 1994) recount the experiences of pioneering women in aviation. Alice Gibson Sutherland's *Canada's Aviation Pioneers: 50 Years of McKee Trophy Winners* (Toronto: McGraw-Hill Ryerson, 1979) is also useful for information on the recipients of the annual award for achievement in aviation.

Among the best biographies of Canadian pilots are Sheila Reid's *Wings of a Hero: Canadian Pioneer Flying Ace Wilfred Wop May* (St. Catharines, Ont.: Vanwell, 1997); Ross Smyth's *The Lindbergh of Canada: The Errol Boyd Story* (Burnstown, Ont.: General Store, 1997), about the first Canadian to fly an airplane across the Atlantic; and Kathleen Shackleton's *Arctic Pilot: Life and Work on North Canadian Air Routes* (Toronto: Thomas Nelson, 1940), the co-written memoir of Walter Gilbert, one of Canada's greatest northern fliers. Carroll V. Glines's *Bernt Balchen: Polar Aviator* (Washington: Smithsonian Institution Press, 2000) is a detailed biography of one of Gilbert's contemporaries who spent much time in the Canadian North. There is no full biography of John A. Wilson yet, but Ernest Stedman published his memoirs (originally written as a series of columns in *Canadian Aviation*) as *From Boxkite to Jet* (Toronto: University of Toronto Press, 1963). *Bush to Boardroom: A Personal View of Five Decades of Aviation History* (Winnipeg: Watson and Dwyer, 1992) is the memoir of Duncan McLaren, who was involved in the Hudson's Bay Company's early flying operations, and Grant McConachie, another pioneering aviation entrepreneur, is the subject of Ronald Keith's *Bush Pilot with a Brief-case* (Toronto: Doubleday, 1972).

There are many general histories of airships and dirigibles. Among the best are Lord Ventry and Eugene M. Kolenik's *Airship Saga* (Poole, U.K.: Blandford Press, 1982); Dale Topping's *When Giants Roamed the Sky: Karl Arnstein and the Rise of Airships from Zeppelin to Goodyear* (Akron, Ohio: University of Akron Press, 2001); Robert Jackson's *Airships: A Popular History of Dirigibles, Zeppelins, Blimps, and Other Lighter-Than-Air Craft* (Garden City, N.Y.: Doubleday, 1973); and Basil Collier's *The Airship: A History* (London: Hart-Davis, MacGibbon, 1974). J. E. Morpurgo's *Barnes Wallis: A Biography* (New York: St. Martin's, 1972) and Nevil Shute's memoir *Slide Rule: The Autobiography of an Engineer* (Toronto: George J. McLeod, 1954) provide useful personal accounts of two of the key designers involved in the British airship program. Patrick's Abbott's *Airship: The Story of the R.34 and the First East-West*

Crossing of the Atlantic by Air (New York: Charles Scribner's Sons, 1973) describes one of the landmarks in dirigible travel. The R-101 has attracted many chroniclers, including Peter G. Masefield, whose excellent book *To Ride the Storm: The Story of Airship R.101* (London: Kimber, 1982) offers the most complete account of the ill-fated airship and its place in the planned Imperial airship scheme. A little different in emphasis is John G. Fuller's *The Airmen Who Would Not Die* (New York: G. P. Putnam's Sons, 1979), a fascinating story of the occult dimension of the tragedy. The successful R-100, however, has been of less interest to historians. The best accounts are Rénald Fortier's *Le R.100 est venu: le Canada et le programme impérial de transport par dirigeables, 1924–1931* (Ottawa: National Aviation Museum, 1998), and Barry Countryman's *R100 in Canada* (Erin, Ont.: Boston Mills Press, 1982).

The action-packed history of transatlantic flying has also produced some fine books. Percy Rowe's *The Great Atlantic Air Race* (Toronto: McClelland and Stewart, 1977) is an excellent account that focuses on the campaign of 1919. The memoir of the winners of that campaign were reprinted as John Alcock and Arthur Whitten Brown's *Our Transatlantic Flight* (London: William Kimber, 1969). The campaign of 1927 is well covered in A. Scott Berg's *Lindbergh* (New York: G. P. Putnam's Sons, 1998). For Lindbergh's own version of his flight, see his hastily written memoir *We* (New York: Putnam's, 1927) and the much better account *The Spirit of St. Louis* (New York: Scribner's, 1953). The best account of the cultural significance of Lindbergh's flight can be found in Modris Eksteins, *Rites of Spring: The Great War and the Birth of the Modern Age* (Toronto: Lester & Orpen Dennys, 1989). Fred Hotson describes another famous transatlantic odyssey of the inter-war years in *The Bremen* (Toronto: CANAV Books, 1988). Transatlantic flying during the Second World War is the subject of Carl Christie's *Ocean Bridge: The History of RAF Ferry Command* (Toronto: University of Toronto Press, 1995), the best and most detailed account of the genesis of the transoceanic service. For a valuable personal account of ferry operations, see George Lothian's *Flight Deck: Memoirs of an Airline Pilot* (Toronto: McGraw-Hill Ryerson, 1979). Two somewhat dated but still-useful surveys are Kenneth McDonough's *Atlantic Wings* (Hemel Hempstead, U.K.: Model Aeronautical Press, 1966) and Alan Wykes's *Air Atlantic: A History of Civil and Military Transatlantic Flying* (London: Hamish Hamilton, 1967). David Mackenzie's *Canada and International Civil Aviation, 1932–1948* (Toronto: University of Toronto Press, 1989) is a much more balanced and substantial account of the opening of transatlantic routes and the subsequent moves toward regulation of the air.

Among the better general histories of Canadian military aviation are Larry Milberry, ed., *Sixty Years: The RCAF and CF Air Command, 1924–1984* (Toronto: CANAV Books, 1984); and Samuel Kostenuk and John Griffin's *RCAF Squadron Histories and Aircraft, 1924–1968* (Toronto: Hakkert, 1977). Much more comprehensive is Larry Milberry's three-volume set *Canada's Air*

Force at War and Peace (Toronto: CANAV Books, 2000), a well-written and lavishly illustrated successor to the earlier works. A useful survey of Canada's air effort during the First World War is Ronald Dodds's *The Brave Young Wings* (Stittsville, Ont.: Canada's Wings, 1980). Alan Sullivan's *Aviation in Canada, 1917–1918* (Toronto: Rous and Mann, 1919) is rather dry but strong on minutiae and contains many good statistical tables. For the Second World War, the three-volume history *The RCAF Overseas*, published by Oxford University Press (1944–49), has certain limitations because of wartime censorship but remains a valuable record. An indispensable history of Canadian military aviation is the *Official History of the Royal Canadian Air Force*, which has been published in three excellent volumes to date: S. F. Wise's *Canadian Airmen and the First World War* (Toronto: University of Toronto Press, 1980); W. A. B. Douglas's *The Creation of a National Air Force* (Toronto: University of Toronto Press, 1986); and Brereton Greenhous, Stephen J. Harris, William C. Johnston and William G. P. Rawling's *The Crucible of War, 1939–1945* (Toronto: University of Toronto Press, 1994).

A number of specialized studies of military aviation should also be mentioned. Spencer Dunmore's *Wings for Victory: The Remarkable Story of the Commonwealth Air Training Plan in Canada* (Toronto: McClelland & Stewart, 1994) and Ted Barris's *Behind the Glory* (Toronto: Macmillan, 1992) both provide excellent accounts of the training scheme that transformed Canada into the aerodrome of democracy. Spencer Dunmore and William Carter detail the operations of Canadian bomber crews in *Reap the Whirlwind: The Untold Story of 6 Group, Canada's Bomber Force of World War II* (Toronto: McClelland & Stewart, 1991).

Readers with a specific interest in military pilots will enjoy George Drew's *Canada's Fighting Airmen* (Toronto: MacLean, 1930), a best-seller that covered the lives of some of the most famous pilots of the First World War. Edmund Cosgrove's *Canada's Fighting Pilots* (Toronto: Clarke, Irwin, 1965) is essentially an updated version of Drew's book that includes the exploits of Second World War pilots. The most recent additions to this genre are two volumes by David Bashow, himself a fighter pilot: *Knights of the Air: Canadian Fighter Pilots of the First World War* (Toronto: McArthur, 2000); and *All the Fine Young Eagles: In the Cockpit with Canada's Second World War Fighter Pilots* (Toronto: Stoddart, 1996).

There are many fine memoirs and biographies of Canada's pilots of the two world wars. Billy Bishop's best-selling *Winged Warfare: Hunting the Huns in the Air* (Toronto: Hodder and Stoughton, 1918), is essential reading, although it contains more than a dash of propaganda. It should be read in conjunction with the biography by Bishop's son, William Arthur Bishop, *The Courage of the Early Morning: The Story of Billy Bishop* (Toronto: McClelland and Stewart, 1965). A valuable complementary work on Bishop's friend and business partner is Wayne Ralph, *Barker VC: William Barker, Canada's Most Decorated War*

Hero (Toronto: Doubleday, 1997). Perhaps the best-known Second World War aviation memoir is George Beurling and Leslie Roberts's *Malta Spitfire: The Story of a Fighter Pilot* (Toronto: Oxford University Press, 1943). Murray Peden's *A Thousand Shall Fall* (Stittsville, Ont.: Canada's Wings, 1979) is a sensitive account of Peden's operations with Bomber Command. J. Douglas Harvey's *Boys, Bombs and Brussels Sprouts: A Knees-Up, Wheels-Up Chronicle of WWII* (Toronto: McClelland and Stewart, 1981) is a little more light-hearted but just as interesting. Dave McIntosh's *Terror in the Starboard Seat* (Toronto: Stoddart, 1998 [1980]) is an excellent memoir of the author's experiences flying night intruder missions over northwest Europe.

Finally, some of the best examples of aviation historical writing have appeared in the pages of the *Journal of the Canadian Aviation Historical Society*, a quarterly publication with a fine mix of first-person accounts and research articles.

ACKNOWLEDGEMENTS

MY FIRST DEBT IN THE WRITING OF THIS BOOK IS TO THE SOCIAL SCIENCE and Humanities Research Council for providing financial support through its standard research grants program. The Department of History and the Faculty of Social Science at the University of Western Ontario were also generous with various forms of assistance and support.

Every historian relies on friends, colleagues and archivists for advice and counsel, input that always makes for a better finished product. My thanks to the archivists who went out of their way to help with my research: Rénald Fortier and Fiona Hale (National Aviation Museum), Garry Shutlak (Public Archives of Nova Scotia), Ainsley MacFarlane (Alexander Graham Bell National Historic Site), Carl Spadoni (McMaster University), Allen Doiron (Public Archives of New Brunswick), Ed Evans (town of Botwood, Newfoundland) and Jill MacMicken Wilson (Prince Edward Island Public Archives and Records Office). I am also grateful to my colleagues around the country who have helped me with suggestions and information, particularly Raymond Blake, Gord Cavanaugh, Terry Copp, Jack Granatstein, Doug Leighton, Peter Neary, Daniel Robinson, Mary Rubio, Maya Shatzmiller and Ian Steele. Finally, I would like to thank the research assistants who put in many hours slogging through microfilm newspapers: Ethan Adeland, Kara Brown, Raymond Farnum, Jennifer Ho, Jonathan Hopkins, Janet Maybury, Joel Porter and Amy Thornton.

I am indebted to Cynthia Good at Penguin and to Linda McKnight for their enthusiastic support of the project at every stage. Charis Wahl did a wonderful job of polishing the manuscript, and the people at Penguin Canada, particularly Cathy MacLean and Helen Reeves, were a pleasure to work with.

Over the course of this project, I was often asked by family and friends why on earth I would write a book about aviation when I was so terrified of flying myself. I wasn't able to come up with a satisfactory answer, but I am grateful to them for asking the question. Perhaps as much as anything, it helped me to think like the average Canadian of the inter-war era who, in the view of the air lobby, was just waiting to be made air-minded.

PHOTO CREDITS

INDEX